2. 2.

1. *Ama Dablam: Kate Phillips arriving at the top of the Ramp during the successful summit bid.* (Brendan Murphy) (p 8)

THE
ALPINE JOURNAL

1991/92

Incorporating the Journal of the Ladies' Alpine Club
& Alpine Climbing

A record of mountain adventure and scientific observation

Volume 96 No 340

Edited by Ernst Sondheimer

Assistant Editors:
Johanna Merz, A V Saunders and Geoffrey Templeman
assisted by Marian Elmes

FREDERICK MULLER

in association with

The Alpine Club, London

IN ASSOCIATION WITH THE ALPINE CLUB

Volume 96 No 340
THE ALPINE JOURNAL 1991/92

Address all editorial communications directly to the Hon Editor (from 1.9.1991):
Mrs J Merz, 14 Whitefield Close, London SW15 3SS

Address all sales and distribution communications to
Victoria Adam
Random Century House,
20 Vauxhall Bridge Road,
London SW1V 2SA

Back numbers:
apply to the Alpine Club or, for 1969 to date, to
Cordee, 3a De Montfort Street, Leicester LE1 7HD

First published in 1991 by Frederick Muller in association with the Alpine Club
Frederick Muller is an imprint of Random Century Group Ltd,
20 Vauxhall Bridge Road, London SW1V 2SA

Random Century Australia (Pty) Ltd
20 Alfred Street, Milsons Point, Sydney, NSW 2061, Australia

Random Century New Zealand Ltd
PO Box 40–086, Glenfield, Auckland 10, New Zealand

Random Century South Africa (Pty) Ltd
PO Box 337, Bergvlei, 2012, South Africa

The Alpine Club, 118 Eaton Square, London SW1W 9AF

Photoset by Speedset Ltd, Ellesmere Port

Printed and bound in Great Britain by
Butler & Tanner Ltd, Frome and London

British Library Cataloguing in Publication Data

The Alpine Journal
  I. Mountaineering
  796.5
  ISBN 0 09 174841 0

Contents

CONTENTS

Illustrations

Appearing between pages 120 and 121

Appearing between pages 184 and 185

South Georgia

STEPHEN VENABLES

(*Plates 19–24*)

I was lying in bed listening to Madam Butterfly, when Lindsay and Brian returned to Royal Bay. It was a stormy night, so I let Julian go and talk to the others while I remained in the tent, warm in my sleeping bag and plugged into Puccini, isolated from the noise outside of wind and rain and belching sea elephants.

Ten minutes later I was roused to go and hear the news. Inside the hut Kees 't Hooft, the Flying Dutchman – our film cameraman-cum-domestic help – was dispensing tea to the two returning heroes who sat dripping in a heap of sodden equipment. Lindsay explained how they had spent three days at the Ross pass, 600m above sea level and 10 miles away, excavating a palatial snow-cave 20 feet up the side of a huge wind-scoop. They had started on Christmas Eve and had continued through Christmas Day in beautiful hot weather. But the temperature had continued to rise and their expanding cave had dripped-dripped alarmingly. On Boxing Day it had rained outside without cease and the wind had gusted to over 100mph. Down here we had giggled nervously at each katabatic gust as it came howling down the valley, swooped up and crashed on to the ridge above. At 600m it must have been frightening. The wind had calmed slightly during the night but the rain had continued. That morning Lindsay had woken at the Ross pass, peered out of the snow-cave entrance and said gently, 'I'm not sure how to put this, Brian.'

'What?'

'Well, you're not going to believe this, but there's a lake out here.'

'What are you talking about?'

'The whole bed of the wind-scoop has filled with water. It's about a foot from the door and I think it's still rising.'

Lindsay had nearly been drowned once already on this expedition, so they wasted no time in packing up to leave the doomed snow-cave, caching all the gear on some rocks high above lake level, and starting back down through the blizzard, groping on compass bearings and finally reaching Royal Bay long after dark. Now Kees, Julian and I received the news of this latest setback with the mixture of incredulous despair and manic laughter that had become our stock reaction to life on South Georgia.

Of course we were warned. If you must choose to go climbing on a sub-Antarctic island, stuck right in the path of the endless procession of storms that crash their way round the Southern Ocean, you can expect to suffer some inclement weather. In a sense the origins of the trip were appropriate. I had known Lindsay Griffin for years, but we had only got to know the other two climbers, Julian Freeman-Attwood and Brian Davison, on Xixabangma, during the Great Himalayan Storm of 1987. Whole camps had been destroyed; Brian had sheltered beside a boulder to find himself the next morning buried alive in a huge snowdrift; Lindsay and Julian had taken two days to struggle across a glacier that usually took two hours. The expedition to Tibet was also an appropriate genesis in another sense. Led by Colonels Day and Blashford-Snell and code-named Jade Venture, it was a great imperial venture, nurturing us for, and providing the contacts for, a visit to the South Atlantic – the last outpost of the British Empire.

John Blashford-Snell gave us the vital introduction to Nicholas Barker, who had captained HMS *Endurance* during the Falklands conflict and kindly recommended us to the present captain. Douggie Keelan introduced us to the current 'C Biffy' (Commander of British Forces in the Falkland Islands) who gave us his full and generous support; and the marvellous thing about the armed services is that, once they receive the vital rubber-stamp from on high, everyone bends over backwards to help a bunch of civilians, however undeserving and odd they may be.

And we were, as Lindsay put it, 'a bunch of weirdos'. He is nearly seven feet tall and a succession of winter epics has left him with a pronounced limp. I was also still a bit lopsided after the loss of some toes. Brian is a very talented climber with a skilful predilection for loose rock, but on the flat he appears completely uncoordinated and is incapable of walking in a straight line. Julian comes from a long inbred line of backwoods gentry, one of whom was the mad Nescliff highwayman who used to attack stage-coaches on the London–Bangor road. Kees, the cameraman, is Dutch and, as if that was not enough, he became known during the expedition as The Poltergeist, because of his tendency to send saucepans and cups of tea flying around confined spaces.

They seemed a little surprised, even alarmed, when we turned up at the officers' mess in the Falklands, but everyone was very friendly. The officers and crew of HMS *Endurance* were equally hospitable during the 900-mile sea passage to South Georgia – three days of glorious weather, wheeling albatrosses and the comforting throb of the ancient five-cylinder diesel engine. The captain, Norman Hodgson, had a busy scientific programme, but as we anchored off the island's military base at Grytviken, he agreed kindly to helicopter half our supplies to the little hut at Royal Bay, 25 miles away. That vital depot gave us the chance to spend several weeks at the southern end of the island and attempt some of the many unclimbed peaks there, including Mount Carse (2331m), the highest unclimbed summit on South Georgia. First we had to get ourselves over to Royal Bay. From Grytviken we were taken across Cumberland East Bay by the garrison's boatswain and then we started walking. We were out of touch with the army for the next six days.

During the two-day journey to Royal Bay the landscape, with its soft greens and browns and that wonderful blend of sea and mountain, reminded me of North-West Scotland. But this was Scotland on a grander scale, with white mountains in the interior and immense glaciers flowing into a sea of brilliant turquoise. And of course there were the birds and animals. On the second day

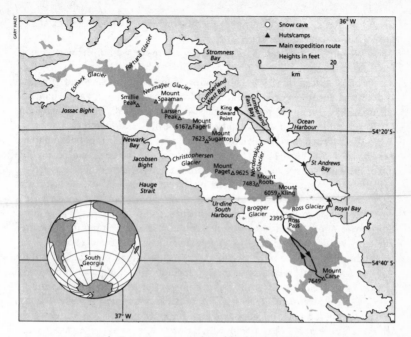

South Georgia. (Reproduced by kind permission of Geographical Magazine.)

we walked for two miles along a beach thronged with tens of thousands of King penguins, so ridiculously pompous beside the shorter dumpier Gentoos. Frisky fur seal pups scampered and growled about our ankles; sea elephant cows stared indifferently out of dark doey eyes, while the bulls reared up their four tons of heaving blubber and opened cavernous snouts to belch forth steaming clouds of halitosis. Their supreme indifference to rain, sleet and snow, and the albatrosses' mastery of the blasting katabatic winds put our own efforts in perspective. We always seemed to be wet and cold. Both Lindsay and I fell in the sea. At Royal Bay we watched helplessly as one of our tents imploded and collapsed into a pile of snapped poles and ripped fabric. When we established our depot halfway up the Ross glacier, we had on some days to abandon load-carries, because the sand-blasting on the beach made it impossible to reach the glacier. Through all this, Kees, who had only just returned from four months 'in the field' with the British Makalu expedition, had to nurture his £30,000 worth of Aaton cine camera, which frequently succumbed to the APD syndrome – All Pervading Damp.

Our strategy was to establish a secure base at the Ross pass and from there eventually attempt some climbing. If we had had sufficient sea or air back-up, we would have done better to use heavy pyramid tents and sledges, enabling us to move as a self-contained unit over the glaciers. However, because of limited funds and uncertain transport arrangements, we had opted for a compromise, carrying only lightweight tents and no sledges. Hence the snow-cave at the Ross pass. Unfortunately the first one was flooded out of existence, putting us back to square one.

We now had to build a new cave, higher up the wall of the wind-scoop. First, down at Royal Bay, we had a late Christmas dinner on 28 December. Marks and Spencer provisions, supplemented by some supplies from Fortnum and Mason, ensured a decent meal of stuffed eggs with caviar, Parma ham and champagne; game soup; goose quenelles with a passable Cabernet Sauvignon; Christmas pudding and whisky butter; port, brandy and Dutch cigars.

We returned to work. Brian and I took 7½ hours to trudge back up to the Ross pass, and on New Year's Eve we started digging the new cave, right at the top of the wind-scoop, well above the frozen lake. When the other three arrived in the evening we had room for them to sleep in the cave. Over the next three days we enlarged and perfected what was to be our home for 23 days. It is probably still there and is a desirable residence, comprising a removable snow-brick front door, leading to vestibule with cupboards, leading to fully fitted kitchen with chimney flue to Ross pass plateau, two main living rooms, seven feet high, with room to pitch sleeping tents inside and ample recessed storage shelves. Architectural features of interest include Romanesque columns and a Gothic niche. Damp needs attention but construction throughout is guaranteed to protect owners from the worst blizzards. This unique property lies in a peaceful secluded neighbourhood, where the only noise is the shriek of the blizzard. There are no local transport facilities but on skis the owners may quickly reach the seaside or explore the glaciers of the hinterland. Because of frequent white-out conditions, they are advised always to leave a line of marker wands on the Ross pass, indicating the approach to the wind-scoop, which can be invisible from 10 yards.

A typical day at the Ross pass would start with the clatter of pans in the kitchen as The Poltergeist prepared breakfast tea. An ice axe shaft through the front door would be enough to ascertain 'hundred per cent blizz conditions' outside and the promise of another day in bed. Soon a gentle slurping noise would indicate that Griffin had taken up his position, statuesque, in the Gothic niche with his morning pint of tea. We read, we talked, I listened to Butterfly, Brian wished he had brought Ted Hawkins as an antidote to 'all those screeching women', Kees tinkered with the Aaton and Lindsay grappled with the jumbo crossword. Periodically one of us would emerge from the drip-shelter tents to take our daily walk round the north and south wings, perhaps stopping to poke another hole in the front door and check blizz conditions.

Every two or three days a lull in the blizz would allow us to emerge from the cave and go down the Ross glacier to collect supplies from the depot or, later, to go climbing. One briefly clear dawn we all climbed The Thing, a shapely blob on the other side of the pass, reaching the summit in a full blizz, and skiing or snow-shoeing home on compass bearings. A few days later we enjoyed a full day of sunshine, dragging everything out on to the plateau to dry, taking turns to pose for Kees's now functioning Aaton and going skiing to reconnoitre a route to Vogel Peak (1352m). The following day we all went across to the foot of the peak. The four climbers, leaving Kees at the bottom with the Aaton and a long lens, proceeded up 600m of snow-slopes, ice terraces, crevasses, little walls and a summit ridge of rime mushrooms, to make the first ascent.

The weather was already closing in again on the way down, but we just had time to glimpse the truly Antarctic expanse of glacial snowfields and unclimbed peaks stretching south down the Salvesen range – the area we had really hoped to explore. Conditions reverted to hundred per cent blizzing and after a few more days' incarceration at the scoop our food stocks dwindled to two days'. Then, at the eleventh hour, when we had virtually given up hope of climbing Mount Carse or anything else, the wind veered round to the east, the sky cleared and we had one final chance.

Finesse is not the word that springs to mind where Julian's skiing is concerned; and Lindsay's leg injuries forced him some years ago to abandon planks altogether. However, at this stage the only hope of climbing Mount Carse, 15 miles south, was to travel fast and take the mountain by storm. So Brian and I headed south with the skis, while Julian and Lindsay took the snowshoes and travelled north with Kees to the closer but harder target of Mount Kling (1847m).

They deposited Kees, tripod and Aaton to record events from halfway up the mountain, then continued up steepening ice slopes which led eventually to a spectacular headwall of loose black rock overlaid with sugar icing. It gave Julian a long hard pitch of protectionless mixed climbing and got the pair of them on to the summit. At least they called it the summit, choosing not to surmount the final 15-foot blade of rotten ice overhanging the great precipice of the NE face. As Lindsay pointed out, the suicidal blade was not a permanent fixture and there is ample precedent on the similar structures of Patagonia for not climbing the final ice blob. Only the most ardent pedant could dispute that they had made the first ascent of Mount Kling. From the summit they had a fine view south along the Salvesen range, past Vogel, Smoky Wall and Paterson to the white pyramid of Mount Carse, 20 miles away, where Brian and I were just about to start our ascent.

We had left at seven that morning on the 13-mile journey to the foot of our mountain. We had to cross a little pass, then skim down to the start of the Spenceley glacier. As we skinned up the Spenceley it was nice to think that, apart from Duncan Carse's initial exploration of 1955, a BAS team in 1974 and the Services expedition of 1982, no one, as far as we knew, had ever been here. Brian, who is always disgustingly fit, set a cracking pace, but by cutting a straight line through his haphazard meanderings I was just able to keep up.

There was a pass to cross at the head of the Spenceley, then a brilliant descent on firm crust, followed by an hour's climb to the third, final pass, with our mountain framed in its vee. One final exhilarating descent took us skimming down on to the Novosilski glacier to pitch the tent in a hollow right at the foot of Mount Carse.

Brian kept up the pressure and we were only allowed a three-hour rest in the tent before setting off again. Knowing the fickleness of South Georgia weather, he argued that the longer we waited to climb the peak, the greater the chance of being caught by a break in the weather: once the wind reverted to normal westerly blizzing mode, travelling back down the Spenceley might be impossible, and we could be trapped 13 miles from base with only two days' food and fuel.

At 4pm we started the 1200m route up the north-west flank of Mount Carse. The climbing was not spectacular, but the occasional ice-wall or crevasse kept us amused and the views were stunning – dagger shadows stretching across the velvet surface of the Novosilski glacier, which merged imperceptibly into the Southern Ocean, studded with glinting icebergs and the dark rocks of the Pickersgill Islands. On the final slopes we could see right up the length of the island, to the towering Mont Blanc bulk of Mount Paget and beyond, right up to the peaks of the far north-west peninsula, nearly 100 miles away. Then the sun set, and it was almost dark when we reached the summit at 9.30pm. A few shivering photos, half a pound of marzipan to refuel our bodies and it was time to descend, rushing down in the darkness to our tent, hot soup and bed.

In the morning we ski'd home. On the Spenceley glacier it took just 20 minutes to skim down ground that had taken three hours to climb the previous day. Then we hit a wind funnel and, on the final pass crossing to regain the snow-cave, we were knocked repeatedly out of our ski bindings. At one stage I was reduced to crawling on hands and knees to make progress, and on the final approach to the cave we were back to the traditional groping through thick cloud on a compass bearing. The journey to the summit of Carse and back had taken 31 hours.

We spent another month on South Georgia, based further north, on Cumberland Bay, but although the weather was better in February we achieved no more climbs. We had had enough of sitting in snow-caves, so we based ourselves at the coast, too far from the action to catch the weather windows. It would have been nice to make some more first ascents and perhaps to climb the island's highest peak, Mount Paget. On the other hand, life at the coast was pleasanter. You can climb a mountain any time, but it is not every day that you can spend a morning watching Sooty albatrosses at their nest, or walk over to see the fur seals playing around the whalers' shipwrecks or film one of the largest King penguin colonies in the world. Anyway, we had made first ascents of various assorted nunataks, as well as three of the island's main watershed peaks, including the mountain named after the island's guru, Duncan Carse, whose private, lightweight survey expeditions of the 1950s had done for South Georgia what Shipton and Tilman did for the Himalaya.

We spent our last week at the Grytviken army garrison. Kees busied himself in the darkroom, while Brian and Lindsay set off on long excursions, tramping tirelessly over every hill and crag in the vicinity; but Julian and I had tired of the 'wilderness experience' and we whiled away whole days in the mess, smoking, drinking and watching endless videos, broadening our cultural horizons with such gems as 'Death Wish IV' and 'The Blob'.

This final week of indulgence was typical of the hospitality of the armed services whose support had made the expedition possible. Nowadays there are normally only two ways for a civilian to visit South Georgia. Either you get a brief glimpse of the island from an extremely expensive Antarctic cruise ship, or you make your own way in a private yacht. Both options were out of the question for us, and our lift with the *Endurance* was perhaps a unique opportunity to spend three months on the 'Island at the Edge of the World'.

Ama Dablam 1990

BRENDAN MURPHY

(Plates 1, 25–29)

Ama Dablam, meaning 'mother's necklace' in Nepalese, is a much admired 6852m peak in the Khumbu Himal of Nepal. Ray Delaney had been inspired by the mountain during his first trip to Nepal and had been talking about climbing it ever since. When I heard that he had finally booked the pre-monsoon slot for 1990, I decided it was time to send him a Christmas card. I was not alone in my cunning as it turned out, for Ray was persuaded to invite not only myself but three of my university contemporaries: Robert Durran, Pete Herold and Kate Phillips. He also signed up two of his Sheffield friends, Richard Haszko and Joe Simpson, as well as his long-time sparring partner, Mal Duff.

Just as preparations were nearing completion, Ray telephoned me to pass on the shattering news: Perpetual, an investment management company, had decided to fund the entire trip. This generous deal (negotiated by the sweet-talking Simpson), combined with the financial contribution made by Mal Duff's supporting trek, meant that the British Ama Dablam Expedition 1990 was in the happy position of being guaranteed at least solvency, if not success.

The first wave of the expedition arrived in Kathmandu on 14 February, to be joined a few days later by the rest of the team and our ten trekking companions. Joe was nursing a broken foot at the time (the result of a drinking accident in England), so the inevitable delay in our departure for the mountains proved rather fortunate. A diet of Nepalese rum appeared to be the prescribed treatment and, sure enough, by the time the last of the bureaucratic hurdles had been overcome, a full recovery had been effected.

The walk-in from Jiri was an ideal start to the expedition, although the effort required to keep up with Kate somewhat marred the experience. We had none of the crowds or leeches that are prevalent at other times of the year, and I felt privileged to be able to experience the delights of Nepal in relative peace and comfort. The contrasts with the Karakoram (the only other part of the Himalaya that I had visited) were stark and numerous: the well-worn paths and the frequent tea houses made the walking almost pleasurable! The Iceberg beer (another marked contrast with Pakistan) flowed at every opportunity, fuelling some of the most outlandish stories I have ever heard; Duff and Simpson must rank as two of the most accomplished raconteurs of our time.

We arrived at Base Camp on 5 March, ten days after leaving Jiri. The green and pleasant meadow that we had been promised turned out to be under a foot of snow, but the location, a quiet side-valley ringed by magnificent peaks, provided ample compensation. We took the opportunity to rest for a couple of days and contemplate our objective, the SW ridge of Ama Dablam. The first section of the route follows a long horizontal rock ridge guarded by occasional gendarmes. Steep mixed ground (breached by the 'Ramp') then leads to an elegant snowy ridge (the 'Mushroom Ridge') and so to the foot of the headwall. The last barrier to the summit is a massive serac band clearly visible from afar (the 'Dablam') which is best turned on the right. This is the original and most popular route up the mountain, and it is surely one of the best.

The ensuing argument about climbing ethics was predictable and doubtless entertaining for our trekkers; alpine-style, capsule-style or siege-style, and what did it all mean anyway? No one wanted to be load-carrying between fixed camps, particularly those who had had bad experiences of this in the past, yet none wanted to find themselves strung out on the mountain in bad weather. After lengthy and sometimes heated discussions, an uneasy compromise was reached, based on the desire to safeguard retreat along the kilometre or so of horizontal ridge. We decided to use a minimal amount of fixed rope and establish a couple of camps: Camp 1 at the start of the ridge, Camp 2 on the 'Yellow Tower' at the end of the ridge. Tactics for higher up on the mountain were to be agreed upon later.

Before concentrating our efforts on Ama Dablam, our first engagement was with Imja Tse (Island Peak, 6189m). This was the prime objective of our trekking party and was seen as a useful acclimatization exercise by the rest of us. In the event, the ascent of Island Peak turned out to be a thoroughly worthwhile experience for all concerned, especially since it gelled the erstwhile disparate groups of climbers and trekkers. Although the normal route is of little technical interest, the summit is a superb vantage point and is at a very respectable altitude. The excursion was only marred by Mal damaging his already-weakened ankle, and he was forced to drop out of the expedition. This failed to dint his high spirits, however, and we left him in Pheriche impressing the locals with his story-telling and beer-drinking exploits.

We arrived back at Base Camp on 13 March and immediately set to work on the mountain. The weather stayed fine, and within a surprisingly short time we had established Camp 2 and consolidated Camp 1. It quickly became apparent that there was a lot of fixed gear already on the ridge, although much of this was in a poor state of repair. This rather detracted from our enjoyment of what was otherwise very fine climbing, but it certainly helped our progress on the lower sections of the route.

It was at this time that an unfortunate indiscretion forced us back to base for a week: Kate started burning our Base Camp rubbish. The problem with this seemingly commendable act is that it brings bad luck, as we were told by our Sherpas, if carried out before the end of an expedition. Bad weather duly followed.

A more serious indiscretion, however, was my suggestion to Gavin that he call in at Base Camp during his trip around the world. I had assumed that the vagueness of the directions I had left him would assure our continued seclusion, but I had underestimated the ability of one who has been travelling for six months to sniff out a free meal. The novelty of his arrival quickly wore off as his true character became known to the rest of the party; our serenity was rudely shattered. I was required to apologize for my blunder at all too regular intervals.

A further potential disaster was only narrowly averted during this period of enforced confinement at Base Camp. Despite the worst of intentions, Joe's attempt at poisoning the ravens failed dismally. These birds were serious pests (they pecked our Goretex tents to pieces), but we later found out that they are sacred creatures and that our survival depended on their well-being! We turned to card-playing to alleviate the boredom in the hope that this would be considered a more virtuous pastime. The democracy riots in Kathmandu that we were following on the World Service seemed to belong to a different world.

As soon as the weather improved, Joe and Ray went back up the hill to explore the route past Camp 2. Pete, Kate and I followed a few days later, intending to consolidate Camp 2 and take over at the front. When the five of us met up at Camp 2, the way looked open to the summit. Joe and Ray had reached the foot of the Ramp, and an alpine push from there looked in order.

Bad weather that night put paid to our hopes. We had a frustrating time the next day floundering through deep powder, and it became obvious that success was not going to come easily. Joe, Ray and Pete decided to return to Camp 2; Kate and I opted to press on regardless. We made a fair amount of progress up the Ramp, only to discover two hours before sundown that the stove was still in Pete's sack. We had no option but to retreat. To cap it all, Delaney and Simpson had scoffed the precious tin of tuna that I had carried all the way from Base Camp. It was April Fool's Day.

The next morning dawned fine. Kate and I quickly regained our high point while the others returned to base. It was great to be exploring new ground as we pitched our way towards the start of the Mushroom Ridge. Just as daylight was failing, we reached the crest of the ridge and were rewarded by the discovery of a comfortable ice-cave bivvy. A further treat was a superb sunset over the cloud-filled valley before the arrival of the evening snow.

Despite the further dump of snow during the night, we decided to forge on, safe in the knowledge that retreat to the tents and gas dump at Camp 2 would be relatively straightforward from this point. Much to my relief, the Mushroom Ridge failed to live up to its name; we had none of the nightmares experienced by the British climbers Cave and Perkins on this section a few years previously. The poor visibility robbed us of any views, but protected us from feelings of exposure. We moved together along this fragile snow-crest, reaching the snow plateau at the foot of the headwall by late afternoon. As we excavated our bivvy in the end of a crevasse, our hopes were high for the morrow. Good weather the next day was all we needed.

I dozed uneasily that night, searching the sky for stars. A lot of low cloud was drifting over and we delayed our departure until dawn. It was bitterly cold. We abandoned almost everything at the bivvy and started picking our way up the headwall. A brief break in the cloud below us allowed our friends at Base Camp to catch a glimpse of two specks moving ever so slowly towards the summit; this was the first sighting they had had of us since we had left Camp 2, and it was to be their last for the next three days.

Crossing a small arête at the top of the lower snow slopes brought us in to a gully at the base of the seracs; it looked like the key to the summit. But as one hard pitch followed another and the hours ticked by, my spirits steadily sank. By the time I had emerged on to the upper snow slopes, I had resigned myself to retreat. Although the last of the technical difficulties was now behind us, I knew we had no chance of reaching the summit and returning to our bivvy before dark. I swallowed my disappointment and discussed the options with Kate, fully expecting her to elect for descent. To my surprise and great pleasure, she was as enthusiastic as ever, seemingly undaunted by the late hour of the day. I pressed on with renewed optimism, convinced now that we would make the top.

For many long hours we plodded upwards, following the steep ice ridge dividing the upper headwall. I could only manage a few steps at a time, pausing regularly to claw at the cold dry air. Intermediary landmarks became temporary goals in an effort to sustain my willpower. Occasional glimpses of the fringing rock buttresses through the swirling cloud were the only way I could gauge our progress. Eventually, and quite unexpectedly, the ridge relented and I found myself collapsed in a heap on the summit. Kate joined me a few minutes later, racked by an evil cough but looking extremely happy. It was 6pm, 4 April 1990.

Any sense of achievement was completely masked by anxiety at the prospect of retreat in the dark. My immediate concern, however, was for the state of my feet which had been numb for much of the day. I spent the few remaining minutes of daylight massaging my toes in a vain attempt to restore the circulation while Kate rummaged for her spare socks. We braced ourselves for an epic.

The six-hour descent was sufficiently harrowing for it to be engraved in my memory for ever. Fortunately, however, it proceeded with clockwork precision and we were spared the ordeal I had feared. I had made a mental note during the day of each of the abseils we would require to get off and, despite failing head-torch batteries and a dropped sticht plate, we made steady progress towards safety. Our biggest worry was the security of the snow-stake anchors, since these could be pushed into the soft snow by hand and tended to wobble alarmingly. Finding the belays in the dark was tricky enough, but the more stressful role fell to the second who was left to watch the inevitable creep of the stake and ponder the merits of unclipping. Our spindrift-swept bivvy was sweet sanctuary indeed.

Warm sunshine and a respite from the howling wind the next morning brought a great sense of relief. I had spent much of the night in a private world of misery, groaning with pain as the blood filtered back to my feet; the improvement in the weather and the opportunity to dry out our gear rekindled my spirits. My pleasure at our success was somewhat tainted by worry about the rest of the descent, but I was confident that we could cope with the remaining obstacles.

The next couple of days were relatively uneventful, if not entirely enjoyable. We continued painstakingly to retrace our steps, ever mindful of the dangers of complacency. The ice-encrusted tents of Camp 2 were a welcome haven and we passed the night in relative comfort. The weather continued to improve the next day and we were quickly spotted by our friends; they had been extremely concerned for our safety. Only years of conditioning allowed me to hold back the tears as we were all reunited at Base Camp. We had been on the hill for eight days.

On 12 April Joe and Ray left their high camp for the summit and topped out in perfect conditions; their patience and experience were rewarded by stunning views and a daytime descent of the headwall! Kate and I went back up to Camp 2 one last time to dismantle our tents and strip a lot of old rope. While some would argue that this was an unnecessary additional risk, it seemed the very least we could do for the mountain.

Perhaps the strongest impression I have, thinking back on the expedition, was the great sense of camaraderie, surely the key to our success. Four of us had the pleasure of reaching the summit, but all of us have fond memories of the trip. Kate and I are especially conscious of our good fortune: our gamble on the headwall paid off. Kate was only the second British national to reach the summit (the other was Mike Ward on the first ascent in 1961); my ascent was the first by an Irishman.

All of us were impressed by the beauty of the Khumbu and appalled by its obvious abuse. Both Base Camps we visited were strewn with rubbish, much of which could have been burned or carried out. Even the majestic Ama Dablam itself is littered with old gear, much of it useless, all of it offensive. Perhaps our greatest source of satisfaction should be the knowledge that at least we left the mountain and its Base Camp in a better state than we had found them.

In the Annapurna Sanctuary

LINDSAY GRIFFIN

(*Plates 2–4*)

So you are planning a brief visit to the Himalaya? Then drive an hour or two from Pokhara along the dusty jeep track that rises gently to the north-west and stop at the wooden shanties of Suikhet. The five-day amble into the Annapurna Sanctuary from this point is one of the country's most popular tourist treks. Along the way you will meet the friendliness and hospitality that is typical of the very best in rural Nepal. You will also find it very difficult to walk for more than 1½ hours without stopping for a welcome brew in one of the many recently established, government-funded, 'Chai houses' that have sprung up along the trail.

What does Jimmy Roberts think now, I wonder? When he first penetrated this dramatic cwm, rimmed by the various peaks of the Annapurnas, the wonderfully named Machapuchare and Hiunchuli, he was the first person other than local shepherds to do so. It was 1956, and Chomrong was the last habitation. Three further days were needed to climb through the impressive gorge of the Modi Khola 'most of the way by dismal bamboo slogging'. Little had changed by 1970, when Haston and Whillans reached the summit of Annapurna 1 via the S face. By the end of that decade, however, the floodgates had well and truly opened. With an annual increase in trekking tourism of nearly 20%, demanding much more than the area can realistically provide, the Annapurna Conservation Area Project is trying hard to maintain the fragile environment. Supplies of kerosene (and also stoves, which can be rented by trekking groups) are stocked at Chomrong. Burning wood beyond this point is normally banned, although the recent Nepalese–Indian trade embargo has gone a long way towards causing renewed destruction to the rhododendron forests.

In the spring of 1989 I was able to explore a small corner of the Sanctuary thanks to the organizational ability of Jonny Garratt – a young upwardly mobile army captain who professed 'connections in the City'. The previous year he had reached the dizzy heights of the Hornbein couloir without supplementary oxygen; a feat that, he was quick to point out, arose from a complete mechanical breakdown in his set rather than from any ethical trait. Martin Doyle, Dave Harries, Mike Woolridge and Jon Tinker, with Kath Slevin as Base Camp manageress, completed this happy team.

Our vote had been cast in favour of a fairly short but interesting approach to Base Camp; quick and easy access from the latter to the bottom of the route, which would lessen the load-carrying; an attractive unclimbed line with a certain degree of technical climbing throughout, so minimizing, we hoped, the occurrence of avalanche-prone snowslopes; a low seven-thousander and preferably an untrodden summit; and for Jonny, whose job it was to raise the cash, something with a familiar ring to it, like Everest! Well, that narrowed it down. In fact it only appeared to leave the E face of Annapurna South!

The first ascent of this previously unattempted 7219m peak fell to a young Japanese team making an inaugural visit to the Himalaya in 1964. They sited their Base Camp, at just over 4000m, in the ablation valley of the South Annapurna glacier – 'a very beautiful place, covered with green grass and pretty flowers, and with crystal-clear pools of fresh drinking water.' We would use the same idyllic location – or would we? The intervening years have taken their toll and the area has been graced with the splendid architecture of the 'Annapurna Base Camp Hotels' – two rather squalid tea shacks and widespread litter.

The Japanese owed a great deal to the considerable expertise of their climbing Sherpas (shades of Rum Doodle?). Massive amounts of rope were fixed up the jumbled depression on the left side of the E face. They finally gained the N ridge at a point between the N and central summits. The highest and S summit was reached on 15 October by Mingma Tsering and Shoichiro Uyeo. 'It was a narrow, snow-covered point that the two of us could not stand on at the same time.' Closer inspection proved that their route, at one stage envisaged as our possible descent, was a singularly unattractive line. The South Annapurna glacier, rising to a small plateau below the face, was far safer and much more straightforward than suggested by its tortured appearance. Above, however, no line seemed immune from tumbling ice. Serac debris of all shapes and sizes littered a vast area – too hostile an audience for our unrehearsed performance.

The safest route of ascent on this side of the mountain appeared to follow the watershed delimiting the left side of this face. Rocky towers just above the col at the base of the E ridge look quite tricky but can be bypassed by following one of the several steep snow ribs on the N flank. The continuation could be straightforward, given reasonable conditions and not the more usual Himalayan fare of windslab or deep unstable snow. It is a much easier proposition than the unclimbed W ridge of Hiunchuli which rises from the opposite side of the col. The E ridge has seen at least half-a-dozen attempts, but only once has it been completed. On that occasion, bad weather terminated the ascent at the central summit. In more recent years attention has focused on the S side. This is undoubtedly the most beautiful facet, and the purity of its ribs and ridge lines has been admired by most travellers who reach the magnificent viewpoint of Poon hill. Attempts, in both summer and winter – mainly by Japanese – have been many; successes have been few. The face rises from the depths of the Chomrong gorge, and access has proved both difficult and time-consuming for laden porters. Perhaps the least-known but most remarkable achievement belongs to the Italian Tessarin who made a clandestine ascent, solo, of a new route on the 2000m high SW face, over three days in August 1988.

On the E face a pronounced pillar leads straight as an arrow to the unclimbed N summit. The bottom bit looks all right: a nice scamper up there in a day from a well-stocked camp at the foot of the face; it might need two trips. The rockband looks hard, and that very steep ice arête above could be rather serious; we might take some rope for that – and I confess to you now, with no little shame, that we took a small amount of rope for fixing. In effect, triple the amount would not have gone amiss! As somebody calculated the face to be 2000m high, it was suggested that acclimatization on Tarpu Chuli (which at 5663m sounds more exotic than Tent peak) and Hiunchuli (6441m) would prove most beneficial.

We reached Base Camp on 12 April and attempted to pitch camp. The 'pretty flowers' appeared to be buried under four metres of heavy winter snow. With no available running water and great difficulty in keeping food fresh, the kitchen became a continual source of chaos and lack of hygiene. Despite the unseasonable problems of access we had privacy rivalling that of Piccadilly Underground Station. Funny how the best-laid plans go astray, isn't it!

In the ensuing days a bright morning would make inroads into the snow depth. Unfortunately, by early afternoon the first flakes would be floating down from an overcast sky and the *status quo* would be fully restored by the following morning. It was easy to convince ourselves that any summits were out of the question for the time being, and instead we slowly began to establish a camp at the foot of the ridge. The long hours of upward toil through deep wet snow were rewarded by a subsequent descent of the same terrain via some monstrous glissades – the most inventive members perfecting a Waikiki surfing technique atop the removable stiffened backpad from a rucksack! Our tents were pitched beneath the overhangs of a rocky outcrop which conveniently deflected any snow-slides well over our heads. After a night there, officially to indulge in the head-thumping joys of premature acclimatization but mainly, I suspect, to escape the unremitting *dahl bhat* at base, we went up for a wee foray. Passing various pieces of old and abandoned equipment, such as obese deadmen of heavy steel plating and similarly constructed 'tent pegs', we came upon the first of the ropes.

Up to this moment we had been blissfully unaware of any previous sortie. Local information later suggested an unofficial attempt – a most unlikely breach of mountaineering regulations, in full view of the whole Sanctuary. This had obviously proved no deterrent to three Japanese climbers who had blatantly fixed the lower ridge with double 7mm hawser. Bleached and rotten, the sections that remained served only to remind us of the subsequent disappearance of the whole team somewhere on the mountain. The rest had either disintegrated or, more likely, had become well buried along with its owners. We progressed with a certain trepidation, afraid perhaps of what we might find.

Quite soon we were afflicted by that well-known ailment that Tilman often referred to as 'Mountaineer's Foot' – a total inability to put one foot in front of the other. An oxygen-starved brain rationalized the problem to be somehow connected with the fact that we were standing up to our thighs in snow. From below we had blithely dismissed this section as offering pleasant front-pointing. The sun had peered over the horizon only a couple of hours earlier, yet we were already too late. Suddenly the *dahl bhat* became wonderfully attractive and we beat a hasty retreat, realizing that we might just have to revise our strategy a little!

All our prior research and extensive photographic information had led us to severely underestimate the difficulties in the lower half. My only excuse could be that, standing there in the raw flesh of post winter, it was hard to recognize the hill from any of those wonderfully bewitching pictures that it had been my misfortune to see. In order to make any headway in the very limited time available for climbing, we would be forced to leave ropes on the mushy snow-plastered slabs of the lower ridge. These would allow a safe descent during daylight hours and could be pulled up once we were all properly established below the middle wall. Already we were giving way to siege tactics and, at this early stage, I think a certain amount of enthusiasm was lost.

A chest infection, contracted either in Pokhara or during the trek, was proving troublesome, though I naïvely assumed that it would clear up in due course. General illness worked through the team on a rotating basis, so that we never seemed to have more than two people on the hill at a time. When Jon and I next climbed the diminishing ice gully at the start of the ridge, a waning moon threw long shadows across the frozen slopes above. We cramponned several hundred metres to reach the first of our recently placed ropes which led up a succession of steep slabs to the crest. Almost immediately we were unhappy, despite reassuring multiple anchors. There would be 10 or 20m gaps in the ropes in order to eke out our minimal resources. That was all right in theory, as the climbing was straightforward, but, in practice, what of these apparently solid lumps of stone hidden under the snow? There was little need for discussion – our philosophies were far too similar. The ropes were rearranged to form one continuous chain, and we felt much happier for it. Unfortunately there were others who, at the time, felt this unnecessary and, at a later stage, the original configuration was restored – with near tragic consequences. The incident occurred on a section I remember well. A 100m rappel, well positioned high above the approach couloir, began with a smooth five-metre slab. This lay above a short slope rapidly turning from névé white to ice grey. Below, a steep gully plunged through a rocky barrier to gain the long wet snow slopes that resembled a giant Nordic ski-jump on to the distant South Annapurna glacier. It was just before passing the base of the slab that one member found himself airborne, describing a graceful backward somersault over that memorable view. The anchors, under the melting influence of the noonday sun, had ripped. With an almost inconceivable piece of luck and agility he landed 'front-points down' on the ice and came to an ankle-wrenching halt, spread-eagled across the slope. I suspect the next few minutes must have been somewhat precarious and mentally absorbing as he carefully slid off his sack, even more carefully balanced it on his head and extracted both ice tools. Not without some further difficulty did he crampon up to refix the anchors, before continuing the rappel in a more traditional style!

Above the ropes, we were left to deal with a steep triangle of rock. Once through this barrier, bizarre formations of snow and ice, admittedly at a more amenable angle, would lead to the middle wall. I remember some awkward balance climbing and a curious little move off a jammed axe shaft. Then I saw it up to the left. I was surprised; perhaps less by the existence of a stainless steel bolt, presumably of Japanese manufacture, than by its placement in a rather wobbly oversized block on a rather undersized ledge. Had I been a modern rock-jock it would have sparked an 'overhead clip' before 'cranking out left on dinkies'. As it was I grovelled up to the right on sloppy mixed ground and reached a section that might well have delighted those *aficionados* of the Kentish coastline, but seemed most inappropriate 5000 miles distant. Remembering my instructional manual, I adopted a technique of 'Piolet Punishment'. Jabbing wildly into the mud above I made a mental note to give Hastings a wide berth!

As the rope went tight I became a coughing wreck, slumped over a rounded snow boss on the ridge. Above, the spine thrust upwards again in a short section of poor conglomerate. I hacked furiously with an adze at a shallow depression on the left side of the rib. The resulting hole accepted a No 2 friend reluctantly – until the hammer was applied (no you're right, it wasn't mine). Selecting the two largest blade pegs, I drove them straight into the mud somewhere above. Was it good enough? Strength and patience had all but gone. I was ill, and I knew it. Gingerly I applied my weight, ever so cautious now but then with more and more abandon until my body convinced my mind. Burrowing my lower limbs into the boss, face down on the snowy pillow, I croaked to Jon to climb.

By the following evening I had begun a course of erythromycin, kindly donated by a trekking physician, and had descended to 3200m. With this powerful combination I found myself learning, yet again to my cost, that rules are not there to be broken. Why should it have been so hard to convince myself that a drop of six or eight hundred metres would make that much difference? The two teashacks that constitute the developing conurbation of Bagar provided a welcome sanatorium. Almost immediately the inside of my chest and sinuses began to smile. Within two days things were well on the mend and a quick reascent on the evening of the third did nothing to retard this improvement.

Alas, it was all in vain. Repeating illnesses throughout the team and persistent snowfall allowed us to get no further than the base of the middle wall at 6000m. Above, the way looked intensely forbidding – black, vertical and mud! We hadn't even scratched the main difficulties, which we now realized to be quite substantial, and the summit was a long, long way off. Heavy monsoon rain beat on our leech-infested legs as we scampered down to Pokhara at the beginning of June.

The line remains to be climbed, and it is a good one. Go late in the year when less snow and lower temperatures should allow climbing for most of the day. In fact, given the easterly aspect and middle range of altitude, it is possible that early winter might provide the most favourable conditions for an ascent. But my advice to you is to take along a few dozen titanium snow-stakes and a big hammer for that middle 'rock' band!

Trekking on Tops

A Kangchenjunga Diary

VLADIMIR BALYBERDIN

(Vladimir Balyberdin participated in the Soviet traverse of the summits of Kangchenjunga in 1989. This article is an extract from his expedition diary. It should be read in conjunction with the account in last year's Alpine Journal *(AJ95, 24–8, 1990/91). Translated by Antoni Marianski.)*

... In the evening of 21 April, in the Forest Camp in Tseram, Ivanov called a coaches' meeting which began with the sentence: 'In my opinion the traverse should be tackled by two groups of five.' Then we sat for over an hour discussing the situation, the opportunities for the team, and offering alternative ideas mainly so as to increase the number of men making the traverse. However, the discussion was terminated by Ivanov: 'I am closing the discussion by stating my own decision that the team shall consist of 10 men.' None of our arguments had been heeded ...

Next day, Ivanov started the meeting with the sentence: 'Well, yesterday we decided ...' I said: 'No, we didn't decide, it was ordered.' Valia said: 'In my opinion we should start by appointing the leaders ...' More tommy-rot. But finally we got down to naming the team members. The coaches were all asked for their opinion, one after the other. Kazbek took into account the difficulties encountered on the south route and suggested that a group for the traverse should consist of those who had worked on it, plus all the members of his group apart from himself, as he was ill. He suggested that we and the Moscow group should have the opportunity to finish off preparing our branch of the centre route. Realizing that he was not including in the traverse party even his best friend Khrichthaty, I was momentarily dumbstruck. I couldn't understand if he was joking or something, or on the point of making another suggestion. But after a few generalizations Kazbek finished. As I see it, Valeri [Khrichthaty] was sunk in his own thoughts at the time and either didn't see disaster approaching or was sure he had misheard.

Vasili Elagin, who was next to speak, naturally did not agree with the role of spear-carrier that had been allotted to him and said that he and his friends had done their bit and had no less a right to do the traverse than others. I think it was actually Elagin who was the first to propose an administrative mechanism for forming the teams: two men from each of our groups. From there on things went smoothly, the pairs were named with very little discussion, and each pair included the group-leader, those leaders all being present. Faces brightened up again, everyone was pleased with everyone else – it was idyllic. But then it was Khrichthaty's turn. Valeri, as a man of principle, was unwilling to go along with a mean-minded compromise which embodied no sporting principles. He suggested a completely new approach, similar to the one I had suggested the day before. Our group to go out with a tent and all the necessaries, start the traverse, set up a bivouac in the couloir between the central and main summits, leave an equipped camp there and complete the traverse using the camp on the west route as a base. In that way we would be satisfying four more men, since the other 10 would still be operating the old plan, and, secondly, we would be solving the thorniest problem of the traverse which was the absence of a proper fifth camp on the centre route. At first Ivanov didn't even want to hear any new suggestions, but at Efimov's insistence Valeri was done the favour of being allowed to have his say. Suddenly Elagin supported him. The coaches were politely mute.

This proposal was news to me, so I had to think while speaking. I said that I liked it. 'How do we form the group of ten?' asked Efimov. I answered that I hadn't climbed in the other groups and couldn't take it upon myself to allocate people.

'But what principles should guide us?' Sergei was again being querulous.

'I have always considered that sporting considerations should be paramount, but I am beginning to realize that the majority here are in favour of an administrative solution. Perhaps they are right.'

'Then tell us who should be taken from each group.'

'No, let the group leaders decide.'

I had always been sure that Sheinov and Klinezki were the best climbers in the Moscow group. But here was Elagin asserting that they were more tired during the sortie and were less ready for the traverse. I had no grounds for disputing that assertion.

The discussion ended there. Two hours later Ivanov announced his decision in front of everybody. There were to be 12 candidates for 10 places, plus two group leaders, Bershov and Elagin. Khrichthaty's proposal was forgotten.

As was to be expected, the reactions of the expedition members were various but relatively unemotional. Some were secretly glad, some were depressed or discouraged or offended, others flared up and quickly calmed down again, yet others covertly denounced the unfairness. Sergei Arsentiev refused to speak with a soul all evening, and next morning went up with Sheinov. Gradually the rest followed.

I was in no hurry and was very sorry that there were so few days to rest in. On the second day of my rest my ECG showed a pulse of 84 – most unusual. We evidently had overdone it on that climb. My bad throat hadn't gone away even though I had been sure that being in the forest would cure anything. No medicine helped.

Towards the evening of the 23rd the whole camp was in turmoil discussing an unexpected situation. The Myslovski-Cherni pair had climbed, with oxygen, from Camp 3 to Camp 5 West and was poised to go for the summit the following morning. Originally they had said they would go and have a look at the climb up the Yalung, but later they said that they would go up along the fixed rope, i.e. towards the main summit.

This caused passions to rage even more fiercely, perhaps, than over the list of men to tackle the traverse. The oxygen-users were crushed. Valeri Khrichthaty, by contrast, flew into a rage and mustered all the sarcasm of which he was capable. The climb up to 8200m, irrespective of the rest of the ascent, had indeed demonstrated what climbing with oxygen meant. Two old men of 52 and 50, with no acclimatization, training or medical supervision, had coolly climbed to over eight thousand and were intending to go even further, confident in their own strength.

But there were also other sides to the situation. Mainly, the safety question. The nearest rescue team was five days away from the climbers. Even in Base Camp, three days away, there was only one interpreter, Vasia Senatorov. At Camp 3 there were, allegedly, three Sherpas who could give back-up. But there was no radio contact with them, so they might as well not have been there. Also, from the point of view of principles and rules and traditions, this action didn't fit any framework.

Next day everybody was on tenterhooks waiting for news from the summit. However, the two men had changed their minds and had come down. The oxygen-users heaved a sigh of relief even though, in principle, nothing had changed, bygones were bygones, and the climbers were coming down to what was called the eight-thousand mark, at 8200m, and spent the night there.

I had still not got better properly, my pulse was still over 70, my throat was sore. But along with the last group I left the Forest Camp on the 24th after lunch. We spent the night in Ramza. Next day, after seven hours of walking plus stops, we got to Base. On the way we chatted with some tourists from the Federal Republic of Germany, and drank tea in the first ice-bound camp.

Next day, 26 April, one group was sent climbing in spite of timid protests from some of its members who had just completed a long journey from down below and had not had a chance to rest. Pastukh's group was given the task of equipping Camp 5 on the centre route. He had Karataev, Khaibullin, Mojaev and Bogomolov.

The same day, at 12 noon, the final list for the traverse was announced: Elagin, Koroteev, Bershov, Turkevich, Vinogradsky, Pogorelov, Lunjakov, Khalitov, Bukreev and Balyberdin. It came to light that there had been a problem of counting out either me or Valeri, and the leaders, Elagin and Bershov, no longer wanted to take Khrichthaty, although they would probably have been pleased to get rid of me too. But that would have gone against the principle of two men from each group. It would be interesting to look at a national football team, recruiting one man from each city. I was shaken. In my opinion Valeri and I should both stay, though I wasn't quite so sure about myself. I started to think feverishly about what I should do.

I could do the traverse in the group, or do it with Khrichthaty, or else I could climb the main summit with him from Base to Base in 24 hours without a stop for the night.

While I was turning this over in my mind, they began to cobble together a group for a quick climb. Its nucleus was Khrichthaty, Suviga, Arsentiev and

Sheinov. Sergei was ready to put on oxygen in order to photograph the climb. Klinezki and Dedii were preparing to help as best they could. They went to the leaders with their suggestion. The negotiations and discussions of the options and the rest of it took 24 hours. Ivanov and Efimov seemed ready to consent, but Myslovski was dead against. It was the usual reason: the risk, which might affect the success of the expedition as a whole. The fact that the lads had calculated everything with hundred-per-cent back-up wasn't taken into account.

In the end the most determined men, Khrichthaty and Suviga, having exhausted all the legal avenues, settled on a final illegal one. They decided to go out at 11pm as planned, even without permission. The rest elected not to go for a direct confrontation and decided to work according to the plan laid down by the coaches.

In the course of this whole struggle Valeri came to me frequently for advice, his latest problem being: 'I'm afraid that they will hold up your group.' I tried to think coolly about this possibility which, on the face of it, seemed absurd.

'Hardly. It would be extraordinarily difficult to justify. Besides, there are Moscow people with us. Would they deprive them of the traverse? At the worst, they'll hold us up for 24 hours. What would be the justification for that?'

'Well, that's a comfort. I'm not afraid of the rest.'

I said that the cameramen were preparing to film their sortie with floodlights. He asked them not to, so as to avoid any unnecessary bother.

27 April

9pm. At supper Valeri has just told me: 'It's all over – I'm staying behind by myself.'

10 May

7.20am. It is very difficult to force oneself to write about the main climb. All that remains is a sense of disappointment, dissatisfaction, mixed with a feeling of unfairness and resentment.

We set off on 28 April. We reached Camp 2 quickly and easily, in spite of having to make tracks after a snowfall. I was loaded down by a cine camera which I had previously taken down for repair, six rolls of film and some food, that is, some 10 kilos. The others had the same without the cine equipment. I was depressed from the very start. I couldn't get used to the idea that Khrichthaty had been sidelined. I myself didn't feel very much like going in the group led by Elagin. It was clear that the combination of oxygen-users and obvious non-users would lead to problems. However, I was still sure that the three of us would survive and do the traverse without oxygen. I kept myself to myself and Vasili, who could see my mood, didn't bother me. And that internal tension was actually resolved during the climb. In Camp 2 I slept very soundly and seemed to be getting fitter. But still there did not seem to have been enough rest days. To this day I cannot imagine why Ivanov was pushing us so hard. Was he trying to synchronize the climb with the May Day holiday? After all, later we simply lived in the Forest Camp in Tseram for a few days, without food what's more. In fact we were half-starving for almost the whole of the expedition. On the 29th we climbed to Camp 3, again in many places we had to establish the track with our feet and we lost three hours 40 minutes on the crossing. I felt great, I did a lot of climbing ahead of the others and had plenty of time for filming.

Meanwhile Pastukh's group was following the centre route: three men were taking both peaks, the other two were going only for the main summit, having completed Camp 5 on the way. Arsentiev's group had climbed up to Camp 4 West.

There was plenty of space in Camp 3, and so as not to be cheek-by-jowl we took over both tents. I was on duty, which is why in the morning I didn't manage to get the camera ready fast enough and was a bit late leaving. The men from Alma-Ata had forged ahead, followed by Elagin, then Koroteev, who turned his oxygen on right beside the tents. Together with us there came two men from Pastukh's group to take away the empty cylinders from under the bergschrund. I filmed Vasili throwing them down. Meanwhile Koroteev had got separated from me but at the bergschrund I caught up with him and filmed the crossing. While I was reloading the camera he vanished again and I didn't catch up with him until Camp 4. Evidently I arrived an hour or so later than the first pair, as they had already prepared themselves to go ahead. They gave me a drink of hot juice. There was nothing to eat. That upset me . . . In all, the crossing had taken seven hours – quite a heavy day's work. I then had no reason to think that I was badly behind the others – after all I had the extra weight, the cine and stills equipment, and my stops were for filming purposes. Moreover, Lunjakov and Khalitov were not only keeping up with Elagin and Koroteev, who were using oxygen, but were actually ahead of them.

The decisive day, 1 May, was ahead of us. We had to go from Camp 5 South to Camp 5 West, via the south, central and main summits. Even before the traverse I had doubts about the advisability of such an intensive day's work . . . But I didn't make any specific objection. For two reasons: who here was going to take my opinion into account? and in my heart of hearts I was hoping to survive without oxygen. Unfortunately, it later became obvious that I should at that point have chosen between filming or doing the traverse without oxygen. The same choice as in our one-day climb without oxygen from Camp 3, when I had taken the sporting option. This time I was hoping for a little bit more. At Camp 5 Elagin told me to take one cylinder, but within an hour I realized that the weight would make me fall a long way behind, particularly as I was again filming a lot. I ditched the cylinder and went faster. On the famous wall, about which there were many frightening stories, Koroteev and I filmed each other. Afterwards he went up and I stopped to reload the camera. When I set off after him the whole group didn't seem very far away. But gradually the gap widened and I couldn't narrow it. On the summit Elagin turned to me indignantly – why was I holding everybody up and not turning my oxygen on? I didn't have any oxygen, that was why. Indignation again. With reason, actually. He gave me a cylinder from the ones lying on the summit. 'What about the others?' I asked. 'They are all using oxygen.'

That made the psychological turning-point easier for me. My great fatigue, and my responsibility towards the group, forced me to abandon my long-standing ambition quickly and matter-of-factly. It all turned out as I had predicted, though I had earlier preferred to disregard my own predictions. My lagging behind had let the Alma-Ata men down. Pointing at me made it easier for Elagin to order them to put their masks on. As they told me later, there was no need for that on the south summit. But I think that sooner or later there would have been. After all, oxygen-users needed only to give the valve a turn or two to leave the most acclimatized non-user behind. On the way down from the summit I met Bershov's group. Bukreev was a short distance in front, though I didn't recognize him through his mask. He immediately started to complain that he had been made to use oxygen and that he had completely lost interest in the traverse. I stopped and waited a good while for the others to appear so that I could film the whole group, but nobody came. Tolia and I said goodbye to each other like companions in misfortune, and we separated. A while later the others appeared in a bunch. I did film them, but in my opinion it was a boring clip because they were all indistinguishable in their masks. Meanwhile our group, who had got as far as the rise up to the central summit, were in difficulties. They had to go up along a fairly narrow crest, over a steep layer of snow and then rocks. 'Why didn't you leave a fixed rope?' I asked Turkevich. 'Because we came down the sheer face, but it's impossible to go up it.' Of course, they could have left one, they just didn't think. All the same, Lunjakov managed that section comparatively fast, fixed a rope and the rest of us followed him. I also hurried off, after observing all this peacefully at a distance. When I went up along the guide-rope Koroteev, who was a rope's length or two away, shouted something down to me. I didn't understand a word, but later noticed a message in a hook. I was to take the guide-rope down and bring it with me. I started taking it out. A bit came and then it got stuck. I was forced to go back, undo the knot at the end and pull it through again.

The extra three kilos did not exactly add to my speed, especially as using oxygen had not given me much relief. You evidently do need to actually work with oxygen constantly, otherwise your system takes a long time to re-adapt after prolonged oxygen starvation. At the central summit I took a few snaps and hurried down. The group were already tackling the main summit. I was sure that I would not get there before twilight; however, the gap closed quite rapidly and halfway up I met Arsentiev's group on their way from Camp 4 West to Camp 5 Centre via the main summit. Khrichthaty was climbing without oxygen, which is why Arsentiev was very angry when we met, because he thought it pointless to wear oneself out on journeys to deliver equipment. Suviga, who was using oxygen and carrying all Khrichthaty's things, was unperturbed. 'Turn the supply up,' he said (I had set it at 1.8), 'the summit's right here, and it is only an hour and a half down to Camp – why economize?' Valeri Khrichthaty was walking as if on to a pedestal, or a scaffold: slowly, with concentration, as if every step was a tremendous event, the outcome (as we felt) of a colossal concentration of all his strength – in other words, he was keeping himself going on will-power alone.

Approaching the summit I suddenly discovered that I could make it while it was still light. Elagin reached the summit at 6pm and I reached it at 6.30.

We took photos of each other, on the off-chance they would come out . . . After coming down from the tower on the peak, we found the fixed ropes fastened by previous expeditions and Valiev's group. But after a while the ropes suddenly ended. It was completely dark, the couloir was carpeted by a thick board-like layer of snow. This meant that, with the absence of ropes and the bad visibility, there was a certain avalanche risk. Trying not to lose the tracks of Lunjakov, who had gone first, we crawled cautiously down each protuberance of rock. Finally I saw that Vasili in front of me had stopped alongside Koroteev, and that they were both at a loss. Lunjakov's tracks had got covered over, there was no answer to their shouts. We had to wait for Khalitov, who was a long way behind. But when he reached us, he took a short while to figure out where we were. It was gone eight when we located the tent. Grisha got in and apparently fell asleep at once. We were astounded at the site Valiev had selected for a camp – almost in the middle of a couloir threatened by possible avalanches. Still, we weren't going to reposition the camp in the middle of the night, after 12 hours of uninterrupted toil . . .

Death at Extreme Altitude

OSWALD OELZ

In October 1988 four Czechoslovak climbers made the first alpine-style ascent of the formidable SW face of Mount Everest, first climbed in 1975 by Chris Bonington's large British expedition. They were equipped with the inner lining of one tent, two sleeping bags, two 40m climbing ropes, four ice axes, two ice hammers, three small cameras, one light video camera, a cooking stove and gas, food for three days and little else. After three and a half days they reached the south summit (8750m) and one climber continued to the summit (8872m). The others began to descend towards the South Col. In the early evening the summiteer rejoined the others at approximately 8300m and radioed that they felt bad and that three persons were nearly blind. They were never heard from again. Americans arriving at the South Col half an hour later could see the entire route to the south summit, but no signs of human activity. Since this area is easy scrambling ground for an experienced climber, the mass disappearance is most likely a consequence of high-altitude cerebral edema which caused the climbers to fall through a cornice or be blown off the ridge.

This is just one recent example illustrating the horrifying statistics on the highest peaks of this globe. To date, 246 climbers have made a total of 275 ascents of Mount Everest; 102 climbers have died on the slopes of this mountain (Elizabeth Hawley, personal communication). This ratio shows no decline in recent years. In the post-monsoon season of 1988, 31 individuals reached the summit of Mount Everest; nine climbers died, seven while attempting the summit without bottled oxygen. 66 persons have climbed K2 (8611m), while 24 have died during the climb. The death toll on 83 British expeditions to peaks over 7000m from 1968 until 1987 was 4.3%. There are repetitive personal tragedies for élite high-altitude climbers like Doug Scott and Krzysztof Wielicki, who survive 10 or more years after two or three high-altitude climbing expeditions per year, while losing most of their close climbing friends who share their passion.

Of the 102 climbers who died on Mount Everest, 49 were killed by falling ice, particularly in the notorious Khumbu ice-fall, and by avalanches. 28 persons suffered a fatal fall and 16 a condition described as 'illness' (exhaustion, exposure), while nine died from unknown causes. In the case of these previously very healthy individuals, 'illness' in most circumstances means high-altitude pulmonary edema (HAPE) and/or cerebral edema (HACE). Falls of experienced climbers on the relatively easy routes of Mount Everest are certainly in part due to hypoxia and/or HACE-induced brain dysfunction. Likewise, 'death from unknown causes' hides hypoxia consequences. Comparable numbers for death caused by HAPE, HACE and unknown causes were found in an analysis of British expeditions, where the chances of death increased with altitude. The recent rash of fatalities in climbers without supplementary oxygen who explore above 8000m further illustrates the crucial role of cerebral hypoxia. On the first ascent of Mount Everest without bottled oxygen, Messner felt 'unusually clumsy' and noted, 'if I had no axe I should simply fall down' and 'we cannot any longer keep on our feet while we rest'.

This ataxia is not surprising if one considers the degree of hypoxia at altitudes above 8500m. The calculated arterial PO_2 in one climber on the summit of Mount Everest was 28 torr; the corresponding value in eight volunteers decompressed over weeks to that altitude in a hypobaric chamber was 30 torr. The arterial oxygen saturation in these subjects was 58% and it dropped to 51% during work.

Can anything be done to reduce the number of victims at extreme altitude? Considering the competitive personalities of these climbers, the fascination associated with long, arduous and dangerous climbs, and the public interest and financial support focused on the most spectacular climbs, it is unlikely that mountaineers will turn great attention to pastoral peaks. Therefore, avalanches and ice and rock falls will continue to kill climbers. The risk can only be reduced by spending less time in the area of danger, as did the two Swiss, Erhart Loretan and Jean Troillet. These men climbed the N face of Everest in 40 hours and returned from the summit to their Base Camp in three hours, making 98% of the descent in a glide upon their backs. However, this style can be practised only by the most extraordinary individuals. Many deaths due to HAPE and/or HACE could have been prevented if climbers had listened to their sick bodies and descended, instead of ascending further. Progressive symptoms of severe acute mountain sickness were ignored, particularly by those who went 'too fast too high'. Sometimes even the most experienced climbers cannot resist the challenge of the summit. Andrew Czok, the first man on Mount Everest in winter, died on Kangchenjunga from HAPE, as did Fritz Luchsinger, the first man on Lhotse, years later on Xixabangma. Both men had suffered from worsening symptoms of HAPE but continued their ascent. Thus, despite the admonitions of climbing physicians, impaired judgement and competitive behaviour will continue to take their toll. Worse yet, catastrophic illness will strike even the wise and prepared without prior warning, as in the recent case of Chris Chandler on Kangchenjunga.

In earlier times, amphetamines were recommended by a few expedition doctors who wanted to give a climber the best chance to reach the summit. Sadly, some of these climbers died while taking an avoidable risk. There is no question that supplemental oxygen reduces the deleterious effects of severe hypoxia and can prevent some deaths due to HAPE and HACE. Falls undoubtedly occur less often in climbers supplemented by 'English Air', as Sherpas on the early Everest expeditions used to call the oxygen bottles. Climbers who run out of oxygen or encounter equipment failure high on the mountain experience great misery due to the sudden drop of tissue oxygen saturation. Previously strong people will have died under these circumstances.

The main problem is that climbing with bottled oxygen is no longer fashionable. Modern light-weight expeditions and alpine-style ascents cannot be performed if one has to carry bulky oxygen cylinders. These factors, and concerns for the environment, have encouraged climbers on the 8000m peaks to forgo bottled oxygen. Diminution of oxygen use for climbing is unfortunately also paralleled by a trend of many expeditions not to carry oxygen for medical purposes.

A pressurized bag has been successfully used in individual cases of severe acute mountain sickness. The time may soon arrive when most large trekking parties travelling with a doctor or well-instructed layperson will carry such a piece of equipment. Still, experience suggests that the bag will be inaccessible in extreme conditions when it is most needed.

Two controlled field studies have demonstrated the efficacy of dexa-methasone treatment in ameliorating the symptoms and signs of acute mountain sickness. Dexamethasone is more effective for the cerebral symptoms of AMS than for pulmonary problems. Nifedipine treatment of HAPE patients results in clinical improvement, better oxygenation, reduction of the widened alveolar oxygen gradient and pulmonary artery pressure, and progressive clearing of alveolar edema. When given sublingually, patients usually report some relief within 15 to 30 minutes, paralleled in certain cases by a marked increase in arterial oxygen saturation. Proper positioning of the patient may allow drainage of alveolar fluid through the bronchial tree. The great advantage of all these modalities is that they can be employed by the climber using lightweight tactics.

This is small progress. The casualty rate will not decline markedly unless over-enthusiastic climbers change their attitudes toward the high mountains and their dangers. Every climber wants to decide how close to the edge he or she may push. Maurice Herzog, who completed the first ascent of an 8000m peak, lost all his fingers and toes, but thought that it was worth it. Climbing to extreme altitude is risky; it is the price of such adventure.

I would like to thank Elizabeth Hawley of Kathmandu for providing statistics about climbers on Mount Everest. This article first appeared in the *Journal of Wilderness Medicine 1, No. 3* (August 1990). Reprinted by permission.

East of the Saser La

Exploring the Aq Tash and Chong Kumdan glaciers

HARISH KAPADIA

(Plates 5–7)

Like many good expeditions, ours began with problems. There are always many bureaucratic obstacles in the way of climbing in the East Karakoram, and this time some added difficulties almost ruined our trip. To begin with, our flight from Delhi hovered over Leh and, because of the cloud cover, landed us back at Chandigarh. So we flew to Srinagar with all the luggage. Muslim Contractor and Vijay Kothari were packed off with it in a truck, and suffered a three-day journey with road blocks, a drunken driver and the other usual hardships. The rest travelled by bus. We all gathered at Leh, five days behind schedule, on 6 July 1989. We contacted the army, and everything seemed to be in order.

Next evening, as we roamed about in the streets of Leh eating kebabs, there was a small riot, and suddenly a furious mob attacked a gompa and a mosque situated opposite each other. This was the start of the four months of riot which were to change the face of Leh. The Buddhists of Ladakh and Shia Muslims were protesting against Sunni Muslims from Kashmir who had cornered the trade. There were bomb blasts, and Leh was put under total curfew for three days. 'This must be the first violence in Leh since the days of Zorawar Singh' (1840), one Ladakhi scholar said sadly. Leh looked desolate and tense, and we felt sad for this Shangri-La which we had enjoyed so much in the past. When we returned in late August there was not a single tourist around. Luckily a settlement was reached later in the year, and an uneasy calm returned.

On 13 July we managed to leave Leh at last, in a private truck. Quickly we crossed the Khardung La (5080m) where we enjoyed an excellent view of the northern ranges. We left Shyok at Khalsar, turned into the Nubra valley and reached Sasoma in time for breakfast with the army there. In the early days caravans took seven days to cover these 158km; now it is a one-day journey. The road ahead leads to the Siachen snout; army convoys pass in both directions with monotonous regularity.

Subedar Raftan, who was in charge of the camp at Sasoma, welcomed us with a firm handshake but discouraging news. We required 12 to 15 mules for crossing the Saser La. First, because of the uncertain weather, the pass, feared by muleteers, was open only intermittently. Secondly, a large army expedition to Mamostong Kangri on our route had already acquired 125 mules, and no other mules were available in the Nubra valley. So we could only wait. Our days were spent quite interestingly with the jawans and subedars, veterans of the Siachen war, whose relaxed routine involved office work, telephone messages and preparation of food for the convoys. In the evenings we played volleyball. Some of us visited the Yarma gompa which is believed to be as old as the Potala. The Nubra river is marked on the map after this gompa as 'Yarma Tsangpo'. The lamas' tradition of painting walls and stones survives in the Nubra valley which is beautiful and full of flowers and poplars, living up to its original name Dumra ('valley of flowers and trees').

After five days the mules finally arrived, and what a happy sight it was for us. We left on 20 July, ready to face the next delay. The track climbs *chhatis mod*. It is hewn into the tough rock, about 550m in height, reaching the Tulum Puti La (3750m) after 36 U-turns. The route, a masterpiece of roadmaking, was constructed in the 19th century from local materials by the engineer Ali Hussain who came from Central Asia. The work was commissioned by the Sultan of Yarkand, after pilgrims on their way to Mecca had complained of hardships on this section of their route. If this story sounds improbable, the unique track into the valley ahead, leading to the base of the Saser La, is even more fantastic. This is what Eric Shipton wrote of the area, which has not changed much:

> From the fertile valley of Panamik, the track climbed a slab of rock, 2000 feet high, so steep and smooth that from a distance it looked scarcely passable for a mountain goat. Beyond it we entered a wilderness of rock and ice surrounded by lofty peaks and by the evening of the second day we reached the foot of a glacier cascading in a series of steep ice-falls from the Saser Pass (17,480 feet). The only way through was up a narrow gully of large moraine boulders between the ice and a vertical cliff. Though this type of ground is familiar enough to any mountaineering expedition, never before had I dreamed that it would be possible to climb it with heavily-laden animals. There was no vestige of a path, and as the ponies clambered up the great boulders, their hooves scraped and slithered agonisingly in their efforts to gain purchase and retain their balance on trembling, bleeding legs.[1]

Beyond the Tulum Puti La we followed the river, crossing it at Umlung over a natural rock bridge. Above it were the plains of Lama Kheti. We crossed the Thangman nala to make a camp at 4054m. We continued along the river, crossing the Lashi and Namlung nalas which come from the south and drain glaciers of the same name, surrounded by peaks up to 6500m high. Of these, only Lashi (6265m) has been climbed. One of the high cols leads to the Chamshen group of peaks which drain into the Shyok and are otherwise difficult to approach. These glaciers are a storehouse of peaks for future climbers. After the open ground of Turtyalak, the track climbed up 280m to Skyangpoche. The Mamostong Kangri glacier was opposite to us in the north. A group of Yarkandi travellers had tried to find a way through this glacier across a col to avoid the much-feared Saser La. They crossed the col at 5885m to the Thangman glacier (Kichik Kumdan glacier). This would have led them quickly to the Chong Kumdan glacier and the Karakoram Pass. But the party perished, and the glacier and the col were called Mamostong ('thousand devils') and Thangman ('glacier of healing'). We camped ahead at the Changmolung nala. The rains arrived, and that gave us our fourth problem. It rained for the next two days, almost as heavily as in Garhwal. The weather in Ladakh is surely changing. Gone are the days of constant blue skies and dry weather. The heavy rain has a devastating effect on the fragile Ladakh landscape. It is difficult to give any reason for the change, though some blame the large plantations in the lower valleys of Ladakh. But the army is very business-like and operates in any weather. They have a simple saying, as Subedar Wani had later put it:

> *Mausam ka illaj nahin*
> *Hukum ka jawab nahin*
> (You cannot rely on the weather,
> you cannot reply to an order.)

On 24 July we could move at last, with the muleteers already grumbling. The route became wilder and steeper. Another aspect was added which all the earlier travellers had written about.

> In the valley leading up to the Pass we had seen the first of the corpses, skeletons and heaps of bones which formed a continuous line of hundreds of miles until we reached the first oasis beyond the ranges.[2]

These skeletons made a gruesome sight but soon we were used to them. Even today, many mules die on the pass and you have to pay compensation. The army can afford it, but a private expedition has to be careful not to press the muleteers too hard. We camped about 2km before the pass, at a camping ground usually used before the crossing. The weather is crucial on the morning of the crossing. If it is cloudy, the snow does not consolidate enough and mules will sink in. As it is, one has to make a midnight start. We did this, and found after one hour that the mules were sinking into the snowfield. The ponies began to weaken, many were limping and several kept collapsing hopelessly. There were blood marks on their legs. We had to return to the camp. Now we were stranded once again, for the pass was not open yet. The only way out of our fifth problem was to ferry our loads to the crest of the pass and arrange for mules from the other side to pick them up. This we had to do for the next three days. It was a gallant effort by the team, more like a desperate attempt to establish a high camp rather than travel on a trade route.

Bad weather persisted, and we appreciated the wisdom of the great explorer Sir Francis Younghusband:

> The Saser Pass was not so difficult at this time of year as it often is. But on the day after we crossed it a terrible squall of snow and rain overtook us, and on looking back I saw the pass hidden in a cloud as black as night; and it is because of these terrific storms that the pass is so much feared.[3]

Finally, on 26 July, we left at 1am with torches. It was a clear night for a change, and walking on the snow was a pleasure. The route went over the scree to the final ice-wall, and traversed across the wall to a plateau above. It is surprising that mules can go at all on such a route, so much like something one encounters on a mountaineering expedition. Whenever we felt concerned about the safety of a mule, the muleteer always reassured us: 'This is a *sharif* (gentleman) horse. He knows where to place his legs. He won't fall.' These sturdy beasts-of-burden, the Karakoram mules, are legendary. They have played no small role in supporting trade and travel, and now defence, in this area. A small temple on the eastern side marked the end of the pass, which was about three hours from our high camp. A steep descent to the Shyok valley led us to the Saser Brangza Camp.

Subedar Dorje and Subedar Wani greeted us warmly. These soldiers had lived for more than a quarter-century in the area and knew it like the back of their hand. They talked of extreme winters, different routes, life at altitude and, of course, about the war. But, surprisingly, no one bothered about the peaks, glaciers, mountaineering history or early travellers. Even in present days a mountaineer-visitor can still explore and gather knowledge about unknown valleys, although people have now lived here for decades. Mountaineers here are not totally useless pains-in-the-neck, as is sometimes thought.

The army at Saser Brangza lent us mules to get all the luggage down from the pass. They also agreed to lend us mules, for two days only, to enable us to reach our proposed Base Camp at the Chong Kumdan glacier. We had to go upstream along the Shyok river and cross two major streams on the way. This route is a shortcut to Gapshan and the Karakoram Pass and is regularly in use. It is fordable up to the Chong Kumdan dam in all seasons, and beyond that only in winter. By this time we were all quite tired and depressed. To fill our cup of misery, the mules stopped at the first difficulty: the crossing of the Aq Tash nala. It was flooded and, as the night was cloudy, the water did not recede next morning. The mules could not wait and so we had to make our base here. The sixth trouble had finally stopped us. We were exactly one month away from Bombay, and still 5km short of our proposed base. We wondered what would have been the reaction of Westerners if this had been a joint expedition. None of the difficulties we faced could have been solved quicker or by better organization. They were all part of the game of climbing in the East Karakoram. In spite of all the support, how could we have stopped the rain, changed the terrain or forced the bleeding mules? As has been said: 'You can change history but you cannot fight geography.' We accepted the situation with oriental fortitude, while a foreigner in a hurry might have been angry and impatient. But how would that have helped?

The Skeleton Trail
The track we were following was the famous Central Asia Trade Route. This historic route was the main trade route between the plains of India and Central Asia. In his autobiography, Sir Francis Younghusband wrote:

The crossing of the Himalaya by the main caravan route to Central

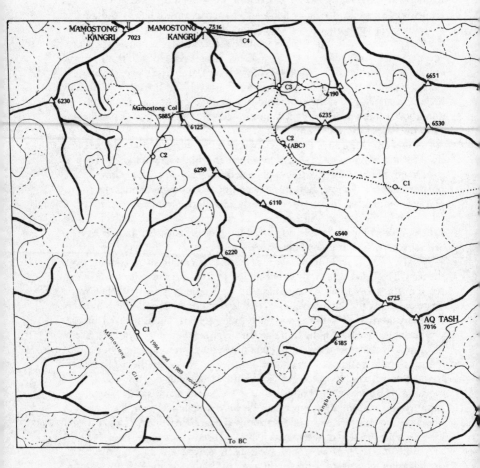

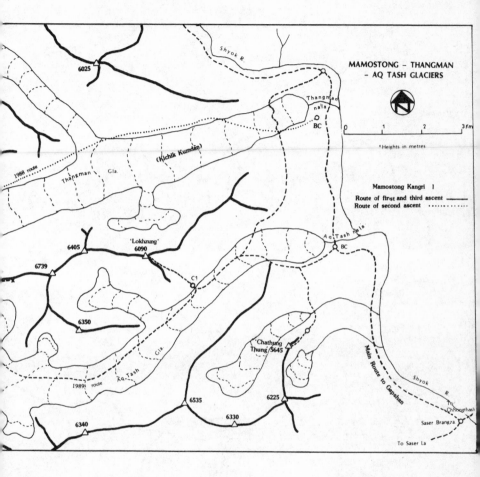

MAMOSTONG – THANGMAN
– AQ TASH GLACIERS

0   1   2   3 Km

'Heights in metres'

Mamostong Kangri 1
Route of first and third ascent ——
Route of second ascent ·············

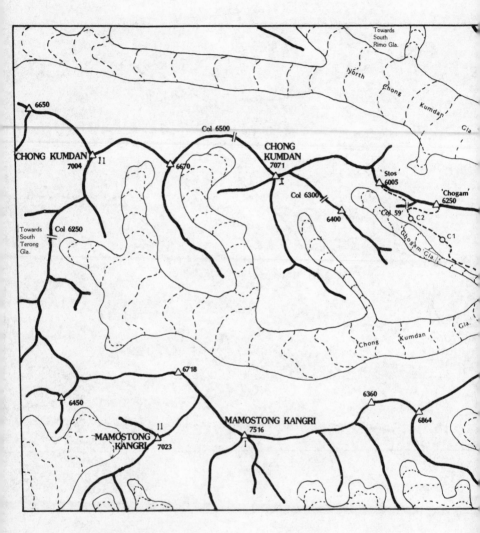

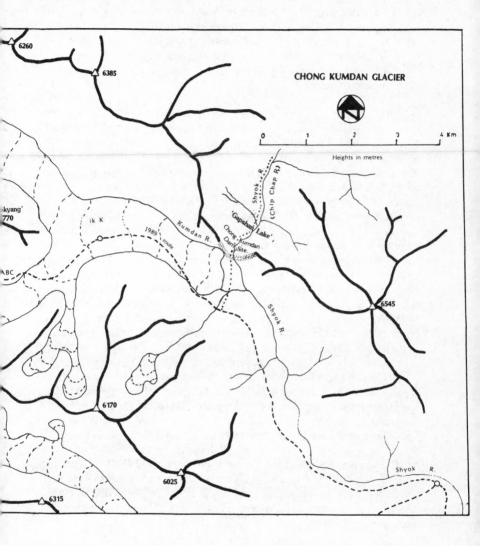

CHONG KUMDAN GLACIER

Heights in metres

Asia over the Karakoram Pass is about as dreary a piece of travel as
I know. The part through Kashmir is delightful. After that, and
especially over the Karakoram Pass itself, the scenery is in-
expressibly dull and as much of the route lies at an altitude of about
17,000 feet, and the pass itself is nearly 19,000 feet, there is a good
deal of that depression which comes from high altitudes. And even
in August the temperature was low enough at night for small
streams to be frozen. It is a hateful journey.[4]

His observations were true. Almost all the early travellers suffered this
way. Diana Shipton called it 'The Headache Mountains', while all the bones of
Ngabong (double-humped camels of Central Asia), men and mules earned it the
name of 'The Skeleton Trail'. The route carried heavy traffic. It was used by the
Yarkandis on their way to Mecca, and on the return many were trapped by
winter and died. Robert Shaw and G W Hayward were the first foreigners to
pioneer this route in 1864, followed by two Forsyth missions. Andrew
Dalgleish was another Englishman to cross the Karakoram Pass; he was
murdered just north of it and was buried at Leh. Dr Ferdinand Stolicza, a
naturalist attached to the Forsyth mission, died at Murgo in 1874 and was also
buried at Leh. A common bird in the area is named after him: Stolicza's Bush
Chat. Literally hundreds of travellers frequented this route, including Ney Elias,
Godwin-Austin, Eric Shipton and Ph C Visser. After 1946 the route was
closed by the Chinese, once they had a stranglehold on Central Asia. Finally, in
1962, a small force of the Indian army was driven back from east of the Saser
La, and some returned via Chong Kumdan and the Saser La to Leh. The area far
to the east is Aksai Chin and under Chinese control. The Indian army now
controls the Shyok valleys and travel is strictly regulated.

The two expeditions allowed into the area before ours were the Indian
Sappers team which climbed Rimo IV in 1984, and the Rimo expedition led by
Col Prem Chand.[5] They travelled by the trail to Daulat Beg Oldi (DBO) and the
Rimo glacier, the latter expedition returning via the Chong Kumdan snout.

At Saser Brangza, east of the Saser La, the track descends to the Shyok.
The winter route from Darbuk and Mandalthang joins it from the south. To the
north goes the route via Chong Kumdan to Gapshan and DBO. The summer
route crosses the Shyok to Chongtash and Murgo to turn north to Burtsa and
the Depsang plains. These plains are a unique feature, extending for many
kilometres; they are now bordered by the Chinese on the east. This is what Sir F
Younghusband wrote:

Of all parts of the world this is the most God-forsaken – dreadful in
every way. The plain itself is over 17,000 feet above sea-level, and
consists of an open expanse of gravel, bounded by rounded, dull,
barren hills. Across it incessantly sweep winds of piercing cold . . .
To add to the gloom the plain is strewn with the bones of animals
who have succumbed to the strain of carrying loads at these great
heights.[6]

Finally all the routes meet at DBO and cross the Karakoram Pass, which is quite unspectacular compared with the terrain already passed. Ahead, over the plains of Central Asia, the route joins the famous Silk Road at Yarkand, running east-west. (Though silk was traded on the Central Asia Trade Route, it was never called the Silk Route. It is a feeder to the Silk Road.[7])

The Indian army officers who are stationed in the area have done extensive trekking. Many relics have been found such as the metal boat, perhaps that of J P Gunn, left in 1929 in the Chong Kumdan lake, the memorial stone of the Visser expedition of 1935, Burtsa stones, remains of caravans and, of course, bones and a few partly-decomposed bodies. Some of these have been air-lifted to army HQ at Partapur, lower down on the Shyok, and are preserved for posterity. Government agencies, geologists, archaeologists and surveyors operate in the area and have collected information and relics.

The final word on the trail is well expressed by Shipton:

Nothing is known of the men who, centuries ago, first ventured across this monstrous wilderness in search of trade or conquest. It is easier to imagine the toil, hardship and frustration they must have endured than to understand what inspired the courage and tenacity needed to discover a way.[8]

Exploring Aq Tash

Considering the time available to us, and our limited strength, we had to improvise. The alternative plan was for Muslim and Arun Samant to enter the Aq Tash glacier, 8km long, and to try out peaks there. Accordingly, on 31 July, they climbed via the right-hand moraine and crossed the glacier to establish Camp 1. The glacier has prominent white stones which give it its name (Aq = white, Tash = stone). As the Yarkandi caravans passed the snout they must have given this simple identification, as in this land of Karakoram (black rock) an Aq Tash attracts attention. For the next four days Arun, Muslim and porters established two camps to reach the col at 6200m on the shoulder of the Aq Tash peak (7016m). This was 'Col 62'. On the other side it offered excellent views of the Thangman glacier. The entire massif of Mamostong Kangri could be seen to advantage. After the 'Mamostong Col' the entire route on the glacier and the E ridge of Mamostong Kangri (7516m) were observed. But the most challenging view was of the Aq Tash peak, lying to the south-west of the col. The ridge rose sharply and was broken. This stupendous monolith is one of the last three unclimbed 7000ers in the area. It would take a strong all-out attempt to climb it. Arun and Pasang Bodh proceeded north-east of the col, following the ridge. They stopped on the sharp 'Aq Tash Tower', at c 6400m. On 8 August all retreated to Base Camp for a rest, leaving all the camp-sites intact.

After two days Muslim and Pasang returned to continue their efforts on the Aq Tash glacier. Their first aim was a peak (6090m) above their Camp 1 (5200m). It took them seven hours to reach the summit on 12 August. The route went up a nala draining from the north and via a snow-gully. A series of false summit humps had to be overcome. A final climb of 150m led to the summit which was christened Lokhzung ('Eagle's Nest'). To the south of the Aq Tash

glacier two small glaciers led to the ablation valley. On the southernmost valley
stands Chathung Thung (5645m, 'Black neck crane'), with a lovely snow-slope
and black rock jutting up like a neck on the top. On 13 August Muslim and
Pasang established a camp on the slopes of this peak, and on the 14th they
overcame three pinnacles to reach the true summit. It overlooked the entire
Shyok valley here and gave a bird's-eye view of the Kichik Kumdan river-block
of yesteryear. They examined the possibilities of climbing the adjoining peak of
6225m but found the slopes avalanche-prone. So by the 16th they were on their
way down and heading towards the Chong Kumdan glacier to unite with the
main team.

Chongtash
After Arun and Muslim had left for the Aq Tash glacier Harish started suffering
from high fever. When contacted, the nearest army doctor arranged mules for
his evacuation to their camp, with Monesh Devjani. Once across the Shyok the
party mounted horses equipped with wooden frames made for carrying
luggage. A painful journey began. The route entered the Chongtash gorge:

> The Saser Pass led us again into the Shyok valley, 160 miles
> upstream from the place where we had crossed it near Panamik.
> Instead of following the valley we plunged almost immediately
> into a ravine, so narrow that the opposing walls also met, 1000 feet
> above our heads, so dark that we seemed to be in a vast cavern.[9]

We were now in this cavern. Ladakhi troops marching with us were fit
and a confident lot. 'Who needs bullets here, we can just throw stones from
above,' they joked. Chongtash ('big stone') was a huge plain with a big rock in
the centre, the only one within miles. Ahead we could see the barren fearsome
mountain walls of Murgo. As strong winds and clouds gathered, a battered
Harish and a suave Monesh were greeted with:

> *Ladakh ki mausam aur*
> *Bombay ki fashion ka bharosa nahin*
> (Ladakh's weather and Bombay's fashion
> cannot be trusted.)

The army was friendly, comforting and literally warm with *bukharis*.
Four comfortable days were spent under the expert care of the army doctor.
After sufficient rest, drugs, video films and the warmth of friendly people,
Harish recovered sufficiently to return to the Base Camp on the Aq Tash glacier.

The Chong Kumdan glacier
We all gathered together on 9 August. Riots and the problems posed by
weather, terrain, sickness and mules had left us only 11 days to visit this
unknown glacier. We divided up, Muslim and Pasang continuing to climb in the
Aq Tash glacier region, while Arun, Monesh and Harish with three porters left
for the Chong Kumdan glacier.

There was a good beaten track leading to the glacier. The Aq Tash nala was now crossed easily, and we trekked along the Shyok bed. The river flowed majestically and very quietly. The Thangman nala (old Kichik Kumdan) was crossed with some difficulty, and in the evening we camped on the plain leading to the historic dam. Arun and Koylu Ram tried to cut across the ice-penitentes of the Thangman glacier with disastrous results. It is very tiring to cut across these pinnacles and walls of about 50m, and they barely managed to cross. The Kichik Kumdan glacier ('small dam') had blocked the Shyok in the past, and we could observe a deep gorge near the eastern wall where the river had broken through. Now the glacier has receded at least 2–3km and poses no danger. The Kichik Kumdan glacier is 11km long; an expedition led by Major A M Sethi traversed it fully to climb Mamostong Kangri.[10]

The Glacier Dam

This is the meeting point of the Chip Chap river from the north and the Chong Kumdan river from the west. The Chong Kumdan glacier has advanced rapidly over the years. A little higher up, the glacier takes a sharp turn; the movement of its mass was so forceful that it pressed hard against the walls. This blocked the flow of the Chip Chap and Chong Kumdan rivers. (The earlier literature [gazetteer] called the latter the 'Kumdan river'.) However, a glacier is liable to retreat and, the dams weakened by the retreat, bursts occurred. All the dammed water rushed out, and death and destruction was caused as far as Attock Fort, about 1200km downstream. Thus the river acquired the name Shyok – the river of death. Such dam-bursts have occurred in 1780, 1826, 1835 and 1839. The dam-waters rose to a peak height of about 125m; the water-marks can still be seen. The dam was studied by Ney Elias and Godwin-Austen in 1877. Kenneth Mason, the first editor of the *Himalayan Journal*, took a keen interest in the dam,[11] collecting much information. The most serious dam-burst occurred in 1929. Mr T Durgi of the Public Works Department was then posted at the dam-site to warn against future bursts. In 1932 he sent two runners to Khalsar over the Saser pass to warn about floods. The flood waters had already reached Khalsar, but by their phenomenally fast trek (130km in 28 hours) the runners did pass on a warning. Kenneth Mason calculated the frequency of advance and retreat of the Kichik and Chong Kumdan glaciers and predicted:

> As I shall not be here to be proved wrong, I will be precise: the Chong Kumdan will advance rapidly during the winter of 1968–9; the Shyok valley will be blocked; a lake will form above it, some 10 miles long; and there will be floods caused by the collapse of the dam in the autumns (July to September) of 1971, 1974 and 1977, the first one occurring probably in the autumn 2½ years after the glacier has advanced.[12]

However, the available records indicate that the last major burst which caused destruction occurred on 16 August 1929. Since then, there were minor bursts in 1932–33 and 1937–39, when the dam-waters escaped slowly and no major damage was caused. Since then, there have been no further bursts or build-up of dams. The Karakoram glaciers in this region are in a state of retreat.

Indian army forces have long been stationed in the area, and their records of the Shyok water-level do not mention any floods.

Is it likely that Mason may still be proved correct about the future?

It must be remembered that it will be a coincidence that the Chong Kumdan and the Kichik Kumdan glaciers will both be at their maximum advance at approximately the same time [1970] and that at their subsequent advances, the Chong Kumdan in 2013 and the Kichik Kumdan in 2005, they will again be 'out of phase'. We can perhaps leave any further speculation to our grandchildren![13]

The Chong Kumdan Peaks

Though the trade route and many caravans passed the snout of the Chong Kumdan glacier, no one seems to have entered on to the glacier. It was first surveyed by E C Ryall in 1862, and a sketch-map was published by the De Filippi expedition in 1914. The glacier is about 15km long, running generally east to west. At the western end lies a high col of 6250m, leading to the South Terong glacier. To the south lies the high Mamostong Kangri wall, with many high peaks that discharge avalanches. To the north of the glacier are the two unattempted peaks of Chong Kumdan I (7071m) and II (7004m). A high col (6500m) between the two mountains overlooks the northern branch of the Chong Kumdan glacier. About 3km from the snout the glacier bifurcates, with the North Chong Kumdan glacier leading towards the South Rimo glacier.

On 11 August we entered this glacier, following the right moraine. A side glacier had cut through, creating a narrow gorge, and we had to climb up to cross it. This opened to our view the entire northern vista up to Gapshan. We moved ahead but after about 2km were forced to descend to the glacier moraine and proceed along it. After the junction of the glaciers we cut across to the north towards the left bank and camped on the glacier late in the evening. Next day an Advanced Base Camp (5040m) was set up on the flat camping ground at the entrance of a small subsidiary northern glacier, christened by us 'Chogam glacier'. While two porters were sent down to ferry more loads, we moved quickly up this northern glacier. On 14 August Camp 1 was placed at 5540m, below a prominent 'dimple' on the ridge. Arun and Koylu Ram left early with their camp, followed soon by Monesh and Harish. We reached a prominent col at 5900m ('Col 59'). Ahead to the NW was Chong Kumdan I, rising from the glacier to a col, then to steep rocks and a tempting rounded summit. The eastern ridge fell sharply to join our peak.

Sir Francis Younghusband was perhaps the first to see it from a distance on his way to Central Asia:

There followed some dreary marches across the summits of the bare and desolate Depsang Plains from which, though 17,000 feet above sea level, the snowy peaks of Saser and Nubra 'appeared above the horizon like the sails of some huge ships' . . .[14]

Nursing a recent fracture Harish found the steep slopes painful to climb and hence opted out. The remaining three followed the steep southern slopes of the peak (6250m). After climbing a pinnacle at the end they were on the summit of Chogam ('a box of holy scriptures'). The panorama extended from Rimo in the north-west to Mamostong Kangri in the south.

On 15 August, Arun and Koylu Ram climbed Stos (6005m, 'goat which gives Pashmina wool') from their high camp. It is a peak between the descending ridge of Chong Kumdan 1 and Chogam.

Our last day of action was 16 August. In the early morning Monesh and Yog Raj left to climb Skyang (5770m, 'wild horse') above our Advanced Base to the north; their energy and speed matched the name of the peak. Going up steep slopes they reached the summit ridge at 9am. On the ridge there were three pinnacles spread over half a kilometre and, to be absolutely sure of the summit, they climbed all three. That evening we built a huge cairn and on a stream 'constructed' our own dam. Exactly 60 years ago to the day, on 16 August 1929, the Kumdan dam had broken with a bang, heard by the Vissers camped at DBO, almost 30km away ('like the noise of a cannon-shot') and by J P Gunn who visited the site immediately from Chongtash. This was the last major burst of a lake which had formed in 1923. That was the year in which Godwin-Austen, crippled at the age of 50, had died, aged 87. A little before he had written to *The Times*, which had just reported another block of the river, vividly recalling his visit to the dam with Ney Elias 43 years earlier.[15] After 1935–39 both Chong Kumdan and Kichik Kumdan went into oblivion and did not cause further blocks or news.

Muslim and Pasang after their satisfying climbs met us at the Chong Kumdan plain. A tired but satisfied party exchanged notes. We were fascinated by the area and even charmed by its barrenness. As Shipton had said:

> As on a long sea voyage, many weeks in the mountain wilderness, remote from the habits and concerns of our former world, had made us intensely sensitive to our new environment.[16]

A tired party staggered back across the Saser La. Subedar Wani has the final quote for us:

> *Kaun kaheta hai ke Mehboob mera*
> *Langda ke chalata hai;*
> *Woh to hushn ke boz se*
> *Lachak lachak ke chalta hai.*

> (Who says my [mountain] lover is walking
> with a limp,
> Because of the load of love [beauty]
> he is staggering a little.)

REFERENCES

1   E Shipton, *That Untravelled World*. London (Hodder & Stoughton), 1969, p143.

2   *loc cit*, p144.
3   F Younghusband, *Wonders of the Himalaya*. London (John Murray), 1924, p131.
4   F Younghusband, *The Light of Experience*. London (Constable), 1927, p54.
5   P Hillary, *Rimo. Mountain on the Silk Road*. London (Hodder & Stoughton), 1988; and *HJ41*, 117–121, 1983–4.
6   F Younghusband, *Wonders of the Himalaya*, p132.
7   P Hopkirk, *Foreign Devils on the Silk Road*. London (John Murray), 1980.
8   E Shipton, *That Untravelled World*, p144.
9   *loc cit*, p144.
10 *HJ46*, 70, 1988–89.
11 *HJ1*, 14, 1929.
12 *HJ12*, 62, 1940.
13 *HJ12*, 63, 1940.
14 G Seaver, *Francis Younghusband*. London (John Murray), 1952, p106.
15 G Morgan, *Ney Elias*. London (Allen & Unwin), 1971, p127.
16 E Shipton, *That Untravelled World*, p145.

Indian Face Arête

A ridge climb on a subsidiary peak of Latok III

SANDY ALLAN

(Plates 8–11)

Pakistan's Latok III (6949m) nestles to the west of Latok I (7145m) and Latok II (7108m), in the Karakoram. Our main objective was the N ridge of Latok II, first attempted in 1978 by an American team consisting of some of the leading exponents of big-wall climbing, Mike Kennedy, Jim Donni and Jeff Lowe. In reasonably dry conditions they reached a high point of 7000m before having to retreat because of illness and severe storms. Rab Carrington led an unsuccessful British attempt in 1982, and in 1987 a French party again made little impression on the ridge. Neither of these expeditions was able to gain the Americans' high point, and both complained of heavy snow deposits which prevented effective progress.

Our expedition, sponsored by Inspectorate, Oilfield Inspection Services Plc, reached Base Camp on 5 June 1990. Although we could see that there was a great deal of snow on the mountain, optimism prevailed at that stage, and we decided to begin our acclimatization for the main objective by attempting some of the other peaks in the region.

Tuesday, 12 June, saw Doug Scott, Simon Yates, Rick Allen and myself camped at 5100m on the Sim La in our North Face Himalayan Hotel which we left at 1.30am to make an attempt on Biacherahi Peak. However, after climbing unroped through a band of seracs and up over the col, we were halted by very unstable snow on the final summit ridge. This was disappointing, but we were appeased by an ascent of an adjacent snow dome which we called Biacherahi Dome (5750m). From here we were rewarded with fantastic views of our proposed objective and its neighbouring Latoks, of the Muztagh Tower, Masherbrum, K2, China and the Ogre, immediately to the east. Our descent was fraught, with great risk of avalanche, and it was late afternoon before we returned to camp; we descended thence to Base Camp, as snow conditions remained treacherous and prevented any further ascents.

Some of us had set our sights on the peak of Hanipispur South, to the north of our Base Camp. On 15 June Simon, Rick, Rick's wife Alison, my sister Eunice, Richard Cowper (a *Financial Times* reporter) and I headed for a high camp on Hanipispur. At 1am the following morning Simon, Rick, Richard and I left camp. After five hours Simon and I came to a high spot on the ridge and admired a panorama of Masherbrum, Latoks and Hushe peaks. Above us, again, there lay steep unstable snow, so regretfully we decided to return to Base Camp.

Between such forays we walked up the Choktoi glacier to view Latok II. We could scarcely believe that we were looking at the same mountain as the one in Mike Kennedy's photographs which had initially enticed us to this area of Pakistan. Doug and I began to realize that the very deep snow was not melting off fast enough to allow Rick and myself to keep to our imposed timetables – work back in Aberdeen's oil world was beckoning.

I had had enough of snow-plodding with heavy sacs and was delighted to join Doug on a superb arête which curved steeply into the sky behind Base Camp, towards the summit of a subsidiary peak of Latok III. We put together a big-wall rack, a haul sac and bivi equipment and headed off to do some exploring. We had only intended to investigate the possibilities, but when we reached the foot of the ridge our enthusiasm took over and we found ourselves on superb clean sun-kissed rock. After four pitches with moves of up to 5c, we stashed the haul sac and abseiled down to the glacier. As we wandered round the base of the arête to check the descent route I saw what looked like the profile of an Indian's face sculpted from the rock high on the ridge, so we named our proposed route the Indian Face Arête. We decided that we could either descend via the crest and rounded ridge to the east, or abseil steeply down a snow-ice couloir to the right of the route.

On our return to Base Camp Rick and Simon announced that they intended to explore the Nobande Sobande glacier and perhaps attempt Bobisighir (6411m). That evening we sat in the mess tent drinking brews of tea and chocolate, and talked about our proposed climbs. For the first time in the expedition we were talking about attaining objectives. Dylan – admittedly sounding rather aged – came from the portable speakers, and life was ace. Doug and I planned to depart very early from Base Camp, climb all day and (Insh' Allah) abseil from the summit in darkness, to return to Base Camp in the early morning. How are the mighty fallen!

9am on 18 June saw Doug and myself at our previous high point on the arête. We had a brew and decided to jettison the haul sac, bivi equipment and some of the rack. We retained the stove and some herb tea bags, boiled sweets and two tracker bars each. Doug did hesitate as he threw the haul sac, but our enthusiasm was so high for the superb feeling of free climbing that we did not really want to burden ourselves with material possessions, even though such things can keep you warm at night!

So we were committed to climbing, and climb we did. It was ace-swinging pitches of 5c, sustained 5c, the rock occasionally flaking but basically very clean. I chose the first main steep aid pitch to take my first-ever leader fall. As I lay face down on a snow ledge beside Doug's stance he told me that I had loosened my peg runners by hammering too much on my highest peg, expanding the crack, and zipping most of the others. But expertise comes with experience, and as I traversed out right and moved up another system I was secretly pleased to belay below a huge overhang and let Doug lead the next pitch. At first it was extremely steep until he went out of my view on, I guessed, a tension traverse, as he shouted 'slack on green and tight on red'. The sound of hammering followed, punctuated with expletives, and a white powder fell on my head. Doug announced that the rock was turning to powder when he tried to place a pin, and he was unable to get a good placement. After two hours the green rope became yellow and the red pink in the light of my head-torch. I lowered Doug off, and we began to search for a bivi.

Doug went down one more pitch and called up that his previous stance was OK, perhaps roomy enough for two. I tied off the rope, hurried down, and cut a ledge in the snow with my hammer as Doug brewed; he was not feeling well. Meanwhile I continued clearing a level space on which Doug could lie down and I could sit. Our meal was tepid herb tea and a tracker bar. We had no bivi gear, but did not want to abseil off. Sleep came intermittently.

The morning found us shrouded in powder snow. My lead was not very pleasant as I climbed in my walking boots to regain my belay stance, tied in and shivered myself back to warmth. Doug came up and was soon back at his high point of the previous evening, again punctuating the Karakoram silence with the pleasing sound of the hammer. Three hours later I started to second the pitch – and was I impressed by Doug's climbing! He had led the pitch by leap-frogging our three blades, with two small 'Rocks' persuaded into cracks and one poor King pin as his only protection. Above, I enjoyed climbing free again, and we were on easier 5b, 5c ground.

We soon came to the ridge proper, with its huge balanced blocks and snow dripping in the sunshine. We changed from our rock-boots into our somewhat drier and more substantial Brasher walking boots and climbed together for a spell, but soon the going became technical again, so we pitched 5b. It was good value to be high up and near the top, although the climbing was becoming progressively bitter. As we approached the summit it was late evening and Doug spied a good bivi. I reversed a scrappy pitch, filled the rucksac with snow as Doug fixed the abseil, and down we went to the bivi site on a rock ledge. Sleep came after cold herb tea and half a tracker bar.

Chattering teeth woke me: I thought they were mine, but perhaps they were Doug's. We contemplated the final steps to the summit, but began abseiling instead. We were happy and felt that we had done all the good climbing. Latter-day views of climbing right to the summit were not for us on this occasion.

Where Poets and Paupers Go

A visit to the West Karakoram

STEPHEN HART

Much searching of *Alpine Journals* revealed that little had been climbed or written about in the Batura glacier region. Situated in the west of the Karakoram, it seemed a suitable area to visit in July/August 1989. We were a small party on the usual low budget, looking for sub-6000m first ascents. Having obtained a copy of the wonderful 1:50,000 Chinese map of the glacier, we could see that the area abounds in such peaks. A standard search followed for cheap gear and reasonable flights, culminating in the sweaty haul from Karachi to 'Pindi. Esajee's shop in Sadaar Bazaar must be world-famous in providing almost any food that an expedition might require, with absolute honesty thrown in free.

The village we made for was Passu, going via Gilgit for the last few items required before entering the mountains. Up in Passu we met Qama Jan, a friend of Doug Scott from the 1978 K2 expedition, who seemed to run things and was an absolute gem in arranging the necessary transportation to Base Camp. The weather up to this point had been quite poor, and when we reached Gilgit we doubted whether we could get up the Karakoram Highway to Passu. However, our worries were ill-founded and we were ready to leave the road-end on a blistering hot day on 25 July.

It is a three-day walk to a Base Camp in a reasonable position for the mountains. Thus we moved into our 'Batura house' in the small summer village of Guchisam at 3740m. Although rather low, set on the lateral moraine of the main glacier, it is well situated for the lower peaks on the northern side of the area. The major drawback to this rather comfortable situation was the use of the village for the pasturing of goats. As a friend's tent had been partially eaten the previous year, we were loath to leave anything outside the house when we were not in residence. The goats also had the nasty habit of breaking out of their rock-walled corral in the middle of the night, creating havoc and of course waking us up.

Our first foray into the hills started with bumbling ineptitude. Warton nala is a side valley some 20 minutes from Guchisam, extending north from the Batura glacier. The path we could see going up a steep scree-slope on the true right bank seemed partially avalanched away, so we proceeded up the opposite bank, climbing steep mud and grass with 25kg sacs, only to watch as a local man skipped easily down the path in question accompanied by his yaks. So much for mountain experience.

We made our first camp on a high meadow at 3920m at the confluence of Warton nala and the Shelin Maidan glacier, sitting out several days of bad weather. An exploratory walk up the terminal moraine of the glacier revealed an array of beautiful peaks, all unclimbed, several of which would give respectable rock and ice routes. The highest of these, at 5973m, looked likely to give the best chance of success, given that my partner Kay Brunger had not been on a glacier before.

From our camp we moved up to make a bivouac at c4900m on the south side of this peak. As a result of too late a start and lack of acclimatization, we failed in our attempt on the peak. Although technically straightforward, this side of the mountain was very avalanche-prone, so we prudently descended from a high point of 5600m.

Meanwhile the other three in our party had gone further up Warton nala and reported that the north side of this peak, while steep, looked relatively safe. They were later to climb a fine trekking peak of 5800m in the western end of this nala. Back in Base Camp we waited out several days, Kay's face needing a repair job after her neglecting to coat it with block on our first attempt. It was the pattern throughout our month in the hills for the clouds to be cloaking the mountains while we had brilliant sunshine in Guchisam. Our guilt feelings were dissipated by stomachs full of chapatis and plenty of chai.

Two further camps at 4420m and 4850m in the eastern end of Warton nala finally brought us under the face on 17 August. After a rest day we set about climbing this finding, as on alpine routes, the best snow during the night. The face of 800m was 45-55% snow, climbing through old avalanche runnels, the only problem being chest-deep powder at the top. This led to a col at 5650m and a mixed rock and ice pitch, followed by a fine alpine ridge. The summit block was a 20m rock monolith surrounded by soft, mushroom-like cornices, not attempted in the light of the danger. A descent of the route gave us 12 hours tent to tent and much satisfaction at having been the first on this mountain.

On our walk back to Base Camp we ran into two British lads looking for something to climb. Although we had met several trekking groups, these two were the only other people, in our time in the Batura, who were there specifically to climb. To my knowledge, having talked with many locals, it seems that we were the only expedition on the glacier this year. With many unclimbed peaks under and over the 6000m mark, there appears to be ample opportunity for making numerous first ascents, especially if a longer time than we had can be spent in the area. The distance between valleys and the need to carry loads are the major drawbacks. But what better way of losing that British pallor and midriff?

Area Information

The best time to visit the West Karakoram seems to be from mid-July to September, avoiding excessive heat and, later, the possibility of heavy snow. Lindsay Griffin has climbed here in November, finding the snow in good condition but experiencing cold days.

The best map of the Batura glacier is undoubtedly the Chinese one in the Sheffield University Geography Library.

In Passu, Qama Jan or the manager of the Passu Inn will arrange porters. They charge 1050 rupees for the trip to Guchisam, non-negotiable. They are the best, most friendly porters any of us had used.

The article by Steve Venables entitled 'West of the Baltoro' (*AJ88*, 194–198, 1983) is a useful reference.

Mountains of East and South-East Tibet

An introduction

MICHAEL WARD

(Plates 12–14)

Topography

Tibet is a pear-shaped plateau, at an altitude of 4000–5000m, its narrow western end being surrounded by the peaks of the Karakoram, Pamir and West Kun Lun, whilst the broad eastern base faces China. The plateau consists of two parts, the Central Changthang and the Outer Rim. On the Changthang, much of it over 4500m, there is internal drainage, and short rivers end in salty or brackish lakes with no outlet. The climate is severe, being cold and very windy even in summer, and there is little vegetation. Temperatures vary between 15°C in summer and -35°C in winter, with a yearly rainfall between 15 and 20cm. Snow falls throughout the year, with hailstorms common in summer, but it evaporates rather than lies, and permafrost is normal. From the Outer Rim, by contrast, the rivers run peripherally, eventually reaching the sea except in the north where they end in the sands of the Tarim Basin.

In the eastern part of the Changthang there is an ill-defined watershed between the internal and external drainage systems, approximately the line of the centuries-old track from the Tsaidam to South Tibet, which is now the Golmud–Lhasa road. In the south the rivers generally drain to the Tsangpo–Indus river system. Vegetation occurs where streams are large and most of the towns, Lhasa, Shigatse and Gyantse are in this southern part of the outer plateau. The climate is milder, with temperatures between 27°C in summer and -15°C in winter, whilst the yearly rainfall is 45cm. There are no forests and trees are confined to watercourses. In favoured ecological niches, however, fruit may be grown, and in Lhasa in the 18th century Jesuits cultivated grapes for communion wine.

The plateau is constrained by two of the world's greatest mountain ranges, the Himalaya to the south and the Kun Lun to the north. Between the eastern extremities of these two ranges lie the Marches of Tibet, a series of river gorges and mountain peaks turning gradually south until they lie at right angles to the general east–west line of the peaks of the plateau. The rivers of the northern section are tributaries of the Hwang Ho which curves north and east around the southern end of the Amne Machen range and then swings through northern China to the Pacific. Through the southern gap, between the Yunnan plateau and the peaks of the eastern Himalaya that end in Namcha Barwa, run the Yangtze Kiang and its many tributaries, the Salween, Mekong, Irrawaddy and Tsangpo rivers, the last four in one place being squeezed into a span of 120km. This gap in the wall of peaks allows the monsoon wind and rain from South-East Asia to blow north up the river gorges to the plateau of Tibet, drenching the south-facing slopes, whilst behind the ranges, in Tibet, it is semi-desert, due to the combination of wind, drought and low temperature. This gap is the 'Gorge Country' of South-East Tibet, a land of precipitous valleys and dark forests, small meadows and snow-capped peaks, of massive scree chutes and flower-covered slopes, of plunging glaciers and calm mountain lakes, and of tempestuous rivers erupting through narrow rock clefts with titanic force. Lonely monasteries and solitary houses are plastered to the sides of cliffs like swallows' nests, and dzongs are perched on spires and rock bluffs over-shadowing the villages at their feet. Covering an area the size of France, the region contains some of the world's most beautiful and varied flowers, trees and shrubs, where arctic flora rubs shoulders with tropical. It is also the most difficult of all mountain countries in which to travel and will always be associated with the plant-hunter and geographer, Frank Kingdon-Ward.

Political Background[1]
General
British involvement in the mountains of Central Asia, and in particular those of East and South-East Tibet, began with the expansion of the East India Company to the borders of Sikkim, Bhutan and Nepal, and the first contact with these independent kingdoms of the Himalaya came in 1766-7 through the survey work of James Rennel in the Bhutan border region. Among Rennel's most important contributions was his contention that the Tsangpo river, whose course in Tibet was appreciated but whose final destination was then unknown, flowed via the Dihang into the Brahmaputra.[2]

The acquisition in 1765 by the East India Company of Bengal coincided with the conquest of most of Nepal by the Hindu Gurkha, Prithri Narayan. In 1767 he invaded the Newar state of the Nepal valley which had close ties with Tibet and the resulting military operations disrupted trans-Himalayan trade. The Newars appealed to the East India Company for help against the Gurkhas and a force under Captain Kinlock was dispatched to Nepal. This, however, was unsuccessful in preventing the subsequent fall of Kathmandu, and the trade route between India and Tibet was closed. The East India Company then started to look for a route through the eastern Himalaya, in Bhutan and Assam, as an alternative means of access to Central Asia.

Warren Hastings began his administration in April 1772 and the following year Cooch Behar, a small state on the southern borders of Bhutan, appealed for help against the invading Bhutanese. Hastings saw his chance and the successful campaign waged by the Company and the intervention of the Panchen Lama of Tashilumpo monastery in Shigatse in South Tibet on behalf of the Bhutanese enabled Hastings to open trade negotiations with the Tibetans. The Bogle mission of 1774 and the Turner mission in 1783 both visited the Panchen Lama at Shigatse but both were denied access to Lhasa, as Chinese influence there was strong and the Tibetans followed an active policy of excluding foreigners. This was partly due to Chinese wishes and partly due to the Tibetans' apprehension at the extent of British control in the Himalaya. In addition, the Tibetans mistrusted the activities of Christian missionaries on the Indian and Chinese borders.

Information about Tibet was extremely scanty during the later part of the 18th and much of the 19th century. Only three Europeans successfully travelled in Tibet during this period. In 1811 Thomas Manning became the first Englishman to reach Lhasa, and two French Lazarist fathers, Huc and Gabet, normally stationed in Peking, reached Lhasa from the north in 1864, having crossed the plateau. After a stay of two months they were expelled owing to the influence of the Chinese Ambans (political representative) and left by travelling through East Tibet to China. In the later part of the 19th century, therefore, information about Tibet and its borderlands depended almost exclusively on that provided by the Pundits, or Secret Native Explorers, trained and employed by the Survey of India, who from 1865 onwards to the end of the century travelled extensively in Central Asia. Several reached Lhasa and a number worked in East and South-East Tibet. Though most efforts to enter Tibet were made from India, some were made from China, and the establishment of a British Consular Office in Kunming in 1877 led to the initial exploration of the Chinese–Tibet border.

North-East Frontier

From 1771 onwards in the North-East Frontier region efforts were made by the East India Company to promote trade with Assam, but these efforts ceased in 1789 because of the civil disturbances. In 1792, at the invitation of the Assamese, a detachment of soldiers was sent by Lord Cornwallis, Governor-General of India, to restore order; this small force was withdrawn in 1794. In 1817 and 1819 Assam was invaded by the Burmese, and as the security of the North-East Frontier depended on a friendly power in Assam the Anglo-Burmese war was fought from 1824 to 1826; following it the British acquired Assam, thus bringing the Raj for the first time into contact with the Himalaya, east of Sikkim and Bhutan. Occupied mainly by primitive tribes, this area acted as a buffer with Tibet, and interest was focused on two main trade routes. To the west one ran from Lhasa through Tawang (east of Bhutan) over the Se La to the Brahmaputra river, whilst further east one connected Rima in East Tibet with Sadiya in Assam by way of the Lohit river; this was the shortest route between Assam and China.[3]

The Assam–Tibet border region was inhabited by a number of tribes, the majority of a warlike disposition. To the west, on the Bhutan border, were the Buddhist Monpas of Tawang who paid dues to Drepung monastery in Lhasa, whilst further east were the non-Buddhist Abors, Mishmis and Apa Tanis who lived along the Subansiri, Dibang, Dihang and Lohit rivers, each a tributary of the Brahmaputra. The British paid these tribes an annual subsidy on condition that they did not raid the plains, and the 'Inner Line' was established in 1873. This ran along the base of the Himalayan foothills and restricted free intercourse between the hill and plains people and also marked the limit of British-administered areas. Initially, exploration of the river valleys and mountains of the North-East Frontier was prompted partly by the commercial possibilities of a link between India, China and Tibet along the Lohit river, but it was also concerned with finding the correct course of the Tsangpo river.

The existence of the Tsangpo river of South Tibet first became known to western geographers through D'Anville's map published in 1737 which was based on the 'Jesuit Map' drawn by Jesuits in Peking (1717–18) from work carried out in Tibet by Chinese surveyors between 1708 and 1716.[4] The upper reaches of the Tsangpo were crossed by Bogle and Turner on their way to Shigatse and by Manning on his way to Lhasa. In about 1860 Colonel Montgomerie of the Survey of India started to train Himalayan natives (Pundits) in survey work and a number followed the course of the Tsangpo in South Tibet on the north flank of the Himalaya in the later years of the 19th century.[5] Of the various tributaries of the Brahmaputra on the southern side of the Himalaya, the Dihang had the largest flow of water, with a minimum discharge of 55,000 cubic feet per second, that is twice the volume of that from the Dibang. For this reason the Dihang was for many years considered to be the continuation of the Tsangpo, although at one time the Irrawaddy was a candidate,[6] an idea that originated from D'Anville's map and the Chinese surveyors. In 1880 this problem was essentially solved by the Pundit Kinthup and the Tsangpo, Dihang and Brahmaputra were shown to be one continuous river.

Although a number of explorers made their way up the Lohit, the development of trade was hindered by the nature of the country and the extreme difficulty of movement and also by the hostility of the hill tribes. In 1885 French Catholic missionaries began working in Szechuan but were continuously harassed by Tibetans. In 1904 the Younghusband mission to Lhasa and the flight of the Dalai Lama led to a political vacuum in Tibet which the Chinese hastened to fill by administrative and political means. They had little success until Chou Erh Feng became commander of the Chinese forces and entered Lhasa in 1910, the Dalai Lama fleeing once again. Chinese activity in East Tibet now extended to Pome and Zayul and this posed a direct threat to the security of the North-East Frontier of India. The murder of Williamson, an Assistant Political Officer, in Sadiya in 1911 forced direct action and a punitive expedition was sent against the Abors. The survey work and exploration during and after this mission was to provide information from which the Macmahon Line in the North-East Frontier Agency was drawn at the Simla Conference in 1914.

In 1913 Bailey and Morshead surveyed the Upper Dihang river and the Tsangpo gorge from the south and then travelled west, north of the Himalaya, to Tawang. This journey proved that the Tsangpo passed between Gyela Peri (7150m) to the north and Namcha Barwa (7765m) to the south, the river then becoming continuous with the Dihang. The Pundit Kinthup's supposition was thus confirmed by the work of Bailey and Morshead and Rennel's hypothesis about the course of the Tsangpo was also proved correct.

Explorers
In the later part of the 19th century information about East and South-East Tibet depended largely on that obtained by the Pundits,[5] and one of their main tasks was to map the course of the Tsangpo river.

One of the first was Nain Singh who in the winter of 1874 travelled along the Tsangpo in Tibet as far as Tsetang; then, striking south through Tawang he crossed the Brahmaputra near Tezpur and returned to India. In 1875 the Pundit 'L', or Lala, set out from India, reached Shigatse and travelled as far as Tsetang. Unable to go any further he returned by his original route. Three years later, in 1878, 'GMN' or Nem Singh, a lama from Sikkim, reached a point 300km beyond Tsetang. He was accompanied by 'KP', or Kinthup, and their measurements of water flow suggested that the Tsangpo and Dihang were the same river. In 1880 KP set out with a Chinese lama; their mission was to throw marked logs into the Tsangpo at Gyala, which would be identified by watchers at the junction of the Dihang with the Brahmaputra. After many hardships which included being sold into slavery by his lama colleague, and his subsequent escape, Kinthup explored the Tsangpo to its Great Bend, discovering in the process the Rainbow or Kinthup Falls,[7] and reached Olon (Onlet), 160km further than any previous explorer's limit. This village was said to be one march from Muri Padam, itself 50km from the Indian plains, whose haze Kinthup could see in the distance. According to instructions he threw marked logs into the river, but none were seen. He returned to India via Lhasa.

Some years later another Pundit, Sarat Chandra Das, described[8] how an inscribed piece of wood which had been found in the Dihang could have come from a monastery near the Tsangpo in Tibet. Finally, Bailey and Morshead at the end of the Mishmi survey operations in 1911–13 discovered Gyela Peri and confirmed that the Tsangpo and Dihang were one and the same river. Previously Namcha Barwa had been found in 1911 by members of the Abor Expedition 1911–12 when its position and height were fixed from the south.

The most famous and remarkable Pundit was 'AK', Kishen Singh or Krishna, who made a series of journeys in Central Asia.[9,10] Living until 1921, the year of the first Everest reconnaissance from Tibet, he made his first journey in 1872, reaching Lhasa from the north after travelling around the Nam Co (Tengri Nor) and describing the Nyenqentangla range, north-east of Lhasa, for the first time.

In 1873–4 AK accompanied the Forsyth mission to Yarkand and Kashgar, and in 1878 he set out on his most famous mission which lasted until 1882, during which he traversed Tibet from south to north, then travelled extensively in East and South-East Tibet. Before he left India he was given instructions by General J T Walker of the Survey of India to 'strike across the Great Plateau of Tibet into Mongolia by any route from south to north which he might find practical and to return by a parallel route over new ground'. He followed these instructions to the letter. 'He was provided with a nine-inch sextant for taking latitude observations, a Tibetan tea bowl for a mercury trough, a prismatic compass for taking bearings to distant peaks, a pocket compass for common use in taking his route bearings, a rosary for counting his paces, a Buddhist prayer-barrel for secreting his field books, an aneroid barometer and some boiling point thermometers.'

From Lhasa, AK followed the main track north, crossing the Changthang and the Kun Lun range, descending to Naichi (Nachatai) and reaching Golmo (Golmud). He then crossed the Tsaidam to Saitu (Tun-Huang). Returning he went through East Tibet reaching Darchend (Tachienlu) and then he struck west through the 'Gorge Country' to Batang, and mentions the 'lofty peaks of Khakarpo' at around 6000m. Reaching Rima he turned north crossing the Ata Kang La (4600m) to reach the plateau again. At Lhojang he joined the official Lhasa–China road and at the Kyichu river he turned south (rather than going north to Lhasa), crossing the Tsangpo and arriving at his original starting place at Khambarji. Finally, 4½ years after leaving, he returned to Darjeeling. The first to provide a reasonable map of Central, East and South-East Tibet, which was drawn from his observations *en route*, he must be considered one of the outstanding scientific explorers of Central Asia.

In the late 19th and early 20th centuries, a number of Europeans travelled in the Tibetan Marches. These included Gill,[11,12] Pereira,[13,14] Teichman,[15,16] Morshead, Bailey,[17,18] Coales[19,20] and Gregory,[21] and they contributed greatly to our knowledge of the region. However, we owe much of our detailed knowledge of the mountain topography to plant-hunters, in particular to two highly talented and formidable botanists, Frank Kingdon-Ward and Joseph Rock.

Frank Kingdon-Ward, who was born in 1885 and died in 1958, is with Aurel Stein, Sven Hedin and AK one of the greatest scientific explorers of the mountains of Central Asia. He worked in the eastern Himalaya and South-East Tibet (Hengduan Shan) from 1909 to 1958, and without his work our general knowledge of this most difficult region would be patchy, of the topography scanty, and of the plants and trees considerably less than at present. As a plant collector he was without peer, introducing a large number of specimens to the gardens of the United Kingdom as well as collecting countless herbarium specimens. The plant for which he is best known is the Himalayan blue poppy, *Meconopsis baileyi*, originally named in honour of Colonel F M Bailey who with Morshead confirmed that the Tsangpo and Dihang were the same river. This plant has now passed through a number of taxonomic transformations, from *M betonicifolia var baileyi* to plain *M betonicifolia*.[22] The business of collecting plants for commercial interests is very different from acquiring herbaceous specimens, and he quickly developed his own methods of doing this which gave him an extraordinarily intricate knowledge of the region in which he worked. His zest for the unknown, the 'blank on the map' and his love of flowers formed the basis of his career.

The Gorge Country was at the time one of the least known and most difficult in which to travel, particularly as Kingdon-Ward was continually having to cross the grain of the country. As he collected plants from higher altitudes for horticultural purposes, this meant that his observations and descriptions of both the topography and the vertical changes in vegetation played a prominent part in his field notes and writing. He really understood the country in which he worked, and mountaineers will always be in his debt for his descriptions of the peaks, passes and glaciers of this unknown land. His topographical descriptions enabled the best commonly available sketch-map of the area in which he travelled to be drawn by the Schweinfurths of Heidelberg University, and his field notes are still being used to understand more fully the region in which he worked.[23] His observations on climate and local wind phenomena are very pertinent, and his division of the country into lower V-shaped, upper U-shaped gorges and the plateau is important, for each represents a different habitat in which different types of vegetation flourished, and this in turn determines the way in which the population lives. In this respect, therefore, he was a geographer of the first rank, though his scientific publications were in the field of botany.

In addition to the physical problems of travel there were also the political problems of sovereignty and suzerainty between Tibet and China in an area where the local people were not inclined to take much notice of either power.

Kingdon-Ward took part in 24 expeditions, wrote 25 books, 705 scientific articles and contributed to many newspapers and magazines. His executor Sir George Taylor FRS, formerly Director of the Royal Botanic Gardens, Kew, who has travelled in this area, told me that Kingdon-Ward was a phenomenon, in a class of his own. It would be difficult to disagree with this assessment.

Joseph Rock, born in 1884, was another erudite and distinguished traveller in East and South-East Tibet. He was born in Vienna and emigrated to America in 1905, finally going to Hawaii because of his health. In 1908 he joined the Division of Forestry and until 1920 worked and collected for the Bishop Museum, which became part of the University of Hawaii. From 1920 onwards for three decades he spent his time in exploration and research in Western China, East and South-East Tibet. His first expedition was to Indo-China, Siam and Burma to obtain seeds of the Chaulmoogra plant for the treatment of leprosy (Hansen's disease). Thereafter he travelled mainly in Yunnan, the Gorge Country, around Minya Konka, and further north in the country to the east of the Amne Machen range.

An exceptional linguist, Rock had learnt Hungarian and Chinese by the time he was 15, and he taught Arabic at Vienna University. He was also fluent in Italian, French, Spanish, Tibetan, Latin, Greek and the language of the aboriginal people of South-West China, and he had a reading knowledge and comprehension of Japanese, Hindi and Sanskrit. He spoke English without a Germanic accent, and for 12 years studied and translated the religious texts of the Na-Khi tribe of North-East Yunnan. For mountaineers his description of the Minya Konka region was an important preliminary to the first ascent in 1932. In his book on the Na-Khi kingdom there are descriptions and maps of the mountain ranges in this area.[24] In addition, he contributed many articles about South-East Tibet to the National Geographic Magazine between 1922 and 1935. In 1949 he was forced to leave China by the Communists and returned to Hawaii where he died in 1962, regarded as the father of Hawaiian botany for his immense contribution to the understanding of the botany of these islands. His main contributions to knowledge were concerned with the flora of Hawaii and the natural history of Western China, and East and South-East Tibet.[25]

Mountain Ranges

Although there are a number of maps of the region (see in particular References 26 and 27), the whole area is hardly known from the mountaineering point of view, and the country is topographically so complicated that a full description will have to wait until many more parties have visited these mountains.

Irrawaddy–Tsangpo Divide

This range is about 200km long and most of the tributaries that are the source of the Irrawaddy arise from it. The highest four peaks appear to be about 5800m high and lie north of the Adung river. There are a number of small glaciers.[28]

The highest peak is Kakarporazi (5873m) at the head of a branch of the Adung river. It is the highest peak in Burma and was first discovered and had its height measured by Indian surveyors in 1923. Possible approaches are from the north and west, via the Diphuk La. Of the various passes over this range, the Diphuk La (4350m) connects with Rima on the Lohit river to the north, whilst further east is the Lachong La (3995m), which is the connection between the Irrawaddy and Salween rivers. The Namni La (4657m) crosses the middle of the range.

In general the country is extremely compressed, with gorges so steep and narrow and ridges so high that it is impossible to obtain extensive views.

Irrawaddy–Salween Divide

The highest peak in this group appears to be Keni Chu Pu, which was described by Rock and Kingdon-Ward.

Tsangpo–Salween Divide

The country between the Tsangpo and its tributaries and the Salween is so complicated that it is impossible to give a good overall description. To the north, between the Po Yigrong river, a northern tributary of the Tsangpo, and the Salween, there are a number of peaks of about 6000m, some sighted by Kaulback and mentioned in his book.[29] One peak (7535m) is marked on the map of the Mountains of Central Asia[26] at 94°E 31°N. This height is taken from an ONC map of the region and may be in error as no large peaks have been described by any European traveller in this region. However, good panoramic views tend to be the exception rather than the rule in this region with its high rainfall and extensive cloud.

Along the Po Tsangpo, a more southerly tributary of the Tsangpo, are a number of peaks mentioned by Kaulback,[29,30] Hanbury-Tracy[31] and Kingdon-Ward.[32] These appear to lie below the 6000m height.

Between the Tributaries of the Lohit River and the Salween

There are a number of peaks in this divide, among them Chombo (6700m)[30], a twin-headed mountain which is south and west of the Ata Kang La and may be the highest peak east of the bend of the Tsangpo. There appear to be a number of summits of around 6000m clustered around Shugden Gompa. The Ata glacier which rises north of Chombo is about 20km long and is possibly the

2. *Annapurna South, 7219m: East Pillar.* (Lindsay Griffin) (p 13)

3. *Annapurna South Face: Top Buttress, British Route.* (Lindsay Griffin) (p 13)

4. *Annapurna South: unclimbed NW face of Hiunchuli from East Pillar.* (Lindsay Griffin) (p 13)

5. *The great bend of the Chong Kumdan glacier. Water-level marks on the walls can be clearly seen.* (Harish Kapadia) (p 28)

6. *The site of the Chong Kumdan glacier dam in 1989. In 1929 the water-level reached 120m. See marks on the walls on the right and on the scree slopes, left.* (Harish Kapadia) (p 28)

7. *Chong Kumdan I (7971m): an unattempted 7000er.* (Harish Kapadia)
   (p 28)

8. *Biachari peak and dome.* (Sandy Allan) (p 43)

9. *Latok II.* (Sandy Allan) (p 43)

10. *Latok II, Ogre and Choktoi glacier from Hanipispur.* (Sandy Allan) (p 43)

11. *View from Hanipis-*
    pur down Choktoi
    glacier to Hushe
    peaks. (Sandy
    Allan) (p 43)

12. *The lake, Shugden*
    Gompa. (Kingdon-
    Ward) *(From the*
    Royal Geographi-
    cal Society archive,
    by permission.)
    (p 49)

13. *Glaciers of Great Snow Range.* (Kingdon-Ward) *(From the Royal Geographical Society archive, by permission.)* (p 49)

14. *Glacier near Shugden Gompa.* (Kingdon-Ward) *(From the Royal Geographical Society archive, by permission.)* (p 49)

15. *The Kunlun Fault, northern Tibet. The Golmud-Lhasa Highway follows the line of a major strike-slip fault that allows the crust beneath Tibet to be displaced to the east.* (Nigel Harris) (p 68)

16. *Nanga Parbat, northern Pakistan. The western bastion and most active mountain of the Himalayan range is being uplifted by nearly 1cm each year.* (Nigel Harris) (p 68)

17. *The Tibet Plateau. Tibet is not a northward continuation of the Himalaya but a rugged plateau that is still being uplifted, bounded by the Himalaya to the south and the Kunlun (seen in the distance) to the north.* (Nigel Harris) (p 68)

18. *Fans of detritus eroded from the rapidly uplifted Karakoram range.* (Nigel Harris) (p 68)

largest glacier east of the Tsangpo, according to Kingdon-Ward. There are several other glaciers, 10 to 13km in length.

Within the Bend of the Tsangpo[32,33]

Here the peaks of the eastern Himalaya end in Namcha Barwa which is surrounded on three sides by the Tsangpo river. The complete ascent has yet to be accomplished but a lower minor summit was reached by Chinese mountaineers in 1983 and 1984.[34]

To the north of Namcha Barwa, on the N side of the Tsangpo river, lies Gyela Peri which was climbed by a Japanese party in 1986,[35] and further north again are peaks to the south of the Po Yigrong river, including Namla Karpo.

Salween–Mekong Divide

The Salween has many tributaries and arises from the south and east portion of the Tanggula range, which runs in an east-west direction across the middle of the Tibetan plateau. The Mekong river rises from the E portion of the Tanggula range, and between the two sources there are a number of high peaks.

Further south in this divide there are many peaks described but not named by Teichman,[15,16] and further south again, around 29°N where rivers are crowded together, are Damyon (5800–6100m), Mts Kagur Pu (Kakarpo), Mo and Drachhen. Of these, Kagur Pu (Kakarpo, Kangkarpo or Meili, 6840m) has had the most attention from mountaineers, with American and Japanese attempts.[36] According to Kingdon-Ward the name means 'white mountain', and it is sacred and famous throughout East Tibet. One of the first to photograph it was Joseph Rock.[37] It is a fine glaciated peak, one of a group and the highest in the Mekong-Salween divide. Another peak in this group is Miyetzimu, also mentioned by Rock.

Between Kangkarpo and Damyon, 80km to the south, there are no less than five scattered snow peaks and several dead glaciers.

Kingdon-Ward[32] describes the peaks of the Mekong–Salween divide as seen from above the village of Atunzu. 'To the west a grand panorama now unfolded itself, about 60 miles of the Mekong–Salween divide'. Far away to the south he caught sight of a snowy peak with extensive snow-fields – the mountains then grew lower until the Kakarpo group was reached – about seven peaks were visible.

Divide between Mekong–Yangtse Kiang and its Tributaries

Topographically this is another extremely complex region. The Pai Ma Shan are glaciated, and Rock and Kingdon-Ward describe two peaks Tsa-Ya and Omagu at about 28°30' N. Near Batang is a group of 'snowy peaks', and further north still at 30°–31°N there are further groups of 'snowy peaks', each described but not named by Teichman.[15,16]

A long way south at 27°30' in the bend of the Yangtse Kiang is the Likiang group of peaks (c5500m), visited by de Beer[38] and Rock. The country is particularly beautiful, with marked slopes of rhododendrons. Recently Chinese and British botanists have worked in this region,[39] and there have been attempts on peaks in the Yulong Shan.[35,40]

Gongga Shan (Minya Konka Group)

This is the best-known range and has been investigated by both mountaineers and geographers. It is a considerable way to the east, being at 102°E and 30°N. The nearest town is Tatsienlu, to the north of the mountain mass.

First glimpsed by American travellers in the late 1920s, it is a very fine group of mountains, with many peaks rising above extensive glaciers. At one time it was thought that there might be a peak of 9000m or more in the area. Articles in the *Geographical Journal*[41,42] go into this assumption in great detail and contain sketches by Herbert Steiner; however, they came to the correct conclusion that a mountain of this height was unlikely. The Gongga Shan supports 159 glaciers, up to 16km in length.[43] The whole area was mapped, explored and photographed for the first time by Joseph Rock and a National Geographic Society party in 1929.[44] A number of peaks were named, including Mount Grosvenor after the President of the Society, and Reddomain Solo (7000m). The highest peak, Minya Konka (7556m) was climbed by an American party, Burdsall, Emmons, Moore and Young[45] in 1932. A panorama from the summit shows a remarkable array of peaks in the group. It has now had five ascents.[34]

Another peak in the area, Jiazi (?6540m), was attempted by a British Army party in spring 1981.[46]

The East Kun Lun Shan (Burhan Budai Shan) and Amne Machin Shan

See article by Ward in the *Alpine Journal*.[47]

TABLE OF PEAKS:
MOUNTAINS OF EAST AND SOUTH-EAST TIBET

Name	Height	Reference
Huzhu	6224m	26
Kekesaijimen	6197m	48 (map)
Yagradze Shan	?	26
Amne Machen		26
Maqen Gangri	6282m	49
Bayan Har Shan	?	26
Nyen-Po-Yur Tse	?	49
Dza-Ra		
No name	5940m	26
Snow Range	?	15, 16
Xiari Aba Shan	?	26
Pk 5931m is close by		
Snow Range	?	15, 16
No name	5850m	26
Chola Shan	6141m	26
No name	20,000 ft	29
Snow Range	?	15, 16
No name	?7353m	26
Snow Range	?	15, 16

No name	6474m	26
No name	6599m	26
No name	6870m	26
No name	20,640ft	29
Pk 20,002ft close by		
Snow Range	?	15, 16
Namla Karpo	?	23 (Map 14)
No name	6010m	26
Minya Konka	7556m	26
No name	20,000 ft	29
Pk 26,450ft close by (??)		
Snow Range	?	15, 16
Gyela Peri	7151m	23
Namcha Barwa	7651m	23
	7765m	
Ningri Tangor	?	23
Kongbo Peri	?	23
No name	6236m	26
Pab Ri	?	23, 26
Temu Tse	?	23
No name	21,660 ft	29
Kang Kar Hlamo	?	31
Dorjet Zenga	?	23
No name	21,680 ft	31
?Kakarpo Range	?	15, 16
Bung Bung Ri	?	26
Chombo	?6840m	23
Damyon	?	23
No name	6290m	26
Kang Pemu	?	23
Konka Ling Range	?	50
Kha Wa Karpo ⎫		
Ka Gur Pu ⎪	6840m	23
? Kang Karpo ⎬		
Meili ⎭		
No name	18,000 ft	24
Pai Ma Shan	?	23, 24
Ka Karpo Razi	?	23
Kaso	?	23
Polon	?	23
Me Tse Mo	?	24
Drachhen	?	24
Ke Ni Chu Pu	?	23, 49
Kanju Shan	?	24
Mizhon Ziga	?	24
Hsin Shih Kuan Shan	?	24
Dapha Bum	?	23

Mungku Hkyet	?	23
Taru Tra	?	23
Likiang Group	?	23, 24
No name	Peaks over	27
	20,000ft	

REFERENCES

1   J G Marshall, *Britain and Tibet 1765–1947. The Background to the India–China Border Dispute*. Bundoora (La Trobe University Library), Australia, 1977.

2   J Rennel, 'An Account of the Ganges and Burrampooter River'. *Phil Trans Roy Soc London 71*, 87–114, 1781.

3   'Mr J F Needham's Journey along the Lohit Brahmaputra between Sadiya in Upper Assam and Rima in South Tibet.' *Royal Geographical Soc Suppl Papers 2, Part 3*, 487–555, 1888.

4   W R Fuchs, *Der Jesuiten-Atlas der Kanshi-Zeit*. Monumenta Serica. Monograph Series IV. Fujen Universität, Peking, 1943.

5   D Waller, *The Pundits. British Exploration of Tibet and Central Asia*. University Press of Kentucky, 1990.

6   J T Walker, 'The Lu River of Tibet. Is it the source of the Irawady or the Salwin?' *Proc Royal Geographical Soc 9*, 353–376, 1887.

7   L A Waddell, 'The Falls of the Tsangpo (San Pu) and the identity of that river with the Brahmaputra'. *Geographical Journal 5*, 258-260, 1895.

8   Sarat Chandra Das, 'A note on the identity of the great Tsangpo of Tibet with the Dihong'. *J Asiatic Soc of Bengal 67, No 1*, 126-129, 1898.

9   J T Walker, 'Five years' journeyings through Great Tibet by one of the trans-Himalayan explorers of the Survey of India'. *J Royal Geographical Soc (N.S.) 7*, 65–93, 1885.

10 *Reports of the explorations in Great Tibet and Mongolia made by A-K in 1879–1882 in connection with the Trigonometric Branch, Survey of India*. Dehra Dun, 1884.

11 W J Gill, 'Travels in Western China and on the eastern borders of Tibet'. *J Royal Geographical Soc 48*, 57–172, 1878.

12 W J Gill, *The river of golden sand*. London (John Murray), 1883.

13 G Pereira, 'Brigadier-General George Pereira's journey to Lhasa'. *Geographical Journal 61*, 124–130, 1923.

14 G Pereira, 'Peking to Lhasa'. *Geographical Journal 64*, 97–120, 1924.

15 E Teichman, 'Journeys through Kam (East Tibet)'. *Geographical Journal 59*, 1–19, 1922.

16 E. Teichman, *Travels of a consular officer in Eastern Tibet*, Cambridge University Press, 1922.

17 F M Bailey, *China, Tibet, Assam*. London (Cape), 1945.

18 F M Bailey, *No passport to Tibet*. London (Hart-Davis), 1957.

19 O Coales, 'Eastern Tibet.' *Geographical Journal 53*, 228–253, 1919.

20 O Coales, 'Economic notes on Eastern Tibet'. *Geographical Journal 54*, 242–247, 1919.

21 J W Gregory and C J Gregory, 'The Alps of Chinese Tibet and their geographical relations'. *Geographical Journal* 61, 153–179, 1923.

22 C Lyte, *Frank Kingdon-Ward. The last of the great plant hunters*. London (John Murray), 1989.

23 U and H Schweinfurth, *Exploration in the Eastern Himalayas and the River Gorge Country of South-East Tibet. Francis (Frank) Kingdon-Ward (1885–1958)*. Wiesbaden (Franz Steiner Verlag), 1975.

24 J F Rock, *The ancient Na-Khi kingdom of South-West China* (2 vols). Cambridge, Mass (Harvard Univ Press), 1947.

25 Obituary of Joseph Rock. *Taxon* 12, 89–102, 1963.

26 *The Mountains of Central Asia* (1:3,000,000 Map and Gazetteer compiled by the Royal Geographical Society and the Mount Everest Foundation.) London (Macmillan), 1987.

27 Operational Navigation Chart 1: 1,000,000, Sheets G7, G8, H9, H10. Prepared by Aerospace Center, Defense Mapping Agency, St Louis Airforce Station, Missouri.

28 F Kingdon-Ward, *Burma's icy mountains*. London (Cape), 1949.

29 R Kaulback, *Salween*. London (Hodder & Stoughton), 1938.

30 R Kaulback, *Tibetan trek*. London (Hodder & Stoughton), 1934.

31 J Hanbury-Tracy, *Black river of Tibet*. London (Muller), 1938

32 F Kingdon-Ward, *The riddle of the Tsangpo gorges*. London (Arnold), 1926.

33 M Ward, 'The eastern Himalaya'. *AJ90*, 10–17, 1985.

34 *American Alpine Journal* 27, 336, 1985.

35 *American Alpine Journal* 29, 295 and 297–298, 1987.

36 *American Alpine Journal* 31, 270–271, 1989.

37 J F Rock, 'Through the great river trenches of Asia'. *Nat Geographic Mag* 50(2), 133–186, 1926.

38 D H de Beer, *Yunnan 1938*. Privately printed, 1971.

39 See the following article in this journal by Tony Schilling.

40 *American Alpine Journal* 28, 303–304, 1986.

41 'Mountains about Tatsienlu.' *Geographical Journal* 75, 345–352, 1930.

42 'Sketches of the Tatsienlu peaks 1930.' *Geographical Journal* 75, 353–355, 1930.

43 B Messerli and J Ives, *Gongga Shan (7556m) and Yulongue Shan (5596m). Geo-ecological observations in the Hengduan Shan mountains of South-Western China*, Chapter in *Natural environment and man in tropical mountain ecosystems* (ed W Lauer). Stuttgart (Franz Steiner Verlag Wiesbaden), 1984.

44 J F Rock, 'The glories of the Minya Konka'. *Nat Geographic Mag* 58, 385–437, 1930.

45 R L Burdsall and A B Emmons, *Men against the clouds*. London (Bodley Head), 1935.

46 H Day, 'Da Xue Shan, Sichuan, China'. *AJ87*, 117–120, 1982.

47 M Ward, 'The Kun Lun Shan. Desert Peaks of Central Asia'. *AJ94*, 84–97, 1989/90.

48   *The Geological Evolution of Tibet. Report of the 1985 Royal Society-Academia Sinica Geotraverse of the Xizang–Qinghai Plateau.* Royal Society, 1988.

49   J F Rock, *The Amnye ma-chhen range and adjacent regions: a monographic study.* Roma: Istituto Italiano per il Medio ed Estremo Oriente, 1956.

50   'Konka Risumgongha, Holy Mountain of the Outlaws'. *Nat Geographic Mag 60*, 1–65, 1931.

ACKNOWLEDGEMENTS

I would like to thank Ted Hatch of the drawing office and Rachel Duncan of the photographic archives of the Royal Geographical Society for their help in the preparation of this article; also Tony Schilling of the Royal Botanic Gardens, Kew, and H Adams Carter, Editor of the *American Alpine Journal*, for their assistance.

A Botanist in the Yulong Shan – the Jade Dragon Mountains of Yunnan

TONY SCHILLING

(Plates 65–72)

The Yulong Shan forms a dramatic range of precipitous limestone peaks, rising to 5600m, riven by deep gorges and containing several glaciers and extensive areas of permanent snow. The range forms the most easterly boundary of the Chungtien Plateau and is bounded on the north-west by the Yangtse river. It seems strange that such a relatively uncomplicated range of mountains, close to a large town (Likiang) in the NW corner of the Yunnan province of China, remains virgin. In fact it has been attempted on at least four separate occasions, the first rebuff being delivered to a New Zealand expedition as long ago as the 1930s. In 1984 a second attempt was unsuccessfully made by a Japanese team, and in the following two years separate American assaults (autumn and spring) were made, again without success. Both these American expeditions appear to have been operating on extremely tight time schedules and were thwarted by bad weather.

In the April–May period of 1987 I spent almost five weeks exploring the mountains, slopes and recesses of this exceptionally rugged and beautiful range of dolomitic limestone as a member of the Sino-British Likiang Botanical Expedition. Two of our members were from the Royal Botanic Gardens, Edinburgh (Ron McBeath and David Chamberlain) and two from the Royal Botanic Gardens, Kew (the author and Chris Grey-Wilson). Four Chinese botanists from the Kunming Institute of Botany made up the remaining members of the party.

Western interest in the Yulong Shan began long before the first serious mountaineers set their sights on its airy summit. Marco Polo visited Ta-Li-Fu, the western capital of Yunnan (Dali as we know it today) in approximately 1283 and may have caught a glimpse of the Jade Dragon Snow Mountains to the north. He certainly noted the botanical wealth and variety of China and remarked upon the country's 'vegetative wonders'. Others who followed over the centuries echoed his comments and brought back seeds, plants and dried herbarium specimens to excite the western botanists of their day.

Most significantly, several European missionaries stationed in China's interior made detailed observations of plants of medicinal importance but, until the Opium Wars of 1842 and 1860 compelled a change in Chinese politics, Westerners were almost completely shut out of the country's interior. Even then, when 'the bamboo door' had been prized open a little wider, travel was often extremely hazardous as feuding war-lords and brigands were common-place. Between 1872 and 1885 the Russian explorer Captain Nicolai Mikhailovich Przewalski made four excursions to China including one to the Tibetan borderlands and left his mark on botanical history. (*Ligularia przewalskii* is but one plant named in his honour.) But it was the now-legendary French missionary Père Jean Marie Delavay, inspired by the Lazarist missionary and innate naturalist Père Jean Pierre Armand, who played the major role in enlightening the world about the botanical wonders of Yunnan. During the 1880s he gathered over 200,000 dried botanical specimens in the north-western part of the province for the herbarium of the Paris Museum, at least 1500 of these species being entirely new to science.

Much of Delavay's time and effort was spent in the Yulong Shan range (referred to in his notes as the Li-kiang) and to serious students of Chinese botany his field notes make exciting and romantic reading. '*Paeonia delavayi* sp. nov [new species] 3,500 metres Li-kiang 9/7/84 Delavay No. 1142 . . . . . . très élégante de la plante lui méritent une place dans les jardins' is but one of his notes which records the very first collection of this deep maroon-red flowered paeonia. Our expedition 'rediscovered' this wonderful species 103 years later and echoed Delavay's sentiments.

The next and most diligent of all botanical explorers of the Yulong Shan was the great Scottish plant-collector George Forrest. Between 1904 and 1932 he made seven expeditions to China of which five were directed to the Yulong Shan and the region centred around Likiang District. He made massive collections of seeds, plants and dried specimens – a practice which would be totally unacceptable today – and by training native collectors managed to spread his collecting-web more effectively.

During these travels Forrest managed to introduce to horticulture many of the plants which Delavay had discovered but had only collected as herbarium specimens. Forrest described the Yulong Shan as follows: 'From the base to the limit of vegetation at 17,500 feet, the range in its whole extent of fully fifty miles is one huge natural flower garden. The extreme height of the range is almost 20,000 ft; there is therefore about 3000 ft of perpetual snow.' With our better knowledge of this range we can now reduce each of these three figures by 1000 feet or so, but otherwise the description is no exaggeration.

During Forrest's third expedition to the Yulong Shan (1912–1914) the intrepid English plant-hunter Frank Kingdon-Ward almost crossed his path as he travelled through Likiang *en route* to other parts of Western Yunnan and the Tibetan Marches. In his book *Mystery Rivers of Tibet* Kingdon-Ward writes of Likiang as being 'a small unwalled city of steep cobbled streets situated in a bowl amongst the hills', and he describes the adjacent Temple of the Water Dragon as being bewitchingly reflected in the water-lilied pool against a background of snowy peaks. On 16 May 1913 Kingdon-Ward left Likiang *en route* to the Yangtse river. This he crossed two days later close to the point where the waters are forced through Tiger Leaping Gorge at the base of the immensely steep north-western ramparts of the Yulong Shan which fall a vertical height of two miles into the river bed. He wrote: 'The great river here flows north eastwards presently to hurl itself into the heart of the Li-kiang [sic] range a spur of which we had just crossed.'

The Austrian-born naturalized American geographer, plant-hunter and anthropologist Joseph Rock spent many years between 1922 and 1949 in China, operating mainly in the Yunnan region. He was an eccentric man of many talents, of great resolve and a natural linguist. His particular talent was for locating particularly fine forms of already known plant species, especially rhododendrons. He only left China when he was forced out in 1949 by the political turmoil of that period.

Having made his home in Likiang he left with a heavy heart, stating that he 'wanted to die amongst those beautiful mountains rather than in a bleak hospital bed all alone', but it was not to be and he died far away in Honolulu in 1962 at the age of 78; to the last he was a lonely, restless figure always travelling and nowhere really at home.

These famous three – Forrest, Kingdon-Ward and Rock – actually met on one occasion during 1922 in the botanical arena of the Yulong Shan; records succinctly state that 'they were wary of one another'. Field botanists are adventurers with egos every bit as sensitive as any 'summit-sighted' mountaineer's, and each of these highly motivated plant-hunters was quick to divert any would-be poachers away from what he considered to be his own chosen patch. Even allowing for this, it is amusing to reflect that, with the whole of South-West China to explore, these three great men found themselves getting under each other's feet on the same mountain. The remaining notable botanist historically to work the Yulong Shan range was Yu Te-tsun, a Chinese plant-hunter and Senior Professor of the Institute of Botany, Academia Sinica, Beijing. He travelled widely throughout China and spent the seasons of 1937–38 in the Likiang region, leading a British-sponsored expedition. Many of the plants which were subsequently raised from his seed collections can be found alongside those of Forrest, Kingdon-Ward and Rock in the many great gardens of Britain, representing a testimony to botanical exploration and endeavour. The main objectives of the Sino-British Likiang Botanical Expedition was to carry out detailed studies of certain genera (with special reference to *Rhododendron, Betula* and *Primula*) and to gain field experience which would directly relate to the cultural requirements of these groups.

As far as records show it would seem that almost all botanical exploration, including our own, has been confined to the eastern flank of the mountain – partly because of its ease of access from the Likiang Plain, but more obviously because the topography of the lower and middle sections of the range is less severe than one would have had to face on the more remote and savage western side. The lower slopes between 2700 and 3000 metres are dominated by the Yunnan Pine *Pinus yunnanensis* which is interspersed with hardwood trees such as Poplar and Lime as well as a very wide range of interesting shrubs. These include several species of *Rhododendron, Hypericum, Buddleja, Syringa, Berberis, Daphne* and the delightful *Clematis montana*, and much more besides. Herbs such as the beautiful George Forrest's primrose *Primula forrestii* with flowers of rich golden-yellow also flourish at this altitude, as does the rare and bizarre-looking slipper orchid *Cypripedium margaritaceum*.

The middle zone of the Yulong Shan between 3000 and 3750 metres is dominated by mixed conifers and deciduous forest and contains some of the finest of all woody species. Conifers include the Yunnan Hemlock *Tsuga yunnanensis*, Potanin's Larch *Larix potaninii*, Armand's Pine *Pinus armandii*, the lower level forms of Delavay's Fir *Abies delavayi*, the Likiang Spruce *Picea likiangensis*, and the Himalayan Yew *Taxus baccata var wallichiana* which is so similar to the European Yew that a galloping yak would never notice the difference! Deciduous trees include Forrest's Maple *Acer forrestii*, Vilmorin's Mountain Ash *Sorbus vilmorinii* and the two major birch species of the region, *Betula utilis* and *B platyphylla var sechuanica*. The list of herbs which grow within this rich area of temperate forest is truly encyclopaedic, for here are to be found such treasures as *Primula bella*, *Iris chrysographes*, *Arisaema wilsonii* and the yellow slipper orchid *Cypripedium flavum*. But it is to the higher slopes that one has to climb, especially those between 4000 and 5000 metres, in order to see the alpine gems which fired the questing spirit of George Forrest and his contemporaries. Here, on the steep alpine meadows and the harsh screes and cliff ledges, are to be found the real treasures of the range. In June the meadows at this altitude are alight with the colour of flowers – *Rhododendron adenogynum* occurs in flowing masses of pale pink, the yellow bells of *Lilium lopophorum* stud the slopes in association with the purple *Lloydia tibetica var purpurescens* (an Asian counterpart of the Snowdon Lily) and the golden *Meconopsis integrifolia*. On the cliffs cling cushions of *Androsace delavayi* and the almost impossibly-named *Solmslaubachia pulcherrima*, one of Forrest's favourite alpines with cress-like ice-blue flowers. On the limestone screes, often in the shelter of boulders, grow dwarf willows, Delavay's Fritillary *Fritillaria delavayi*, *Rhododendron telmateium*, and cushion saxifrages, the finest of which is *Saxifraga calcicola*.

Best of all is the exquisite dwarf alpine 'Blue Poppy' *Meconopsis delavayi* which Kingdon-Ward described as 'a shimmering bluish-violet flower with the texture of Japanese silk'. Higher still in the north-facing base-rich wetter flushes the seemingly uncultivatable *Primula dryadifolia* shows its mauve-pink flowers against broad prostrate mats of foliage (25cm across), accompanied by three 'sisters' of the same genus, *Primula pinnatifida*, *P secundiflora* and *P pseudo-sikkimensis*.

One of the most spectacular areas of the Yulong Shan is the tortuous and mysterious valley of the Gang-ho-ba which drives itself deeply into the eastern recesses of the range to end in a great cul-de-sac of moraines, detritus, hanging glacier and soaring cliff faces. This is the inner sanctum of the Yulong Shan and the region which inspired us the most, both for its floristic wealth and its mountain majesty. Our greatest disappointment was in not being able to camp in the alpine zones. Our Chinese hosts mystified us by preferring to base the expedition in Likiang and to set forth each day from the hotel. In consequence we were constantly obliged to ascend and descend the mountain by a different route, and after a period of 3½ weeks of near-perfect weather we calculated we had notched up a collective up-and-down climbing figure of well over 36,000 metres! It is appropriate here to refer to a paragraph by S B Sutton from *In China's Border Provinces* where she states: 'As Rock's, Kingdon-Ward's and Forrest's harvests proved, the river gorges and mountains of western China were sufficiently fertile to keep a man busy for a lifetime or at least as long as his legs held out!' The Likiang region is currently open to tourism and, what was until a short while ago a little-known part of SW China, is fast becoming just another point on the Asian overlander's itinerary.

In 1913 Frank Kingdon-Ward amusingly wrote: 'If the day ever comes for the publication of a Tourist Guide to Yunnan we may expect to see something like this, – from the pass an extensive view is obtained of the Li-kiang range (highest peak 20,000ft) which has hardly received at the hands of climbers the attention it merits. Guides cannot be obtained locally, as the people do not mountaineer.' Almost 80 years later the summit of the Yulong Shan still awaits the attention of a successful climber and the little-known north-western slopes still hold secrets for the naturalist.

REFERENCES

Journal articles
C A G Jones, *American Alpine Journal* 28, 303–304, 1986.
E S Perlman, *American Alpine Journal* 29, 297–298, 1987.

Books
A Franchet, *Plantae Yunnanensis*. Extract from *Bulletin de la Société botanique de France* 1886.
F Kingdon-Ward, *Mystery Rivers of Tibet*. Seeley Service & Co Ltd, 1923.
E H M Cox, *Plant Hunting in China*. London (Collins), 1945.
S B Sutton, *In China's Border Provinces*. New York (Hastings House), 1974.
R L Lancaster, *Travels in China*. Antique Collectors' Club, Woodbridge, 1989.

ACKNOWLEDGEMENTS

I express my thanks for their assistance to the librarians of The Royal Botanic Gardens, Kew, The Royal Botanic Gardens, Edinburgh, and The Royal Geographical Society.

The Geological Exploration of Tibet and the Himalaya

NIGEL HARRIS

(Plates 15–18)

The Great Himalaya stretches for nearly 3000km in an arc from Namcha Barwa to Nanga Parbat, forming the southern rampart of the Tibetan Plateau (figure 1). Before the second half of this century, the British Raj was the political power of the southern Himalaya, whereas to the north an independent Tibet controlled the trade routes. Today the world's highest mountain range spans the boundaries of five sovereign states, China, India, Pakistan, Nepal and Bhutan. It is the complex politics of the region during the past 40 years, as much as the forbidding terrain, that has determined the geological exploration of the region. Even today, intertribal disputes in Sikkim and Assam, the everlasting Indo-Pakistan hostilities over Kashmir, and the disputed frontiers between India and China east of Bhutan, leave very little of the Himalaya accessible to scientific expeditions.

Although the first tentative explorations of Tibet by European travellers began in the 17th century, it was not until the 19th century that systematic exploration of Tibet's geography began. By this time, interest in Tibet was precipitated by the mutual distrust between the British and Russian empires. The Survey of India recruited agents, later to become known as Pundits, from

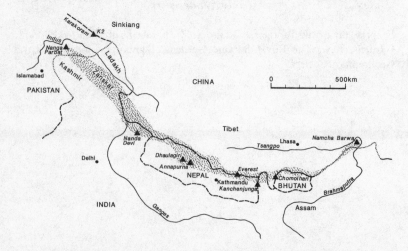

Figure 1. *The geopolitics of the Himalaya (stippled). Disputed* de facto *national boundaries are marked as dotted lines.*

the eastern Himalayan tribes to explore Tibet as systematically as possible, given its rugged topography and the suspicious Tibetan authorities. Pace and compass techniques were used to measure distances (the Pundits were often disguised as monks and prayer beads served to keep track of large distances), and altitudes were estimated from the boiling-point of water. Their results have proved to be remarkably accurate. In 1882 a Pundit known as AK (like all true secret agents, Pundits were identified by initials only) measured the altitude of Lhasa as 11,910ft; this compares with the correct value of 11,970ft (3650m).

The geographical exploration of the Himalaya and southern Tibet identified geological problems that remained unresolved for over a century. Tibet was established as a plateau, 2000km across from south to north, that rarely drops below 3000m above sea level (figure 2). Such a vast and high plateau is unique on this planet, although there are some similarities with the altiplano of the Andes, and it demands a geological explanation for its uplift. Another observation made by the early explorers is that the Himalaya is not a watershed; several major rivers, including the Tsangpo which emerges in Assam as the Brahmaputra, rise in Tibet and cut through the Himalaya through a spectacular series of gorges. The observation that major rivers cut through a mountain range is unusual; it is true neither of the Andes nor of the Alps, and it implies that the rivers first flowed before the mountains were there. As uplift occurred, the rivers increased in potential energy and cut through the incipient hills, forming deep gorges. This is only possible in young active mountain ranges.

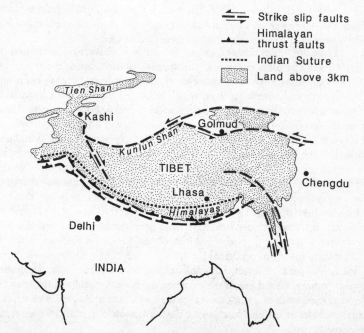

Figure 2. The structure of the Tibetan Plateau.

In some ways the geological exploration of Central Asia during the second half of this century has mirrored the geographical exploration of the last century. Although most of the Himalaya and Tibet have been inaccessible to scientific study until recently, select regions of the southern Himalayan slopes have been surveyed by geologists for much longer. The most detailed area of geological study has been in the western Himalaya of northern Pakistan, the same region that had been surveyed by Colonel Alexander Gardiner in the first half of the 19th century. It was here that in 1964 Augusto Gansser, the distinguished Swiss geologist and Himalayan explorer, discovered fragments of oceanic crust near the Indus river. But like the European explorers of the previous century, western scientists had to stay on the southern Himalayan slopes. Tibet was off-limits until about a decade ago.

Modern understanding of the geology of the highest mountains on Earth really began with the exploration of the ocean floor and the formulation of the theory of plate tectonics about a century after the early expeditions of the Pundits. Since the early 1960s, earth scientists have realized that oceans were transient features, growing from sinuous volcanic ridges such as the mid-Atlantic ridge; these are largely submarine but occasionally form spectacular volcanic islands, such as Iceland today. Oceans not only grow but also shrink, due to a process called subduction, and in the contraction of ocean basins the continents on their opposing sides converge. The final stage of this process is collision between two continents. Continental crust is less dense than oceanic crust, and much less dense than the mantle beneath it. The low density means that continents cannot be subducted far beneath the surface. The result is that, although the processes of the Earth's plates can create crust at subduction zones, they cannot get rid of it. So after continental collision the crust crumples and thickens.

Professor John Dewey, now at Oxford University, identified the Himalaya as a possible example of continental collision during the 1970s. One of the lines of evidence for a collision model came from geophysical results, from gravity and seismic surveys, which indicated that the crust beneath the Himalaya is over 60km thick, twice the normal thickness for continental crust. A head-on collision between two vast continents will obviously crumple and thicken the leading edges of the continents. This explains why the Himalaya is so high – the low density of the continental crust means that the surface of thickened continents is uplifted to great altitudes. Like a block of wood floating on water, the thicker the block the higher it will stand above the water-line (and the deeper are its roots). So the low density of the continents means that crust which has been thickened will be uplifted. The great thickness of the Himalayan crust can be seen not only indirectly from geophysical surveys but also from observing the rocks themselves. Most of the Great Himalayan peaks are sedimentary in origin, deposited by the sea that has now disappeared. But on some of the peaks, Everest, Chomolhari and Manaslu for example, granites appear to have melted out of the surrounding rock. Crustal melting may be a direct consequence of a thick crust; the high radioactive content of continental crust provides an internal heat source that causes melting of rocks deep within thickened crust.

Earth scientists have also traced the movement of India before its impact with the rest of Asia. About 100 million years ago, India lay in the southern hemisphere where it fragmented from a vast southern landmass, rifting from Madagascar along its western coast and from Antarctica along its eastern coast. India drifted north at a velocity of about 20cm per year. Impact with the rest of Asia occurred 50 million years ago. The fragments of oceanic crust found by Augusto Gansser in the Indus valley are the remains of a vast ocean floor which was folded and crumpled within the suture zone that now separates the former continental masses.

This simple model of collision between two continents explains the formation of a narrow high mountain range such as the Himalaya, but does not obviously explain the Tibetan Plateau. Like the Himalaya, Tibet is supported by an unusually thick crust. A related problem is the continued northern movement of India. Since the initial collision the two continents have not simply fused into a single supercontinent. India and the rest of Asia have continued to converge at an average rate of 5cm a year, amounting to over 2000km since the ocean was first closed by subduction. Three models have been proposed to account for such a staggering convergence between continents in the absence of an intervening ocean.

Firstly, the crust can be squeezed out sideways. The idea was first put forward in 1975 by Peter Molnar of MIT and Paul Tapponier of the University of Paris. On satellite images they spotted long faults dissecting the Earth's crust in northern, eastern and western Tibet. From analysing the seismic waves associated with earthquake activity that result from movement along the faults they determined that the Earth's crust is moving sideways across them. Such faults are called strike-slip faults (figure 2). The Molnar–Tapponier model for crustal deformation in Tibet predicts that movement across these strike-slip faults allows wedges of continent to move out sideways, particularly to the east, clearing the path of the converging continents.

Secondly, the Indian crust may be thrust under Tibet by a series of faults which dip towards the north; such faults which result from compression of the crust are known as thrust-faults (figure 2). Field-work in the Himalaya has identified a series of such faults. The devastating earthquakes that plague the lives of inhabitants along the southern slopes of the Himalaya result from movement along these thrust-faults. Although no single fault carries a slice of continental crust more than a few tens of kilometres beneath another, their combined effect is to thicken up the crust. Some mountains owe their altitude to movement on such faults. Nanga Parbat, for example, is an extraordinary mountain in that it is a long way from any other 8000-metre Himalayan peak and stands proud of its neighbours by several thousand metres. This is partly because it lies on a finger of the Indian plate which points north into the Asian landmass, and is riding upwards on thrust-faults to the north, east and west.

A third theory for the mechanism of India's northward movement suggests that the crust may shorten by stretching vertically, as a piece of plasticine is lengthened when squashed from the side. The vertical stretching model is not needed in the Himalaya because much of the convergence can be explained by the major thrust-faults, but it could account for crustal shortening across the Tibetan Plateau.

By the beginning of the 1980s the broad-brush geology of the Himalaya was known from geological exploration, but Tibet itself was known to the West only from satellite images, and from occasional samples retrieved by 19th-century explorers (John Dewey's early papers on continental collision in the Himalaya cited evidence for recent volcanic activity within Tibet from samples collected in 1916 by the Swedish explorer Sven Hedin). The reasons for Tibet's inaccessibility have changed through time. Until this century the Himalaya was largely successful in protecting Tibet from visitors from the south, and the hostile plateau protected it from visitors from the north. Tibet's geography, however, could not maintain its isolation for ever. A brief incursion to Lhasa by a British military expedition in 1903 marked the beginning of Tibet's brutal acquaintance with modern life. The British mission did not stay long, partly because the fears of Russian influence in Tibet proved to be groundless, but in 1951 Lhasa was again occupied, this time by the Chinese. Since then Tibet has been incorporated into China and governed from Beijing as an Autonomous Region of the People's Republic of China. Over the past 40 years, entry to Tibet for scientists and mountaineers alike has depended on international relations between China and the West.

The first major international geological expedition to Tibet was a Sino-French study of southern Tibet from 1980 to 1983. This established the details of the northern boundary of the Indian plate which follows the Tsangpo (Brahmaputra) river along much of its length. A trail of oceanic fragments has now been traced over 2000km from northern Pakistan to south-east Tibet which marks the suture between India and Eurasia (figure 2). At about the same time an expedition across Tibet was conceived, jointly funded by Academia Sinica in Beijing and the Royal Society and led by Professor Robert Shackleton of the Open University and Professor Chang Chenfa of Academia Sinica. The geotraverse team was made up of 22 Chinese and western earth scientists. During 1985 they surveyed over 1700km of the plateau from Lhasa to the town of Golmud on the edge of the deserts of Central Asia. Results from this study draw together evidence from palaeomagnetism, palaeontology, sedimentology and geochronology for the movement of the tectonic plates that make up Tibet. They indicate that there was no single collision 50 million years ago, and several earlier collisions have now been identified. The Kunlun mountains of northern Tibet, for example, saw a continental collision 300 million years ago, and since that time at least two distinct collisions have occurred before the final convergence of India. Because of inclement weather and minor accidents one of these possible collision zones was never visited by the geotraverse team, but two years later a group of second-year geological students from Cambridge found their way to this remote spot in central Tibet and returned with both samples and a geological map. The age of amateur scientific exploration is not quite dead.

Results from the geotraverse expedition also help to unravel the way in which the Tibetan crust has been uplifted and thickened. The expedition found little sign of active or recent thrusting across the Tibetan Plateau, in strong contrast to the Himalaya. An erosion surface that planes off the peaks of many of the mountain ranges of central Tibet was found to be at least 10 million years old and yet virtually undeformed; this rules out strong folding in the recent history of the Tibetan crust. Field evidence therefore argued against internal shortening of the Tibetan crust by folding or faulting.

Geologists have also been able to make some deductions about the timing of uplift of the plateau. Measuring uplift is not easy; there are three principal methods, none without its problems. Firstly, fossil plants can indicate the approximate surface altitude at which they grew. Chinese palaeontologists working in Tibet have identified a switch from sub-tropical to alpine flora about 25 million years ago. Secondly, geomorphology can provide evidence for rapid uplift periods, particularly from deeply eroded river terraces. Thirdly, a recently developed technique called fission-track dating allows an estimate to be made of the rate at which rocks have reached the surface of the crust based on the preservation of microscopic tracks left by nuclear fission. Fission-track data indicate that in the Himalaya Nanga Parbat is being uplifted very rapidly, about 7mm a year, almost double the uplift rate for most of the Himalaya. Combination of results from all three techniques indicates that Tibet has been uplifted in two distinct phases. Initially it was uplifted relatively slowly to an altitude of about 3000m, reached earlier than about 25 million years ago. Subsequently it was uplifted to its present average altitude (5000m) during a period of very rapid uplift over the past five million years. Interestingly, the period of most rapid uplift is a period of little internal deformation of the plateau.

This two-stage uplift history fits what is now known about the geophysics of colliding continents. Collision will thicken up both the crust and part of the upper mantle beneath, known together as the lithosphere, but this process cannot go on indefinitely. The thermal structure of the underlying mantle places an upper limit on how thick the lithosphere can become. In time the base of the thickened lithosphere will heat up and will effectively be absorbed by the convecting layer underneath it. In other words, the lower and denser part of the lithosphere will be removed through thermal processes. The result is rapid uplift, known as isostatic rebound. Application of this model to Tibet shows that crustal thickening more than 25 million years ago was largely from vertical stretching of the lithosphere, and the more recent period of rapid uplift results from the rebound caused by dropping off the lower, denser part of the lithosphere.

In retrospect it appears that the international scientific expeditions to Tibet during the first half of the 1980s were made possible by a brief rapprochement between China and the West, and by an easing of Chinese military rule in Tibet. Even before the Beijing massacre in 1989, martial law in Lhasa had been reimposed by the Chinese military to control civil unrest. Most of what western geologists know about the geology of central and northern Tibet results from a single north-south traverse, coupled with interpretation of satellite imagery. There is much work still to be done in understanding the best example of continental collision on Earth, and although the construction of major roads across both central Tibet (the Lhasa–Golmud Highway) and the western Himalaya (the Karakoram Highway) has simplified the logistics of geological exploration, the geopolitical problems of Central Asia are probably more intractable now than they were in the 19th century.

BIBLIOGRAPHY

C Allen, *A mountain in Tibet*. Futura, MacDonald & Co, 1984.
P Fleming, *Bayonets to Lhasa*. Oxford University Press, 1986.
J Keay, *When men and mountains meet*. Century, 1987.
R M Shackleton (ed), 'The geological evolution of Tibet'. *Philosophical Transactions of the Royal Society A327, 1988*.
M Ward, 'Across Tibet'. *AJ91*, 84–89, 1986.

Around the Nam Tso

MARGARET CLENNETT

(Plates 73, 74)

It was a back-of-the-envelope plan, our trip to Tibet in the summer of 1987. An A4 envelope, admittedly, but quite large enough, given the limited information we had about our chosen area, and our non-technical ambitions. With our time restricted to four weeks, and the assumption that a visit to Lhasa was inevitable, we had chosen to trek in the Nyanchen Thanglha, a range of mountains some 80km N of Lhasa. There were four of us, each with a special contribution to make. Sheila Cormack did the organization and operated her idiosyncratic primus, Annabelle Barker negotiated with the locals, Jay Turner carried the heaviest sack, and I booked the flights and was chief hypochondriac.

In retrospect, the Bangladesh Airways flight to Kathmandu was not the best approach. Halfway through a jet-lagged, eight-hour interlude at Dhaka airport a mullah started to lead his flock of Mecca-bound pilgrims round and round the transit lounge, all chanting enthusiastically. At Kathmandu we discovered that our ski-sticks had not left London, and that a devastating flood had washed away two villages and a substantial stretch of the road to the border. Instead of reaching the Friendship Bridge in a day, we found ourselves well short at 7.30pm, stumbling in the pouring rain and pitch dark into a virtually foodless and totally bedless Tatopani, where the offer of a small dish of noodles and a floor to sleep on was gratefully accepted.

At Xhangmu we had our first taste of Chinese bureaucracy. Tourists were passing through all day, wanting to change money, but the bank did not open until 5pm. We spent the afternoon in a chai shop which accepted Nepalese rupees, and where the western music and pocket calculators (used to show us our bill) were in stark contrast to the primitive shack in which we sat.

Our plan to stop at Nyalam (3750m) to acclimatize was abandoned when we discovered that transport out of Xhangmu was at best erratic. Official CMA-approved expeditions and 'organized' trekkers had vehicles laid on, but as independent travellers we joined the free-for-all to board the first truck out of the village for two days. With about 40 other sardines, mostly westerners half our age, we committed ourselves to two days in an open truck, crossing three passes over 5000m, in order to reach Shigatse. With memories of going too high too quickly in Kenya, I swallowed a Diamox and crossed my fingers.

After a bumpy day and a grim night at the dreary, inhospitable army barracks at Tingri we set off on the second morning in heavy rain. Judicious placement of one's umbrella meant that the water was channelled on to someone else, or their gear, until the balance of power shifted. Cowering beneath our brollies in the now muddy lorry we could see little, then nothing at all, as the rain turned to snow and then a white-out. We passed other lorries, stuck, then an overturned minibus, its western Buddhist occupants smiling unperturbed as they stood in the snow in their sandals. On our truck there was a lower discomfort threshold, and tempers were short, until the need to deal with an incipient case of hypothermia restored a community spirit. The victim, clad in little more than a T-shirt, had expected Tibet to be hot!

A day's recuperation, a bumpy bus ride, and we were in Lhasa, where little remains of Harrer's city, which is now engulfed in a concrete sprawl. After a sleepless night in a downtown hotel my face was swollen out of recognition, and my body was covered in blotches. Bedbugs? Fleas? But on studied reflection it could only be a Diamox allergy; so much for trying to cheat on acclimatization. Weevils crawled out of a bag of porridge as we packed our gear; morale was low.

A week of precious time had gone when at last we clambered on to the Golmud bus, and the driver was puzzled when we insisted on alighting, apparently in the middle of nowhere, a few kilometres past Yangbajing. We had seen a valley cutting deep into the mountains and, in the absence of a detailed map, we hoped that it was the approach to the Goring La which we wanted to cross, reversing Harrer's route of 1946 over the Nyanchen Thanglha. Only in retrospect did we realize how crucial it had been to have a clear day; for most of the next fortnight the mountains were shrouded in mist, and maps were barely better than sketches, being on a scale of 1: one million, or worse.

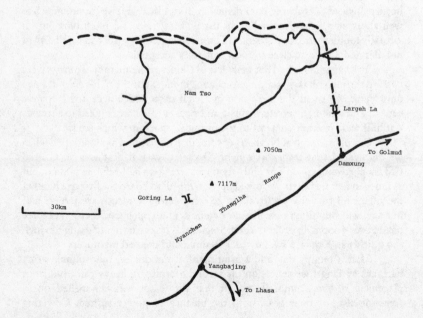

As on previous trips, we planned to hire porters or animals to carry our gear, and so had not made efforts to pare away surplus weight. Thus we took several hours to stagger to a nearby village, negotiating two rivers, ankle-twisting tussocky grass and barbed wire *en route*. But we *were* in the right place, and over tsampa and butter tea we negotiated the hire of two men and three horses for three days.

For two days we walked up the grassy main valley, with the added interest of a thigh-deep, fast-flowing glacier stream to cross on the second afternoon. On the third day, in cloud and drizzle, we turned up a side valley, traversed below a glacier, then began a rising traverse, horses too, up across the ice. The horses went well until a steepening some way below the col, where they stopped, but our ever-helpful porters heaved and pushed sacks up slippery snow for a few more precious metres before waving goodbye. The col itself (5800m) was rocky, and bedecked with tattered prayer-flags. In the grey light we saw snowy mountains all round, but we had only limited distant views and wondered what Harrer had seen on his southward crossing towards Lhasa. Traders and nomads still use the route, and there was a good track down a moraine on the northern side.

We were prepared mentally, if not physically, for humping our gear for the next two and a half days, by which time we would, according to our porters, reach encampments and be able to hire more porters. Downhill we plodded, to stop at the first grassy spot, suffering from the weight of our sacks or from the altitude.

The valley widened, and after two days we were on a flat, green plain. We had begun a 'half an hour at a time then stop' routine as a temporary measure. Only Jay was able to lift her sack on to her back unaided, so woe betide the last person if she got left behind or wanted an emergency stop. As predicted, we passed nomad camps, but despite Annabelle's dramatic gestures, Jay's drawings and my appearance of misery and exhaustion, no porter, yak or horse could we hire. The performance was repeated several times before we gave up; the half-hour routine became permanent.

Our situation was reassessed. We did not want to recross the Goring La but knew of no other pass in the vicinity. We were at the SW corner of the vast Nam Tso lake, but the locals were adamant that we should not try to traverse its southern shore, the shortest distance to a known pass. We never found out why.

We took their advice and opted to circumnavigate the lake; there was a road marked on our map on the N side, and we hoped to hitch a lift along it. Such innocence! The decision made, we waded a couple of silt-laden rivers, bowed our heads against the wind and drizzle and trudged northwards across the plain, not reaching more water until 6.30pm. The weather cleared, and two horsemen rode out of the sunset, passing our camp. A greeting, and they galloped away eastwards, like cowboys in a spaghetti western. Next morning the great Nyanchen Thanglha itself was towering above the now distant range, a shining, icy Matterhorn. This tantalizing peak of a respectable height (7117m on our map) was usually shrouded in cloud; it could make a fine objective for a climbing holiday, given reasonable weather.

Another day and a half and we saw the Nam Tso, a vast inland sea and, at

4590m, supposedly the highest named lake in Tibet. We continued northwards along its western flank, watching the water change from brilliant blue to ultramarine, to leaden grey and then back again. One evening, having passed no fresh water all day, we camped on the lake shore, resigned to a thirsty night. Like the Ancient Mariner, we looked out over an ocean of salt water – until Annabelle dipped a mug into it. True, the tea was over-salty, but next morning's porridge was excellent. Fresh water was to remain elusive; one evening's trickle, found with difficulty, had dried up by the time we had finished our meal.

Shortly after midday on the fifth day after crossing the Goring La, in cloud and drizzle, we reached a dirt track which was the road. Empty. That night we saw a lorry pass, and next morning as we walked along there was another. Exuberantly I stood in the middle of the road and waved my arms; in disbelief we watched the lorry swerve past, accelerating. Stillness returned. The road snaked inland, and hopeful of more traffic we followed it. Now low hills hid the lake and mountains, and we plodded on across immense green plains, grazed by occasional yak herds. People who describe Tibet as brown have seen the country from Himalayan peaks, but it can be vivid shades of green, as far as the eye can see.

Descending, drenched, into a valley at a wet lunchtime, we saw stationary lorries and two large tents, one elaborately decorated. Inside this mobile gompa were women and children at worship. Their menfolk in the plain tent gave us salt tea in return for a look at the Dalai Lama pictures in our *Tibet survival guide*, but they were travelling in the opposite direction and not interested in a joyride back the way they had come.

Later that day a large lake came into view to the north, and hopes rose; we must be further on than we had thought. Inevitably, though, it was the map that was wrong, and we realized that at our snail's pace we would miss the plane home unless we could hitch a lift. Now jeeps began to taunt us as they visited settlements which were specks in the distance, or as they actually drove along the road, the wrong way, their noises echoing across the plain. At one village, touched by our obvious disappointment at finding yet another lorry going in the opposite direction, locals brought us drinks as we sat resting by the roadside.

That afternoon, the fifth we had spent on the road, salvation arrived in the form of a small jeep, already carrying two passengers, but happy to shoe-horn us in as well. To our delight, the driver offered to make a detour from his journey for us, on eastwards, then back up and over the low hills, and down to the Nam Tso again, taking us much further than we could have walked in a day. We were now almost at the NE corner of the lake, and one more day's walking took us southwards along the shortest side. The morning we finally left the lake behind us, the Nyanchen Thanglha ahead had a dusting of fresh snow, but the road was a quagmire of deep mud. No wonder there had been so little traffic. We floundered up to the Largeh La, and were able to hitch a lift down the other side on a roadmender's lorry. That last night we ceremoniously ate our last tin of sardines, one fish each. At least we were not carrying excess food back.

We knew that civilization was near when, some hours after a final frugal breakfast of oatcakes, we met a large party of chic, well-groomed French trekkers, carrying minuscule day-sacks. Their luggage followed behind on a herd of unruly yaks. Another lift took us to Damxung, on the main road, and as the bus rolled back to Lhasa we looked out at the bank of impenetrable cloud which hid the Nyanchen Thanglha. Just where was the Goring La?

Orina

The Aldenham School 1989 Expedition to the Chinese Pamir

DAVID MACGREGOR

(Plates 30–35)

> He took the [road] to the mountains.
> He ran through the Vale of Cashmere,
> He ran through the rhododendrons
> Till he came to the land of Pamir.
> And there in a precipice valley . . .
>
> Robert Frost: *The Bearer of Evil Tidings*

Camels can be oddly attractive creatures, evoking happy memories of childhood trips to the zoo. If you were standing, however, as I was in July 1989, on the sandy fringes of the Karakol lakes, lying at 3600m on the Karakoram Highway between Kongur (7719m) and Muztagh Ata (7546m), and were watching these ill-tempered, spitting, braying, smelly brutes being loaded by their Kirghiz masters and if, as I did two days later, you were watching these same animals and drivers, now about 24km up the Konsiver river valley, dump our 1743kg of food and equipment on the rocky ground before deserting without a backward look or word of regret – having been hired for 20 days more than they stayed – then your good opinion might have been severely tested. The fickleness of camel and Kirghiz, indeed, forced a radical change in our expedition plans, much, as it turned out, for the better: 14 days later, almost everyone in our party had achieved the first ascent of one or two 5500m peaks, as well as having completed a quite extensive exploration of this obscure corner in China's 'Wild West'.

That hot afternoon's crisis brought the inevitable disruption to two years of hard, yet relatively smooth-flowing preparations. A characteristically crisp remark by colleague Sally Westmacott – subsequently our official 'adviser' – along the lines of 'I've always wanted to look at the Kashgar area', led to the initial research. It was followed by my wife's more calculated observation, 'Well, if anyone can get us to Xinjiang, you can', intoned in a way which suggested wholehearted scepticism about the likelihood of getting much further than Ben Nevis: not exactly an encouragement, but at least a stimulus. The Alpine Club's China Symposium at Plas y Brenin in November 1987 confirmed for me that this expedition could really happen. Ten young stalwarts, aged then between 16 and 18, who had demonstrated their mountaineering abilities on school expeditions, as well as their capacity for getting on with each other, were chosen; anxious parents were persuaded that the venture was genuinely 'educational' and not wholly lunatic; Chris Bonington kindly agreed to be our Patron; by February 1988 we were ready to start training.

July 1988 saw us prussiking up the seracs of the Glacier Blanc in the Dauphiné, under the baleful gaze of John ('Some day, mountain will win') Brailsford. Technical exercises were followed by a brisk ascent of the Pic du Glacier d'Arsine (3383m) and a mass excursion up the straightforward snow-trail to the Dôme de Neige des Ecrins, in order to prove that everyone could breathe above 4000m. Success brought its own problems. John's programme opened up a fundamental split in the party: do we learn through further technical exercises, or simply go for more summits? The party divided: one group followed John and Nick Parks (soon to become Climbing Leader, and instrumental to our final successes) up the Coolidge couloir to Pointe Puiseux (3946m), the highest point of Mont Pelvoux; the others benefited from the vast experience of Mike Westmacott in reaching the Col du Sélé (3278m) from the Sélé glacier, learning a good deal about how to 'read' a glacier on the way, before tackling the rotting arête of the Boeufs Rouges N ridge. A similar division surfaced in China over mealtime discussions at Advance Base Camp: were we there primarily to get to summits, or should we be concentrating more on exploration and field-work? Fortunately the split never became acrimonious.

Our Dauphiné experiences, useful as they were, had to be reinforced: some typically shin-barking, mud-enveloped night-navigation exercises on Kinder Scout, and crevasse-rescue practice off Froggatt Edge therefore followed in November 1988. This weekend came a month after signing the Protocol with the Chinese Mountaineering Association in Beijing – an educative experience in itself through our subsequent discovery that, instead of paying for a couple of returns on a 747 and a hotel room, we could have negotiated directly with the Xinjiang Mountaineering Association using only letters and telex! On our second major training expedition in February 1989 we were decanted from the Euston–Fort William sleeper at Tulloch, on the northern fringes of Rannoch Moor, for a test of morale and the integrity of our equipment under the appropriate atrocities of Scottish winter conditions. The intention was successfully realized in that a particularly spiteful hurricane blew our tents apart and thereby proved their uselessness for the Pamir! This obliged us in May to carry out a profitable tent-replacing sponsored 24-hour traverse of the Welsh 'Munros'. Other, more informal training events took place: four boggy days across the Cairngorms; a painful introduction to Koflach 'Ultras' on Ben Alder; a brisk winter round of the Snowdon Horseshoe; an exhilarating traverse of The Saddle in Glen Shiel; extensive use of Harrow School's climbing wall, and so on. By the time we were ready to leave for Islamabad we had a fair idea of each other's mental and physical strengths and weaknesses, and could be said to be generally technically proficient, except for river-crossings . . .

On 13 July the Advance Party, having completed the joyous business of customs' clearance for our 49 barrels in 45° heat, via nine dingy government offices and as many power-cuts, met the Main Party at Islamabad airport, with the smell of blood heavy on the streets: it was the time of the 'Id Festival', an occasion for ritual slaughter, great dinners and mighty gatherings of buzzards above the wayside carcasses. In true monsoon conditions we left Rawalpindi for the Karakoram Highway – a part of the expedition which in the intensity of the experience surprised us all.

First, one crosses lush, rolling hills before reaching the Indus gorges at Thakot Bridge. From the coach window, the angle between observer and river – a waterway of mythological proportions, even 900 miles from its mouth – approached the apparently vertical, down 1000 feet of vertiginous and unstable-looking cliff. Our PTDC guide, the nonchalant Anwar, informed me as we ground on towards Gilgit that the section ahead was 'rather bad'; I noted the driver's loyalty to the notion of 'Insh'Allah' rather than any belief in the causal relationship between good driving and long life. On the return journey, Anwar's words took on a greater irony: from Gilgit, the driver and his gearbox had enjoyed a relationship normally reserved for sumo-wrestlers; below Chilas, the gearbox gave up. As it lay on the roadside, like an old and much-despised armadillo, a passing cattle-truck was stopped and politely commandeered. The bemused Pathan drivers, their own perception of the gorge's dangers blurred by the inhalation of exotic substances, carried us over pot-hole and under overhang for eight bone-shaking hours, much of it in the dark – an odyssey of terror which will live with me for ever. On the Chinese side of the Kunjerab pass, however, the Highway descends from 4703m across a desert plateau, passing the Karakol lakes at about 3600m before tumbling through the Gez Defile to the oases of Kashgaria at only about 1200m – a much more agreeable experience on countryside distinctly less susceptible to upheavals in the Earth's crust.

Two final stages of our preparations remained. At Gulmit, north of Hunza, we organized a test match against a local XI, with the Indus for a boundary, and the typical Karakoram ant-hill spikiness of Tupopdan (6125m) rising behind long-off. A day's walking above the mulberry bushes and apricot trees in Karimabad was followed by a trot up the true right of the Passu glacier at about 3000m; we had a fine view of the 'penitents' before the rain came. Three days later, on the purple and brown dustbowl surrounding the Karakol lakes, we tested our radios, went on overnight bivouac in the desert, and tried a square search, all to get our lungs working – as well as to avoid the increasingly uninhibited prying of the Kirghiz. Our camel-train was then assembled, and we struck off up and across the Konsiver – thigh-deep but safely 'braided' – *en route* for Aktash.

The plan was to cross the Karatash pass (c5000m), about 10km east of Aktash, and explore the country around the Chimghan Jilgha (valley) which drains the unvisited glaciers to the east of Kongur. This pass was first crossed by a Westerner – Ney Elias – in 1885, although it is just possible that Alexander Gardiner may have done so some time in the late 1820s. Sir Aurel Stein reached it from the Karakol side in 1900. Tilman crossed it ('an easy pass for animals') on his way to meet Shipton for their 1947 attempt on Muztagh Ata. Some members of the SMC 1988 Shiwakte expedition made the first return crossing, and in the same year a single Frenchman crossed it with Zhang Xongwen, our Liaison Officer, *en route* for Chat before returning to Karakol via the old trade route and Torbelung valley. Trekking specialist David Hamilton crossed a path

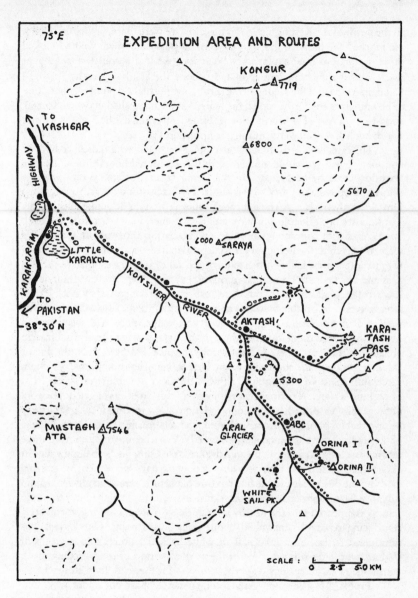

EXPEDITION AREA AND ROUTES

to the north of the Karatash two months after we were there, in October 1989. He reached the hitherto unexplored Terzöse Jilgha on which we had looked down during our final exploratory excursion. We had permission to attempt two peaks of approximately 5700 and 5500m, the first being in the Terzöse–Chimghan area and the second being (probably) the highest point of what came to be known as the Orina range, the massif on the watershed between Kongur and Muztagh Ata. (The word Orina was frequently used by the Uighurs we met at Advance Base Camp. Its meaning is uncertain.)

The camels' desertion at Aktash, however, required a radical rethink of our plan: since we could not cross the Karatash without camels, all our attention came to be focused on the Orina range; reconnaissance was the priority. I led a small party to the Karatash ('Black-stone') area, to assess the Orinas' northern slopes. The approach valley is pretty, not unlike Glen Affric. The hills are not difficult: blunt pyramids or domes, long sharp ribs and deep bowl coires with widespread moraine, and glaciation above about 4600m. We were misdirected (the best map we could obtain had a scale of 1:250,000) by a Kirghiz into a presumably hitherto unvisited valley just to the north of the real pass and reached, after a very laborious ascent over steep, trackless moraine, a spectacular col at about 5000m. A second reconnaissance, led by Nick Parks, after two uncomfortable bivouacs at 4200m and 4700m, reached a col on the west end of the Orina range, above a vast gorge, until bad weather and uncertainty about the state of the snow on the narrow ridge ahead combined to preclude further progress. A third reconnaissance, led by expedition doctor Dave Arathoon to the south side of the Orinas, being less ambitious, was more successful: polaroid photographs showed the clear possibility of access from Torbelung valley. (Previous expeditions to this area have used polaroid photographs to establish a friendly relationship with the locals; now they believe that all photographs are polaroid, and relationships deteriorate when a photograph cannot be immediately handed over.) The information from these reconnaissances led us to set up an Advance Base Camp in Torbelung valley at about 4200m, and the next few lung-extending days were spent in ferrying loads up the dusty track to the fine mixture of pasture, scree and glacier around Advance Base. Our departure from Aktash exposed the lacuna in our training: James disappeared into the nearby river during a (roped) crossing, fortunately resurfacing relatively unscathed about 80m downstream. Our arrival was scrutinized by an inquisitive pair of white-backed vultures and a group of Uighurs who later offered some of the boys a portion of their evening meal: marmot stew in dumplings – another triumph for the schoolboy stomach!

From ABC a second, lesser reconnaissance phase got under way. One party reached the head of a coire at about 4800m above ABC and reported poor snow and loose rock – no summit route there. Another party continued up Torbelung valley and ascended the valley wall to a delightful area of perfect turf subsequently nicknamed Twickenham. Looking across the valley to no fewer than seven tributary valleys, a route was discerned up to the glacier within the cirque containing the apparently highest peaks in the range.

More digesting of information led to a plan for the summits. A climbing party reached 'Glacier Camp' at about 4800m on 6 August, and next day they followed a typical mountaineering route for this area: a laborious clamber over moraine on to a steepening mixed rock and snow ridge, leading to a long, heavily-corniced summit snow ridge at an easier angle. This party of 12 reached the summit of Orina 1 (5450m) after four hours from Glacier Camp, on a route which merited a PD-grade. After a long, elegant descent of the shapely W ridge most of the party carried on down to ABC. The summit panorama, in perhaps uncharacteristically clear weather, embraced the 3000m E face of Kongur and much of the Karakoram. During this climb my wife and I had remained with one invalid at ABC, retaining radio contact with the climbers through the day. We also had time to make a botanical excursion up Torbelung valley for about 10km and were able to see the steep-sided Chichilik pass which leads contortedly to the unexciting town of Tashkurghan ('Stone Fort') between Karakol and the Kunjerab. Lammergeyers of vast wingspan surveyed us as they lounged on their air-currents.

On 8 August our turn came, and an ankle-straining few hours brought us to Glacier Camp, pitched on the very tongue at a height similar to Mont Blanc. Even more satisfying was our perfect degree of acclimatization. In the night, our Phreedome 3000s were put to the test in a gusty gale which blew about 10cm of fresh snow off the rather stubby glacier at the base of the Orina amphitheatre. Some suspicious cracking and booming underfoot next day (the gale had abated about 4am) did not impede quick progress up Orina II, opposite Orina I and nicknamed Moby Dick: a beautiful snow peak with a long, undulating and, as we soon discovered, sensationally exposed summit ridge. Deep cornices hung on the right, while a suspiciously convex lee slope descended steeply on the left for about 600m to the glacier. Swirling mist prevented a view comparable to that from Orina I, but Kongur and the western outliers of the Kun Lun Shan figured prominently for a while, as did the magnificent W face of Chakragil (6727m). The rare and wonderful excitement of making a first ascent – a respectable 5360m – was to some degree compromised when one member of the party discoursed at length on how quiet it was!

Appetites were now thoroughly whetted: the gourmets celebrated on the Glorious Twelfth with vegetable soup, Baxter's delicious Grouse in Port Wine with new potatoes, and Scottish raspberries; a passing Kazakh donated some pungent goat's cheese to go with the oatcakes. The climbers, more importantly, returned to 'Twickenham' for a few days. At the foot of the hanging glaciers on the beautiful White Sail Peak (5436m) they practised a variety of skills and extended their understanding of avalanche awareness before making the ascent of several small 5000m tops, above as delightful an alpine playground as one could hope to find.

Two camp stools, 50m of old rope and a vacuum flask gained us the hire of two Uighur donkeys for the day; on a snowy morning, we struck ABC and regretfully descended to Aktash to be met by Meng and Gu (the Beijing University postgraduates who had joined the expedition to help with the geology field-work; they eventually gave us a poignant insight into the horrors of the Tienanmen Square events). This highly likeable pair had had the foresight to roast a whole sheep before our arrival, to celebrate our summit successes. Over this dinner, accompanied by shredded potato, onion and peppers, and followed by luscious water-melons, some members felt that a bit of tourism was now called for. For this group, a hefty one-day walk-out to Karakol ensued; they then hitch-hiked down to Kashgar in the back of a horse-truck with two sheep, a goat and five Hungarians. Sightseeing in this turbulent city was much enjoyed, but the quantity of polyester among the bales of 'silk' in the fabled Sunday bazaar testified to the way in which industrialization has encroached on the Uighurs' otherwise horse-drawn society.

The others, however – the self-styled 'Cream Team' – had decided that they were ready for more exploration. They ascended the gorge next to Aktash called Uzun Jilgha on Sir Aurel Stein's map, bivouacked at a cottage-sized boulder at about 4700m, then continued to a camp on a col astride the main South Kongur ridge, at about 5200m. The view of the little-known E face of Kongur was particularly striking in the sunrise, as was the first sight of the unexplored area around the Terzöse Jilgha, leading the eye to the glittering spires of the Shiwakte range (c6000m). A number of minor tops above this col were reached, and a route connecting the Terzöse and Konsiver valleys (referred to by Sir Clarmont Skrine in *Chinese Central Asia*, p275) was ascertained before further exploration was cut short at 5am on the second morning by a slab avalanche coming off the party's tracks.

Despite the camels' late arrival for the return trip from Aktash to Karakol, both the Uzun Jilgha and Kashgar parties were successfully reunited at the CMA bothy on Little Karakol. A party of Homeric dimensions followed before we set out on our disrupted journey to Rawalpindi. Some enterprising members even managed to take in a 24-hour trip to Peshawar, near the mouth of the Khyber Pass, in order to make purchases at Pakistan's finest carpet bazaars, while I languished in an Islamabad customs shed. British Airways then brought us home.

Maurice Herzog's observation, *Il y a d'autres Annapurna dans la vie des hommes*, has always seemed rather metaphysical for my tastes, but reflections on the expedition should consider its consequences. The effect on the boys has been profound: they have gained a deeply memorable experience to build on, and the way they have extended their knowledge and understanding of their world and its people would gladden any teacher's heart. I have been equally moved by the disinterested help given by so many members of the Alpine Club in encouraging these young people to go out and face challenges of this sort. But the proof of the successful outcome of this expedition, if any were needed, is that plans are already under way for an attempt in 1992 on a 6500m range in a particularly remote corner of north-west Tibet.

Descending Peak Lenin

DAVID HOPKINS

(Plates 36–39)

David Hopkins and Marloes Hopkins de Groot made a high camp at 6500m on the NW ridge of Peak Lenin (7134m) on 22 July 1986. Their ascent to this point had been achieved alpine-style in very poor weather. In the face of worsening conditions and lack of food and fuel, they descended 2000m to the Lenin glacier on 24 July. Theirs was the highest point reached by any of the international climbing teams, involving some 60 climbers, who were attending one of the two International Mountaineering Camps arranged annually by the USSR Sports Committee in the Pamir range. This is the story of their descent . . .

It was a peculiar dream. I was trapped in a dungeon; it was claustrophobic; it kept moving; and I was suffocating. There were a few people milling around but I only recognized Kafka. I asked him why I was there – he did not know. I thought that I should know, but I could not remember; if only I could remember, then everything would be all right. I gradually woke up; it was almost dawn. We spoke a few words, and one of us looked out of the tent; it was still snowing, and the horizon remained invisible. 'Let's go down,' she said. 'OK,' I replied, and we dozed a little more. When we reawoke, we confirmed the decision and made the radio call.

We were trapped in a small tent at 6500m on the Radelzny ridge of Peak Lenin. It was the third day, and we were beginning to feel the strain. Although the storm had been with us for the past week, the weather had not been so bad as to preclude our moving slowly upwards to Camp IV. We arrived in a gathering storm which eventually stabilized but effectively prohibited any further progress. In good weather the summit would have been a mere three to four hours away, but in these conditions it could have been on the other side of the world. We had virtually run out of food; our alpine-style tactics limited the amount we could carry. We had been sharing a packet of freeze-dried food containing 500 calories between us for the past few days. Consequently we were beginning to lose strength and, although we felt strong enough to descend that day, we wondered how long that feeling would last.

I emerged into the blast of wind, orientated myself to the stinging opaque greyness of our world, and made my way across to the Russian tents. We had been befriended during our ascent by six Russian guides who were also attempting to climb Lenin. They represented the cream of Russian mountaineers and knew the mountain well. We were all that remained of the 60 or so climbers who, with their eyes fixed on the summit, had arrived at the Achik-Tash Base Camp some weeks before. I told them of our decision to descend. They asked if we would make it, and I shrugged equivocally. Two of them volunteered to descend to Camp III with us.

We froze our fingers and faces while breaking camp and then moved tentatively towards the buttress edge. Our friends, whose decision to accompany us was based more on Marloes' charm than concern for our safety or their need to exercise, plunged down into the gloom. We followed on a short rope, balancing our loads against the spiteful wind.

As we descended the buttress we marvelled at the contrast with our ascent some days before when, in brief but glorious sunshine, we enjoyed our most euphoric day on the mountain. We had been moving well, felt strong, revelled in the climbing, and knew that we had the summit in our grasp. We were magnificent, we told each other, and so we were – but that was nothing compared with the descent.

When we reached the col, our friends took us to their colleague's igloo in the lee of an enormous cornice. They gave us our only food of the day (smoked salmon and toast), toasted Marloes' courage and tenderly left us. Their congratulations on our attempt were flattering but irrelevant as we continued downwards.

We struggled up towards Radelzny Peak. Fancy having to climb over a 6200m summit on our descent! This proved to be one of the most testing experiences of my mountaineering career. There were no maps or landmarks and it was a complete whiteout. I thought we could always retreat to Camp III by following our footsteps. When we were totally committed, however, Marloes shouted that my steps were obliterated after 10 metres, and because of the storm she could not even see me some 15 metres ahead.

Our joy at finding the slope which eventually led to Camp II was heightened by meeting the two Bavarian brothers whose bold exploits on the Lipkin ridge of Lenin, although eventually unsuccessful because of the storm, had held us in awe. We hugged each other and, with profound respect, wished each other well. A silly mistake prevented them from going much higher, but our relative successes convinced us that, in climbing as well as in many other things, commitment is everything.

The international contingent at Camp II plied us with hot drinks, took our photographs and encouraged us to continue down. It was here, I remembered, that, with the arrival of the storm, I made my last diary entry: 'I cannot let myself think or write too much. I prefer to be in suspended animation until it is all over – one way or the other.'

It was now almost over. Tired as we were, we thought we could descend the remaining and comparatively easy 1000 metres in a couple of hours. But, as we pressed on in the encroaching darkness, our composure was badly shaken. We came across massive avalanche debris. The avalanche had been triggered a few days before. It was colossal, easily the most extensive I had experienced during a half-life spent in the mountains. We traversed it for at least a kilometre. It was after nine that evening when we staggered, in the dark, on to the glacier. I

19. *South Georgia, L to R: Lindsay Griffin, Stephen Venables, Brian Davison and Julian Freeman-Attwood on Vogel Peak.* (Stephen Venables) (p 1)

20. *Nordenskjold Peak and Mt Roots from King Edward Cove.* (Stephen Venables) (p 1)

21. South Georgia: Brian Davison on Novosilski glacier. (Stephen Venables) (p 1)

22. *Brian Davison near the summit of Mt Carse.* (Stephen Venables) (p 1)

23. *View NW from Mt Carse.* (Stephen Venables) (p 1)

24. *Mt Paget from Cumberland East Bay.* (Stephen Venables) (p 1)

25. *Ama Dablam from below Camp 1. SW ridge is the left skyline.* (Brendan Murphy) (p 8)

26. *Brendan Murphy silhouetted against Ama Dablam.* (Kate Phillips) (p 8)

27. *Ama Dablam: looking W from below Camp 1.* (Brendan Murphy) (p 8)

28. *Looking towards The Ramp and Headwall from Camp 2.* (Brendan Murphy) (p 8)

29. *Ray Delaney jumaring up steep ground above Camp 2.* (Kate Phillips) (p 8)

radioed our friends at Camp II and told them we were safely down.

The resident doctor and Master of Sport at Camp I gave us fruit and vodka. We were very wet, cold, and beyond exhaustion. On finding the tent we piled wet clothes into a corner, and crawled into damp sleeping bags. As we tried to sleep, we held each other close and, as our coughs racked our bodies, their sound penetrated the storm outside.

Daniil Gauss's Ascent of the Volcano Kliuchevskaia Sopka

The Origins of Russian Mountaineering

A Kh KHRGIAN, V V SHER and D M DANILENKO

Between 1785 and 1794 a large Russian expedition led by Captain J Billings and Lieutenant G Sarychev recorded a detailed description of the shores of north-eastern Siberia, Kamchatka and the Aleutian Islands, and the adjacent waters.[1] The expedition had reached the ocean using the route known at the time – by river to Irkutsk and Iakutsk, along the Maia and Iudoma rivers and by portage on to the river Okhta, then along that to Okhotsk. This fairly large expedition included the mining engineer Daniil Gauss whose name is linked with the first ascent of the volcano Kliuchevskaia Sopka (4750m) in Kamchatka.

Daniil Gauss's description of his ascent has come down to us through Dr O de Huhn of Riga who published it in French in 1809.[2] That paper was based on a copy authenticated (against the original report) by Matvei Ignat'ev, secretary of the province, in the presence of Captain Timofei Shmelev as witness. (Shmelev was well-known for his earlier descriptions of the volcano in 1773.[3]) The copy was authenticated in 'Ichiginsk,' or 'Ischinsk', a settlement on the western shore of the peninsula, or else in 'Gizhiginsk', as some contemporary authors suppose. The publication does not indicate how the manuscript came into the possession of de Huhn or the Moscow Society of Naturalists.

Gauss's description is accompanied by a diagram depicting the volcano as seen from the settlement of Kliuchi Kamchatskie, together with a detailed legend describing the route of the climb. That diagram (*reproduced right*), as is obvious to anybody familiar with the area, fully authenticates Gauss's description of the settlement and of the climb up the volcano itself.

It should be noted that Gauss's climb is not mentioned in either the description of the expedition published by G A Sarychev in 1802, or in the reports compiled by Martin Sauer, the secretary/translator of the expedition, which in 1802 were published both in London and, in a French translation, in Paris.[4] Most of the members of the expedition were at the time busy transporting its main equipment to Okhotsk, building boats there, and so forth. Information about Gauss's activities is furnished by later writers.[5,6] For instance, it is they who mention his participation in 1787 in Elistratov's hydrographic expedition which left a description of the western shore of Kamchatka from Tigil to Penzhina and gathered a large collection of minerals. The available facts, however, leave no room for doubt about the accuracy of the description of the climb. On the map which forms an appendix to Sarychev's

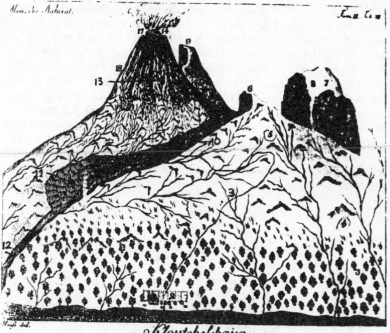

Kloutchefskaia.
Volcan du Kamtchatka

book a dotted line marks the route of the expedition which followed the western shore of Kamchatka and then turned east, towards the volcano.

Gauss's ascent was made in the company of two unnamed fellow-climbers between 4 and 8 August 1788 (the exact date was not mentioned in his 1789 report). He describes how the group slowly moved upwards, 'expecting to meet (their) doom at any moment' owing to the snow-slips and the stones lying upon the ice. Nevertheless, 'his curiosity got the better of him and impelled him to the summit of the mountain with the desire to leave for his descendants the description of such an interesting place'. The climb took all day, hampered by a strong wind and the clouds which had gathered. Towards the summit it was as cold as in winter. Upon reaching the summit, Gauss saw the walls of an enormous crater about a kilometre across, roughly triangular in shape, and surrounded by massive blocks of black and rock-marked lava. Along the edges of the lava-blocks one could see, besides the main crater, many large openings from which vapours and flames were erupting. When those vapours reached me, the author wrote, there was a strong smell of sulphur. That was what caused Gauss and his fellow-climbers to start their descent at once, and afterwards they felt ill for several days.

The history of that description of the first major mountain ascent in Russia has not been a happy one. For a long time it was forgotten, only to be mentioned in 1940 by Academician V I Vlodavets.[7,8] In his large book *The Kliuchevskaia Sopka Volcano and its Eruptions of 1944–1945 and Earlier,*[9] B I Piip is the first to quote Gauss in detail. He points out that there is no doubt that Gauss had planned his ascent in advance, and cites later authors on the subject. Piip also addresses some of the doubts about the authenticity of Gauss's story, for instance those entertained by Friderizzi, a member of Kruzenshtern's expedition, who in 1804 had made an admittedly unsuccessful attempt on the volcano. However, as we have already observed, both Gauss's description and his route map, and the oblique data from Sarychev leave no doubt that 1788 was the year of Russia's earliest planned and successful ascent of a high and wonderful peak.

REFERENCES

1 G A Sarychev, *Puteshestvie flota kapitana Sarycheva po severovostochnoi chasti Sibiri, Ledovitomu moriu, i Vostochnomy okeanu. Ch I. Ot nachala ekspeditsii s 1785 po 1790 gg Ch II. So vremeni otpravleniia iz Petropavlovskoi gavani do okonchaniia ekspeditsii.* (The Journey by Captain Sarychev across the north-east Part of Siberia, the Arctic Sea, and the Eastern Ocean. Pt I. From the Beginning of the Expedition, 1785, to 1790 inclusive. Pt II. From the Departure from the Peter and Paul Harbour to the End of the Expedition.) St Petersburg, 1802.

2 O de Huhn, 'Déscription d'une montagne volcanique au Kamtschatka'. *Mém Soc Naturalistes de Moscou, Vol II,* 1809, pp189–197. (A copy of this article, giving Gauss's detailed description [in French] of his ascent, is in the Alpine Club Library.)

3 T Shmelev, 'Kratkoe opisanie o Kamchatke, uchinennoe v iiune mesiatse 1773 g. Kamchatskim komandirom kapitanom Timofeem Shmelevym' (A Brief Description of Kamchatka, written in June 1773 by the Kamchatka Captain-Commander Timofei Shmelev.) *Studies of the Free Russian Society of the Imperial Moscow University, Pt I,* 1774.

4 M Sauer, *An account of a geographical and astronomical expedition to the Northern Part of Russia performed by Commodore Joseph Billings in the years 1785 to 1794, narrated by Martin Sauer.* London, 1802.

5 P Lesseps, *Lessepsovo putechestvie po Kamchatke i iuzhnoi storone Sibiri* (Lesseps' Journey across Kamchatka and the Southern Part of Siberia). Moscow, 1801.

6 A P Sokolov, Ekspeditsii k Aleutskim ostrovam kapitanov Krenitsyna i Levashova v 1764–1769 gg'.(The Expeditions to the Aleutian Islands by

Captains Krenitsyn and Levashov in 1764–1769.) *Notes of the Moscow University Hydrographic Department, Pt10*, 1852.

7   V I Vlodavets, 'Kliuchevskoi vulkan' (The Kliuchevskii Volcano). *Zemlevedenie Vol I (XI)*, Moscow, pp9–15.

8   V I Vlodavets, 'Kliuchevskaia gruppa vulkanov' (The Kliuchevskii Group of Volcanoes). *Studies of the Kamchatka Vulcanology Station, Vol I*. USSR Academy of Sciences, Moscow, 1940.

9   B I Piip, 'Kliuchevskaia sopka i ee izverzheniia v 1944–1945 gg i v proshlom' *(The Kliuchevskaia Sopka Volcano and its Eruptions of 1944–1945 and Earlier). USSR Academy of Sciences, Moscow, 1956 (Studies of the Academy of Sciences Vulcanology Laboratory, Vol II).*

(Translated by Antoni Marianski. This article appeared in the Proceedings of the Academy of Sciences of the USSR, Geographical Series, No 5, *Moscow, 1988. We thank Dr E Gippenreiter and Mrs V V Sher for communicating the article and for permission to publish.)*

Mount Wilhelm

DAVID J BROADHEAD

The rain finally started about noon, soon after I had reached the hut. Across the coire, through gathering cloud, the waterfall feeding Lake Aunde indicated the direction of tomorrow's route until it too was swallowed up by the mist, focusing our attention inside. Now little more than a shabby bothy, the wooden hut with its ubiquitous corrugated iron roof had once been a research station for the Australian National University. As welcome as any bothy in bad weather, the place was soon bustling with activity as the soaking stragglers arrived, claiming their bit of floor space before changing out of wet gear and organizing food and hot drinks for themselves and the Chimbu carriers. Activity gradually slowed down in the afternoon as the carriers headed back, leaving the rest of us to come to terms with the altitude of 3480 metres, having left our homes at sea level the previous morning. Although we were close to the equator, it was cold enough at this height to endure the smoky stove for the evening before retiring early in preparation for an alpine start, despite the rain which was still drumming on the roof.

When I first applied for a post in Papua New Guinea I had only the vaguest idea about this country, located just north of Australia. New Guinea, I soon discovered, is the world's second largest island, divided by a complex colonial history into two separate nations. Fascinating, but what of the climbing possibilities? The mountains which drew Heinrich Harrer and Peter Boardman lie in the western half, Irian Jaya, a troubled province of Indonesia, while independent PNG seems to have attracted more than its share of gold prospectors, missionaries, war heroes and anthropologists, judging from a browse through my local library. I learned more of interest from one of my earliest hillwalking companions who had forsaken the Munros to spend several years there, becoming President of Lae Explorers Club. This mainly expatriate group of outdoor enthusiasts have been active for many years organizing regular outings ranging from 'four-wheel drive picnics' and local bushwalks to longer trips in the Highlands. After a fascinating evening pouring over maps, slides and photo-albums, I accepted the post and was able to pack my rucksack in confident anticipation of some interesting trips ahead, particularly since I had been appointed to a post in Lae.

Engineers have yet to tackle the challenge of building a road across PNG, whose terrain is usually described in superlatives. Lae, the second city, lies on the north coast, accessible from the capital Port Moresby on the south coast only by air or sea. Long delays on the popular direct flight gave me an unexpected introduction to a fantastic kaleidoscope of cloud and rain forest from the window of a cramped 'Twin Otter', skimming over sharp green ridges spilling silver ribbons of waterfalls into dark craggy gorges as we flew via Wau.

Two months later I had enjoyed a few short bush-walks in the rugged hills around Lae, seeing nothing more of the Highlands until Easter 1986 provided a rare four-day weekend and the opportunity to join a trip to climb Mount Wilhelm, at 4509m the highest peak in PNG. Covering about 100km^2, the Wilhelm massif is enormous but fortunately relatively easy of access. For many years the colonists of New Guinea had dismissed the rugged jungle-clad mountains rising up from the coast as an impenetrable and sparsely populated wilderness. As recently as the 1930s gold prospectors exploring the interior with the help of aeroplanes were astonished to discover a series of densely populated fertile valleys which were not really opened up until the 1950s. Now the paved Highlands Highway links the interior with Lae and the outside world, carrying down Highlanders looking for wider opportunities and the lucrative coffee beans which have transformed the Highland economy, growing so well in their temperate gardens. Back up flow the trappings of modern civilization which the versatile Highlanders have been quick to adopt. Sadly, this fascinating blend of ancient and modern is not without its problems. Hold-ups at shotgun point have become alarmingly common on the Highway, making travel after dark unwise. Explorers Club trips occasionally had to be cancelled at the last minute on the advice of the local *kiap* (government officer) when rascal gangs literally took to the hills in areas we planned to visit. The traditional custom of 'payback' still applies, giving an added incentive to careful driving, particularly through the many roadside villages where pigs are still a symbol of wealth and prestige, roaming unrestrained and apparently oblivious to traffic. Hitting a pig would require immediate compensation, while an accident involving a villager would have much more serious consequences.

We left Lae on a wet Good Friday morning, my first venture along the Highway beyond the trade store at 'Forty Mile', following the broad flat Markham valley for 130km until suddenly the road seemed to tire of avoiding the surrounding mountains, turning to drive straight at them, twisting and climbing over the Kassem pass into the more open rolling landscape of Eastern Highlands province. From the town of Goroka the Highway climbs again over the Daulo pass into rugged Chimbu province. The imported baseball cap, T-shirt and jeans have been universally adopted by the men of PNG, but while we waited for the rest of the party to rendezvous in Kundiawa town I noticed an old man in traditional 'arse grass'. This venerable stooping old bodach wore a cuscus fur hat, a moon-shaped mother-of-pearl amulet across his bare chest, a ragged sort of apron in front, backside covered by a withered bunch of tangket leaves, his only concession to the 20th century an incongrous threadbare jacket that had once been part of a blue lounge suit: a poignant reminder that the Stone Age is still living memory here.

The Chimbu people called it Enduwa Kambugu, but the surveyors of German New Guinea chose instead to name the highest point in the Bismarck Range after their Kaiser. The territory was under Australian administration when the first known summit climbers, patrol officer L G Vial and two anonymous Papua New Guineans reached the top on 15 August 1938; their route is still the standard way.

We left the Highway at last for the final stage of our approach which required four-wheel drive, following a dusty rough road up the right branch of the Chimbu gorge. This is one of the most heavily populated areas of the whole country and a patchwork of vegetable gardens spreads up every hillside. By late afternoon we had reached our destination at Keglsugl (2510m) where we settled into 'Herman's Tourist Accommodation', a clean neat bunkhouse. Herman himself was a German who had spent 27 years in PNG and seemed happily settled with a Chimbu wife and half-a-dozen children.

To judge by the crowd milling around outside at dawn, Herman was not the only member of the local community hoping to benefit from Wilhelm climbers. Ignoring the disparaging comment in the guidebook that 'anyone who cannot lug his pack up the 1000 metres from Keglsugl to Pindaunde hut should not be doing the climb', we took the advice of seasoned veterans and employed carriers and a guide. Resting my rucksack beside the front gate while I took a few photos of the splendid clear morning and the colourful crowd, I turned round to see it heading up the road on eager unsolicited shoulders. We were actually able to motor a few kilometres more, past the new Provincial High School to the road-end where villagers were appointed to look after the vehicles and carriers selected. Our already large party of 16 adults and five youngsters swelled considerably, taking on a holiday carnival atmosphere as many of the hopeful carriers who failed to get a pack to carry came along anyway. We quickly spread out along the narrow trail, climbing steeply through thick rain-forest. It was pleasantly dry underfoot, and occasional breaks in the trees gave glimpses of the hills beyond: a very enjoyable start to our climb. After a couple of hours we broke out of the forest at about 3200m, turning into the lower reaches of the Pindaunde valley, dotted with tree ferns. Morainic debris on the hummocky valley floor is a reminder of the glacial ice which filled the valley 15,000 years ago, while above us the rocky outcrops of Mount Wilhelm began to dominate the surroundings through the cloud which had been building up all morning. A rocky step gave a final short steep climb leading at last to Lake Aunde and the hut.

It had been a rare pleasure the previous evening to feel cold enough to snuggle into a sleeping bag again. Now the novelty had worn off and the combination of altitude, smoke and 'night before' butterflies made sleep difficult. Success or otherwise depended on the weather, so it was a relief to wake at 1am to silence and be able to look blearily out into a dark but dry night. Our local guide had returned home the previous afternoon to attend a christening party, and true to his word was back in time for our 2am start. The line of torch-lights started stretching immediately, skirting the lake through some awkward bush before a short steep climb up another rocky step led to higher Lake Pinde. These nocturnal stumblings were planned to fit in with the notorious Wilhelm weather: a regular clear sky can be expected for a few hours around dawn, which occurs at about 6am throughout the year. As we climbed slowly west towards Wilhelm's southern Bogunolto ridge the rising moon soon made the torches unnecessary. By now the party had built up some rhythm, the tail-end having turned back to join those satisfied with reaching the hut. We joined the ridge briefly at 4020m, glad of woolly hats, gloves and anoraks in a bitterly cold wind. Fortunately the route soon turned off to the sheltered E side, skirting below rocky buttresses. None the worse for having been up most of the night, our local guide proved worthwhile as the route was neither clearly marked nor easy to find. Another small party which had set out ahead of us wasted a lot of time and energy finding its way. Shortly before dawn we saw the tinkling lights of Madang town on the coast, 100 or so kilometres away to the north-east. The final climb to the rocky summit provided some entertaining scrambling over rough gabbro, and despite my headache I found I had enough pidgin to rephrase Patey's celebrated epigram:

> Mount Wilhelm, Mount Herbert, Sepik-Waghi divide
> Em i gudpela trainin long Cuillin bilong Skye.

We reached the summit at 7am, and already a little cloud was starting to build up in the valleys. Luckily the wind had dropped and we were able to sit and admire the magnificent panorama at our leisure before turning around to begin the long descent back to the coast and to work again on Tuesday morning.

FURTHER INFORMATION

New Guinea by Roy Mackay in the Time–Life Books *World's Wild Places* series gives a colourfully illustrated background to the scenery and wildlife, while Lonely Planet's *Papua New Guinea – a travel survival kit* by Mark Lightbody and Tony Wheeler and *Bushwalking in Papua New Guinea* by Riall Nolan are both packed with useful information.

There must surely be some interesting rock-climbing on the gabbro buttresses of Mount Wilhelm and its neighbours, and I would like to have returned with some climbing gear in the June–September period when the weather is supposed to be better. I heard rumours of activity by other parties, but never got round to searching out further information.

I do not know if I will ever return to Papua New Guinea, but my feelings are summed up in this quotation from *Among The Cannibals of New Guinea* by the Rev S McFarlane:

> When every mountain in the Alps has been scaled, and even the Himalayas made the scene of mountaineering triumphs ... it comes with a sense of relief to visit a country really new ...

Mountaineering Eden –
The Southern Alps

J G R HARDING

(Plates 40–46)

New Zealand, the Gift of the Sea, a green oasis in the wilderness of the Southern Ocean, was the last of lands to be discovered by man. When Polynesian seafarers first set foot on this temperate Pacific island, barely 1000 years ago, it was as close to earthly paradise as existed. New Zealand's age of innocence ended abruptly 800 years later with the coming of the Europeans who felled the primeval forest for sheep runs and indiscriminately imported a ragbag of alien fauna and an aviary of European birds. This fatal impact irrevocably altered the balance of nature and consigned to oblivion a unique range of indigenous flightless birds who had roamed the country unmolested by natural predators. The North Island has borne the brunt of this 19th-century ecological disaster but the South Island, the land of the Long White Cloud uplifted high by the Southern Alps which support the world's biggest glaciers outside Asia and the Polar regions, remains one of the world's least spoilt natural wonders.

I had previously climbed the Southern Alps in 1970, so a re-match during my 3½ month sabbatical in 1988 was inevitable. As time was short, objectives were limited to Mount Aspiring and the Mount Cook National Park. In New Zealand, all mountaineering activity is in thrall to prodigious storms that can blight climbing for weeks on end. Inevitably, our visit had to coincide with early November, traditionally a touch late for ski touring, too early for climbing but generally unsettled. Yet I banked on memories of that first visit when I had struck lucky in November and in finding three New Zealanders to climb with – Mike White on Phipps, Mike Brown on Cook and Jim Wilson on Rollaston. This time round, medieval mountaineer recognized the inexorable logic of Hamish Nichols's advice to hire a guide.

NZ guides are a helpful, friendly breed whatever variety you opt for. But once *in situ*, Carl 'Thomo' Thompson (ski guide/pilot/Antarctic veteran) reckoned that my man for Aspiring was Nick ('Guide Anywhere Anything') Cradock, contactable exclusively through his sports shop sponsors 'Macpac'. Only after our telephonic deal did I discover that Cradock was New Zealand's 'Mountaineer of the Year', fresh from Cerro Torre. We met for the first time on 6 November in Christchurch when he fetched up with a hired car for the drive south. Answering to 30 (give and take), Nick was lean, laconic, rolled his own, had chosen to climb and had once been Alpine Guides Mount Cook's chief instructor. Now he did his own thing.

For the past two months, the Southern Alps had been stormbound but though it rained throughout our journey south, the forecast was for a change to Southerlies, NZ's high pressure winds. At Twizel, once a hydro town and now a dormitory for Mount Cook guides, we stopped for tea and a wad with Gary Ball, leader of the NZ 1988 Everest Expedition for the latest on Lydia Brady's claim to have become the first woman to climb Everest solo without oxygen.

The Mount Aspiring National Park, one of ten in NZ, was conceived in 1935, established in 1964 and now covers 288,000 hectares. The Maori name for the region is Titiraurangi, 'The Land of Many Peaks Piercing the Clouds' – which aptly describes this wild country of forest-clad ridges, hanging valleys and heavy glaciation where bad weather and access problems transform any climb into a minor expedition. The mountain itself they called Titita, 'The Uprising, Glistening Peak' – as evocative as the name 'Mount Aspiring' given to it by John Turnbull Thompson, NZ's first Surveyor General, in 1857. Aspiring (3027m) was first climbed in 1909 by Major Bernard Head (AC) – killed six years later at Gallipoli – with the NZ guides J M Clark and Alex Graham. Few other peaks in the area were climbed before the 1930s, none in the Haast range until after the Second World War, and several others not until the 1960s and 1970s.

We reached Wanaka – an ingenuous resort on a site rivalling Annecy's at the end of a 50 kilometre lake – towards evening, signed in at the Park's HQ and for the next hour bumped up and along the Matukituki valley in swirling mists and deepening gloom by a dirt road which forded countless streams up to and over the car's hubcaps. Everything was awash from a myriad cataracts cascading down the hillside like a skein of white ribbons. In the valley bottom, flocks of sheep grazed unconcernedly while seagulls wheeled and swooped amidst the paradise ducks. Cradock, ever economical in his conversation, pronounced that seagulls on a south wind augured well. From our road head we walked another two hours to the NZAC's Cascade hut and next morning, 7 November, awoke to a perfect day. Sunlight now bathed a swath of hoarfrost-bleached meadows running to the valley's edge before merging into the matt green beech forest. At the head of the valley the snow cone of Mount Bevan gleamed like a beacon. Were ever the European Alps so green or their snows so white?

With the costs clock ticking, Cradock's plans for Aspiring – a mere 3027m peak – seemed indulgent. One day to make the Lucas Trotter hut (1465m), 1000m up the French ridge: another half-day to cross the Bonar glacier to the Colin Todd hut. Only the third day was earmarked for Aspiring itself. But any resemblance between NZ and Alpine hut marches is coincidental. The normal route into the Aspiring massif up the Matukituki valley past Shovel and Pearl Flats twice crosses the river by suspension bridges and then takes flight up the French ridge by a path so resembling a rope ladder that it deserves a grade of its own. With food enough for a fortnight we needed all of seven hours to reach the hut. The weather looked good but the night was disturbed by the antics of keas repeatedly sliding off the tin roof. This iron-beaked alpine parrot – capable of killing a sheep and persecuted remorselessly for the trait – is one of NZ's few indigenous species to have survived the European. Intelligent, fearless, curious and destructive, the kea has become the cult bird of NZ mountaineers.

From the Lucas Trotter hut there are three ways to get to the Colin Todd hut of which the fastest is via the 'Breakaway' – another way of describing the ice cliffs that spill off the Bonar glacier between Mt Joffre and Mt French. Threading a way through serac debris, I remembered the hut's memorial plaque to Ruth Trotter and Ralph Lucas, killed 18 years ago almost to the day by an ice avalanche while attempting this passage. After 2½ hours we emerged on to an ice plateau to be confronted by the gleaming white pyramid of Aspiring 3km dead ahead, rising 1200m sheer from the glacial moat of the Bonar, Therma, Volta and Kitchener glaciers.

In NZ you are always looking over your shoulder to the west for hogsbacks and other bad weather harbingers. Today the sky was cloudless and, with hindsight, our best bet might have been to go for Aspiring while the weather held. But I was not psyched up for this and nor perhaps was Cradock, who earlier had let slip that he had once climbed with someone even older than me. He too was weighing up what he had let himself in for.

The wind which got up later that afternoon was still blowing strongly next morning, 9 November. We made abortive starts at 4am and 6am and finally got off at 8.45am, bound for the NW ridge. This 1225m *voie normale* is rated 10 hours in the guidebook, though Samuel Turner's epic first ascent in 1913 took 60. To get on to the ridge Cradock festooned an ice ramp with a succession of ice screws but after half a dozen pitches, with the ridge seemingly within grasp, he broke off the engagement with the news that the wind was so strong that, even if we reached it, we would certainly be blown off. You need a special confidence to gainsay a guide on his home ground, but to yield ground so hardly won created within me an unresolved inner conflict. Cradock suggested that, to salve something of the day, we knock off Rolling Pin (2245m), the most southerly peak of the Haast range. This ran away to the north, a jagged line encrusted with double cornices billowing out a sheer 1000m above the Therma glacier like the square rigger's topsails from which their names derive – Main Royal, Sky Scraper, Star Gazer, Spike and Moonraker. Rolling Pin, only climbed in 1948, looked an improbable prospect *en face* yet yielded with grace. Dropping down to the hut from the ridge which gave a grandstand view of Aspiring's NW face, I allowed myself a moment's musing on what might have been as the sun beamed down out of an azure sky and the wind scarcely raised a murmur.

Back at the hut, besieged by keas, we braced ourselves for another crack at Aspiring next morning. But long before our 4am reveille, the North-westerlies were rattling and rocking the hut. The issue now was not how to get up but out. Food was no problem but, with a guide, a short stay in even the meanest hut is like a five-star hotel with none of the comforts. In any event, both of us had deadlines so we launched out at 10.15am into the blizzard aiming for Bevan Col. Cradock's last caveat was that descent might be impossible and retreat likely. For the next 1½ hours we marched on a 220° compass bearing, rope-length after rope-length, me in front and Cradock at rear semaphoring to maintain dead-reckoning. We reached Bevan Col as planned and now began a

dodgy diagonal traverse across the glaciated S face of Mt Bevan to knock off
Hector Col. Everything hinged on navigation. To wander off east into the
Waipara gorge guaranteed a three-day walk out to the coast: a variation west,
an unwitting parapente off 1000m bluffs overhanging the upper Matukituki.

At 12.30pm Cradock announced that we were lost and the situation
serious. As we sat down to ponder with altimeter and map, I noticed Nick's sac
turning a couple of cartwheels before taking off like a chough. Nick's speed
from a sitting start was impressive, but his sac was even faster. This normally
taciturn man now gave vent with a *Heldentenor*'s vocal powers but with a
libretto limited to prosaic four-letter invocations. He reaped only the wind but,
with sac, snow shovel, bivvy bag, sleeping bag, stove and a fortune in
ironmongery at the bottom of the Matukituki gorge, he lifted his game and
within half an hour of furious activity we had reached and positively identified
the upper gorge of the Matukituki. By 1.40pm we were off the mountain,
striding down the valley through sleet, rain and a tangled undergrowth
occasionally relieved by the white splashes of the Mount Cook lily. Wading
knee-deep through the Matukituki river as if it never existed, we reached the car
at 8.15pm and slept that night in Nick's homely lorry/log cabin convertible at
Wanaka.

After three days back in Christchurch juggling flight schedules, I caught
the 8am Mount Cook Airline's bus bound for the Mount Cook National Park.
Our driver Paul had long exhausted his limited gamut of superlatives by the
time we stopped for the mandatory view of Mount Cook across the glacier-blue
waters of Lake Pukaki. At Mount Cook Village most passengers got off at the
Hermitage – now a US/Japanese redoubt – while I rendezvoused for a projected
ski tour with my guide Shaun Norman, a former Brit accredited with more
Antarctic seasons than most have done Alpine. In NZ mountain lore, the
country's first skiers were immigrant Norwegian miners. Mannering and
Dixon, on their sixth unsuccessful attempt on Mount Cook in 1893, fashioned
skis from the hickory blades of an old reaper and binder. But the history of NZ
ski mountaineering proper begins in September 1936 when Colin Wyatt,
Britain's outstanding ski mountaineer for three decades, teamed up with
Hermitage guide Mike Bowie. Their double traverse of the Main Divide set
standards by which all subsequent NZ ski tours have been judged. Downhill ski
resorts are not yet an intrusive feature of the Southern Alps but there is endless
scope for both heli-skiing and ski mountaineering, and most NZ mountaineers
regard skis as an indispensable tool to mountaineering.

Early November is usually the close season for Alpine Guides Mount
Cook. For months the weather had been appalling, but today the skies were
quite clear. Thus, barely arrived, I was rustling up an equipment package of
primeval crampons and clod-hopping Salomon downhill boots – the only pair
in stock. To catch the good weather we had to reach the Tasman Saddle hut that
same afternoon. This, the best mountain base from which to explore the
National Park's ski hinterland, sits uneasily on a precipitous bluff at the top of
the Tasman glacier, 48km away from Mount Cook Village. When the sun
shines you don't waste two days doing on foot what can be done in 45 minutes
by plane. A dozen of these sat out on the airstrip quivering to get airborne but,

due to a gusty wind, only Shaun and I got off that afternoon, skis strapped under the wings and cockpit filled with food. For this 'Flight of a Lifetime' the trick was to fly straight at the mountainside and only back off when the passengers started screaming. After two dummy runs we landed at 5.30pm at 2303m, dumped sacs and skinned up to the Aylmer Col to see the sun sinking into the Tasman Sea.

Down at the hut, a pair of hard-eyed Yankee girls with an assortment of guides and others were generally in good heart for having climbed Elie de Beaumont (3117m) earlier that day. This was our objective for tomorrow – weather permitting. NZ weather preoccupations get tedious, but ten laboured hut-book pages spinning out the frustrations of the Keen Brothers trapped for 11 days a month earlier added substance to such hallowed sagas as H E L Porter's 18 days' incarceration in the Malte Brun hut and Austrian guide Conrad Kain's three successful ascents of Mount Cook in 25 attempts.

Next day, 15 November, we set off at 5.45am for Elie's S face. Shaun now made a sacrifice. To cope with the uncompromising Salomons, I would carry them and climb in my own boots. In descent we would swop: Shaun would ski the Salomons and I his Dynafit 'Tourlites'. On the steep approach slopes, Harscheisen would have been handy but were evidently regarded as pansy. At 7am we dumped our skis under an ice block and, after negotiating a selection of bergschrunds, reached the summit at 9.30am to make Shaun's fastest ascent. Later on in the season, open crevasses and bergschrunds can make the route virtually impossible. From the summit, the mountain backbone of NZ stretched away north and south as a progression of icy crests – cold, remote and altogether wilder than anything in the Alps. A cloud sea enveloped the western approaches, but to the east the eye of faith might have discerned the Pacific.

Next morning we again stole away from the now deserted hut as the sun's first rays lit up the ice dome of Elie de Beaumont. Shaun's plan was to cross the Tasman Saddle, ski down the Murchison headwall and glacier to its junction with the Classen glacier and then climb into the Classen Basin for a tilt at Mount Mannering (2637m). The previous night I had had an uneasy dream about this Murchison headwall. The reality – a glinting sheet of ice riven by bergschrunds – was no better than the nightmare but, once past it, we sped down deeper and deeper into the shadowed bowels of the glacier – skis clattering, thighs tightening, straining for breath in the icy air. One mountain in particular dominated the scene – Broderick, a 2637m pillar of rock buttressed by ice cliffs.

We donned crampons 750m lower and meandered through a staircase of crevasses up to the Classen Saddle. Mannering took shape as a spiralling snow cone surmounted by a vertical ice topping. It looked hours away. At my urging, we opted instead for the SE face of Broderick. Dumping our skis, we climbed up through yet more bergschrunds to a brèche which led on to the teetering ice wafer of the summit ridge. I reckoned that this tightrope, dropping a plumb 1200m to the Whymper glacier, was an hour's worth: Shaun bet seven minutes. We did it in eight to reach the top of Broderick exactly five hours after leaving the hut. Five kilometres across the sensational abyss of the Whataroa gorge the E face of Elie de Beaumont, yesterday's mountain, rose a clean 2000m from the pit of the Whymper glacier. We descended swiftly down soft, treacherous snow, ski'd through the Classen's crevasses and dropped down again to the Murchison glacier – now a cauldron in the afternoon sun. But success was our fan as we stormed back to and over the headwall to make the hut by 3.55pm. In under ten hours we had descended and ascended almost 2000m and snatched the prize of Broderick.

The weather forecast of Northwesterlies for the following afternoon determined that our last shot would be an eight-hour descent of the Tasman glacier. You wonder how this restless river of ice – 29 kilometres long, 3 kilometres wide, over 100 square kilometres in area and up to 600m deep – can exist in the middle of a Pacific island at a latitude equivalent to the Pyrenees. But the genius of the place lies not in its skiing – only the top third is normally skiable – but rather in its backdrop of colossal ice mountains delineated by the galactic skyline of the Main Divide that runs 30 kilometres from Elie de Beaumont to Mount Cook. And it is at the foot of Aorangi, 'the Cloud Piercer', here soaring almost 3000m above its glacial base, that all journeys in the Southern Alps should end. In Maori legend this great mountain was the boy turned to stone on the shoulders of his grandfather, the Earth itself. And it is this vision of youth that leaves the most lasting impression of New Zealand's mountaineering Eden where nature has so unstintingly lavished her favours.

In the Footsteps of Gervasutti

SIMON RICHARDSON

(Plates 47–51)

The 1930s have come to be regarded as one of the golden ages of alpine climbing. During this period there was a huge surge in standards, and the great N faces of the Eiger, Grandes Jorasses and the Matterhorn were first climbed. Competition was fierce for these prestigious ascents, mainly between German and Italian teams, and each nationality achieved notable successes. Firmly established within the Italian camp was Giusto Gervasutti. Widely regarded as one of the most talented climbers of his generation, he made first ascents of several of the finest routes in the Western Alps. Today, his climbs are not as well known as Cassin's, for example, but whilst Cassin succeeded more often by careful planning and determination, Gervasutti's routes were imaginative and often very modern in concept. His greatest rock routes carry their reputation to this day for difficulty and seriousness.

Reflecting over my own 15 years of alpine climbing, I realized that Gervasutti's climbs, more than any other, have provided some of my most challenging and satisfying ascents. I must admit to a love of wild and empty places, and the desire to visit these is often as strong as the urge to climb itself. This perhaps explains why Gervasutti's routes, which are often remotely situated, have such an appeal. For others who share my fascination with some of the less well known corners in the Alps, I have tried to give a taster below from some of my own experiences on Gervasutti's greatest rock routes. Those with a keen sense of alpine history will realize that I still have to climb the Right-Hand Pillar of Frêney and the SE ridge of Pic Gaspard to complete the collection!

North-West Face Olan (1934)

1934 was an important year for Gervasutti. He followed an expedition to the Andes with a good summer season and his first major alpine new routes. After making the first ascent of the E face of Mont Blanc du Tacul by the couloir that now bears his name, he met the French climber Lucien Devies. Soon after, Devies suggested they set off to the Dauphiné to attempt the NW face of the Olan.

The ascent of this 1100m high rock wall, on their first attempt, was remarkable since neither of them had seen the face before. They climbed the well-defined spur to the right of the huge central couloir, although they did briefly consider taking the direct line up the impressive steep wall to the N summit. (This direct route was climbed in 1956 by Desmaison and Couzy.) Hard rock climbing in the Dauphiné in the early 1930s was unheard of, and there were no climbs in the TD category on the French side of the Alps at all at that time.

My own experience of this route began in August 1990, when Guy Muhlemann and I crossed the little Maye glacier. After several years' absence from summer alpine climbing, I had forgotten about the hollow-stomach feeling during the pre-dawn approach to a big climb. However, as always, this soon disappeared after we had crossed the bergschrund. We moved together up the initial 300m slabs, with a peg every ropelength or so to point the way. At the first steepening I belayed and Guy led through up a steep IVsup corner. I always seem to find pitches of IVsup desperate, and this one was no exception, with steep out-of-balance moves on loose awkwardly spaced holds. Guy found it hard too, and we wondered how we would find the pitches of VI higher up the route.

Above, easier climbing led to the Yellow Tower, the 150m crux section. Uncertain of where the exact line lay, we traversed right and then back left to enter a compact dièdre system. This led to the very crest of the spur, probably some way to the left of Gervasutti's line. The rock, which up until now had been on the loose side, now deteriorated alarmingly. Guy made a very delicate lead up the steep arête, gently pushing the rock back into place and taking care not to dislodge several huge and precariously poised blocks with the rope. Following, I was unable to reproduce Guy's finesse, and several large blocks went crashing down the face below me.

The rock improved only slightly above, but the angle eased. To our left, on the Couzy route, we could see the two French climbers we had met the day before. We had spent a convivial evening together, whilst Serge, the hut guardian, fussed over us and cooked a magnificent dinner. Shouting across, we exchanged greetings. The sight of the two tiny red dots below the immense headwall added to the savage atmosphere and accentuated the vastness of the wall.

Near the top of the face we entered the great couloir and arrived at the *brèche* below the central summit. Gervasutti and Devies descended the complicated W ridge from here, but we were keen to reach the top of the 'Dru of the Dauphiné'. The climbing up to the central summit and traverse across the higher N summit was easy but spectacular. To the north and east the Dauphiné mountains were spread out before us, and it was a real privilege to be alone on the top of such a wild mountain.

We descended the N ridge, traversed across the top of the Sellettes glacier and crossed the Brèche de l'Olan to take us back below the N side of the mountain. We stopped to watch the sun setting on the route. The climbing and quality of the rock had been poor, but the savage grandeur of the face had made it a deeply satisfying day. Happy and content, we raced down to the Fond Turbat hut, wondering what delights Serge would have prepared for dinner that night.

Croz Spur, Grandes Jorasses (1935)

The following year Gervasutti was one of the main contenders in the race for the N face of the Jorasses. Much of the early attention was focused on the Walker Spur, but Gervasutti was convinced that the central spur leading up to Pointe Croz would prove the easiest route. In 1933 he had climbed the couloir running up behind the first two towers at the bottom of the spur, but a storm forced a retreat. Gervasutti then tried in 1934, when three other teams were on the face, but again bad weather made them descend.

By 1935 the face was still virgin, but international interest was so great that when he arrived at the Leschaux hut on 30 June there were German, Swiss and French parties already on the face. His companion Chabod was so upset that he wanted to go down and climb elsewhere, but Gervasutti was insistent they try anyway, and see if they could catch the leaders up. That afternoon the French and Swiss teams descended, leaving only the two Germans, Peters and Meier, on the face. Later that evening, the Swiss guide Lambert with Loulou Boulaz arrived at the hut, and all four started the route together the following morning.

The mountain was in remarkably good condition for so early in the season and they made good progress, but were hit by a violent storm about half way up the face. They bivouacked near the notch above the upper icefield, and the following day Gervasutti led the party up the final icy 150m to the top to make the second ascent. This one had got away: Peters and Meier had beaten them by two days.

7pm, 13 October 1983, Grandes Jorasses: Our bivouac site, in the notch above the upper icefield, was probably very close to where Gervasutti must have stayed. As I wriggled into my sleeping bag, I thought back to the lucky sequence of events that had got me there. I'd arrived in a deserted Chamonix with a week's holiday on the off-chance of finding a partner. Kevin Doyle, a Canadian who had spent the summer ticking off many of the famous alpine faces, was keen to add the Jorasses to his impressive tally before returning home. With a day and a half of good weather forecast we decided on the Croz, but our tight schedule went awry from the very beginning. We spent the first good day drying our clothes outside the Leschaux hut after being caught in a wild storm on the glacier!

Kevin had been confident of climbing the route in a day, but a late 8am start meant we were now well short of the summit ridge. However, the climbing had been superb. The icefields had been perfect névé, the couloirs choked with squeaky white ice, and the crux slabs had iced over to give two sustained 50m pitches. So far the Croz had been like climbing two Orion faces, stacked on top of each other on a super Ben Nevis.

According to the forecast the storm should have already arrived, but the weather still appeared good. I had a faint suspicion that the stars were not twinkling as brightly as they should, and spent much of the night worrying how much longer the weather would hold.

The first wisps of cloud appeared from behind the mountain at 6am. As predicted, the front was moving in from the south. By 6.30 it was snowing hard, the mountain was completely clagged in and we were frantically stuffing gear into our sacks in the dawn gloom.

The final 150m of the Croz is generally reckoned to be the crux. There are two alternatives: one can either follow the crest of the spur directly to the summit of Pointe Croz, or, more easily, take a steep gully system about 50m to the right. There was no discussion about which option to take, and we immediately set off traversing right towards the gully. Already 15cm of fresh snow was piled on the rock, the protection was poor and the rock suspect. Our progress was slow. After what seemed an age we entered the gully and clawed our way up steep black ice and shattered rock all covered in a deep white blanket. At midday we pulled out on to the summit ridge and were met by the full force of the southerly gale.

We couldn't stand in the wind which was wrapping the ropes around the rocks on the ridge, so we unroped and crawled over the summits of Pointe Croz and Pointe Whymper. Snow slopes now led to the col where we could descend the icy slopes of the S face. Visibility was reduced to only a few feet and we were relying on my memory of descending the mountain the previous summer.

By the time we reached the Rocher du Reposoir we were floundering through waist-deep snow. What had been a sustained scramble the summer before was now more like a swim, but eventually we slid down the lower rocks to the Grandes Jorasses glacier. Unable to find the hut we spent the night in a crevasse.

The following morning the storm had stopped, but the visibility was still poor. We soon discovered that we had spent the night less than 100m from the hut, but we weren't bothered now as the valley was in sight.

I don't know why, but well below the hut we looked back at the way we'd come. There was a tiny pocket of blue sky above the Croz, and as we watched a red dot appeared in the centre of it. I joked to Kevin that it was a rescue chopper. The red dot traversed the summit ridge, and then started to descend following our tracks. We were two days overdue, and it didn't take us long to realize that this really was a helicopter looking for us. We waited and soon it was hovering above us with a soldier from the mountain gendarmerie being lowered down to meet us.

'*Bonjour*,' he said, 'where 'ave you come from?'

'Grandes Jorasses.'

'Which route?'

'The Croz.'

'Who 'as called out the 'elicopteur?'

I was stunned. How on earth could we possibly know?

'Er . . . Jules,' I stammered, 'Julian Mills.'

The name of the only person we both knew in Chamonix seemed to be the right answer, for he signalled to the winchman to get ready to haul us up.

'But we're OK, thank you very much. We don't need rescuing.'

The gendarme looked at us hard, nodded, signalled to the winchman, and disappeared back up into the helicopter. Within seconds it had gone and there was total silence again.

We had mixed feelings. It was touching that someone cared and was worried about us, but the incident had disturbed our sense of isolation. We both desperately wanted to finish our adventure by ourselves.

The Val Ferret road was blocked by snow, and we had to walk to Entrèves where we caught a bus. We were the only passengers, and the driver was so excited to hear that we had just climbed the Jorasses that he took us through the tunnel for free. Later that evening I went to the Chamonix rescue to thank them for coming to look for us. Rather than scold us for knowingly climbing in such atrocious weather, they raved about the winter-like conditions on the face and wanted to know every detail of our ascent! It had been a good week away from work.

North-West Face Ailefroide (1936)

The NW wall of the Ailefroide was the culmination of Gervasutti's partnership with Devies. Their route is often referred to as the Walker Spur of the Dauphiné, but it is infrequently climbed with perhaps only two or three ascents each season.

The face is huge, over 1000m high and more than a kilometre wide. Although it had not attracted the same attention as the Jorasses, it was very much in 'the last great problem' class. Eager not to miss out again, after being so close on the Croz the year before, Gervasutti started the route despite an accident on the glacier where he broke two ribs. To add to their problems, on the climb itself Devies suffered from appendicitis.

The route takes an elegant and logical line, following the pronounced spur in the lower half of the face. They climbed the blank slabs above, and found a way through the impregnable looking headwall. The bottom of the climb is very serious, for to reach the foot of the spur you must cross the Coste Rouge couloir, a notorious stonefall shoot.

3am, 4 August 1990, Coste Rouge glacier: It started as a rumble but soon a huge echoing roar shook and filled the glacier basin. We had been woken yet again by a large rockfall. It was as though a dumper truck on the summit ridge was emptying tons of rock down the face. Guy Muhlemann and I had joked the evening before about 'Messerschmitts and Spitfires' zinging down the face, but we didn't expect major rockfalls well into the night. Guy suggested that we should wake early as planned, and if a single stone fell whilst we were making breakfast we would abandon our attempt. For my part, having seen more rocks fall down the face than I had in the whole Alps put together, I decided that a dry 1990 summer meant the route was definitely off. I was bitterly disappointed but kept my thoughts to myself.

At 5am Guy started making coffee and we ate our breakfast in silence. All was quiet. Another cup of coffee . . . still silence. Slowly we packed our sacks, roped up and without a word crossed the glacier to the foot of the face. Guy stopped at the glacier edge. A single stone bounded lazily down the rocks and landed in the snow beside us. We spoke for the first time.

'We're committed once we cross the "schrund",' Guy said.

I paused. It was already light, we were late and I knew my silent decision last night was the correct one. My reply came as more of a surprise to myself than to Guy.

'There's only been one stone, let's go for it!'

We changed up a gear and were soon moving together up the initial 100m slabs. Hearts in mouths we crossed the Coste Rouge couloir and continued moving together up slabs to reach the base of the spur. At the first steepening we lost the way and took a harder variation to the left before regaining the crest of the spur. 'You have to pretend you're Gervasutti, and always take the easiest line,' I grumbled to Guy at the top of the excellent but unlikely pitch. We continued up the spur and six hours after crossing the bergschrund we arrived at the foot of the Grey Slabs.

Still no stones had fallen down the face and it was tempting to relax a little, when a huge rockfall roared down the full length of the Coste Rouge couloir below us. Two climbers silhouetted on the summit ridge were clearly the cause, but the event unsettled us and we felt very small and vulnerable in the centre of the vast wall.

There was no obvious line up the smooth slabs above which were scarred with pock-marks from thousands of falling stones. Guy led off on what had now become the psychological crux of the route. The route-finding was difficult, the protection well spaced and our position felt very exposed. Only two stones fell, but nevertheless it was two relieved climbers who arrived on the crescent-shaped ledge three pitches later.

The headwall was now bathed in the afternoon sun, and despite reports we'd heard to the contrary the rock was firm with good holds. We made good progress, and the pitches improved with height. In particular, an absorbing ropelength up an icy chimney with rock-boots carefully positioned on ice-free rock stood out as being particularly enjoyable. Above, the route took an unlikely and spectacular finish heading towards an immense overhang which was avoided at the last possible moment with a tricky rock-wall on the left.

We neglected to go to the W summit and descended the ridge a little way before dropping down to a bivouac on the Ailefroide glacier. The following day we made a leisurely descent, dropping into the Sélé hut to record the second ascent of the season. As we walked through the pinewoods below, I reflected that never before had I come so close to failing on a route without even leaving the bivouac. It was two very satisfied climbers who toasted their luck over dinner in Ailefroide later that evening.

South-West Face Gugliermina (1938)

Gervasutti was determined to make an attempt on the Eiger during the summer of 1938, but following Heckmair's success in July he immediately switched his attention to the last and perhaps the greatest prize of all – the Walker Spur. It was not until August that he was able to make an attempt, only to learn on the walk up to the Leschaux hut that his fellow countrymen, Cassin, Esposito and

Tizzoni were already established on the face. Gervasutti and Ottoz started the route that afternoon nevertheless, but a storm when they were in the region of the Rébuffat crack sent them down to the glacier. Meanwhile Cassin and his Lecco team were sufficiently high on the face to be able to force their way to the top. Later, Gervasutti said that his disappointment was softened by the fact that victory had gone to Cassin, but it must have been a bitter pill to swallow, for none of the Lecco party had ever even seen the Leschaux cirque before.

In his autobiography[1] Gervasutti writes philosophically about being beaten yet again to a major first ascent on this face. One can sense the relief, however, that the race for prestigious lines was now over, and there was no longer any need to compete. Of the Walker and Eiger N face ascents he wrote:

> There did not now seem to be any other wall whose ascent would constitute a problem big enough to warrant its becoming an object of competition on a national scale. So mountaineering once more became a personal affair, and a new route the private creation of the climber.

On his return to Courmayeur he met his old friend Gabriele Boccalatte. They decided to attempt the SW face of Pointe Gugliermina, an elegant rock pillar on the S side of the Aiguille Blanche de Peuterey. Of all Gervasutti's routes this is perhaps the one that is best known today. Apart from a pendulum high on the face, they climbed the route almost entirely free. Subsequently it was hailed as the most technically difficult pre-war rock climb in the Mont Blanc range. Later ascents confirmed the beauty and delicate nature of the climbing and, unusually for a major Gervasutti route, the climb has achieved a fair degree of popularity. It is even included in one of the recent topo guides to Mont Blanc, retaining a modern TD grade and rubbing shoulders with the bolt-protected desperates of the 1980s.

Roger Everett and I made an ascent in the summer of 1983. In common with many of Gervasutti's routes the approach is a long one, and the crossing of the Col de l'Innominata and ascent of the chaotic Frêney glacier to the foot of the face demands a certain degree of mountaineering ability. Therefore we were surprised and a little disappointed to see a party of three already bivouacking on a series of ledges at the foot of the face.

We spent a comfortable night on a glacier rognon and made an early start the following morning, taking the other party by surprise as we quickly caught up with them. They turned out to be two guides with a well-known French lady client. The charm of the lady was contrasted by the aggressiveness of the guides who would not let us pass. They eventually let us through when they realized that Roger spoke fluent French and understood their bad language, and that we seemed quite prepared to move together up pitches of V whilst still carrying coils. Above, we resumed a more conventional style, and wearing rock-boots and carrying minimal sacks we made fast progress and were on the top well before midday.

The descent, with EB's crushing tired toes, down the loose Schneider couloir seemed to last forever. Eventually, six hours after leaving the summit, we reached the rognon and our bivouac gear. Gervasutti had taken half that time to descend. I'm sure he would have laughed!

East Face Grandes Jorasses (1942)

This route was undoubtedly Gervasutti's greatest climb, not equalled in difficulty until the 1960s with the American routes on the W face of the Dru and S face of the Fou. Gervasutti had no competition for this line, and he made four attempts spread over five years before he was eventually successful. Even today, Gervasutti's route carries a reputation for seriousness that has few parallels in the Mont Blanc range.

2am, 19 July 1982, Frebouze glacier: Nick Kekus banged shut the wooden door of the empty little Gervasutti hut, and slowly we wound our way up the contorted glacier to the Col des Hirondelles. We were astonished to find two French climbers bivouacking there who said they were also going to climb the E face. I couldn't believe that, after only six ascents in 40 years, two teams were going to be on the face at the same time! The spell and aura of the route's inaccessibility began to dissolve in front of me, until further questions revealed that they were going for the Hirondelles ridge after all.

The ascent to the col had taken three hours and we were already behind time. Our success depended on being able to avoid the stone-swept 'Y' couloir in the lower third of the face. Once we were established on the concave bulging walls above, the stones would fall well out into space behind us. The French Vallot guide had provided the key to avoiding the couloir, with a description of Marmier's winter variation (climbed on the fourth ascent), which took a circular line to the left. Our strategy involved climbing this before dawn when the first of the sun's rays would start the barrage of stones down the lower part of the face.

From the col we traversed left, crossed the bergschrund and climbed a small icefield. We traversed left again and then back right as dawn broke and the first stones began to fall. Fortunately we were now following a ramp sheltered from above by an overhanging wall. We quickly crossed the 'Y' ledges, avoiding the whining stones, and were soon established on the central wall. We were now safe, but our satisfaction was tempered after the second difficult pitch by a violent hailstorm. It was still early, and we were hopeful that the storm would soon pass. After all, the normally cautious weatherman at the Chamonix meteo had promised *grands beaux temps*. When the hail turned to snow we knew we were in for a long wait, and we retreated under our bivouac gear. Well into the night we were blasted by another ferocious hailstorm. The weight of the ice between us and the rock pushed us off our ledge and we were left hanging on the belay.

I spent much of the night thinking of reasons why we had to continue the following day. Retreat down the face would be too dangerous, I argued, and the hard pitches above would soon clear in the morning sun. I hadn't climbed before with Nick who was surprised that I should be worried that he might want to descend. There was no question, we would continue.

Our persistence was rewarded by an immaculate series of pitches up steep cracks and grooves on the left side of the wall. The pitches were sustained at V+ and VI and we were grateful for our rock-boots. The snow had melted quickly from the ledges, but often the cracks were streaming with water. We had been concerned about whether our meagre supply of pegs was up to the A2 aid pitch on blade pegs, but this proved reasonably straightforward with wired nuts. The slab above, however, provided the hardest lead on the route, and involved teetering over a series of wet streaks with minimal protection.

We bivouacked on the terrace at the top of the slab, but not long after nightfall we were treated to a storm even worse than the night before. At first the storm centre was behind us, somewhere over Mont Blanc, but suddenly it moved very close. Without warning there was a deafening bang and we were both thrown up into the air. My head felt as though it had been hit with a sledgehammer, and I was aware of a strong smell of cordite. We realized we'd been struck by a ground current, and it was at least an hour before we had stopped shaking enough to get to sleep.

Dawn was a misty, murky affair, but before long we were heading up towards Pointe Walker with fresh snow covering the upper part of the Tronchey arête. Later that evening, back in Chamonix, we found a scorch mark on my helmet and three burn holes in the hood of my bivvy bag. We'd had a lucky escape, and I have been particularly wary of lightning ever since.

Epilogue

Describing the moment when Gagliardone and he reached the summit of the Jorasses after their successful ascent of the E face, Gervasutti wrote:

> We felt no shiver of joy, no ecstasy in victory. We had reached our objective, and already it lay behind us. How much finer it would be . . . to long for something all one's life, to fight for it without respite, and never to achieve it!

Down in the valley again, he decided that he 'should at once look around for another goal, and if it didn't exist . . . create it!'

Sadly, this was Gervasutti's last great climb. He died in 1946 whilst trying to free a jammed abseil rope when retreating down a rock pillar on the E face of Mont Blanc du Tacul. This had all the makings of a typical Gervasutti climb, being a fine line in a remote and serious situation. The pillar was climbed five years later, and today it is considered to be one of the finest routes in the Mont Blanc range. As a tribute, it was named in memory of Gervasutti. Ironically, with the ease of access from the Midi téléphérique, the route is now more popular than any of his actual ascents.

REFERENCE

1   G Gervasutti, *Gervasutti's Climbs* (translated by Nea Morin and Janet Adam Smith). London (Hart-Davis), 1957. (Reprinted, Diadem, 1978.)

More about the Fifties

JOHN HUNT

(Plates 52–55)

Hamish Nicol's personal account of his climbs in the 1950s (*AJ95*, 85–94, 1990/91) is a useful contribution to the annals of mountaineering, for he records some of the activities of a promising young generation whose first opportunity to extend their skills as rock-climbers came with the ending of the Second World War; some of them have achieved great deeds in the past 30 years. In following the lead provided by Hamish my motive is, admittedly, indulgence of a personal nostalgia. But it may be of interest to add to his reminiscences the doings during those years of some of us from an older generation who first saw the Alps shortly after a previous war which ended in 1918. Our ambitions and achievements were more modest and our failures were probably more numerous, but I doubt if we lacked any of the enthusiasm for the Alps which was evinced by Hamish, when we first returned there after 1945. He wrote: 'When I first saw the Alps in 1949 I nearly fell out of the train in my excitement.' So did I! I recall my emotions in August 1949 as being akin to a renewed love affair, as the little red train carried me up the Nikolaital to join Douglas Side at an Alpine Club meet in Täsch; it was one of several meets which the Club organized at that time to help alpine beginners. I stood, in a state of euphoria, on the open platform at the end of the carriage, the better to view the meadows and forests and to catch a glimpse of the great peaks at the head of the valley.

During the following week of fine, hot weather our climbs were attuned to the lack of experience of our clients and to our proper sense of tutorial responsibility. We traversed the Allalinhorn and the Alphubel; followed the splendid ridge of Hohberghorn, Stecknadelhorn, Nadelhorn and Lenzspitze, and climbed the Dom before moving up to Zermatt, whence some climbed the Matterhorn. The week ended on a high note with a traverse of the glorious SW ridge (Rothorngrat) of the Zinalrothorn. By a lucky chance George Finch, one of my boyhood heroes, with his wife and daughter Bunty, with whom I had climbed on Skye three years earlier, were at the hut when we returned. With them was Josef Knubel of St Niklaus, then in his seventies, famed for his exploits with Geoffrey Winthrop Young and other British climbers of that earlier generation.

During 1950–52 I was serving on the Allied Staff at Fontainebleau, and this provided many opportunities for my wife and myself to make short sorties to the French Alps. I longed to return to the Dauphiné, where I had spent three seasons more than 20 years earlier. We were joined by another companion from that holiday on Skye, John Hartog. In July 1950 we headed south through Bourg-Saint-Maurice and drove up towards the Col du Lautaret, pausing in La Grave to make enquiries of my guides of those early years, who had accompanied me over the Meije, the Tour Carrée de Roche-Méane and other climbs. The names of Jouffray and Dode featured on several tombstones in the graveyard: 'fusillé par les Allemands'. I was relieved to discover that Paul and Georges had survived, but 20 years were to pass before we were to meet again. From the col we drove down to the village of Ailefroide, the hillsides fragrant with the scent of lavender, and pitched our tent on the Pré de Madame Carle; it was a peaceful alpine pasture at that time.

We had set ourselves a strenuous programme for the first week: a traverse of the three peaks of the Agneaux, of the Pelvoux by the Arête de la Momie, followed by the Ecrins and down to La Bérarde to meet Bryan Donkin and a formidable quartet of fellow *Bleausards*: Pierre Allain, Bernard Pierre, Jean Deudon and Dr Jean Carle. While we were there, I was delighted to meet again my old guide Elie Richard of Saint-Christophe, who had led me over the Ecrins and on other climbs 20 years earlier. In the following week our Anglo-French party traversed the Râteau from the Brèche de la Meije and the Aiguille Dibona by its E face (Voie Boëll). On our way back to Ailefroide we enjoyed a stroll up the Pic Coolidge. The need for that relaxation was mainly due to the truly appalling weather we had experienced.

The Pelvoux traverse had been made in a drizzle of sleet and near-zero visibility. On the upper rocks of the Momie arête a ledge had collapsed and precipitated me down the mountain. Joy, hugging her holds for dear life, had checked my fall after some 40 feet. On the Râteau, to which we had turned after finding the Grande Muraille of the Meije plastered with new snow, we were struck by an electrical storm near the summit. All that had contributed to an exciting first alpine season for Joy. But there were more excitements in store. A few days later we were struck by lightning during a traverse of the NW and central summits of the Ailefroide, experiencing several heavy blows on various parts of our anatomy before we managed to find shelter. I have seldom felt more thankful than at the moment when, in mist, darkness and by chance, we reached the cairn marking the ordinary way from the Col des Frères Chamoix and groped our way down to the Sélé hut after a 19-hour day.

The final adventure for us during that dismal month of July took place on the Drus, from which the weather had earlier forced us to retreat. Some distance up the Petit Dru Joy received a nasty head wound from a rock dislodged from above us: helmets were not in fashion in those days. Fortunately we had a 'shell' dressing in our first-aid kit and she valiantly insisted on continuing the climb. But we were much slowed down; other parties far outdistanced us during the somewhat indeterminate descent from the Grand Dru, and we lost more time in route-finding. Among those who passed us were Hermann Buhl and Kuno Rainer, who had come up the N face. We reached the Charpoua hut in full moonlight at 10.30pm. Messrs Saxby and Viney were there, and they told us that Tom Bourdillon and Hamish Nicol, who had been in the hut when we had made our earlier attempt, had bivouacked beneath the N face and were to attempt it next day.

The weather had the last word that season. John Hartog and I had left the Leschaux hut to traverse the Rochefort ridge over Mont Mallet. But the clouds rapidly built up and we were delayed by the intricacies of the Périades glacier. In despondent mood, we made our way towards the Montanvers. It was just as well, for a spectacular storm overtook us, unleashing some major rock-falls and dispatching a few giant boulders down the mountainside from the foot rocks of the Grépon. It was a truly Wagnerian display of natural forces, such as I have seldom seen before or since.

Chamonix was then, as now, a great meeting-place for British climbers. Michael Ward was there with an Oxford party; so was Basil Goodfellow with a group from the Rucksack Club. And we met many French friends: Gaston Rébuffat had just returned from Annapurna, and our meeting that summer gave rise to several climbs and ski-tours during our subsequent visits to Chamonix. Our meeting with Basil led to our climbs in 1951, when we joined him and his companions Michael Wilson, Ian Charleson and Frankie Mayo in the Valais. That was a season of happy memory, blessed by good weather and unattended by alarms. We camped at Saas Almagell, traversed the Allalinhorn by its pleasant E ridge, and the Rimpfischhorn from north to south. From that mountain we descended to Zermatt, whence we climbed the Zinalrothorn and that delightful little near-fourthousander, the Schalihorn. It had been our intention to traverse that peak in order to reach the Weisshorn hut, but fresh snow would have made that move dangerous. So we returned to the Rothorn hut and, with Charles Warren, traversed the Obergabelhorn over the Wellen-kuppe and the Arbengrat. Two days later, on the summit of the Dom, a majority decision in our rope of three not to follow the ridge across to the Täschhorn caused dismay to the leader, but my spirits were revived when, after another false start, Basil Goodfellow and I traversed the Weisshorn by its E and N ridges. We were enveloped in mist on the summit of the Bishorn and had to spend a most uncomfortable night among boulders above the seracs of the Bis glacier. Little did I realize that this partnership with Basil, who was then the Secretary of the Alpine Club, would lead me to the Everest expedition two years later.

Military duties and the preparations for that expedition almost ruled out any climbing in the Alps in 1952; among the few opportunities, attempts on Mont Blanc on skis from the Grands Mulets and on the traverse of the Trois Cols from the Albert Premier hut were thwarted by the weather. But at the close of the year there was one light-hearted success, when Charles Wylie and I climbed the Mönch in December from the Jungfraujoch, while we were testing equipment for the Everest expedition. We had so many samples of high-altitude boot on offer that we resorted to wearing a different boot on each foot, during each of the four days of those trials.

After Everest, it was a great joy to return to the Alps. Notwithstanding his touch of *amertume*, I felt some sympathy with Eric Shipton, who is on record as having said at that time: 'Thank goodness, Everest has been climbed. We can now get back to some real climbing.' But 1954 was another dismal year for us.

Bad weather dogged most of our plans around the Chamonix valley, and the record was largely of failures. Wilfrid Noyce, Michael Ward, David Cox and I were forced to turn back within a few hundred feet of the summit of the Peigne by its NW ridge. A similar fate attended Noyce and myself on the Frontier ridge of Mont Blanc; the summit was a scene of turmoil and we had no choice but to return on the more sheltered side of the mountain to the Col de la Fourche, after arriving close to the summit ridge. But these were satisfying failures, for we had pushed the attack to the limits of common sense. In that miserable season, we were even grateful for such trivialities as the Aiguille de l'M, the Petits Charmoz, the Clochers Clochetons and the Aiguille de Belvédère. Our only success of any merit was the double traverse of that superb snow arête, the Rochefort ridge from the Géant and back. My reverse in 1950 made this success the sweeter.

1955 made ample amends for the previous year. I have described our climbs from Les Contamines, and the double traverse of Mont Blanc, from the Durier to the Torino huts and our return over the Voie de la Sentinelle, in *AJ*93, 123–128, 1988/89. While waiting for the weather to improve for that return journey, we greatly enjoyed a social round in and around Courmayeur. It was a joy to meet again Toni Gobbi and his wife; it was Toni who had led a group of guides from Courmayeur to greet Hermann Buhl and some members of the 1953 Everest expedition, during the celebrations in Genoa for the 500th anniversary of the birth of Christopher Columbus. We met Roger Chorley and Ted Wrangham, who had returned from the Peuterey ridge; Roger was suffering from frostbite. Ubaldo Rey, recently returned from K2, was at the Pavillon de Frêtey. Una Cameron gave us a welcome hot bath in her chalet while she cruised around in her cold swimming-pool, smoking her habitual cigar. A German party entertained us in their camp beneath the Brenva face, where they had been waiting for 10 days to climb Mont Blanc. We were besieged by hordes of ecstatic Italian holiday-makers who pestered us for autographs. But despite all this *dolce vita* we did manage to climb the Aiguille de la Brenva by its E face and Grand Dièdre.

After the return to Chamonix over Mont Blanc, our last climb that season was the *intégrale* on the Moine by its SW and N ridges, a most satisfying expedition during which, I recall, we made at least nine rappels on the descent to the Talèfre glacier, in a thunderstorm. On that high note I was able to join the celebrations of the *Fête des Guides* in Chamonix with all the more zest, in the good company of Maurice Herzog, Lionel Terray, Louis Lachenal, André Frison-Roche, André Tournier and Gaston Cathiard – not to mention the dazzling Denise Perrier, 'Miss World' in that year.

At the end of July 1956, David Cox and I were about to set off for the Strahlegg hut to climb the Schreckhorn, having climbed the Wetterhorn and the Klein Schreckhorn by its interesting W face. We called at Alfred Bhend's shop in Grindelwald to leave our spare baggage. 'Have you heard the news?', he asked. Two British climbers had been killed in the Baltschiedertal; one of them was a member of the British Everest team. Of course I knew this was Tom Bourdillon, who had told me of his plans a few days earlier in London. Stunned by the tragedy, David and I caught the earliest train to Brig, whence we were taken to Visp by the head of the Swiss rescue service. Hamish Nicol has recalled the event in last year's journal, so I will not attempt to describe the shock and sorrow of the whole British climbing community during that period. I was much involved in the funeral arrangements and in contacting friends and relatives at home, in Chamonix and Zermatt.

Despite our sadness, it seemed best to resume our programme. Robin Hodgkin had joined us and we returned to Grindelwald, going straight up to the Guggi hut, *en route* for the Jungfrau by that route. The weather was very bad next morning and we could do no better than reconnoitre the way up the Kühlauenen glacier; it provided us with some useful practice in ice techniques to negotiate some of the crevasses. The Guggi route has an evil reputation for its crevasses and we took the precaution of further practice from the rafters in the hut that evening. The morning of 4 August brought little comfort but we decided to ignore the forecast and, retracing our steps, pushed on over the Schneehorn and up the notorious Giessen glacier to the Silberlücke. By now the weather had worsened and visibility was closing in as we started up the final ridge towards the Jungfrau.

It soon became clear that a traverse of the mountain to the Jungfraujoch was out of the question; indeed, the only option open to us was to retrace our steps and beat a hasty retreat. But our up-tracks had already been obliterated; in a near whiteout, David Cox suddenly disappeared and fell 60 feet into a hidden crevasse. Our rehearsals of the previous day now stood us in good stead, but David was very fortunate to emerge with little damage. According to my diary, it was 'the nearest possible thing to disaster'.

Messrs Eggler, Reiss and Reist of the successful 1956 Swiss expedition to Everest were in Grindelwald when we returned, and David and I accepted Ernst Reiss's invitation to accompany him to Mürren, with the promise to take us up a sensational new route which he had just made on the Gspaltenhorn. This venture proved to be a hilarious fiasco, for our host succeeded in losing his way in thick mist, on his own home ground. The outcome was a sleepless night in a cowshed among a herd of heifers, to the accompaniment of bells and bellows. Next day we emerged into the same pea soup of mist and drizzle, and there was nothing for it but to cross the Sefinen Furka and descend to Spiez. It was sheer bathos, but Ernst is one of those endearing companions whose endless cheerful chatter can compensate for any disappointment.

From Spiez we took the train to Chamonix to join Gaston Rébuffat, Noyce and Ward, with the Innominata ridge of Mont Blanc in our sights. Once again we were thwarted, for on reaching the Col de l'Innominata we found the rocks covered with new snow; it was raining hard. We made a start across to the Col des Dames Anglaises on the Peuterey ridge but, seeing a large group of climbers already on the Brèche, we realized that the refuge would be full. So we retreated to the Gamba hut in high dudgeon. Alan Blackshaw and Bob Downes, whom we had met earlier in the day while descending on foot from the Torino, had arrived and, next day, we all returned to Courmayeur. It was some compensation to meet other British friends there. Alfred Gregory had returned from making a new route on the Tour des Grandes Jorasses with Ghiglione; Roger Chorley and Alfred Tissières were also in the town.

Our party then moved up to the Requin hut, having decided to climb at a lower altitude for the time being. We hoped to trace a route on the E face of the Requin, which was described in vague terms in our guidebook. 12 August turned out to be a beautiful day, but the route eluded us at about half height on the face, at a point where we found two pitons. Surmising that this must have been the highest point reached by the would-be pioneers, we moved across to the excellent Mayer–Dibona route on the right and followed it to the top. Our fruitless searches had delayed us and we arrived with the onset of darkness, which forced us to spend a cold and cheerless night wedged in the Cheminée Fontaine. Somehow we survived this ordeal, helped by two prunes, a few lumps of sugar and a packet of glucose. I recall a slow and insecure descent next morning on the steep, frozen slopes, with no crampons and only one ice axe in the party.

My last summer season in the 1950s was, appropriately, the Centenary Meet of the Alpine Club in Zermatt in 1957, when I was President. Joy and I enjoyed a number of climbs in the good company of Swiss and British friends. An Anglo-Swiss party which included Edouard Wyss-Dunant (leader of the first Swiss attempt on Everest in 1952), Anthony Rawlinson, John Tyson, Joy and myself traversed the Lyskamm. After the return to the Bétemps hut, another joint climb was made over the Breithorn via that superb route, the Kleintriftje ('Young') Grat. My companions were Eggler and Luchsinger of the 1956 Everest expedition, Fritz Ganssen, Band, Brasher, Hobhouse and Tyson. A few days later, Tyson, Hobhouse and I, with Mike Banks and two Marine corporals, made the direct finish of the S face of the Obergabelhorn. Towards the end of the meet Joy and I, with John Hobhouse, were involved in a dramatic rescue of another British 'rope' which was stranded overnight on the summit of the Alphubel. We climbed that mountain by its Rotgrat, and effected the rescue of our marooned compatriots just before a team of guides came up from Saas Fee, with Geiger circling in the mists above us.

There had also been high drama on the Obergabelhorn. On the final pitches a local guide, Elias Julen, with a French client, whom we had met on the Breithorn, were stranded and *in extremis* on a slab beneath the final chimney. They were exceedingly fortunate to have a rope thrown down to them from the summit by another party which had just arrived there over the Wellenkuppe and E ridge. But perhaps the most enjoyable events during that eventful season were modest family affairs. With a few Alpine Club colleagues, I was able to introduce our daughter Susan to her first alpine climbs, on the Pointe de Zinal and the Untergabelhorn.

Among the many alpine seasons which I have enjoyed, I recall with the greatest delight the months spent in the Alps during the early part of the decade of the fifties. The good memories are not only of our climbs, our successes and failures, nor of the alarms which accompanied some of those excursions. At least as happy was the background: the environment and ambience in which we walked and climbed, uncrowded by hordes of tourists, undistracted by the noise of traffic, undismayed by commercial development in the valleys, unaided by the ugly technology of the skiing industry. For myself, at the end of the 1940s, there was that sense of wonder in rediscovering a world to which I thought I had bidden farewell at the onset of the war.

Yet Another High-Level Route

DAVID BRETT DUFFIELD

(Plates 56,57)

Seven years ago I had the good fortune to be able to make a 'Grand High-Level Route' from La Bérarde in the Dauphiné Alps to Heiligenblut at the foot of the Grossglockner, over a period of 44 days, solo, and taking in several good summits and over 30 major passes and cols. (Accounts of this route appear in *Climber and Rambler* for April, May and June 1982; *AJ87*, 41–45, 1982; and my book *High Level, The Alps from End to End*, Gollancz, 1983.) Then, looking across through breaks in the cloud as I stumbled along through the Valais and Lepontine Alps, I would imagine another, shorter, but more intensive excursion, running the length of the Bernese and Glarner Alps, from Lake Geneva towards Liechtenstein. This I have now managed to complete, despite mishaps and bad weather. It has taken me two attempts, and I haven't done it clear through in one push, as it ought to be done. But here it is, for anyone else to try. It offers a remarkable, varied and punishing experience.

For a variety of reasons I have done these and other high-level routes alone. This is not a good idea unless you have both the temperament and the experience, and these are two imponderables that one can hardly assess for oneself. The less said about solo glacier travel, the better. In my view the expedition described below would be a superb three-week tour for a party seeking to get all-round mountain experience and enjoyment. There is much to be said for a party of four, since that allows for all sorts of contingencies; but it would require from everyone the same hard-nosed commitment.

Here, then, is a description of a 'Northern High-Level Route'. The aim is to get from west to east by the most direct route through the mountains north of the Rhône–Rhine trench; to take in summits, and to have as many mountaineering days as possible within about three weeks. The starting line is the Col du Pillon above Les Diablerets; the finish is the head of the Linthal valley. For most sections this is the best direction, and it ends with an ascent of the Tödi. The best time to start is early to mid-July.

Section One: Wildstrubel etc

1. From the Col du Pillon, walk or ride up to the Cabane des Diablerets. From here, by far the most pleasant way is to descend north-east, toward the Olden alp, and round to some excellent camp-sites on the snowy terrace below the E face of the Oldenhorn. In the morning, climb the Oldenhorn (3125m) by the face and the E ridge. Early in the season this is a pleasant snowy mountain; later it becomes a heap of loose shale. Descend on to the Tsanfleuron glacier. Descend

30. *Wedge Peak, c6410m, an eastern outlier of Muztagh Ata.* (Matthew Cobham) (p 80)

31. *Orina I, 5450m, from Orina II. The ascent followed the spine left of centre.* (Matthew Cobham) (p 80)

32. *White Sail Peak, 5436m, from Torbelung valley. The ascent was via the snow ridge on the left.* (Stephen Edwards) (p 80)

33. *Nick Parks approaching the summit of White Sail Peak.* (David Arathoon) (p 80)

34. *The N face of Muztagh Ata, 7546m, from the Uzun Jilgha valley.* (Stephen Edwards) (p 80)

35. *Crossing the Konsiver river between Aktash and Karakol.* (David MacGregor) (p 80)

36. *Marloes Hopkins de Groot approaching the 'Pass of the Travellers'.* (David Hopkins) (p 87)

37. *David Hopkins on the Radelzny ridge: the buttress above the Radelzny-Lenin col.* (M H de Groot) (p 87)

38. *The summit of Peak Lenin.* (David Hopkins) (p 87)

39. *Peak Lenin: ascent from Camp 1 to Camp 2.* (David Hopkins) (p 87)

40. *Southern Alps: looking N from Elie de Beaumont.* (John Harding) (p 98)

41. Southern Alps: Mt Aspiring, 3027m, from the south. (John Harding) (p 98)

42. The Haast range, with Nick Cradock, guide. (John Harding) (p 98)

43. *Rolling Pin, 2245m.* (John Harding) (p 98)

44. *Elie de Beaumont, 3117m, from Mt Broderick.* (John Harding) (p 98)

45. Southern Alps: Classen Saddle, looking NE. (John Harding) (p 98)

46. Mt Broderick, 2637m. (John Harding) (p 98)

the glacier and follow a shallow valley, taking a cairned path leftwards across limestone pavements down to the Col du Sanetsch. There is a small chalet restaurant some distance down the track south of the col that is worth visiting, because for this long section you have to be carrying food for three nights and four days.

2. From the Col du Sanetsch walk up the long but pleasant shaly ridge to the east until you come to a level shoulder below the Arpelistock (3035m). This can be easily climbed from here. Traverse right across steep snow at the head of a cwm, toward point 2598m; cross over the col and traverse hummocky ground toward the lake at 2471m. This can be tough going if the snow is lying deep. Good camp-sites. Walk up snow and moraine into the enclosed south-western cwm of the Wildhorn. Climb up steep snow and bands of loose rock to gain a level shoulder below the last of the rock-towers that descend from the southern summit of the Wildhorn. A magnificent viewpoint! Descend into a boulder and snow-filled hollow and then traverse on scree and steep snow below two prominent pinnacles (some stonefall). Climb up to a level shoulder and then round the foot of a buttress. Beyond, follow a snowy valley on to the upper part of the glacier plateau, from which the summit (3248m) is easily reached by a pleasant ridge. Descend north-eastward by easy snow and rock outcrops, and go down into a curving snow and scree-filled valley. Take to its left slopes to traverse well above the small lake, making toward a rocky shoulder above the lake. In thawing snow this can be an unpleasant section. Follow cairns across limestone pavements and hummocks round to the track over the Rawilpass. Wide meadows provide beautiful camp-sites.

3. Do not go as far as the pass, but head off east of a marshy depression. Follow a steepening cwm that leads to the Wildstrubel hut and the radar station. A well-marked path leads up and over to the Plaines Mortes icefield. Trek across this polar landscape, a marvellous place in the early morning, and climb the Wildstrubel (3244m) by its easy SW ridge. Descend the Wildstrubel glacier to the Lämmern hut. Thence follow paths down to the Gemmipass and Leukerbad. In bad weather you can escape south by retreating to point 2808m on the rim of the icefield and, by passing east of the easternmost stream, descend on very steep scree and steep snow into the cwm known as Les Outannes. From below this cwm an intermittent track runs across steep slopes to the Varner alp, and finally, by means of a *via ferrata*, descent can be made into the Leukerbad valley. Camp-site and provisions.

Note: if there is much late snow, these three days will have been hard work. In cloud some of the route-finding requires great precision.

4. Take a pleasant path up toward the Gitzifurrgu. Reach this little pass by the snowy terrace on the south side of the valley, below the Ferdenrothorn (3180m). This peak can be climbed by a snow couloir that rises from the terrace about half a mile from the top of the pass. Descend steep snow to the Lötschenpass, where there is a small hut. From here, the Hockenhorn (3293m) S face is a recommended route. Take good paths, well marked, down to Lauchernalp, Weritz and either Blatten or Fafleralp. There are no supplies at

Fafleralp, but a useful bus runs up and down the Lötschental. The walk down to Fafleralp is extremely beautiful, with wonderful vistas. There are numerous good camp-sites in the upper valley, but especially at or shortly beyond Gugginalp.

Section Two: The Bernese Alps

This is the highest section of the route, and is extensively covered in the appropriate guidebooks which should be used together with these notes. The route follows a well-established line and there will usually be tracks on the glaciers. It will certainly be best to use the huts and to send your camping gear round by post-bus.

1. Reach the Hollandia hut by the Lang glacier. This glacier is much crevassed and could be nasty; make sure you are on it and off it before the sun is up. The Hollandia hut is usually without a guardian in July.

2. Descend the Aletsch glacier to Konkordia; the section around the promontory on which the hut stands requires care later in the day. If the conditions are good, continue on without stopping, over the Grünhornlücke to the Finsteraarhorn hut.

3. From the hut take the little path and snow-slopes that lead over the steep rocky Gemslücke and across an easy glacier to the Oberaarjoch and its hut. From here descend the Oberaar glacier and walk lengthily to the Grimselpass. A long day.

   The number of peaks that can be climbed on this section depends, of course, on the ambition and ability of the party. The great prize is the Finsteraarhorn (4274m) but other tops, well within most capabilities, lie directly above the line of travel and do not require an extra day. This is the finest, most entirely high-mountain environment in Europe, and to cross it in good weather is a wonderful experience.

   In bad weather there will be problems; if it is very bad, you will have to descend lengthily down the Aletsch glacier to Fiesch. To descend the Fiescher glacier seems to be a really bad idea; it is very crevassed and awkward. An interesting alternative would be to cross over the Beichpass from the foot of the Lang glacier and descend to Belalp.

4. Establish yourself either at the Grimselpass, or at camp-sites at Oberwald or Handegg, south or north of the pass. There are buses four times a day back and forth.

   Take a day off. Have a beer. Sleep. Eat. Eat some more!

Section Three: Furka

Up to now the route has been extremely direct; around the Furkapass there is no obvious line to follow, but there are three or more worthwhile alternatives.

(a) From the Grimselpass reach the Rhône glacier by way of the rocky hills known as the Nägelisgrätli; good paths. From the foot of the Rhône glacier, climb the Dammastock (3630m) and descend its E face to the Damma hut and the Göschenen valley.

(b)   From Handegg or the Grimselpass, reach the Gelmer hut. Climb the Tieralplistock (3383m) and traverse the ridge between the Rhône and Trift glaciers all the way around the Dammastock summit; then descend as in (a). At the right time this is superb.

(a) and (b) are both substantial mountaineering days; they would certainly be better in the other direction, because going west to east one must descend the Dammastock E face late in the day. This face has three or more steep but apparently straightforward snow-ice and mixed routes on it, which are quite often climbed from the Damma hut. My intention was to follow alternative (b); but the weather was vile and so I went by (c)! This gives two short mountain days (or one long one), with access to the Galenstock (3583m) and many good smaller peaks.

(c)   From the top of the Furkapass (reached pleasantly by walking from Oberwald or the Grimselpass, or by bus) take a good path toward and across the snout of the Sidelen glacier to a small hut; then up a slope of snow and rocks to cross the Unterbüelenlücke. Descend into the glacier cwm beyond and pass below the face of the Gross Büelenhorn and across the snout of the Tiefen glacier toward the Albert Heim hut. It is not necessary to climb up to the hut; cross moraine to find a well-marked path leading round below a rocky promontory. When it starts to descend to Realp, watch out for a painted sign on the rocks reading 'Winterlücke' and 'Lochberglücke'. The Winterlücke leads to the Damma hut; the Lochberglücke track, after a while, winds up across terraces to reach a col west of point 2865m; from here it descends below the Lochberg to a moraine lake at point 2515m, and then down toward the dam. In good weather a traverse of the Lochberg (3074m) from the Winterlücke to the moraine lake is a popular route locally. There are excellent camp-sites below point 2515m on slabby terraces, or on the meadows below the dam.

    This alternative is full of interesting peaks. The Gross Büelenhorn (3206m) has two fine ridges and a face on which there is now a 'modern' route demanding a rack of gear. The Winterstock (3203m) is very attractive; a miniature Dru. The Müeterlishorn peaks are superb and easily reached from point 2515m; they give a wealth of excellent routes on good rock. The area is well worth a visit.

    The meadows below the dam are popular with German rock-climbers visiting the Salbitschijen; there are great roadside crags in the valley with routes of all standards. There are occasional buses to Göschenen, and a pleasant valley path.

Section Four: Glarner Alps
1.   From Göschenen (where there is no camping) one is faced with an immense task – climbing 1700m up the Riental, to cross the Rientallücke into the upper Fellital. This brings the Bächenstock (2944m) and the Schijenstock (2885m) into reach, but this route will be taken only by the purist. The rest of us will take a train through the gorges to Andermatt (where there is camping), and then, with mechanical assistance, reach the Stöckli and follow the military track above the Oberalppass road, to cross the Fellilücke. Fine camp-sites halfway

down the Fellital. From this valley there is much low-altitude climbing to be done; the Diederberg peaks to the west have many summits, and a complete traverse would be a great expedition. To the east there are the face of the Fedenstock (2985m) and the spurs of the Sunnig Wichel. There are new routes to be done here.

2. Descend toward the Tresch hut and climb lengthily and steeply up to the Börtlilücke; there is a wonderful camp-site half-way. Descend to Spillaui Alp and thence to camp-sites below the Etzli hut. A great day of tough walking. The Sunnig Wichel (2911m) is a fine rock-peak; it can be climbed from the pass directly. The Piz Giuv can be climbed from Spillaui by crossing below the little lake and scrambling along the N ridge until at around 2800m it becomes steep and loose; from a small col descend leftward on to the glacier, ascend it and climb by steep snow and loose rocks to the summit (3096m).

3. From below the Etzli hut climb the stony track over the Chrüzlipass and down steeply into the upper Val Strem. Here there is magnificent camping; one can descend easily to Sedrun for supplies. The peaks around the Chrüzlipass are pleasant in July, but stony wastes in August. The S ridge of the Witenalpstock (3016m) is impressive.

4. Climb up grass, moraine and steep snow to reach the col 2841m south of the Oberalpstock (3327m); from here, climb to the summit by a glacier route. A very fine stubby mountain. Descend across the Brunni glacier to the Cavardiras hut. The upper part of the Val Cavardiras is very bleak and stony, but there is good camping further down at Alp Cavrein.

The best break for supplies on this section of the route is to cross the Brunnipass and descend by the pretty Lag Serein to Disentis, returning the same way. There is a first-class organized campingplatz one mile outside Disentis on the Lukmanier road; very good in bad weather.

5. From Alp Cavrein the most direct way is to take a faint trail round into Val Russein and follow paths up towards the Sandpass. There is an excellent 'shelter stone' in the upper part of the Val Russein after which the path and the paintmarks cease. The pass is reached by following a rising grass terrace past an obvious small pinnacle, and then climbing steep snow and loose rocks. On the other side, descend diagonally across the Sand glacier to its left hand (northern) bank and follow the path down, very pleasantly, to the Ober Sand chalets where there is perfect camping on meadows below fine glacier scenery.

The more mountainous alternative is to take the Fuorcla da Cavrein and reach the upper part of the Hüfi glacier and traverse across to the Planura hut (usually no warden). This way, several good climbs can be made – notably, the Düssistock (3256m), the Piz Cambrialas (3208m) and the Clariden (3267m). There are also more serious ways still.

6. From Ober Sand a traversing path rises and falls round the flanks of the Tödi, to the Fridolin and Grünhorn huts, from which the Tödi (3614m) may be climbed to give a magnificent finale to the whole journey. Thence descend at length through fine gorges to Tierfed and the town of Linthal (where there is no camping).

An alternative to this would be to climb the Tödi from the Val Russein by one of the huge couloirs and high cols that lead on to the upper Biferten glacier; this is a very substantial undertaking, full of interest and originality. Though the summits in this region are not very high, the vertical intervals match most places in the Alps.

Beyond Tierfed one could extend the traverse over the Hausstock and as far as the Piz Sardona, but there is no natural line to take. All things considered, Linthal is the best conclusion to a remarkable expedition.

The length of time to be taken will depend on the combination of the weather and the ambition of the party, but three weeks would be a good period to set aside. My time of 24 nights was spread over two attempts, both with some very bad weather.

Equipment? This is essentially old-fashioned mountaineering, made easier with modern materials. The basic rule is – MINIMUM GEAR, MAXIMUM FOOD. The more food you can carry the less you will be rushed and the more choices you can make; thus you have both greater pleasure and more safety. On the whole, British parties carry more gear than they need or use. The only place you will want more than the minimum may be in Section Three, where a good range of rock-climbing can be had; in this case, have a spare sack and send it ahead of you by post-bus. One long axe per rope is a very good thing to have; or better still, a metal ski-pole with detachable basket. A helmet is a nuisance but a rain-cape is a good idea. Yeti-style gaiters should be discarded for short 'stop-touts'. Spare sunglasses and ample sun and lip cream are essentials. The crucial ingredient is the right attitude. Never hurry. Get up early. Think. If is as hard to make the right decisions in this as in any other form of mountaineering. The only way to learn is to get out and do it. Once you have successfully completed a high-level route of this kind, you know you have got very close to an understanding of the mountains.

Of course, the really big one, the Grand Slam of all alpine high-level routes, begins at Nice and ends in Trieste . . . any takers?

A Night in a Hole in the Ground

ALAN HARRIS

The lightning and thunder were getting closer to each other, and therefore to us, and our ice axes were tuning up. It started to hail, so we hastily discarded the axes and slithered down the rock to be well away from them.

We were at the highest point of our walk, at Babilonia (2990m) on the rock shoulder south-east of Pizzo Bianco, which is south-west of Staffa, Macugnaga.

After the hail came torrential rain. We stood through it all. Eventually the storm moved away. We were wet and so, more importantly, was the rock. That slowed us considerably once we had recovered our axes and started moving again. We descended 575 metres, crossing from Babilonia; it took a long time.

By 10pm we were still high on the south-west side of the Val Quarazza. It was too dark to continue safely and we had to admit that our return to the rest of our party at Pecetto that night was impossible.

Jim found the hole. It was clean and dry, about eight feet long, inclined downwards from the entrance into the mountainside and just wide enough for the two of us. The entrance enabled us to slide through, one at a time. Once inside it was barely possible to sit upright. If the weather worsened during the night we should be well out of it.

Supper was eaten in the open, for the wind had dropped, and by 10.30pm we were in our shelter and lying full-length with arms wrapped round each other. 'Hypothermia is now the only slight risk we run, even at this time of year,' (early July), I had said – this was our first night out together – 'so we must keep as warm as possible.' Both of us were shivering, but after a while that stopped.

'Babilonia is certainly an appropriate name for the place where the storm hit us,' said Jim, 'but why us? We've hardly feasted from forbidden vessels, either on our way across the snow or outside this hole, and concubines are out of the question these days.' 'That was the writing on the wall, Jim. We have been weighed in the balances, and found wanting, or we wouldn't be here.'

Our climb from Pecetto up to the col near Pizzo Nero had taken slightly less time than I had estimated, which was satisfying. But the plain fact was that we should have started at least three hours earlier than we did. Fancy waiting for the Post Office to open before going on a 12-hour walk! Our enthusiasm had overrun judgement. Certainly the storm had been a major contributory factor, otherwise we would have returned to wife and friends before midnight – too late for dinner, but at least we would have slept in our own beds.

We dozed intermittently and uncomfortably on our rocky floor. Every so often we had to change position: as soon as we separated we started shivering, which died away some minutes after we were clasped in each other's arms again.

'I can see lights,' said Jim. His position enabled him to see out of the hole – I could not. 'Must be lightning,' said I. 'Funny kind of lightning, for there's no thunder.' 'It's a long way away, that's why.' 'They're out looking for us,' said Jim, a possibility I was loath to concede. Nevertheless, we scrambled out. It was midnight.

There were lights, indeed, and we watched them for a while. They resembled sheet lightning more than anything else, but with rare bursts of light high above us. They had no obvious origin or direction and, what seemed most relevant, there was no discernible pattern to them. 'Simply a meteorological phenomenon,' I said dismissively. 'Or perhaps the Italian army is on manoeuvres with searchlights.' Jim insisted: 'If people are looking for us what should we do?' 'Stay by our hole and, if you want, blow the standard signal on your whistle, while I will find a vantage point from which I will flash the signal with the torch.' So that is what we did for half an hour. I could scarcely hear Jim's whistle for the noise made by a stream, while I shone the torch into cloud drifting below as well as above us. We soon felt the futility of what we were doing, but the issue was decided for us by the onset of severe shivering, so we crept back into our hole. This time it was quite long before the shivering faded. Before getting back I had rearranged our ice axes on a flat rock, just in case Jim was right.

'Must move again,' said Jim, 'there's water dripping into my ear.' 'Often?' was my unfeeling response. 'Just move your head.'

We spent half the night talking, of course, particularly about what our party might be thinking and doing. My wife would, rightly, be angry because I had misjudged things so, as well as anxious because of the storm, and our friends would share her anxiety. They were not to know that we were sheltered, uninjured and not lost – if only we had had a radio-telephone! So we talked and dozed and shifted our bodies . . .

'It's light,' said Jim, waking me. We shuffled out and shook ourselves, ate most of our remaining food and, at 5.30am, started walking again, though very unsteadily at first. After half an hour or so we had warmed up, and our progress was faster. Then we heard a helicopter below us. I prepared to signal to it with the torch, but we never saw it.

The Sentiero Terzaghi, which had been our route from Piani alti di Rosareccio (above the Anza valley), ends by Bivacco Lanti on the mule-track north of Passo Turlo. We reached the shelter at 7am and knew that all we had to do was walk down Val Quarazza. 30 minutes later we met three mountaineers, one of three superbly equipped teams looking for us. They told us that one of the other teams had already reported finding the few steps I had cut in the ice on our way up to the col by Pizzo Nero. The one thing we had done right before departure had been to say where we were going! After satisfying themselves that we were unhurt and could still keep going, they escorted us down the path. Within a few minutes the helicopter reached us. Our rucksacks were thrown into the cabin, the crewman pulled Jim and me in and then the team leader. We flew down the valley and exactly five minutes later jumped out on to the public car park at Pecetto. There a doctor examined me thoroughly and declared me none the worse for our adventure. She just looked at Jim, who is young, tall and handsome. Clearly there was nothing wrong with him that a hot shower would not put right.

The appropriate flight details now appear in my flying log-book. The 'remarks' column reads 'Pronto Soccorso Alpino (after a night in a hole in the ground at 2500 metres with Jim Hart)'.

REFERENCE

Map 1: 35,000 Macugnaga e il Monte Rosa, published by Azienda Autonoma di Soggiorno di Macugnaga (1976).

A Zermatt Retrospect

PAULA BINER

(Plates 58, 59)

The Hotel Bahnhof was built by our father Alois Biner, around 1900. He married Bertha Varonier from Varen, a little village in the Rhône Valley above Leuk, in 1898. After managing the Buffet de la Gare in Visp for some years, my mother with her mother and sister moved to Zermatt. Here they rented the Hotel Gornergrat and ran it. Father Alois got his guide's certificate in 1892 and worked as a guide for more than 60 years. He was a guide with all his heart and never intended to become a hotel-keeper.

The newly-built Hotel Bahnhof was rented out to the Seiler Hotels as an annexe of the Hotel Victoria for a very long period. Grandmother and mother, who had both been in the hotel business, would have been prepared to take the Bahnhof into their hands, but taking care of a large household and raising seven children kept them more than busy. So we spent a wonderful youth in a quiet, unspoiled village and enjoyed the family life at home for which we are thankful to our dear parents and ancestors.

Our brother Bernard also became a guide in 1924 and worked in his profession with extraordinary skill and much love for the mountains. Both father and Bernard were great friends of the British climbers. With a large number of them they entertained a considerable friendship which our family still gladly remembers. Among so many others, I would like to mention the Rev Lord Gordon who climbed with father for a long period, year after year. Lord Gordon stayed at the Riffelalp Hotel and went climbing with his guide Alois all around the Alps, including the traverse of the high alpine passes with snow-shoes in spring. We also remember with much love the late Rt Rev Bishop of Leicester, Dr Ronald Williams and his wife, the late Mrs Cicely Williams, who were both great friends and climbing partners of father's as well as of Bernard's. They came to Zermatt regularly for very many years; Mrs Williams's last visit was in 1985, the year she died.

It was in 1951 that we took over the Hotel Bahnhof which had been rented to the Seilers up till then. It all started with a talk that Bernard had up at Riffelalp with Mrs Emeline Zschokke-Seiler, then manageress of the Riffelalp Hotel. She had received an enquiry from a French priest in Lyons who was looking for cheap accommodation for a group of students. Mrs Emeline encouraged Bernard to offer them room at the Bahnhof which had not been opened for some summers. The facilities there did not provide the necessary comfort as an annexe of the Hotel Victoria any more. In those days I myself worked at the tourist office in Zermatt, and I saw the great demand from tourists for a cheap place to stay. I felt sorry, knowing that at our hotel the shutters were closed. Bernard agreed to Mrs Zschokke's suggestion and told her that she could offer the accommodation to the college priest. But he then forgot all about it and never mentioned this to anyone in our family. On 28 July 1951, a fine summer day, the French priest knocked at our door at the Haus Rosa and asked for the promised lodging. Our surprise was great, the rooms were not ready and we were not prepared. But the group insisted, so with my parents' agreement I went to the Seilers' central office to collect the key. The management was quite prepared to release the contract and off I went and opened the entrance door of the Hotel Bahnhof. With the help of my sister we got the rooms ready, and this is how the family Alois Biner started running the Bahnhof.

Soon after this French group had left, climbers came to the door and asked for lodgings. In those days the hotel was the first building at the entrance of the village. Below it there were only meadows and fields. Many tourists came by bicycle and the first cheap place they saw they happily chose for spending the night. To more and more British climbers the Bahnhof became their favourite inn while in town.

Very soon we all realized that my sister Bertha and I were not able to cope with all the work that needed to be done, so Bernard too came to work with us. To our great surprise, even he got interested and helped wherever possible. After a serious illness, Bernard was not allowed to do hard climbs any more and it became his aim to undertake the necessary alterations to the building into which he put many hours of work and great skill. Yet he never gave up climbing completely.

My personal work at the hotel was a wonderful experience and with all of Bernard's help a real pleasure. Luckily, our dear father was still able to see how the hotel became a place much in demand by climbers. During our first summer season, he would come for a visit and watch with pleasure the start of our little family enterprise. It was in May 1952 that he passed away. Mother too was very happy to see how we managed. Her support and moral assistance helped us a great deal. It was good to know that our parents appreciated what we did. Mother died at the astonishing age of 90, in 1964.

At Easter 1952 we opened the hotel for the first time for spring skiing. The previous autumn Bernard, together with a friend, had installed electric heating. From then on the house was ready to receive winter guests as well.

Much sadness and worry overcame us at the sudden death of dear Bernard in April 1965. What will the Bahnhof become without him, and how am I to manage? After serious reflection and with advice from family members, I decided to carry on. Especially my brother-in-law, Elias Lauber, and his wife, my sister Pia, were of considerable support henceforth.

The summer of 1965 with its centenary celebrations of the first Matterhorn ascent will never be forgotten. Many climbing friends of Bernard's came to visit and to encourage me. This will always be gratefully remembered.

During the summer of 1966 many British climbers contributed to a commemoration plaque. It was unveiled in front of the hotel by the Rt Rev Bishop Williams in August 1966 in the presence of many English alpinists, of family members and of Bernard's friends. The inscription reads as follows:

GRATEFULLY REMEMBERING
BERNARD BINER

29th December 1900 – 9th April 1965

HIS BRITISH FRIENDS
COMMEMORATE WITH THIS TABLET
A GREAT GUIDE
AND A GOOD FRIEND TO ALL CLIMBERS

On 19 August 1986 the plaque was replaced by a new one made of Scottish granite with the same inscription. We treasure that gift and it gets lots of appreciation and praise from the hotel guests and from passers-by.

I myself was offered a fine present containing a watch, a barometer and a hydrometer with a very dear inscription. It has been of indescribable value for giving weather information to our guests. We consult it daily with success and feel grateful to the donors.

In 1960 the British mountaineers presented Bernard with a book for entries of successful climbs. It now contains a great number of entries and descriptions of exceptional interest, made by famous climbers from all over the world, and it evokes many fine memories.

During its existence the Bahnhof has known many highlights associated with successful climbs. The first British ascent of the Matterhorn N face occurred in summer 1961, the one of the S face in September 1966. Ever since there has been a Bahnhof, and up until today, very many important, difficult climbs and first ascents were undertaken by alpinists staying there. Besides the British, all possible nationalities are represented, such as the Austrian, German, French, Italian and Spanish, the Polish, Slovak and Czechoslovak, the American, Japanese and Korean and, of course, the Swiss. After their big achievements, it has been our joy and pride to welcome the happy climbers back to the hotel decorated with their respective national flag.

Of course there have also been sad times, with accidents occurring in the mountains. We have spend many worrying days waiting for climbers to come back and many a prayer has been sent to our Lord for a safe return. During those long hours, I felt most how helpless I really was without the assistance of Bernard who used to advise and inform the climbers before they set off for the hard routes.

You might like to know what changes there have been observed in the mountaineering scene during the past 40 years. Nowadays, among the alpinists who intend to reach one of the surrounding peaks, especially the Matterhorn, there tend to be more and more of those who underestimate the seriousness and dangers of the mountains. Earlier on, climbers liked to spend more time acclimatizing and getting themselves prepared for a demanding ascent.

Numerous were and still are British mountaineers as well as mountaineers from all over the world who enter our door and who keep coming year after year, renewing our friendship. We only hope that the young generation will also keep up with this tradition and consider the Bahnhof as their home. They must know that they will always be very welcome.

The 125th Anniversary of the First Ascent of the Matterhorn

and a personal Reminiscence

JOHN HUNT

(Plates 60, 61)

It was 25 years ago that my wife and I, with other members of the Alpine Club, attended the festivities in Zermatt and Breuil which marked the centenary of the first and second ascents of the Matterhorn, on 14 and 16 July 1865. Bad weather somewhat marred the excellent Swiss programme, not least an attempt on the Hörnli ridge by an Anglo-Swiss rope composed of Albert Eggler and Fritz Luchsinger (members of the first Swiss ascent of Everest in 1956), with my wife and myself. We had to abandon the climb after ascending about 800ft, the ridge being covered by deep snow, with fresh snow falling.

The Matterhorn has always held me in thrall, as it has the millions of people who visit Zermatt or Breuil to gaze in awe at what George Finch called '. . . surely the most wonderful mountain in the world'. My last encounter with the mountain was in August 1966, when Jo Kretschmer and I climbed the Hörnli ridge in a storm. I was intent on avenging my defeat in the previous year. The weather conditions were almost identical, but this time we pressed on regardless and were greatly rewarded. Only one other rope – a British foursome – reached the top that day. In the late afternoon we emerged above the wind and the gloom into bright sunshine, a few hundred feet below the top; only Monte Rosa and the Weisshorn among the surrounding peaks stood above the sea of cloud. The experience exacted its price. We missed the last lift at the Schwarzsee and reached Zermatt at about midnight, exhausted, having lost our way in the dark. But that adventure remains as one of my best mountain memories.

The 1990 celebrations in Zermatt (8–15 July) – under different management and with better fortune with the weather – were a most successful and enjoyable affair. In 1965 the Swiss Alpine Club and the Swiss Tourist Office had played a leading part in the organization; this time the planning and management were undertaken by the *Gemeinde* of Zermatt. The programme was arranged in three parts. There was a series of events for the general public which continued throughout the week, consisting of art exhibitions and climbing demonstrations; there were showings of mountain films and a jubilee concert. Events during the weekend overlapped with the other two programmes for invited guests and for the International Association of Mountain Guides.

British alpinists were represented by Tony Streather and Mike Esten on behalf of the Alpine Club, by John Whyte and Peter Ledeboer for the ABMSAC, by Stephen Venables who represented the BMC, and by myself. Nigella Hall and Tim Woodgate were present as descendants of Whymper, but Major Hadow had to cry off on grounds of ill-health. The national clubs of France, Italy and the Netherlands were represented by their Presidents, and a distinguished member of the Japanese Alpine Club also attended. Pat and Sylvia Limerick were also present with a group of fund raisers for the Royal Marsden Hospital; they planned to make a number of sponsored ascents of the Matterhorn.

We feasted sumptuously at two evening banquets in the Monte Rosa and Zermatterhof Hotels, each occasion being preceded by a large outdoor reception. We lunched *al fresco* at the Schwarzsee and in the Hotel Pollux. We listened to many long speeches, to which Tony Streather, John Whyte and I were called upon to contribute. We took part in a splendiferous procession through the town, looking very British in our dark blazers and sporting small Union flags; we were honourably positioned behind a large banner bearing the legend GROSSBRITANNIEN (as though it was not self-evident!), one end of which was held by that good friend of all British climbers, Paula Biner. Ahead of us marched two bands and a platoon of attractive drum-majorettes, unfortunately obscured from our view by the nearer of the two bands. As we made our way through the narrow streets, crowds of tourists and many local people demonstrated their enthusiasm. It was an emotional experience.

But apart from all this wining, dining and junketing, meeting old friends and making new ones, a serious note was struck. Services of remembrance and thanksgiving were held: outside the little chapel beside the Schwarzsee, over which the Bishop of Strasbourg presided; and in front of the main church in Zermatt, conducted by the local priest and assisted, among others, by our own Bishop of Dunwich. A number of addresses were given at these ceremonies, inspired by the story of the first ascent. Our bishop preached on the lesson which this provided for brotherhood and unity among the Christian churches. A third service of dedication was held in the English church of St Peter.

The Catholic services were notable for their pageantry and colour. Beside the Schwarzsee chapel a quartet of long Swiss horns boomed sonorously and a female choir sang, dressed in traditional Walliser costumes. Outside the Zermatt church the Swiss and Italian mountain guides, and the Chief Guide from Chamonix, looked smartly professional in their formal uniforms; the Swiss guides provided both a choir and an orchestra. Banners were prominently displayed. Beside the altar stood a large painting depicting climbers tackling the final few feet below the summit of the Matterhorn. After that service a procession was formed and we moved down to the cemetery, where the renovated tombstones of the four pioneers who were killed during the descent were blessed by the presiding priests. Members of the Club will be aware that the AC had contributed towards the cost of restoration.

Other events took place on the mountain itself. On the 14th a number of special guided ascents were made, whose arrival on the summit was reported by radio-telephone to the crowds gathered at the Schwarzsee. Among the climbers was Ulrich Inderbinen, a 90-year-old guide who, after an interval of eight years since he had made his 125th ascent of the Matterhorn, reached the top in four hours from the Hörnli hut. Not surprisingly, he was the centre of many admirers and much media attention that evening, during a reception outside the Zermatterhof Hotel.

All in all, this was a most successful and memorable event in the long history of the mountain. Much tribute is due to the *Gemeindepräsident* Daniel Lauber, the *Bürgerpräsident* Erwin Aufdenblatten, the Chief Guide Hermann-Josef Biner, and many other hospitable local officials of Zermatt.

Tony Streather made a gift of a handsome bound copy of *Scrambles amongst the Alps* (1900 edition) and John Whyte presented a Visitors' Book to St Peter's Church. We felt privileged to represent British climbers at an event which recalled a milestone in mountaineering history.

Festivities analogous to those at Zermatt also took place later on the Italian side of the Matterhorn. They followed somewhat simpler lines, but were extremely enjoyable and friendly. Mike Esten and Peter Ledeboer were able to attend and were entertained most generously. The Alpine Club was greatly honoured to receive an invitation, from a descendant of Jean-Antoine Carrel, to unveil a plaque in the main square of Valtournanche to the memory of the two great local guides, J-A Carrel and J-J Maquignaz, with whom the first ascent of the Matterhorn is so inextricably connected, and who both died within the space of a few days 100 years ago. Mike Esten performed the honours and made the leading speech (in French) which was well received.

Alpine Meet 1990

MICHAEL BINNIE

(*Plate 62*)

When I told friends that I was going on the AC meet to the Bernina they all enthused about the Biancograt. 'Lovely route . . . you must do it . . . can't give it a miss,' etc. Muriel Derry, who lives near us, remembered it vividly. 'Fourteen hours on a single ham sandwich shared between Jack and me. But that was a *long* time ago,' she concluded wistfully.

I hadn't climbed in the Alps (ski'd, yes) for over 20 years and for once my wife and I decided to make it a joint venture. 30-odd years ago I took Carol up Flying Buttress and Spiral Stairs and she was, well . . . impressed. 'Please,' she had said, 'never let me do anything like that ever again. Please.' Yet here we were, discussing the Alps. 'Look,' she said, 'you go up and do your thing on the high peaks and I'll potter about the valleys sketching, pressing flowers. That sort of thing. I'll be fine. *Really*.' Well, that was the sport-plan.

We crossed the Julier pass at 7 one morning in late July and stood by the roadside, entranced by the view to the south. The Biancograt, of course, dominated the skyline and already I saw myself climbing it, boldly leading a party to the top accompanied by Vaughan Williams's music for 'Scott of the Antarctic'.

Later that morning we found a motley crowd of Brits in the nicest, shadiest part of the Morteratsch campsite and plans were soon afoot. A sizeable party was going up to try the Piz Morteratsch the next day, so we decided to join them. Carol, too. Forget the flower arranging: 'I'll just go up to the hut.' It was her first-ever hut-bash, first-ever load-carry, but she gave it, as they say, her best shot and we got there, if slowly.

At 4.30 next morning it was far too warm when I, Tom Sancha and Daphne Pritchard (in that order – but see below) set off up a well-worn track, headed for the Boval Col. An hour later we tried to be clever and cut off left for what appeared to be an easy snow gully. It was, but the snow was already like melting sugar and I suddenly began to feel awful. Tom, who'd been in the Alps a week para-ascending, or para-descending, I forget which, cruised into the lead and shot up the gully with disgusting ease, while Daphne was soon to glide past me.

Eventually we reached Morteratsch's main north-south ridge and were faced with the choice of either going up a steepish nose which led directly to the summit, or an easy but boring-looking plod to the left which avoided the nose. Most parties were choosing this latter route whose track had now become a knee-deep trench.

'Shall we try the nose?' asked Tom, full of bounce and eagerness. Daphne was definitely on. I gave a feeble nod of assent. 'Right, then,' said Tom, 'no need for a rope, is there?'; he then bounded off like some stripling chamois and was soon but a speck on the horizon. Daphne clunked efficiently up while I laboured along in the rear. Halfway up this slope, at one of my many rests, I decided to put on my gloves as any attempt to arrest a fall would have been painful without them, if not impossible. I found one glove and then proceeded to unpack the entire rucksack in a vain attempt to find the other, getting myself into a fearful muddle. I looked down. The slope was steep but not *that* steep, was it? I mean not steep-steep as the Kangshung face is steep?

John Town was somewhere near the summit of Piz Tschierva at about this time. In a campsite conversation a day later he let slip that 'there were a few parties doing that steep nose. At one point I looked across and there appeared to be someone all by himself, having an epi.'

There was. Me.

I was gasping for breath. I could only find one glove. Tom and Daphne had long since disappeared, and to cap it all I began to get the shakes. Somehow I got it together – ('dammit, I'm on an alpine doddle, not K2') – crammed everything into my sack and staggered upwards. The other two were waiting patiently at the top where the nose flattened out and shepherded me to the summit, where I slept for an hour. When I awoke, a dapper Swiss said, 'I am admiring your classical English clothing.' I shot him a glance. Did I detect just the tiniest hint of irony? I was wearing baggy cords, an old check shirt demoted to gardening and climbing and a rather down-at-heel Norwegian sweater (an article made of wool which one pulls on over one's head – I write this by way of explanation to all those who have been reared on zip-up fibre piles). I now realize what the Swiss alpinist meant. For classical, of course, read shabby.

Two days later at midday Tom, Daphne, Carol and I were being driven up the Val Roseg in a horse-drawn conveyance bound for the Coaz hut. Coffee and cakes delayed us in the hotel at the roadhead and there followed the long walk, up past a little hamlet of alpine pastoralists who produced delicious creamy yoghurt for us in earthenware bowls, along a high, beautifully flat shelf, to the Coaz hut perched on a rock buttress at the head of the valley. It was a glorious scene, dominated by Piz Roseg.

There was no stopping Carol, who was determined to bag a peak, and an hour before dawn the next morning the four of us were stumbling up scree bound for Il Chapütschin (3386m). Carol was clutching my long-shafted hickory ice axe, 1960 vintage, and would shortly strap into an ancient pair of ten-point crampons borrowed from a friend. Daphne and Tom moved rapidly ahead; this allowed us to take our time, which we did, lots of time, meandering over the glacier, peering into crevasses, wading through soft snow, tackling a little ice slope, until we finally negotiated a jumble of boulders, crampons screeching, to the summit of this modest but thoroughly worthwhile little mountain, 32 years after Flying Buttress. It was a moment to savour and Carol was smiling and snapping photographs; half an hour later she was still smiling ('from relief') before we plodded down, taking our time, to rejoin a much relieved pair of friends at the hut. It had been a memorable day.

Tom and I joined forces for what was to be my final climb, the North Pillar of the East Peak of Piz Palü. I noted that its first British ascent, in 1947, was by Everesters J O M Roberts and C G Wylie and, as my guidebook had once belonged to Anthony Rawlinson (kindly presented to me by Lady Rawlinson), himself a reserve for the 1953 expedition, I felt, somehow, quite illogically, drawn towards the route. It had fewer so-called 'objective' dangers than its two parallel pillars, and, frankly, looked easier.

The next night Tom and I dined in the Diavolezza Hotel with superb views of our peak surrounded by about a hundred other Piz Palüers. John Town had assured us that nearly all of them would be going for the ordinary route, but we were determined to make a flying start.

At 9pm the dining room emptied. All the proles like us trooped off to the barrack-like concrete dormitory block and at four the next morning rose to a man and silently paraded for breakfast. No unseemly rush or noise. A vast throng of climbers patiently waiting for their rolls and coffee. It was curiously impressive – and very un-British!

We managed to get away amongst the leading group and at 4.45am were cramponing across the Pers glacier in third place. It was a magnificent morning, perfectly still, if a trifle too warm – but that was the summer of 1990. We noted the rocks strewn across the glacier below Piz Cambrena. Not a place to be, later in the day. An hour after our start I looked back. A silent army of alpinists was strung across the glacier in single file. However, a party of three, ominously, appeared to be gaining on us. Correction: *was* gaining on us. We stepped up a gear and just managed to reach the foot of the climb ahead of them in a flurry of sweat and heaving chests. The party of three had somehow become five. Oh *dear*.

I led the first pitch and was just tying on when the young *bergführer* guiding the first party shouted up at me to take in my rope quickly! I yelled back, a little testily, that I was *not* going to hurry; and Tom joined me. The guide's clients were competent and he himself turned out to be quite helpful, so all was well. However, we were not going to have the route to ourselves. A pair of young Swiss were also hard on our heels.

The North Pillar of the East Peak is a fine, clean route. Solid, chunky granite provided excellent holds, and we appeared to flow up it. We moved together throughout, except once when I went off route and made a pitch. The Swiss then went ahead, whereupon we slowed down and began to enjoy ourselves. The climbing was very straightforward, about AD to AD sup, and I think we both felt, perhaps, a little unchallenged. We paused at the end of the rock section to don crampons and refresh ourselves and then crunched up the final snow arête to reach the summit at 8.50am, very nearly halving the guidebook time of five hours. The climb reminded me of North-East Buttress on the Ben.

For the next eight hours we footled about, traversing the Central and West summits of Palü, abseiling sections of the Fortezza ridge in log-jams of humanity, descending the wrong bank of the Pers glacier, constantly arriving above cliffs of vertical grass and rubble before collapsing outside our tents at 5pm. Nice climb; shame about the descent.

The next day Carol and I packed up and meandered gently home in nine days, pottering about the Oberland and enjoying walks in the Jura. Each night we slept under the stars. It had been the perfect holiday for us both. The Biancograt? It'll wait. A few days after Palü, Tom did it; and not without incident. Perhaps he'll tell us about it in some future article?

Avalanche Birth

EDWARD WILLIAMS

Axe thrust in easily,
Stopped with ominous wrist-wrenching scrape;
Boots sank fluffily,
Precarious ice-surface hold, gaiters out of sight;
Jelly feel of side slip
At next forward step on infinitude of sloping white.

Gently I firmly grip,
Carefully rub in my boots and slowly undo my longest screw
Then I hold it neat
Between my feet and clip on a crimson sling;
Breath held, then sighs,
As well-aimed blows bury it deep in the ice.

A hiss comes up behind,
Each step-hole joins to the next and the snow here and below
Wrinkles like skin
Of aged hand, fragile and thin, it breaks silently,
Crumples and undulates,
Moving and spreading: a sea leviathan disturbed.

Then as a spent wave
Retreats from the shore the hollows and crests
Move inexorably,
Innocently, down, break and tumble in terrible turmoil,
Gathering a silent power
Feared and fearful, in seconds unstoppable, irresistible.

For Whom the Chopper Chops

ANNE SAUVY

(Translated by Edward Peck)

Never send to know for whom the chopper chops
It chops for thee
(with apologies to John Donne)

Happy memories flooded into Isabel's mind. Morning in the woods, with slanting shafts of light . . . paths carpeted with pine needles and criss-crossed with knotty roots. Clear torrents chattering down, sometimes gouging out deep pools where you could draw fresh water in your cupped hands. Sometimes the shade was so thick that no plants grew below the high stands of spruce. Sometimes you walked through green and sunny glades where ragwort, cow parsley and briar roses were bursting into flowers . . . And very far away, very high up, there was ice and snow glistening in the rays of the brightest of suns.

All these wonders were for tomorrow . . . Tomorrow! What a delight. Into the scattered luggage went trousers and light dresses, the tartan bathing suit and her thick grey sweater. Isabel smiled with pleasure as she found with her fingers the familiar little roughness on the right-hand lock of the big suitcase. Everything would be ready this evening when Luke came home. He would only have to tidy up a bit his odds and ends of ropes, slings, pegs, étriers and nuts stacked up in a corner of the room. And tomorrow at dawn, they'd be off.

One year earlier Isabel had been thinking rather gloomily about this kind of departure. Holidays far from the sea seemed to her a cruel kind of punishment. And the letter sent by her godmother had been like a cold shower.

'Although the operation has been successful,' it read, 'the doctors have not concealed the fact that I cannot expect to be fully myself this summer, and in any case I could not spend my holidays alone in my beloved Chamonix. If perchance Isabel could spare a little of her time for the poor invalid that I have temporarily become, she would be doing me a very great service. And perhaps she would find in our mountains some delights she has so far ignored . . .' Etc.

'No! No! Damn it!' Isabel had exclaimed. Nonetheless there she was, a few weeks later, sighing as she got ready to pack sweaters, boots, anoraks and above all some books intended to cheer up a bit this sacrificed holiday.

Her forebodings proved correct, and she was bored stiff for the first two weeks. It rained a lot, it was cold. She had no friends, and, in spite of her efforts to show a kindly face to the old lady, who for her part seemed to be returning to life, Isabel was forced to count the long summer days one by one.

The only person at all young who came to the house exasperated her to the highest degree. Devoted to climbing, Pascal had a morbid taste for stories of mountain accidents, with which he tried to capture her attention.

'A fall of 800 metres! . . . They were found in little bits . . .'

'You're worrying Isabel,' said the godmother. 'Tell us about the climbs that end all right!'

'But, Aunt Anna, that's part of mountaineering, too. Look, in this morning's *Dauphiné*, there's a report of another six dead.'

And then one day, Pascal arrived together with Luke and a new tale of woe, to which for the first time Isabel listened with a sympathetic ear.

'I've brought along a friend, Aunt Anna! A great bloke! Yes Luke, you are! A natural! . . . The poor chap has just broken an arm on the North face of the Mont Blanc de Cheilon! In a stone-fall! He was belaying his partner and went on holding him in spite of the rock that had just wounded him . . . Otherwise they'd have dropped some hundreds of metres and they would have been buggered. Sorry, Aunt Anna . . . There'd already been two killed on Mont Blanc de Cheilon the week before, and this would have made four. So that's buggered his climbing for the season . . . Oh, sorry, Aunt Anna . . .'

Luke had stayed to dinner. And then he came back often with Pascal, in whom Isabel began to take a new interest. The fine weather helped. They went for long walks together. Isabel soon got to know all the parts of a valley which now seemed splendid to her . . . They came home in the evenings with sacks full of mushrooms or baskets of blueberries, with bunches of marguerites or scabious, with stories and laughter that echoed through the old house.

The summer passed happily. The pink flowers of the willowherb turned into stems of purplish pods, then into tufts of down, with bits of fluff floating away in the light at the slightest breath of wind.

At last there came the day when, having escaped from Pascal, Luke and Isabel went up to the source of the Arveyron. All the details of that walk remained vivid in Isabel's memory. The woods where the shafts of sun came through the branches of the fir trees, making a pattern of clear patches on an emerald bank of thick moss . . . The track as smooth as any in a park . . . The golden insects dancing their weird ballet in the sunbeams . . . The flight of a jay . . . They had reached a remote and romantic spot, dominated by the Dru and the splendid rugged wall of the Flammes de Pierre. Far away over the valley there was a low-lying mist suggesting the onset of autumn. A light wind ruffled Isabel's hair. Luke explained that in the last century the glacier had at this point formed a great arch of ice, but that its retreat had revealed the series of narrow gorges down which the Arveyron plunged into basins of bluey-green water and foaming waterfalls. And then he had said nothing at all, except a bit later: 'We'll soon have to go our own ways . . . Unless . . .'

They were married that December. The year had been a whirlwind of preparations, purchases, presents, invitations. They had had to fit out a little office, work desperately hard to prepare for long-neglected exams. Sometimes in the evenings they brought a few friends together and, inevitably, the conversation turned to the mountains. Isabel did not understand all this endless climbing talk, but it brought back to her happy memories of time spent between the Col de Voza and the Col de Balme, the interplay of clouds and sunshine, the tops powdered with snow, and she felt herself in harmony with this talk as she grew more and more familiar with it . . .

'A Grade V pitch, but bad as anything, a sloping chimney full of verglas. Not a hope of wedging up it with a sack. We sweated like pigs. All that with belaying and climbing through on one piton . . . well. You just had to *feel* safe, you couldn't afford to come off. Guy had called "Slack on the red!", and at that moment there was a stonefall. We were lucky, they fell a few feet away, if not . . .'

'And if not,' Pascal intervened, 'they would have found you at the foot of the slabs, in the bergschrund. Well I never, that makes me think of the accident Max had two years ago. But still, what fun we did have that day. Poor chap. I liked him so much!'

The start of the holidays was delightful. For the month of July, Luke and Isabel had been lent a chalet in the upper part of Les Frasses. They had to mow the lawn, weed the garden, clip the hedges and water the flowers . . . They went for walks again, waiting for James to arrive; he was Luke's usual climbing partner.

'You'll see,' Luke had said to his wife, 'we'll hardly be separated at all. Between climbs, we'll have a break. And then there are all those days of bad weather! I hope you'll get to love the mountains more and more.'

It was quite true. She became aware of her growing attachment to the alpine world and could no longer think of any other kind of holiday. Butterflies were collecting nectar in the meadow. Sparrows had made their nest under the eaves of a wooden barn and were flying about to feed their cheeping nestlings. The chalet was filling up with sheaves of lupins. Every evening they lit a wood fire and beside it they chatted and laughed as they ate their supper, recalling memories of many things they had already enjoyed together and making a mass of plans for the future . . . To be able one day to buy this chalet . . . To fill it with the laughter of children.

James arrived at the end of a week. Luke welcomed him eagerly, since a whole period of fine weather had just gone by and nothing had been done. That evening, with James dining in the chalet, the talk was all of climbing.

'We'll go up to the hut tomorrow,' said Luke decisively. 'My dear chap, let me get my breath,' James protested. 'You've been resting for a whole week, and you're well sun-tanned! Here am I, just arrived, pale as a ghost, shagged out. Let me have a day to get myself organized in the campsite, and enjoy the delights of doing nothing. The weather forecast is good. Don't panic! What would you say to a climb, the day after tomorrow, taking the first cable car up the Aiguille du Midi? That'll give us a good start without our having to get up too early! Then we can tackle something more serious . . . We might begin with the Seigneur route on the Peigne? I don't think you've done it and neither have I . . .'

Luke explained to Isabel, who was looking a bit worried, that they'd only be away a very short time.

'The Peigne, that's above the Plan de l'Aiguille which you know. A tiny little mountain. Not high, not long, not dangerous. We'll be home in the afternoon. You'll hardly have time to fix a dinner for two starving climbers before we're back! Go on . . . Smile!'

The day after next, Luke got up early and disappeared without a sound. For Isabel, the day was endless. She tried to read, tried to knit, tried to write postcards, went for a short walk, got bored stiff, went back to the chalet . . . At five o'clock she was still alone and at the end of her patience. She decided to go to wait for the two men at the cable car station: if James's car was not there, they would have passed each other on the way and she would come back to the chalet. But the car was still there. Isabel parked her own car alongside and waited. The situation was becoming more interesting. Each cable car disgorged a little group of noisy tourists and of climbers whose efforts showed in their faces. Isabel felt proud to be waiting for one of them.

From one car or another, rather like the winning ticket in a lottery, Luke would get out, surprised and happy to be welcomed like this . . . And then they'd laugh together . . .

Time wore on. Isabel went to the information desk to ask when the last car was due.

'It's on the way now, Miss!'

Luke was about to arrive and the wait was delightful. But the men were not in the group that came out of that car. Isabel went round the station, looked about and asked again.

'Don't get so fussed, dear!' was the answer she got. 'Your husband will have been delayed and missed the last car down. That happens every day! He'll come down on foot. It's not serious. Just go home. He'll be there sooner than you think!'

The chalet now seemed a gloomy place. Two hours went by. Isabel, finding the loneliness unbearable, began to think the worst. The only person in the valley she could think of to tell her anything was Pascal, with all the tales of accidents he brought with him . . . At nine o'clock, she couldn't stand it any longer; she grabbed the telephone and, her words broken with sobs, poured out her tale of her day of waiting and the inexplicable delay.

Pascal was very good, even optimistic. Indeed he boosted her morale. Like the cable car man, he too seemed to find it all quite normal.

'Happens all the time . . . Don't fret . . . Anything could have happened to him without it being at all serious . . . No reason to panic, I tell you . . . He could be here in five minutes . . . In any case, keep me posted . . . Don't hesitate to disturb me. Just call me as soon as he's back, or if you get too bored!'

Isabel set about waiting again. She called Pascal several times on the phone. At eleven o'clock, she was weeping copiously.

'All right!' said Pascal. 'I'm not worried yet. But all the same, we'll do something. I'll telephone the Mountain Rescue to make sure they haven't had any accident reported to them, and I'll ask them to make a helicopter recce tomorrow morning, always assuming James and Luke are still not back down.

Now it's dark and there's nothing else one can do. Go to bed, take a sleeping pill. I swear there's nothing so far really out of the usual.'

Luke arrived about midnight. Isabel threw herself into his arms, sobbing wildly.

'But what on earth's the matter? What's the matter?' he asked. 'Has anything happened to you?'

'No. It's you, Luke. I thought you were dead . . .'

'. . . That I was dead? What a ridiculous idea! Do I look dead? . . . No! So what? . . . But am I tired? . . . And I didn't expect to be welcomed home with a fit of hysterics!'

This remark unleashed another flood of tears from Isabel.

'But you said you would be back down by the afternoon! How was I to know? . . . With all these stories of accidents which Pascal has been telling us . . . And the newspapers . . . By the way, Pascal has asked for the helicopter, for tomorrow morning . . . I was so frightened . . .'

'Hell!' exclaimed Luke, grabbing the telephone . . .

Then he understood, from his wife's distressed face, that it was all his own fault, for not having explained things better to her. The poor girl simply didn't understand.

'It just happens, my dear little Isabel, that one gets held up . . . We had some unforeseen snags, and in particular we lost hours helping a rope of three youngsters to get down. Absolutely knackered, they were, and inexperienced, to have set off like that . . . If we hadn't looked after them, they would have had to bivouac . . . Here, take my hankie. Look out, it isn't very clean . . . In normal circumstances, we should have spent the night at the Plan, instead of pushing on down on foot in the dark . . . It's for your sake we came back now . . . But I didn't expect to find you in such a state . . . Don't cry any more . . . I'm here well and truly alive and kicking . . . I love you . . . It's all over . . .'

Three days of rest followed. Isabel remained slightly ashamed of her panic. The next time she would know how to behave as a real climber's wife should . . .

The next time was not long in coming, but Luke was wise enough to take the necessary precautions.

'This time, I'll put you in the picture. It's going to be a longer climb . . . We're going to do the north face of the Triolet. We'll be gone at least one night. I'll explain the route to you: we climb a rather steep ice face above the Argentière glacier, and we'll come down by the normal route, an easy one, towards the Couvercle hut and then by the Mer de Glace to the Montenvers. I shan't be able to telephone you from the Argentière hut the first night because there isn't any Argentière hut! It's being rebuilt this summer and we shall have to bivouac. But when we come down, I can call you from the Couvercle. Now you know all that's involved. It could go quite fast. But now you begin to understand what it's all about. Sometimes the unexpected happens or the face can be in bad condition. If we've got to belay each other, it'll take longer, you understand, and in that case we may be home late. Or we might even spend a second night at the Couvercle. Not very likely – but just so that you've been warned . . . And don't let your imagination dwell on these accident stories!

Pascal is a fine lad but he does pile it on a bit . . . And he ends by scaring himself so much that he hardly dares to go climbing himself . . . Just think of him spending his nights in huts, with all those catastrophes buzzing round in his brain . . . What a nightmare! There you are, you're laughing, that's right. I hope I'll find you still laughing when we get back.'

Putting up with this new departure was in fact much easier. Isabel dined alone and spent the evening at the cinema; on returning home under the stars she thought dreamily of Luke and fell fast asleep at once. Next morning was fine and all must be well on the mountain. She went for a swim in the pool. It wasn't so bad after all, waiting down below, and she was surprised at herself for getting used to it so quickly. She spent the rest of the afternoon making a peach tart which, if it was no use that evening, would do splendidly for the next day. Isabel had refused an invitation to dine with Aunt Anna, so as to be home if Luke turned up or if he phoned.

The evening was a bit dismal, with no news of any kind. Isabel ended by going up to bed, but it was some time before she fell asleep, thinking she heard noises on the ground floor, the click of the door-latch, the noise of a car engine, voices . . . But it wasn't Luke . . .

At nine o'clock in the morning, on the third day, there was still nothing. Isabel needed reassurance but hesitated to bother Pascal. She had made the acquaintance of the wife of a guide, who lived nearby. She went to ask her, as a neighbour, what could be the reasons for the delay. She was lucky enough to catch the husband, packing his sack for a Mont Blanc trip.

'They've certainly not been quick!' he reckoned, once he had been put in the picture. 'But if you're worried, it's easy, you've only got to telephone yourself to the Couvercle. Ask for the warden and tell him it's from me: we've known each other for ages! He'll certainly let you know if they've been seen passing by, or if they're on their way down. It's quite easy.'

It wasn't as easy as all that. Fear once more gripped Isabel's heart. What should she say to this warden at the hut? And Heaven knows what he might tell her?

Eventually she rang Pascal. He was more surprised than he had been last time.

'North wall of the Triolet? Well, in fact, they should have been here last night! Of course, all sorts of things can happen . . . But it's a good idea to ask the Couvercle . . . You daren't? Come on, don't get in a state; I can hear the sob in your throat. Good, just wait, I'll ring myself. I'll understand the answer better than you will . . .'

He rang back ten minutes later.

'That's it . . . Don't panic Isabel . . . There's something I don't under-stand, but above all don't panic! . . . They haven't seen them yet at the Couvercle . . . And they haven't spent the night there either.'

A wail was heard at the other end of the line.

'I told you not to get in a state! They've probably had to bivouac . . . But there's something that worries me a bit . . . A roped party did the normal route up the Triolet this morning, very early, and is already back. I caught one of them on the phone. It seems they didn't see anybody, nor any tracks coming off the north face. A bit funny, it seems to me.'

'But what if they've fallen off the other side,' moaned Isabel.

'Don't assume the worst, not just yet! They could have . . . well, I don't know . . . Gone very high up on the face and not been able to get over, and had to climb down again . . . I don't know . . . Or they might have had a slight accident which held them up . . . Just a tiny one . . . Nothing serious! Hang on, don't cry. I'll come round . . . It was silly of me to tell you that . . . They'll be here soon . . . There'll be some explanation. Or else you'll have a call . . . I'll come, I'll be round in a minute. Don't cry like that.'

Pascal was really more worried than the last time. The timing was long, very long and it all seemed to show that Luke and James could not have reached the top of the Triolet.

Isabel was a terrible sight. She was twisting her handkerchief between her fingers, and was shaking her head continuously from left to right, as if refusing to accept what he had said, while tears streamed down her face.

'I should never have let him go! I should not have!' she sobbed.

'But you didn't know!' retorted Pascal, his arguments exhausted. 'Oh, what can have happened? Don't cry like that, it doesn't help . . . What a business. No. I beg of you, don't look at me like that . . . Good! Are we agreed? I'll call the helicopter.'

And, a little later: 'They'll make a recce over the Argentière basin at two o'clock . . . Now, calm down.'

Luke arrived back at ten to two and sized up the situation at a glance.

'Oh no! Not again!' he sighed.

While Pascal phoned to cancel the flight, Luke tried to calm down Isabel, who was racked with sobs. Then he began explaining things. Yes, they had had some idiotic mishaps. And revolting conditions . . . A covering of loose snow on ice for hundreds of feet . . . The way through the seracs had been bad . . . They'd got out of them at nightfall and had had to bivouac a bit lower down, on the south side . . . A roped party on the normal route? No, they hadn't seen it . . . It had probably gone over the summit before they'd even woken up . . . Not surprising that the party hadn't seen any tracks, especially if they weren't on the look-out for them . . . The route out was all in sheer ice and anyway there were several ways out . . . As for themselves, they had got down as quickly as possible . . . They were worn out after the day before and simply hadn't had the heart to climb up to the Couvercle just for a telephone call . . . They'd sooner get down as fast as they could . . .

As Pascal had disappeared, Luke looked at Isabel and nodded his head.

'Well,' he said, 'you do make a fuss . . . Now, don't begin crying again. Smile instead . . . I'm still alive, once more . . . I'm delighted to know that you love me so much . . . It's very flattering, you know. I must be the most appreciated husband in the whole valley of Chamonix. But mountain time-tables, you must understand, aren't like railway timetables . . . Do you get it, now? . . . Well, there we are. Don't wipe your tears on my shoulder, please . . . You must take a grip on yourself . . . And I must have a good bath and the kip I've been dreaming about for the last two days. Tonight I'll take you to dine at the Monchu Restaurant, in honour of the north face of the Triolet . . . That'll be nice, won't it?'

Of course it was all right. And the affair was nothing more than a joke which went the round of climbing circles.

'Hallo, Isabel? Do you want me to call the Mountain Rescue?' Pascal said every time he rang up his friend.

It had begun to rain. They organized consolation dinner parties. And, when the fine weather returned, Isabel repeated to herself the little lesson she was not ready to forget . . .

Luke explained to her his next climb.

'This time, we'll do the Aiguille Verte by the Y couloir. I daren't promise that we'll be back in good time . . . And, above all, don't raise the blood pressure of those chopper pilots! You won't, will you, my dear Isabel?'

He left home, reassured. Isabel went down to Geneva to dine with a bunch of friends. This time she seemed completely at ease. And so she was . . . She certainly spent a better night than Luke, who got up at some unearthly hour when she wasn't even in bed, in order to tackle the wearisome trek up the glacier in the dark, and to manage the crossing of some particularly evil-looking bergschrunds.

Isabel woke late, lay lazing a bit, thinking that once more the weather was fine, despite the slightly threatening cirrus clouds of the day before. Luke was in luck. If only she could find time to do, before his return, all the things she had set out to do . . . First of all it was Saturday, the day of the entertaining market. With her basket on her arm, and joy in her heart, Isabel went from stall to stall . . . A smile came to her lips as she remembered the anxiety that had harrowed her throughout the day of the trip to the Peigne. How long ago that now seemed . . . She'd learnt a few things since . . . Hallo, there are already mirabel plums on sale . . . !

The accident happened very early on the climb, and unforeseeably. Even so, it was freezing hard. But the loose stones had suddenly zoomed down, sweeping straight down the centre-line of the couloir. It was impossible to avoid them. Luke and James had been moving together when they heard them. No time to find the least belay. They had both been carried away and their fall had been savage, punctuated with jerks by the rope. Luke didn't even know whether he had fallen into the bergschrund or into a crevasse lower down. It seemed narrow, where he was, for a bergschrund. But deep enough to fill him with horror. His sack had fortunately stopped him by hitching at his back on a blade of ice. He felt pain all over . . . Of James no sign at all . . . The rope must have been cut by the stones. James must have finished up, him too, in the bergschrund or in a crevasse. And in what sort of a state? . . . Luke had lost his ice axe and one of his crampons . . . It was the sheerest chance that he'd kept his sack, that the waist-strap had held and that the whole thing held him up miraculously suspended on this blade of ice . . . With his remaining crampon, he tried to get a foothold on the other side of the wall of the crevasse . . . The arm-strap of his sack began to crack . . . No! better not budge . . . not move at all . . . his balance was too precarious. The sack wouldn't hold for ever. Luke had blood in his mouth. He was frozen. Mustn't get too cold, but there was no means of moving . . . Mustn't move, that's all . . . Wait for help . . . But how long would Isabel take to panic, this time round? What had he said to her? . . . Surely

nothing very nasty . . . Oh yes, he had joked about the chopper pilots' blood
pressure . . . God! If only they knew! . . . How long would it take Isabel to call
the chopper? How long?

Oh My God, We're Dead!

JOHN C WILKINSON

I bumped into Guy on the balcony of the Monzino hut. He was off to do some multi-day route on Mont Blanc, whereas I had only come for a training climb on a nearby pinnacle. But I could see he was unimpressed by the Ottoz route on the Aiguille Croux, even for the first route of the season. *Faut faire la Gugu, c'est à vaches.* I certainly didn't think that meant that the Gugliermina would be a walkover, if only because it is a three-day outing. But Guy's remark did work its way through the filing cabinet of my mind until, in the course of the next few days, it pushed *la Gugu* out of the 'not for me' dockets into that of the 'possibles'. Simon does not have such a wimpish section in his climbing classifications and so, once I had tentatively mentioned it to him, I knew that I was committed.

We left Chamonix rather later than we should have done. It takes a full day, in August, to get through the tunnel, find somewhere to park, flog up the screes and cables to the Monzino, carry on as far again to the Col de l'Innominata, get down the other side, and cross the horribly tortured Frêney glacier. Even if one is planning to nip up and down the route itself in a day, only carrying a chalk bag, there are still going to be two bivvies on the Vires Schneider, which means carrying large and heavy sacks to the foot of the mountain. That is why, of course, one does not find the rock-jocks anywhere near it: just the superfit, like Guy, and the over-ambitious, like me.

So it was getting late when we saw the plaque on the Col de l'Innominata commemorating the death of the last victim of the 1961 Central Pillar epic. Now the whole trip took on a serious air. Behind us were the easy and tedious slopes up which we had slogged under a sweltering sun all afternoon. A steep abseil down the tottering blocks on the reverse of the col landed us on the glacier. I tried to put on my new crampons but Jules had adjusted the right one far too tight. In the shop it had seemed a good fit, but here it simply would not go on. Eventually we managed to hammer out the front retaining pieces sufficiently to get my boot in. It was an inauspicious start, and we had not much more than an hour of daylight left to find a way through what appeared to be an impossible ice-fall.

Slushy snow treacherously covered the lower part of a serac that seemed to give access to a passage above the first crevasses. I remarked to Simon that a fall here would be fatal. Shortly afterwards we found ourselves at a dead end, with vertical drops on all sides. There was no time to try and force our way further. We were less than halfway across and we would be benighted. Never mind, we could bivvy somewhere near the col and start again early next morning. Nothing would be lost.

We returned to the key serac and Simon started to climb down. There was no question of a belay. Besides, we had no ice screws and only one ice axe each. So when Simon reached the slightly less steep, mushy far edge, diagonally below me, I threw down the last useless coils and, with both hands free, started teetering down the 60° top section high above an impressive crevasse. Suddenly I saw Simon's feet shoot from under him and he started slithering helplessly. I knew exactly what was going to happen. 'Oh my God, we're dead,' I shouted, as the rope came tight on to my harness and tugged me off. It was, as Simon subsequently said, a very defeatist remark. I suppose I must have tried to brake down the serac face with my single ice axe, for I was still clutching it as I shot over the lip into the crevasse. Suddenly I jammed and the snow piled in on top of me. In a situation like this one's mind seems to operate at two different levels: so this is what it's like to be buried alive in an avalanche, I thought dispassionately. Disinterestedly, I looked up at the overhanging wall of ice above my head and knew that there was not the slightest chance of getting up it.

'Are you all right John?' an anxious voice yelled from somewhere in the remote world outside. 'Well, at least I'm alive,' I replied laconically. As I tried to turn round, a shooting pain cut through my side; my feet flapped in space and I felt my ribs glugging in liquid. Now I could see into the depths of the crevasse yawning to my right. If I had fallen three feet further along, both of us would have been dead. Perhaps for the first time in my climbing life I was afraid, *really* afraid. 'Simon, for God's sake hold me!' I yelled in uncontrolled panic. I managed to stay wedged as I turned around, and I could see that the ice wall behind me did not look quite so steep. But if I was to climb it I had to move fast, for in my now febrile state I was convinced I had punctured my lungs and would run out of strength. I had read enough of such situations to know that fear lends wings and I had to make use of that fear as an ally. 'I'm going to try and climb out,' I shouted, 'just keep pulling all the time as I move up.'

'Can you stay where you are?' Simon yelled a few moments later. 'No! For God's sake just keep me tight,' I peremptorily instructed. Concerned only at my own predicament, I could not understand his querulous tone. What I didn't know was that my companion had managed to brake to a halt and was now holding me across the tip of his ice axe still embedded in the slope. In fact, if I had not wedged, I would surely, in turn, have pulled him off and down into whatever lay below us. But now, from his precarious position, Simon was trying to pull me up. I started to climb. Suddenly the slope flattened out to a hidden ledge and I realized I could walk out of the side of the crevasse. 'OK, Simon, you can move now.'

As we joined together in safety, the reaction set in. I desperately wanted nursing over the easy ground back to the edge of the glacier. But it was dark by now, and we had to find somewhere to bivvy. There was no question of doing so under the Col de l'Innominata with its massive unstable blocks. Elsewhere the encasing walls were vertical and the rubble at their base showed that they were less than solid. But we had no choice, and Simon managed to find a crack where we could at least wedge ourselves into a sitting position. Fortunately we had no shortage of warm clothes, having come prepared for two bivvies. The trouble was that I was still suffering from shock. Instead of explaining, for instance, that I wanted my rucksack passed over, I could only stutter out a staccato 'ru-ru-rucksack'. Believing that I must have struck my head in the fall, Simon determined that I should not go to sleep. His efforts to keep me awake were not without humour. As the shock wore off I was able to explain to him that my only worry was the liquid gurgling around my lungs. Half reassured, he relaxed his attempts to keep talking me awake and I began to think that perhaps I had not done any great injury to myself after all. But Simon need not have worried. Every time I began to nod forward, the pain from my broken ribs shot me awake again.

Next morning Simon climbed back over the col and down to the Monzino hut to call the helicopter. It was pleasantly warm, but as the clouds built up I began to realize what it must mean to be without help. I knew that if I absolutely had to I could eventually get myself back to the Monzino. But if my lungs were punctured? I had plenty of time to reflect. I remembered, after a forced retreat in the Himalaya, playing a game called 'VI Sup' in Base Camp and triumphantly producing my helicopter card when I got stuck, and how we all suddenly stopped laughing as the same thought crossed our minds. Roger and Nick were still up on the col in the hope of a summit push and the weather had again clamped in: no helicopter card for them to play. And in Peru, just a year ago, I had at one stage been in a position where I believed the others to be in trouble and, far from help, was faced with the problem of organizing rescue. A few days later, leaving for home, we had come upon the remains of a small American team from Dartmouth, who had befriended me when I was ill. They had just located Randy, who had been crawling for three days with a broken hip at over 6000m, after falling on Huascaran and seeing his companion killed. No helicopter to get him down.

The wait became interminable. With every sound of an aeroplane I anxiously scanned the clouding sky for the helicopter. Eventually the *deus ex machina* of the Alps arrived, and I was attached to a cable and lifted off the glacier. As the helicopter circled to climb out of the Frêney basin, the centrifugal force swung me in ever greater circles and I had an incomparable view of the savage pillars on Mont Blanc and the W face of the Noire. They were not appreciated. I closed my eyes as the cable jerked me in excruciating pain and swung me in a terrifying dance high above those menacing crevasses. Suddenly warm and gentle arms reached down and pulled me into the cabin. The winching was over and a few moments later we picked up Simon from the Monzino. In the clinic at Courmayeur it was discovered that I had merely a couple of broken ribs and nothing dramatic like punctured lungs. It had all been so easy, I reflected; I had played my helicopter card but in 'VI Sup' one is only allowed to use it once. Should I have tried to play the hero and avoid the indignity of being saved for such a trivial injury?

At least the location where my mini-drama had occurred sounded good. Later, René Ghilini caustically summed up the experience: *C'est aussi bête de tomber dans une crevasse sur le glacier du Frêney que sur la Mer de Glace, mais ça fait moins sarpé!* (It is equally stupid to fall into a crevasse on the Frêney glacier as on the Mer de Glace, but it is less bumbly.)

Jura – the Unsung Mountains

KEV REYNOLDS

(*Plates 75, 76*)

To most alpinists, I guess, the Jura are no more than green-rucked hills forming the borders of France and Switzerland, whose fame rests solely on the fact that they've given their name to a geological period. The TGV from Paris rushes through with barely a blurred glimpse; from the air they form a doll's house landscape, pastoral, wooded and gentle; by road they frustrate with fragmented views and tease with unfulfilled promise. And it is only by taking to the footpaths and plunging into their heartland that their true worth is at last revealed. Then, ah then ... then you'll find they have a charm and elegance sufficient to warrant a closer examination.

The Jura range stretches for something like 250km from a point a little south of Basle in the Rhine valley to the valley of the Rhône east of Lyons; a banana-shaped range, narrow at either end and broadening to about 50km in the centre. Produced by the same forces of upheaval that built the Alps, they are the classic expression of folded mountains with a series of parallel ridges imitating one another in character, but in fierce competition with regard to depth of greenery and pastoral splendour. Woods flank the hills and crown many of the summits, while other crests stand bare like the exposed skeletal spines of long-dead dinosaurs. These are limestone mountains, of course, dry on the surface but with fine rivers gouging transverse valleys (cluses) and creating dark defiles here and there. Lakes adorn some of the longitudinal valleys. Cave systems mystify others. Flowers dazzle the meadows and cluster for attention in the crevices of crag and wayside outcrop. Butterflies thrash the air in their summer toings and froings among them; hawks hang motionless overhead; black cherries dangle with temptation from meadowland trees; the woods are sumptuous with wild strawberry, raspberry, blackberry and bilberry – and the only glaciers are those that drape a far horizon, those of the Oberland far beyond the chequered plains of lowland Switzerland, or of Mont Blanc across the sea-like Lake of Geneva.

Remember Belloc in his *Path to Rome*?

> For below me, thousands of feet below me, was what seemed an illimitable plain: at the end of that world was an horizon, and the dim bluish sky that overhangs an horizon ... One saw the sky beyond the edge of the world getting purer as the vault rose. But right up – a belt in that empyrean – ran peak and field and needle of intense ice, remote from the world. Sky beneath them and sky above them a steadfast legion ...

He wrote that of the view from the eastern Jura crest at Weissenstein (1284m), above Solothurn. And all along this edge, this highest ruck of ridge, one gambles the opportunity for such views – a bonus in itself, for Jura scenery lacks nothing in its own inimitable landscape of delight.

This edge, it would appear at first glance, holds little for the climber – not along the crest, at least. But that is a misguided judgement, for what it does have of immense value to the crag-happy is, for example, the huge cirque of the Creux de Van near Neuchâtel. It's a horseshoe well, two kilometres long, 1200 metres wide and with a wall some 500 metres high on which some challenging artificial routes have been developed. (Creux de Van is now protected as a Nature Reserve populated by marmots, chamois and ibex, and at certain times of the year climbing is restricted there.) The rim of the Creux (about 1460m altitude) levels to pasture broken by stretches of limestone pavement from which you gaze over the high plateau of La Bied, a strange broad high valley seeming to contain a world all its own.

Climbing opportunities in the Jura are far more numerous and varied than one might expect. (See *AJ78*, 146–152, 1973, which contains 'Mountain landscape – the Jura', an article by Maurice Brandt and Edward Pyatt, outlining the great rock-climbing potential here.) There are classic routes on polished arêtes, steep walls breaking free of forest-clad valleys and enough overhanging roofs to satisfy most tastes when the rain falls on more open, exposed cliffs. But what is missing here is notoriety. One can climb on the Jura's mostly sun-warmed limestone for half a lifetime without finding anyone at home who'll have even heard of the crags you've been working on. Yet the Jura is not without its advocates.

For the walker these hills are second to none. (How can you compare one range with another?) Not hard alpine walking with snowfield and ice-slope to contend with, I'll grant you, but with footpaths that lead to the most delectable of belvederes in order to reveal the rich bounty of nature. Since there are maximum altitudes of not much more than 1700 metres, there'll be vegetation – and a rich and memorable one at that – practically all the way.

The classic walk is the *Jurahöhenweg*, the High Route which runs along the easternmost Swiss ridge. It begins a little to the east of the Jura corrugation in the village of Dielsdorf, midway between Zürich and the German border, and works its way south-westward for 299km as far as Borex, a small village near Geneva. On its way it passes over all the main summits of the Swiss Jura: Mont Tendre, La Dôle, Chasseral and Chasseron among them. It traverses meadow-land and forest. It visits remote agricultural villages full of colour and personality, yet strangely missing from calendars and the lids of chocolate boxes. There are wonderful isolated farms long hours from anywhere where the walker may find an overnight bed on a mattress in the hay and play at pioneer, and long sections of ridge-walking on which there are few signs of man. Everywhere you walk there are huge vistas to enjoy, either of hills plunging steeply to the Mittelland that runs off to the Bernese Alps, or of ridge upon green ridge folding away into France.

It's a grand walk that will take care of a fortnight's holiday. Along it you pass from German-speaking to French-speaking Switzerland, a divide as architecturally and culturally significant as it is linguistic, and the unfolding of each day's panorama brings with it an hourly challenge. Practically the only other walkers, it seems, are Swiss. They've come up from the plains to weekend in one of several CAS huts dotted along the route, although we had the pleasure of sharing one such refuge with a Dutchman who was so passionate about these unsung mountains that he spends at least one weekend per month walking among them, and was by far the most travelled of all the members of the CAS section he'd joined. It was not difficult to appreciate his enthusiasm and his commitment.

This is a corner of Switzerland (and of France) that time has passed by. Development is there, to be sure, in the form of an occasional ski-tow, but by comparison with the neighbouring Alps it's largely unknown territory. Unknown, unsung, but not unloved.

In winter the region becomes a ski-touring Mecca, and it is then almost inevitable that a far greater number of visitors will be met than on a summer walking tour or climbing trip. Cross-country skiing in the Jura is probably safer than almost anywhere else in Europe, but is in no way a soft option. On the French side there are some 10,000km of prepared pistes, yet it's easy enough to break away from marked trails and take to the higher crests off-piste, although for travel through forests it takes a practised eye to detect the route of a path buried under a metre of fresh snow. Navigational difficulties can occur in poor visibility even in the long open combes, so those who stray from the machine-pisted trails should be prepared to cope with an assortment of challenges.

There are some magnificent tours waiting to be made by ski. By using an assortment of gîte, hut and village hotel such routes as the five-day Circuit of the Val de Joux, the 170km Grande Traversée du Jura (GTJ), or the 149km of the Swiss equivalent, the TJS (Traverse of the Swiss Jura) become a realistic aim.

So what of the Jura mountains? If it is stature, altitude or stark glacial sculpture that are your main requirements, you'll pass them by, as have countless others on their way to more notable peaks. But if you seek somewhere a little different, somewhere whose charm is to be found among more subtle elements, yet bearing an unquestionable charisma, if you care less for the obvious than for a spirit of place that works its magic in the most unexpected of quarters – then the Jura will reward a visit in a truly surprising way.

GUIDEBOOKS

Guide d'Escalades dans le Jura, Vol 1: Sainte Croix-Val de Travers-Bienne.
Guide d'Escalades dans le Jura, Vol 2: Moutier-Raimeux-Bâle-Olten. (Editions du CAS, CH8304 Wallisellen, Switzerland.)
The Jura by Kev Reynolds and R Brian Evans (Cicerone Press) gives detailed route descriptions of the Jura High Route and of winter ski traverses.

The Pirin Mountains –
Kingdom of the Thunder God

JERZY W GAJEWSKI

(Plates 63, 64)

We were coming in to land and the plane circled the area where the city of Sofia was presumably situated. I was sitting by the window with my camera ready to take pictures either of the Balkan mountains to the north or of the Vitosha mountains to the south; but clouds, like swirling cotton wool, obscured the earth's surface. A few minutes later the aircraft descended through drifting white vapour, and suddenly the tyres hit the runway. The hills surrounding the city were a uniform grey, drained of colour. This was not how I remembered the sunny capital of Bulgaria from 13 years ago.

I had first come here, by train, in 1976. We had approached Sofia from the north, where the railway cuts through the Balkan mountains following the valley of the Iskir river. I remember it as a long, beautiful canyon, framed by honey-coloured rocks which turned golden in the light of the setting sun. The next day we had ascended the nearest available summit of the Vitosha mountains, Mount Kopitoto at 1348m, by the newly-built cable railway, before embarking on our main adventure in the Pirin mountains.

These mountains are part of an extensive range running along the Bulgarian–Greek border. Their name derives from Perun, the old Slavonic god of thunder. The Pirin range is divided into three parts – northern, central and southern. The northern area, the largest and the most interesting for hikers, has a main ridge 42km long. The central and southern parts are much lower, the highest peak, Mount Oryelek, being only 2099m. This afforested area, near the Greek frontier, is closed to tourists.

Most of the northern part of the range has been proclaimed the Pirin National Park, with a protected area comprising 27,500 hectares. Camping and the lighting of fires are now prohibited, but I remember how, in 1976, we camped not far away from the Vihren refuge and, since it usually snowed at nights even in August, we made a fire every evening from branches of the dwarf mountain pine. It is still possible, today, to wander at will outside the marked trails – but for how much longer?

The Pirin mountains are not the highest in Bulgaria – the Rila mountains are higher, with Mount Musala at 2925m. But the only goal for the majority of tourists is Mount Vihren at 2914m. The Pirin mountains are popular because of their alpine character, with rocky peaks and numerous lakes, and they are visited in force by hikers as well as by mountaineers. Winter climbing, in

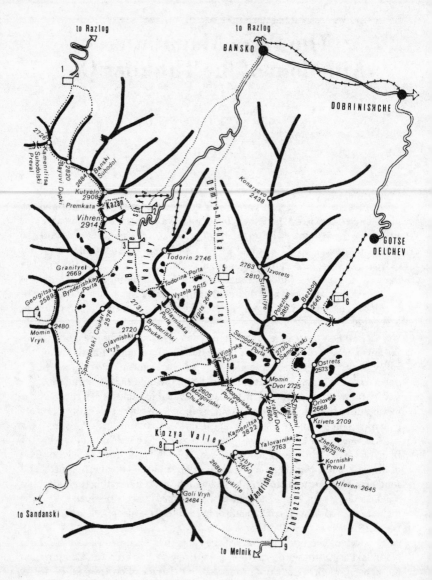

particular, is becoming increasingly popular. Bansko is the main starting point for the highest summits, such as Vihren, Kutyelo and Todorin. It is situated at the entrance to the Bynderishka valley at the foot of the highest mountain ridge. Two mountain huts and a small leisure resort are well placed for climbing Mount Vihren. This fact, and the building of chair-lifts to the N ridge of Mount Todorin and to Chyrna Mogila (1976m), have intensified the popularity of the area.

There were 12 in our own party – really too many for the small coach which transports tourists to the Bynderishka valley. But we all packed in somehow, with other passengers mostly from Germany and Poland. The winding road finishes 14km beyond Bansko at the Bynderitsa hut (1810m). 30 minutes' walk further on there is the other refuge of Vihren at 1950m. Although this hut is preferred by the Bulgarians, both huts are usually crowded. But we were in luck and spent the next two nights in the Bynderitsa hut. The interior was typical: a steep staircase, creaking wooden floors, closely-packed bunks and a cooking area in the basement – or outside in the yard. Fast-moving grey clouds from the invisible main ridge and a cold wind reminded us that we were in the heart of the Pirin.

Our first trip was to Mount Todorin, 2742m. 13 years ago we had climbed it directly from our camp near the Vihren refuge, up the couloir running straight down from the top. From below this had looked easy, but in fact it was steep and monotonous and we had to hack our way through the almost impenetrable branches of the dwarf mountain pines. The summit cone turned out to be a big heap of stones. Today a chair-lift runs up the N ridge to within 400m of the top. As the lift rises, more and more superb views are revealed of the white pyramids of the Vihren and Kutyelo peaks. From the summit we were lucky to have a good view of the Vihren main ridge framing the panorama to the west. Green wooded slopes descended to the north while, to the south and east, a sea of rocky peaks faded away into the blue distance. In the Vasilyashki cirque and in the upper part of the Bynderishka valley, the stony desert landscape was enlivened by masses of green and gold lakes, glittering, like tiny mirrors, in the sunshine. We descended by the classic route down the SW ridge to Mount Malka Todorka (2710m), and steeply down again to the Todorina Porta (2580m), an important pass between the Bynderishka and Demyanishka valleys. Our route back to the hut passed near the lakes of Ribno and Dolgoto which reflected the last rays of the sun as it vanished behind Mount Granityel (previously Mount Muratov, 2669m).

The next day was our only chance to climb Mount Vihren, which was especially important to those who had not done it before. Unfortunately the morning was gloomy and cold, so that only a few of us decided to venture out, hoping, optimistically, that some blue sky would show up later. Two trails lead from the huts to the top: one runs over the Kazan cirque and up the N ridge, while the other passes over the pleasant hanging valley of Dylbakoto Dere to the Vihrensky Preslap pass (which separates the marble and granite parts of Pirin) and the S ridge. An experienced hiker should reach the top in 3 to 3½ hours. On this gloomy morning we quickly attained the ledge of the lower Kazan cirque. The wind dropped and the leaden clouds seemed to be standing still. An oppressive silence enveloped us as we stood in the centre of the grassy arena surrounded by marble walls and gazed up at the Golyam Kazan, a stone cirque closed off by the 400m high NE face of Vihren. We crossed the N ridge of Vihren in heavy mist which parted only for a few seconds to reveal green passes and meadows on the southern side of the mountain. To reach the top in clear weather would be an exciting moment indeed.

The top of Vihren is easy to reach in summer. The first winter ascent was made on 9 January 1925 by T Atanasov, D Stoikov, B Bainov and N Bodzhilov. The first climbers on the NE face were Germans: W Mosyl and F Auer in September 1934; the first winter ascent of this face took place on 15 February 1949 (A Byelkowski and V Lobidin). In 1976 we observed many climbers on the white walls of Vihren but in 1989 we did not meet any climbers at all. Possibly the National Park regulations prohibit rock-climbing or perhaps, nowadays, mountaineers find the area of Malyovitsa in the Rila mountains more attractive.

The NW ridge of the Pirin mountains runs from the Vihren over Kutyelo (2908m), Bansky Suhodol (2884m), Bayuvi Dupki (2820m), Kamyenititsa (2726m), to Mount Pirin (2593m). Their N faces run down to other big cirques full of caves. The whole of this area is protected, as the Bayuvi Dupki-Dzhindzhiritsa reservation. The most frequently visited parts are the long trail running over the highest summits to the Predel pass, and the area around the Yavorov hut (1740m), accessible from the north from the town of Razlog.

A less visited area lies more to the east: the Demyanishka valley with the Demyanitsa hut (1895m) and, further east still, the resort of Gotse Delchev (1450m). Our plan was to attain this resort and the Bezbog hut (2237m) above it, and to cross the main ridge of the Pirin to the S side, finishing the trip in Melnik, a small town with marvellous, unusual scenery. In 1976 I finished my trip in Melnik, too, but by a different route. We crossed the main ridge straight from the Bynderishka valley via the Byegovitsa hut (today named Kamyenitsa hut), lying in forests on the S slopes of Pirin. This is a good starting point for Mount Kamyenitsa (2822m), shown in the guidebooks as an attractive pyramid reflected in the lake, which I climbed in 1976. I remember that we were surprised, after crossing the main ridge to the south, to find a changed landscape of soft green hills used as pasture for sheep and donkeys. The climate was different too: the air was warm and dry and it grew hotter and more stagnant as we approached Melnik. We had left the cold wind and snow behind.

In 1989 we made our way to the Bezbog hut above Gotse Delchev by train, taxi and on foot (because the new chair-lift was out of order). We spent the next night in tents on the banks of the Byezbozhko lake (2240m), but at midnight a strong wind blew up, damaging the tents and forcing us to evacuate ourselves to the hut (an unforgettable experience for the younger members of the party). We spent a day exploring the peaks of Bezbog (2645m) and Polezhan (2851m) which, from the valley, looked rocky and inaccessible but which were actually quite easy. After boring climbs to the passes we enjoyed the route-finding and scrambling over the stone cirques and ridges.

Next morning we set out on our longest trip. First we came down over the Bezbozhki Preval pass to Lake Popovo, the largest of the 158 lakes of Pirin. Situated in a wide valley, this lake is the junction-point of marked trails from the

Demyanitsa hut (over the Samodivska Porta pass previously known as the Dzhengalska pass) and from the Bezbog hut over the Zhelezni Vrata pass (previously Demirkapya) and the Zheleznishka valley. The lake is set in a wide, open landscape, quite different from the Vihren area, with clear views to the peaks of Samodivski (previously Dzhengal, 2730m), Momin Dvor (2725m) and Kralev Dvor (2680m) on one side, and of Ostrets (previously Sivriya, 2593m) and Orlovets (Dzhano, 2668m) on the other.

The Zhelezni Vrata pass, which was our goal, could be seen from the lake as a trapeze-shaped depression on the skyline. We came upon it almost unawares: suddenly, to the south, lay another world. To our right, the rocky peaks of Kamyenitsa and Yalovarnika, topped with white clouds, framed the Zheleznishka valley; while, to the east, on our left, the tops of Orlovets, Krivets (previously Chengenchal, 2709m), Zheleznik (Demirchal, 2673m) and Hleven (2645m) rose above a long and deep valley. A winding footpath threaded its way along a stream, towards the twin lakes of Argirivo and Mitrovo, and the Demirkapiyski cirque. We knew that the Pirin hut, situated at the far end of this valley , was still a long way away.

As it was such a nice day, two of us decided to make a detour by climbing over the E ridge and descending the hills more or less in the middle of the valley where we would rejoin the rest of the group. This was a very good idea indeed and we look back upon it with pleasure. The precipitous ridge finished at the top of Orlovets and we moved above the valley from top to top without trouble. To the east, the Pirin mountains sloped down to the Mesta river valley and the green hills of the Rodopi mountains; to the west, rugged rocky peaks reminded us that we ourselves were among them, at the same height. Afraid of missing our comrades, we turned straight down towards the valley, following a precipitous route among rocky ledges and unaware that a comfortable footpath ran down from the next pass, the Kornishki Preval, to the bottom of the valley where the rest of our group was waiting for us.

Our walk on the final day of our trip was along tracks through the dense forest, with dry ditches running alongside them. At one time these had probably been used to irrigate the lower areas and villages. Five hours later we reached the Rozhenski Monastery, with its Orthodox Church full of the subtle smell of thin wax candles and the murmur of oft-repeated prayers. Now a fascinating trail ran through deep canyons hidden deep within the soft southern mountainside of the Pirin. Soon the view to the south, towards the Slavyanka range which lay on the Greek border, disappeared behind the curtain of yellow hills surrounding Melnik. Our journey through these sandstone pyramids and tetrahedrons, with their rocky towers and pinnacles, left us with an unforgettable memory, and it was not surprising that our day ended in the local winevault! Indeed, our visit to Melnik was the highlight of our trip, and anyone travelling through the Pirin mountains should make a point of going there.

The Grosse Spitzkop –
Matterhorn of Namibia

A Climbing History

MICHAEL SCOTT

(Plates 77, 78)

With Namibian independence in terms of UN Resolution 435 a reality from 21 March 1990, it seems an appropriate time to publicize the territory's mountains – and in particular the remarkable Spitzkop.

Like a shimmering mirage, the peak rises towering above burning, arid plains in the heart of Damaraland, 50km from Usakos, the nearest town. This rosy granite inselberg has an altitude of 1728m. Its proud pyramid shape has been flattened on a north–south axis to form a mile-long serrated ridge behind the summit cone. Vast sweeps of smooth walls rise for some 700m sheer out of the plains, and massive columns of blistered crumbling rock give little encouragement to the climber's eye seeking an easy line.

Legend has it that a German party forced a way up, sent a smoke signal, then failed to return. No proof of this enterprise exists, and the mountaineering discovery in modern times is credited to the redoubtable Dennis Woods, who cited it as the most memorable landmark on his trip through the deserts in 1938.

Woods returned in 1940 with Servie le Roux and I C Smith. The soaring, conical shaft of pink granite towering above the surrounding wastes reminded them of an elephant's tusk or rhino's horn. To Woods it was '2000ft of naked stone piercing the blue of the firmament like a great scimitar'. He perceived the summit curving over in a manner reminiscent of the Matterhorn, and commented that 'the changing shades of pink and purple lighting the precipices in the glory of the sunset, or flush of dawn, are unforgettable'.

The group made two attempts on the peak. After the first, having followed a system of gullies choked with huge boulders on the E wall, Woods returned with a wrenched knee. Smith and le Roux continued the line and fought their way up ledges and corridors, climbing hard jam-cracks and chimneys of rough crumbling rock, to be stopped by the massive, unclimbably smooth gendarme block behind the summit. This block was to prove the nemesis of many other parties coming later. Frustrated like this, it is small wonder that Smith felt the peak's magic had turned hostile, the poisonous, prickly vegetation on the hot slopes lying like a curse on the unwary.

In 1945, a party of German climbers from Swakopmund tried the peak by the same route, prepared to force their way with all the post-war climbing aids, but they got no further.

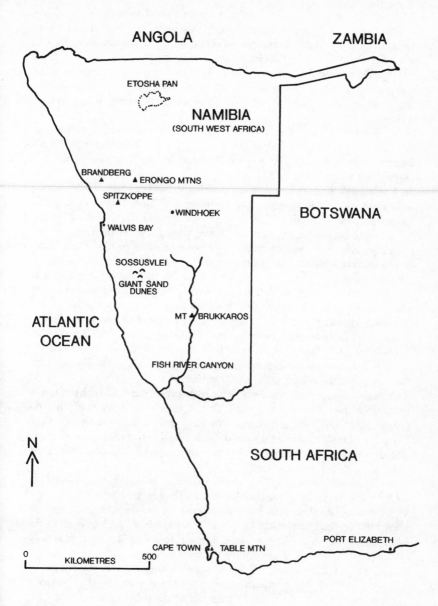

July 1946 saw a strong contingent from Cape Town arrive: P O'Neill ('Peggy'), Les Schaff and O Shipley (Ship). They were lured by this mysterious spire, to make the nightmare journey via train and lorry through dust and sun-scorched desert. Camp was between the towering red granite walls of a canyon nearby. They noted that unfamiliar techniques were required on these holdless slabs. They could friction-walk only up to an angle of 50° in their 'tackies' (tennis shoes), and otherwise had to follow cracks and chimneys if they were to advance at all.

The first attempt was on the W wall, where they friction-walked the whaleback formations avoided by earlier parties, and followed Servie le Roux's beacons on the ridge to the 20m eggshell-smooth block. To cross it required an engineering feat, and they tried to abseil 30m on either side to get past, with no luck. Although the N face looked impossible and had been totally ruled out by earlier parties, O'Neill's party had no other alternative left. They were surprised to find camouflaged gullies, chimneys and wormholes behind jammed blocks, which led to a cathedral-high narrow leaning passage cutting right through the mountain. This now famous three-step chimney takes a bend in the middle, which means the crucial last portion is done in darkness, before one emerges on to a platform approximately 25m from the summit. Above this the rock is blank, and the party descended the gully below it to a tree and made an 18m abseil on to a large ledge strewn with boulders which led to easier breaks on the W corner. However, a 10m bulge blocked entry to any of the breaks. A bivouac and another day's attempts failed to get them through. With the thought of 'so near and yet so far' came the agonized soul-searching, culminating in O'Neill's words: 'If the mountain will not yield to ordinary methods, we shall violate the rules of mountaineering and *cut* our way to the top!'

Four days later the party was back with hammer and cold chisel. During those four days they endured hardships of a different nature. Having no transport of their own, they started the long trek back across the desert to Usakos, and took the wrong direction. Some time later a farmer picked up the dehydrated group; with all the thirst-quenching required in Usakos, buying the chisel took longer than expected!

When they descended the fixed rope on the abseil once more, the unthinkable happened – the rope broke and Shipley tumbled 10m on to the ledge, bruised but alive. They reflected on the state of their equipment, and on what their predicament would have been if the accident had happened to the last man on the rope. The free-climbing pitch to get up the abseil was only opened in the 1960s by Brian Honey, wearing modern friction boots, and he graded it a protectionless F3 (USA-5.8) – not a proposition for the 1940s.

Using some rope gymnastics and support from a home-made massive piton hammered behind a flake, O'Neill and Schaff balanced precariously for two hours and managed to chip four steps. At this stage storm clouds were rolling in, and they retreated in gale-force winds. After seven days of battling against the Spitzkop defences, the peak was baring its fangs in final defiance. O'Neill had few regrets, as he felt they had unlocked the weakest link in the peak's closely-guarded chain of secrets.

Some months later, during November 1946, Hans and Else Wongt-

schowski arrived. They were known as the Wongs in much of the literature –
their full surname was too difficult. With them was a young Jan de Villiers
Graaff and a non-climbing companion, Rex Dey. Led by Hans the three
climbers set off. Following the normal route they were soon belaying off the
large piton. Then the leader stood on the second man's shoulders to reach the
first two steps. They are fairly spacious, but nearly three metres up. (Nowadays
this is F2 in friction boots, although the steps have been considerably enlarged
over the years, and F3 if one avoids the steps altogether.)

Jannie Graaff wrote that it must have required exceptional balance to
have stood there in tennis shoes cutting the steps, and was probably
unjustifiable without the support of the piton. Initially they were unable to
move higher than the second set of two steps, which were only toe size, and on
their second day's attempts they managed to chip a fifth hold, with some
difficulty. The red, weathered surface has first to be cleared off, to expose the
hard blue granite underneath. Stepping on to the vague depression made, the
leader could friction-walk to easier ground. There followed a series of cracks
and chimneys; the last one – a fierce struggle for large people – was mastered by
handing over the lead to Jannie, and then they were on the summit.

Until April 1960 the route of the original climb remained the only one to
the top. It took over 10 years until the second ascent was accomplished, by Dave
Smith and Graham Louw on 2 January 1957. They were followed in June 1957
by the third ascent party, comprising Horst Lachenmann and Rosalie and Ken
Bethune. The latter were to figure prominently in the formation of the South-
West Africa mountain club, whilst Horst later participated in the opening of the
W face route.

A year later, in July 1958, Lachenmann accompanied Friedrich Schreiber
up the *voie normale*, carrying three sections of metre-long angle-iron which had
formed part of a worn-out Herkules windmill that pumped water for 50 years
on a nearby farm. It had been imported from the Dresdener Windturbinen-
werke in the old German colonial days. From the girders they erected a summit
cross which was still standing proudly in July 1966, when I made the 19th
ascent of the peak in Colin Inglis's party. On my second visit, in December
1989, Barrie Cheetham and I formed the 235th party, and the cross was gone.
The records tin was damaged by lightning, and finally, in September 1988, the
cross was taken down by Adam Roff and Duncan Elliot. They felt an
uncluttered summit was preferable.

Lachenmann, Schreiber and Bethune waited two years before they
returned on 13 January 1960 and climbed the E wall via a number of chimneys
to a point below the nek between the infamous gendarme and the peak. They
did not wish to use mechanical means or top-roping to get over the smooth 8m
overhang blocking their way, so instead they made the 10th ascent via the
normal route and got on to the 'unclimbable gendarme' at last, from the back.

Restraint with mechanical aid was abandoned when Schreiber and
Lachenmann, now with the addition of Richard Helm, on 16–17 April 1960
pioneered the weaknesses of the W wall – long thought to be the smooth and
impractical side. They used 40 pitons and twice needed rope tension to aid them
across awkward traverses. At one stage they formed a precarious climbing tree,

when all three men stood on each other's shoulders like the Bremer town musicians, so that the leader could reach the holds. Their route gave them problems with loose rocks, crumbling piton cracks and strong winds which blew one hat right off the owner's head. On the second day after their bivouac at the gendarme nek, the wind strengthened to gale force, so a fixed rope was used to bypass the gendarme, and they finished up the final chimney crack used by the first ascensionists. Even so, the route was recognized as a separate ascent line, but it was not attempted again for 14 years.

This was the 11th ascent of the peak, and the first by a new route up a peak that at that stage had been climbed by only 19 different people, three of them ladies.

No new climbing was done for 10 years, until in 1970 the American Dr Tom Choate came touring SWA with Val and Anne King. They climbed a N face gully variation to the start of the normal route, then avoided the cut steps on the crux section by traversing on friction climbing over to the left, where a layback move got them into a crack and gully which joins the usual route higher up.

Two University of Cape Town students, Tim Hughes and Rodney Lichtman, who had practised on the granite of Lion's Head in Cape Town, visited the peak in November 1972. They did a NE Frontal, apparently somewhat to the right of the 1960 E face attempt, by following parallel cracks up two huge columns leaning against the peak. Tim remarked that from the correct angle one could see right through a gap behind the columns. They ended on top of the blocks above the three-step chimney on the original route and, hanging precariously and boldly off two bathook moves, they could reach moderate climbing to the top. Back on the peak after two years' break, Tim and Rodney repeated Schreiber's 1960 route, eliminating most of the aid and, more significantly, avoiding the traverse on to the standard route by climbing the smooth 8m overhang at grade F3 on 18 December 1974.

It was inevitable that the exploratory rock-climber Eckhard Haber would get to the Spitzkop, and he did so in 1982, when over three days he opened the 550m-high SW wall route with Clive Ward. Totally modern in style and approach, it has desperately hard, thin climbing with bold leads, where protection consists only of a few bolt hangers far apart.

Since then the climbing explosion on the main peak and on the subsidiary Pontok (or Pondok) Spitze has resulted in a guidebook to the area, along with, somewhat more sadly, better roads, meaning easier access, more litter, more denudation of vegetation, and less chance nowadays that you will have the Spitzkop all to yourself for a memorable climbing trip on a unique mountain.

BIBLIOGRAPHY

MCSA Journals 1940, 1946, 1960, 1970, 1974.
D Bristow, Mountains of Southern Africa. Cape Town (Struik), 1985.
J Burman, A Peak to Climb. Cape Town (Struik), 1966.
D Coulson, Mountain Odyssey. Johannesburg (Macmillan), 1983.
E Mountain, Geology of South Africa. Cape Town (Books of Africa), 1968.

Descents
(for Gill)

TERRY GIFFORD

Always I stayed too long up there,
in too deep, out too far
on the highest places,
turning on those pinnacle points
towards snow, lakes, woods
and whole ranges of colour,
soft High Sierra skylines
of cloud shadowed strata –
red rounded Dana
or the white Minarets.

But the descents were yours
in more than just direction,
or my guilt, or sheer speed
flowing down the dust scree
off Mount Hoffman, then loping along
the last hidden meadow
before jogging round rocks
to May Lake and shouting
your name, echoing
across the still water.

And from Cathedral Peak
reading boulders like chessmen
across grooved glacial slabs
to pick up the trail, panting
but feeling antelope-fit
over the logs of Budd Creek
and sensing the Meadows road
getting closer and closer,
three hours late from my solo
but through darkening trees
calling your name again
and again . . .

You'd brought beer in the car
and wanted no nonsense
like 'The summits are mine
but the descents are yours.'

Christmas on Chimborazo

MICHAEL BINNIE

*When I was but thirteen or so
I went into a golden land
Chimborazo, Cotopaxi
Took me by the hand.*

In my case I was twenty-three or so and my journey, unlike the imaginary one of Walter Turner in his *Romance*, was substantial, though hardly less fantastic. It was to the Cordillera Carabaya in Southern Peru that five of us were spirited in 1960 where we were privileged to make seven first ascents in a range that had barely been explored. That was my magic hour, all those years ago – and I hadn't been on a 'real' expedition since.

So when I read in the November 1989 AC circular that a second person was wanted on an expedition to go to Tierra del Fuego, leaving on 1 January for six weeks, I became suddenly excited. There was a telephone number. Then I thought about it. Of course I couldn't go. I couldn't afford it, nor could I get the time off from work. It was quite impossible.

So I rang the number . . . Another man had been found.

That night I toyed with my dinner and my wife asked me what the matter was. So I spilt the beans and she, bless her, suggested I consider somewhere that would take up less time. So I thought of Ecuador. None of my old climbing friends could make it ('if only you'd thought of it earlier'), but nothing was going to stop me – dammit, I would solo Chimborazo if need be – and then I thought of Will Gault. He is 20 years my junior, a City man and, crucially, a bachelor. I rang him at work.

'Doing anything at Christmas?'

'Not really. Anything on?'

'Want to climb a mountain in Ecuador?'

And, after a very short pause, 'Yes, OK.'

We flew out of Heathrow on 18 December and the return date on the ticket was exactly 14 days later. Chimborazo (6300m) was first climbed by Whymper in 1880; by his, the normal, route there are no technical problems. But would we acclimatize in a fortnight? There was much umming and ahing by climbing friends. Diamox was advised, and taken.

We arrived in Quito (2800m) at 7.30am on the 19th, on the first of 14 brilliant mornings, temperature 75F each day, all day. We found a cheap but adequate hotel in the old, colonial quarter and proceeded to explore the plazas, baroque churches and markets. Was this really happening to me? Classic cliché – could this be a dream?

> *I walked home with a gold dark boy,*
> *And never a word I'd say,*
> *Chimborazo, Cotopaxi*
> *Had taken my speech away.*

We climbed a hill behind the hotel and there it was, Cotopaxi, suspended above the city, the perfect volcano, a faultless cone, its glacial tongues hanging from its crater like the frayed edge of a distant, hazy petticoat. Each day we took a bus out of the city and made a four or five-hour walk on the surrounding hills, increasing the height each day by approximately 500m so that on the third day we reached 4200m. We were treated to wonderful views of Cayembe, Antisana (both first climbed by Whymper), as well as Cotopaxi. By 11am, even earlier sometimes, the peaks were obscured by cloud and for the rest of the day their positions were detectable only by the banks of cumulus, bouffant clouds, piled thousands of feet into the sky.

The countryside was full of interest. There were women in traditional, full, black skirts, scarlet shawls and wide-brimmed sombreros tending little herds of tethered pigs and cattle; a man ploughing with a team of oxen. We passed one farmer wearing an industrial hard hat hoeing the steepest field of potatoes I had ever seen. He was pleased to be photographed (this was not always the case), as was a woman weaving baskets outside her mud-walled, tin-roofed hut. Sometimes we passed through eucalyptus groves, and a lasting memory will be the sound of strands of peeling bark, caught by the wind, clattering softly against the trunks of these slender, graceful trees.

Day four was Saturday when we made a trip to the famous Otavalo market and crammed our rucksacks with bargain sweaters as presents for everyone we could think of back home – and so ended the honeymoon period. For the next day we would travel to Chimborazo. I remember saying to Will, for whom this was his first major climb: 'From now on it will be Hell.'

I hadn't enjoyed my day at 4200m and, while lying in the grass at that height and fitfully dozing, I experienced the rather alarming phenomenon of Cheyne-Stokes breathing. We had another 2000m to make up, and only a week to do it in.

On Christmas Eve we staggered to Quito's main bus terminal under enormous rucksacks. Will is well over 6 feet tall and towered above the neat, diminutive Ecuadorians. We looked somewhat ridiculous in all our gear, climbing breeches and enormous boots. At the bus station a shoeshine boy offered to clean mine for me.

We boarded a bus for Ambato and thundered south along the Pan-American Highway, wildly overtaking anything that moved. The windscreen, rent by an enormous crack which threatened to cave in on the driver at any moment, was plastered with crucifixes and images of the Virgin. The conductor, a boy of about 14, fought his way down the bus through the mass of humanity and eventually reached us where we were being hurled wildly about above the wheel arches. The fare for the two-hour journey was 50p. 'A rip-off,' said Will.

So we reached Ambato, which was destroyed by an earthquake 50 years ago and looked it, and negotiated a price with a taxi-driver to take us on the next leg – a two-hour drive to the Whymper hut at the foot of Chimborazo.

It was then that we remembered about the paraffin. Will had traipsed round several garages in Quito without being able to get any. Our stove ran on it. Rumour had it that there might not be any gas at the hut. I wasn't looking forward to my space-food dinners in any case, but *cold* space food . . . and on Christmas Day?

'*Quiero comprar paraffin,*' I said to the driver. We had stowed our rucksacks into the boot and were all ready to *vamos*.

'Paraffin?' He looked nonplussed.

'Si, paraffin.' Total incomprehension.

Will: 'Try kerosene.'

'Kerosene?'

'Kerosene?'

'Si, kerosene.' I went through a pantomime – lighting a match, pumping a primus, stirring a pot, sipping a hot drink. 'Kerosene.' We had started to drive but suddenly the driver, Luis, stopped.

'Kerex?' he asked hopefully.

Now it was my turn. 'Kerex?'

'Si, kerex, boom, boom,' and he threw his hands in the air in the manner of minor explosions. We drove slowly round the town, Luis muttering 'Kerex' to himself and looking about him, shaking his head and shrugging his shoulders. 'Domingo,' he said, and indeed it was Sunday, and lunchtime, and Christmas Eve. An awful lot of shops looked ominously closed. We stopped at several garages. No kerex. Luis was genuinely concerned. Then he looked hopeful.

'In pueblo?' he suggested.

We drove out of town into the parched countryside, past steep little fields of withered corn (for it hadn't rained for months). We stopped frequently at roadside stores and a garage. But always the same answer, 'Kerex no hay.' At one village we drove up a track to stop outside an unprepossessing hovel. By now Will had unpacked his rucksack, the contents of which were strewn all over the back of the taxi – ironmongery, spare clothes, packets of food – in order to get out the primus which he was now using as a visual aid. He was not amused. Luis ushered him into the hut. I remained outside entertaining some children and a drunk old man. Will reappeared in five minutes.

'I've got it,' he said.

'Do you think it's the right stuff?'

'I've no idea.'

The whole episode had made us ridiculously tense.

We drove on, climbing steadily, past the last trees and hamlets into the paramó, a region of sandy soil, cinders and tussock grass. Families tended flocks of sheep, a cow or two and even a few llamas by the roadside. Eventually we crossed a wide, shallow pass and there, ahead of us, crouched the squat bulk of a mountain enveloped in cloud. It was a bleak scene.

'Chimborazo,' said Luis, hoping to cheer us up.

He drove us for several more miles up a dirt-road and dropped us at the hut around 2pm that afternoon. We were at 4700m and at the lower of two huts, the upper being a mere half-mile away and 200m higher up the mountain. We decided to carry half our gear to the top (Whymper) hut and to return and sleep at the lower one. The next morning, Christmas Day, we established ourselves at the higher hut and took stock of our situation.

It was still only our sixth day in the country. Neither of us felt anything like our best. Fully acclimatized parties, those in effect which had previously climbed Cotopaxi or Tungurahua (over 5000m) or both, went as a rule straight to the top hut and climbed the Whymper route, starting at midnight and making a round trip of 8–12 hours. We discounted this plan and decided to sleep two, possibly three, nights at the Whymper hut, spending the intervening days training on the mountain. We would thus acquire, we hoped, at least adequate acclimatization to make a two-day assault on the route, bivouacking the first night at about 5500m.

The Whymper route is technically easy but long. It starts with 300m of scree to the SE of the hut to gain an easy ridge which runs north to the main bulk of the mountain. Then a short steep wall, rent by half-a-dozen gullies, provides a minor obstacle. None of these gullies is difficult, but they nevertheless constitute the steepest part of the climb. We planned to bivvy here. On Christmas Day we got as far as the gully systems (known locally as the *canalettos*) and on Boxing Day we climbed about halfway up the Thielmann glacier. At the end of that day we reckoned we could 'go for it'. Meanwhile, back at the hut, there was Wayne; and Anna.

Wayne and Paul were from California and, like us, were spending several days on the mountain, acclimatizing. They had left a tent and provisions on the ridge leading to the canalettos and were planning to make a two-day ascent, at approximately the same time as us. However, Paul was very out-of-sorts and had decided to pull out. We invited Wayne to join us. Anna was a Venezuelan and a student at Caracas University. Hers was a long story, the gist of which was that she had travelled across Venezuela, Colombia and Ecuador by bus to join up with a group from her university climbing club. Somehow wires had got crossed, and here she was on Chimborazo by herself. Umm. She had climbed Cotopaxi the week before and was, we couldn't help noticing, rather beautiful. She spoke English in an attractive Hispanic-American accent, interspersed with the odd delightful malapropism. We were definitely charmed by Anna. Would she like to join us on the climb? She would be delighted.

Next day, 27 December, we left at midday for our respective bivouacs. Wayne and Anna would camp a little below us and we agreed that they would join us at two the next morning. Will and I proceeded up to the canalettos and after scouting around found ourselves a couple of crumbling ledges below the red wall. As the afternoon advanced a magnificent cloud sea developed below us, lit finally by a short, spectacular sunset. Suddenly it was night, the temperature dropped dramatically and within a few moments the glacial stream beside us had frozen. We leapt for our sleeping bags. Then a boulder trundled off the cliff above to land dispiritingly close to our ledges, an inconvenience which was to continue intermittently all night. At one point during the wee hours I noticed that the clouds below had dispersed, and I enjoyed the sight of the lights of two towns shining thousands of feet below us – Ambato, I supposed, to the north and Guaranda (see Whymper) to the south. They were rather comforting.

Reveille at 1.15am, a forced breakfast of a few dried apricots and orange powder squash, dressing and kitting up by torchlight while balancing on our ledges occupied the next 45 minutes; but at two o'clock Wayne's pinprick of torchlight was still a long way off. We stamped about on our ledge, beating our arms and still shivering. At last, at three, we were joined by Wayne and Anna and we realized why they had been so long. Anna had no torch. She was also complaining of the cold and I could see at a glance that she had lost the will to do the route. Fortunately she realized this herself and, as Will had a spare hand-torch, she was quite happy to walk back down the ridge on her own to Wayne's tent. The three of us now tied on to a single rope and I led two pitches up the gully, belayed by the other two who then moved as a pair to join me. Thereafter we moved together up a wide featureless snow slope.

I was climbing painfully slowly, clearly affected by the altitude; Wayne was not going well either and asked for frequent stops. After 20 minutes he called a halt and suggested he go down. I persuaded him to give me his rucksack – we had left ours at the bivouac – and we continued to plod up, but after another rope-length or so he again called out to me. 'I don't want you to bust your ass for me,' was how he put it. 'I know I'm holding you guys up.' We all felt very disappointed but he insisted on untying and returning down. I'm quite sure we could all have made it to the top.

The route now made a long traverse left beneath some seracs on the summit ridge. Because of these seracs which occasionally fall across the traverse line in the heat of the late morning, the route is climbed at night. Apart from a few small crevasses and ice cliffs, easily avoided, the traverse was uneventful. Dawn was just breaking as we gained the summit ridge. Above stretched a seemingly endless snowfield up which we crept slowly, stopping frequently. We reached the top at 8am. Only it wasn't the top. We knew all about this, for the Whymper summit is half a mile away and a mere 40m higher. Many parties return from the lower summit, for Chimborazo has effectively been climbed. The decision to go on was unspoken. All Will said was: 'I suggest we de-rope here,' and I owe it to him that we reached the true top for, left to myself, I might easily have turned back. We descended into a shallow basin and then up on to the dome-like summit. By now I was coughing frequently and bringing up a lot of nasty-looking phlegm, but Will seemed in good shape. Forty miles or so to the north Cotopaxi thrust up through the sea of cloud. The round trip from summit to summit had taken us an hour. It was 10 days since we had left London. And the kerex *had* turned out to be the right stuff.

During the descent I dropped off to sleep at the frequent rests. I reached the hut at about 1pm, where Will had been for a good hour. He came out to meet me.

'Anna has gone,' he said.

Ah, well . . .

Paul had arranged a lift for us to Riobamba which we reached that evening. Oh, the delights of a hot shower in the – where else – Hotel Whymper (there is even a street in Quito named after the great man). At dinner that night Paul said: 'When I got to my room I looked inside the sleeping bag and there were *sheets* in it!'

Early next morning I went on to the hotel roof to get a last view of the mountain. The view from the south-east across the rooftops of Riobamba was as perfect as I could have wished for. After breakfast I came up again. The clouds were creeping up the sides and only the summit dome was visible. I dashed down to my room to get my camera for a final, final shot but when I returned Chimborazo was no more.

> *The houses, people, traffic seemed*
> *Thin fading dreams by day,*
> *Chimborazo, Cotopaxi*
> *They had stolen my soul away!*

The Seven Summits

On the highest mountains of all continents

OSWALD OELZ

(Plates 79, 80)

The Swiss climber Dölf Reist was the first to succeed in climbing the highest peaks of five continents. He reached the summit of Mont Blanc in his early years, climbed Mount Everest in 1956, Mount McKinley in 1961, Kilimanjaro in 1969 and Aconcagua in 1971. At that time the highest point of Antarctica, the Vinson Massif, was inaccessible; and Mount Kosciusko in Australia was considered too insignificant to justify such a long trip from Europe. The Japanese climber Naomi Uemura later repeated Dölf Reist's feat.

In 1981 Dick Bass, a millionaire from Texas, created the idea of climbing the 'Seven Summits' which include the Vinson Massif and Mount Kosciusko. Furthermore, Mount Elbrus in the Caucasus replaced Mont Blanc as the highest peak in Europe. Although it took Dick Bass more than four years, instead of one year as planned, to climb his Seven Summits, his achievement which culminated on the summit of Mount Everest in October 1985 was most remarkable, particularly if one considers the fact that Bass was not a mountaineer when he started thinking about the Seven Summits.

The Canadian mountaineer Pat Morrow competed with Dick Bass for the first full set of Seven Summits. He lost the race because he was unable to raise enough money to hire a plane for Antarctica. However, he introduced another hurdle by claiming that Carstensz Pyramid in Irian Jaya is the highest peak of Australasia. He argued, as did others such as Reinhold Messner, that Mount Kosciusko, whose top can be reached by car, should not be regarded as the highest point of that area but rather Carstensz Pyramid, a much higher and more difficult limestone mountain which is almost inaccessible for political reasons. Pat Morrow succeeded with his version of the Seven Summits on 7 May 1986, when he reached the summit of Carstensz Pyramid. Half a year later, on 27 November, Messner completed his collection with the Vinson Massif, having climbed Carstensz Pyramid already in 1971. The Dick Bass version of the Seven Summits was subsequently repeated by two more mountaineers, Gerry Roach from the USA and Gerhard Schmatz from Germany, but the version of Morrow and Messner with Carstensz Pyramid had not been repeated by February 1990.

Mount McKinley (Denali, 6194m), Alaska

After several attempts by various groups the highest peak of North America was climbed on 7 June 1913 by Hudson Stuck, the Archbishop of the Yukon Territory, together with three others. The thankful mountaineers said a Te Deum on the summit at a temperature of -14°C. In the meantime Mount McKinley has developed into a major goal for North American climbers and is attempted every year by several hundred mountaineers. The peak is considered to be one of the coldest mountains in the world, and temperatures far below −50°C have been measured.

Mount McKinley was my first big mountain. In June 1976, Reinhold Messner and I landed at the traditional place on the Kahiltna glacier and ascended the normal W ridge route in three days to the plateau at 4200m. There Messner identified an ice and snow couloir that led directly to the summit area and had not been climbed before. We decided to give it a try and started on 6 June at 2pm. We climbed gaining 200m of altitude per hour and had agreed not to wait for each other, never to sit down, and to turn round if our altitude gain dropped to less than 200m per hour. We carried neither rope, food nor drink. Messner led all the way and reached the summit half an hour before midnight, while I followed almost exactly at midnight. During our descent, which followed the route by which we had come up, we experienced the Alaskan sunrise at 30 minutes after midnight. The 'detachment from the world so far below', which had already impressed the archbishop and his colleagues, was an intense experience.

Mount Everest (8872m), Nepal

On 29 May 1953, Ed Hillary and Tenzing Norgay reached the summit of Everest for the first time. Although Everest has by now been climbed more than 300 times, the success-to-death ratio on this mountain is still terrible: for every three climbers who have reached the summit there is one who has died on the slopes of the mountain. The statistical chances for an individual climber to reach the summit during any one expedition are below five per cent. When I was a member of the Austrian Everest expedition in 1978, the chances for Messner and Habeler to reach the summit 'by fair means', that is, without bottled oxygen, were considered to be even lower. Furthermore, many experts had predicted that Messner and Habeler, even if they got to the summit at all, would be victims of irreversible brain damage. On 9 May I had the privilege of examining them 16 hours after their summit success at an altitude of 7400m. It was a pleasure to ascertain that they had retained their mental capacity intact. My climbing partner was Reinhard Karl who was at that time the most original and most successful German mountaineer. He died in 1982 in an ice avalanche on the S face of Cho Oyu, during our next climb together. However, in 1978 we were two very happy, although breathless, human beings when two days later we stood on the summit of the world after a 6½ hour climb from the South Col.

Vinson Massif (4895m), Antarctica

The Vinson Massif was first climbed on 18 December 1966 by an American expedition, with substantial support by the US navy which provided the essential transport to the Base Camp. After that, private journeys into Antarctica were strongly discouraged by all nations running scientific (and pseudo-scientific) operations on the seventh continent. In the autumn of 1986 Messner, having climbed all the 14 eight-thousand-metre peaks, succeeded in organizing the money and transport for our long-desired journey to Antarctica. The legendary Giles Kershaw, the best pilot of Antarctica, took us together with some Americans to the foot of the mountain. It was the most exciting and impressive flight that we had ever had in our life. 33 hours after landing we reached the highest point of Antarctica and enjoyed the splendid isolation and a unique environment reduced to just light, sun, ice, cold and fog far below.

Aconcagua (6960m), Argentina

After having climbed three of the most difficult peaks of the Seven Summits, my appetite for the others grew. On our return journey from Antarctica we were forced to spend six days in Santiago de Chile. We used this for a quick trip to Aconcagua which we climbed in 2½ days from Puente del Inca. It was an easy way to come back to this mountain, where I had spent one month on the S face in 1974 and was forced back just below the final slopes because a friend had developed cerebral oedema. It was also quite a contrast to the adventurous first ascent by Matthias Zurbriggen from the Valais Alps who summited alone on 14 January 1897. His expedition leader, Edward A Fitzgerald, had become a victim of acute mountain sickness and was almost unable to stand on his feet in their last camp at 6400m.

Kilimanjaro (5895m), Tanzania

The highest peak of Africa was climbed on 6 October 1889 by the German geographer Hans Meyer, together with Ludwig Purtscheller from Salzburg. This success was a result of Meyer's perseverance. At his first try in 1887 he had had to turn back at the edge of the crater, and during his second try in 1888 he was captured by rioting natives, put in chains and transported back to the coast. Meyer noted with German pride: *'es erschien mir fast als eine nationale Pflicht, daß der Gipfel des Kilimandscharo, wahrscheinlich des höchsten afrikanischen und zweifellos des höchsten deutschen Berges, der von einem Deutschen (Rebmann) entdeckt und von einem Deutschen (von der Decken) zuerst näher untersucht wurde, nach allen Bemühungen englischer Reisender doch zuerst von einem deutschen Fuss betreten werde.* He planted *auf dem verwitterten Lavagipfel mit dreimaligem, von Herrn Purtscheller kräftig sekundierten Hurra eine kleine, im Rucksack mitgetragene deutsche Fahne auf,* and joyfully proclaimed: *Mit dem Recht des ersten Ersteigers taufe ich diese bisher unbekannte namenlose Spitze des Kibo, den höchsten Punkt afrikanischer und deutscher Erde: Kaiser Wilhelm Spitze.*

When I stood, together with my wife, at this very spot in the autumn of 1987, the opening pop of a bottle of champagne seemed to me a more appropriate sound to celebrate the moment.

Elbrus (5633m), USSR

Craufurd Grove, Horace Walker, Frederick Gardiner and the Swiss guide Peter Knubel were the first mountaineers on the highest peak of Europe on 28 July 1874. They found the ascent over endless snow slopes to be 'exhausting and utterly unexciting'. They thought that their prostration was due, not so much to the thin air, but rather to 'not being in fit bodily condition for severe walking' and to the 'enforced abstinence from any kind of wine whatever and the total change of diet'. Nevertheless, Grove noted after their success that the only remaining question was 'how soon it will be practicable to ascend another peak'. I had similar thoughts when, standing on the summit of Elbrus in April 1989 in an icy storm, I noted many future mountain goals in the Caucasus. At that moment my wife and I celebrated my seventh summit in the style of Dick Bass, opening a bottle of almost freezing champagne from the Crimea. Three months earlier I had walked up to the summit of Kosciusko after a long flight to Australia.

Carstensz Pyramid (5030m or 4883m), Irian Jaya, Indonesia

The highest point of Australia/Oceania, first seen by the Dutch sailor Carstensz from the sea in 1623, is located in the central highlands of Irian Jaya, the Indonesian part of New Guinea (the exact height is uncertain). It is surrounded by almost impenetrable forests, and it took Heinrich Harrer, the first ascender in 1962, several weeks to get to the base of the mountain. He was supported by Dani porters who were at that time still living in a pure stone age culture. Harrer noted that the climbing was very rewarding because of the excellent firm limestone. Reinhold Messner made the second ascent in 1971, approaching the mountain from a missionary station in the highlands. Later hopefuls met even more difficult obstacles, because in the meantime the Indonesian government had started a joint venture with an American company to exploit the extremely rich copper sources of the area. With enormous effort and much money a road was built to a potential mining site, and the exploitation was started. Since the natives were not satisfied with the payments by the mining company they started some small sabotage actions. The Indonesian government reacted with machine gun fire and bombs from helicopters based on battleships, aimed against the Dani warriors armed with bow and arrow. Since then the area has been hermetically sealed to foreigners. Only a few Indonesian climbers and some daredevils have climbed Carstensz Pyramid since 1971 [*Editor's note:*

amongst them the Alpine Club members Richard Isherwood, Jack Baines and the late Peter Boardman.]

Reinhold Messner had told me about his adventurous journey to Carstensz Pyramid in 1971 and I had long waited for an opportunity to climb this mountain. Various attempts to get a permit all failed until I finally heard of an American climber with unusually good contacts in the US government who was apparently able to get such permits. After some transatlantic telephone discussions I met him and seven other North American climbers, among them Pat Morrow, at Biak, Irian Jaya. Five days later we finally got our special permit and approached the mountain through the mining area. Local porters assisted our transport for two days to the start of the climb. Subsequently the Danis rapidly retreated since the temperature dropped towards freezing and the continuous rain changed into snow. Carstensz Pyramid was not visible through the fog. We spent the following days climbing in almost constant rain and snowfall. Waterfalls seemed to block access to the higher parts of the mountain on all sides. On two days I reached the summit ridge but was forced back each time by storm and 30cm of snow on the rock. I spent most of my time sitting in my tent and drying my clothes over a candle. The penultimate try ended, several hundred metres west of the summit, on vertical rock plastered with ice. None of us had expected such conditions, and therefore our equipment was simply insufficient. While drying my clothes yet again over the candle flame I started to meditate, wondering whether Peter Matthiessen was right when, on his journey to Dolpo where he never sighted the longed-for snow leopard, he concluded that the journey was all the more successful because he did *not* reach his goal. However, I was not yet mature enough to accept this attitude with more than faked conviction.

On 16 March 1990, together with Pat Morrow and the British Antarctic veteran Martyn Williams, I started on a last attempt. Eventually we traversed the long ridge to the main summit, leaving a rope in place at a 40m high abseil site. After that we were in a white land where all the fantastic rough rock on the equator was plastered with ice. Reaching the summit in such conditions was a particularly rewarding culmination.

Mixed feelings

Climbing the five summits was a natural development for Dölf Reist because of his lifelong passion for mountaineering. The Seven Summits were an opportunity for Dick Bass to demonstrate that an American businessman in excellent bodily condition, with the help of money and a good portion of luck, can achieve almost anything. In the meantime climbing the Seven Summits has become a status symbol for executives and climbers. Actually, anyone with little more than average strength, the patience for long air journeys and some money in his bank account can without too much trouble climb five of the Seven Summits: Elbrus, Kilimanjaro, Mount McKinley, Vinson and Aconcagua. Carstensz Pyramid is still reserved for daredevils or people with very special political connections. Mount Everest is the eye of the needle, passable only by those with the fitness and experience resulting from long years of mountaineering. In addition, a good portion of luck is required at the decisive moment. Several mountaineers with five or six of the Seven Summits have yet to climb Everest. Thus the Seven Summits are not entirely buyable.

The original reports of the first ascenders of these mountains arouse nostalgic feelings. It took them months or even years to reach their goals; their expeditions were real in the sense of the Latin word *expeditio*, which means travelling to foreign unknown hostile country where the outcome is uncertain. I envy Stuck, Grove, Meyer, Zurbriggen, Hillary, Harrer and all the others for their adventures which are not repeatable any more. However, I am happy to have had the privilege of spending many moments above the clouds in another world which, as Herbert Tichy has written, seems not to have been made for human beings, and to have been able to experience the feeling of utter detachment from the world so far below.

(Translation, in slightly modified form, of an article in the Neue Zürcher Zeitung *for 10 May 1990. We thank Dr Hansjörg Abt for permission to publish this translation.)*

To Bolt or Not to Bolt

MICK FOWLER

The ethics involved in the sport of rock-climbing have long been a major source of debate in the letters pages of the climbing press.

Pitons, hold chipping, top-rope inspections ... all have been generally recognized as undesirable and have raised passionate feelings at some time or another. None, though, have succeeded in provoking as much heated debate as the ubiquitous expansion bolt.

Why, then, does the use of the bolt cause such a problem?

To those in favour of using bolts for protection (or even – God forbid – the occasional aid point) they would seem to offer the best of all worlds. Safety margins are increased, less gear has to be carried, standards can be raised and more routes are made available to the masses.

The anti-bolt lobby, though, does not see things this way. It strives to retain the traditional flirtation with excitement and danger which has always been an integral part of British rock-climbing. Their view is that, as bolts can be placed absolutely anywhere, their use means that even the most intimidating and featureless lines can be degraded to mere gymnastic exercises. Bolts in the eyes of the anti-bolt lobby are alien pieces of ironmongery which simply reduce the degree of boldness in a climb to the level that the first ascensionist can cope with.

In Britain at present we are at a curious halfway stage compared with the freely bolted French and Belgian crags just across the Channel. Some crags (Malham, slate etc) have bolts as the norm, whereas on others (gritstone, mountain crags etc) the odd bolt may exist, but bolting in general is very much frowned upon.

Regardless of their personal feelings about bolts, I think that very few anti-bolt climbers would seriously suggest removing all bolts from crags where such protection is now well-established. Pro-boltists, though, do see the possibilities for bolt-protected free climbing in currently bolt-free areas. A clash of interests is therefore unavoidable, and the subject is ripe for heartfelt debate and more.

In considering the best way forward, it is perhaps logical to look first towards France and Belgium and see what effect widespread bolting has had there.

Many crags in these countries now have a bolt every six feet or so (or less!), regardless of the amount of natural protection available. Bolts are expensive, and in an effort to maximize safety local clubs often take on the responsibility of making routes safe. A deal will often be struck with the bolt manufacturers, climbers being employed to place bolts where they are felt to be necessary. On a recent visit to the Continent it was explained to me that the policy often extends beyond just making hard new routes completely safe. Routes which have been established without bolts for many years are now hearing the hum of the cordless drill as novices and enthusiasts alike are encouraged to practise the sport in safety and without the additional worry of having to place their own protection. The whole bolt-protected ethic is one with which many Continentals feel far from comfortable, and one which raises justifiable concern that bolt-bred climbers are more likely to injure themselves when they visit areas without fixed protection. Many Continentals are also uncomfortably aware that they are turning their magnificent natural crags into giant replicas of man-made climbing walls.

It is reasonable to assume that, if the spread of the bolt is allowed to continue unchecked, then British climbers will soon see them appearing on classic crags and classic climbs. Cloggy, Gogarth, Cornish granite and Glencoe have already seen their first bolt placements. In the often inconsiderate and egotistical race for new climbs many leading activists feel that, if no other protection is available, bolts are justified – regardless of location. As we have seen on the Continent, the next step will be the bolting of routes already climbed without bolts. I believe the number of bolts on Tequila Mockingbird (Chee Tor) has already increased since the first ascent, and rumblings have been heard that Johnny Dawes's Indian Face would benefit (?!) from a bolt, in that more people would be able to enjoy its technical climbing. Beyond that, experience on the Continent shows that it is only a matter of time before Longlands and the Idwal Slabs hear the hum of the drill.

The time has clearly come to take stock of the situation, and to try to lay down some guidelines which will keep the majority of climbers happy in the future.

In Britain, areas now fall into three categories of bolt protection, and it is logical to consider each in turn:

1.   *Well-established bolt-protected areas (mainly slate and limestone)*
One only has to spend a day at Malham or in the Llanberis slate quarries to see that these are popular areas where many climbers enjoy being able to stretch themselves to their limit in bolt-protected safety. Also the blank slate and limestone walls are often devoid of cracks and there are no possibilities for natural protection. It follows that, if the bolts were removed, the routes would not be climbed and many keen climbers would be understandably upset at being deprived of so many fine quality climbs. A few years ago, when there were very few bolt-protected routes, my attitude would have been unsympathetic and very much in the 'if you can't do it without bolts, leave it for someone who can' mould. Now, debolting the popular bolted crags would be akin to debolting Verdon. It would upset too many people and be a virtual physical impossibility. Bearing in mind that the overall aim must be to keep as many people happy as possible, the anti-bolt lobby must accept that debolting in these areas is not now an option. They must also accept that many future routes will be bolt-protected.

2.   *Bolted routes in generally bolt-free areas (eg the Tunnel Wall routes in Glencoe, Atlantic Ocean Wall, Lands End etc)*

Here we are not looking at blank featureless crags offering no natural protection, but are considering routes forged up sparsely protected lines adjacent to traditional climbs. We have to stand back and ask ourselves whether we really want our traditional crags turned into bolt-protected gymnasiums. In researching this article I became convinced that the groundswell of feeling is against such routes, and my personal view is that all such bolts should be removed. If we allow such acts of bolting vandalism to continue, no new bold climbs will be established in Britain, and our climbing will lose much of its unique and rewarding flavour.

Having stated my own opinion, I have to concede that it is not up to any one individual to dictate what future policy should be. After all, it is a (nearly) free world, and anyone is legally entitled to place (or remove) a bolt wherever he/she likes. Local clubs clearly have their ears closest to the ground as regards local opinion and should therefore do their best to enforce the wishes of the majority of climbers in their area. However, on such a vital issue it would seem important for the British Mountaineering Council to test national feeling and to be represented in popular or contentious areas. This is imperative in our major climbing areas such as Cloggy, Scafell, Ben Nevis etc which are enjoyed by climbers from all over the country and not just by local activists. Before sanctioning bolting on such crags, we would need to be as certain as we could be that the action was in line with the wishes of the majority of British climbers.

If it ever happens, it will be a sad day for British climbing.

3.   *Non-bolted crags*

Here the policy for the future would seem best handled by local clubs in exactly the same way as detailed in the preceding paragraph. If any activists step outside 'no-bolt' policy guidelines, they can be ridiculed in the press and the offending bolts removed.

Such measures do seem rather drastic and bureaucratic, but we must make sure that we learn from the experience of Continental countries before it is too late. We must act now to preserve the sense of adventure and excitement in British climbing, and yet at the same time embrace the bolt-protected gymnastic side of the sport.

If we just ignore the problem, then five years from now we could see the BMC sponsoring bolt protection on Stanage.

Think about it. It differs little from the sponsorship by the Belgian Alpine Club of the bolting of the magnificent limestone crags at Freyr.

Mountains, Genes and Time

TED MADEN

(*Plates 81, 82*)

Several years ago a friend and I, after climbing some peaks in the Gran Paradiso area, planned to finish our holiday with an ascent of Mont Blanc by the Old Brenva Route. We arrived at the Trident hut in clear weather, but cloud to the south suggested unstable conditions, and nocturnal flickering of lightning across the Val d'Aosta deterred us from setting out in the early hours. When dawn came, the expected bad weather did not materialize. Instead we watched a perfect sunrise, pink turning to gold on the highest slopes of Mont Blanc, and stealing down the features of the Brenva face and the Peuteret ridge. Swallowing our disappointment, we turned our backs on the Brenva and climbed the Little Gervasutti couloir on the Tour Ronde instead.

When my colour slides came back from processing they recalled vividly the hues of sunrise on the great Brenva face. They also interacted with my thoughts at work. I was writing a research paper about a piece of sub-microscopic machinery that plays a central role in living cells. So central, in fact, that large parts of its structure have hardly changed at all during 65 million years of mammalian evolution. I looked at the slides again. Where was Mont Blanc 65 million years ago?

The answer, of course, is that it was nowhere to be seen. Entire mountain ranges, including the Alps and Himalaya, were built within this time-scale. The fact that features in the design of some biological structures should be more stable than the Earth's great mountain ranges is not intuitively obvious. What is the explanation?

Mountain building

Mountains are thrust up by colliding plates of the Earth's crust. The plates are in a state of continuous, slow movement relative to each other, carrying the continents raft-like on a substructure of basalt that spreads out from the mid-ocean ridges. The primary driving force for the movement is convection of heat generated in the Earth's interior, largely by the decay of naturally occurring radioactive atoms.

The rates of sea-floor spreading have been estimated by magnetic measurements, and are in the region of two to five centimetres per year.[1] The movements are transmitted through the rigid crustal plates. At boundary zones where two plates are being pushed into each other, one plate goes under, the other overrides, and folds and crumples. The detailed consequences depend upon additional factors including whether continental land is involved on either side of the collision zone. Collisions involving continental masses on one or both sides of the colliding zone generate land-based mountain ranges; colliding oceanic plate boundaries generate island arcs and ocean trenches. The general point is that two to five centimetres of relative movement per year add up to 20–50 *kilometres* per million years, enough for very extensive folding and crumpling. Add to this the attritional effects of weathering and glaciation, and it becomes obvious that great geographic changes occur at plate boundaries even in one million years.

The Southern Alps of New Zealand have been thrust up in the last few million years. India had not yet collided with Asia 65 million years ago, the interactions that have pushed up the Alps had not yet happened, and the Atlantic, with America moving away from Europe, was little more than half as wide as it is now. The face of the Earth was very different then.

And yet the design of the particular component of living machinery that I and my colleagues had been studying had remained virtually unchanged through all this time. Immortality does not reside in the component itself, however, but in the blueprint for its construction. The blueprint is a gene. The essential features of genes that determine their immortality can be illustrated very simply.

Gene replication

Imagine a long string with red, yellow, green and blue beads. The order in which the coloured beads are arranged carries coded information, eg:

red, blue, green; red, red, yellow; blue, green, red; etc.

Then imagine a second string paired with the first. On the second string the beads are arranged so that at each position the colour is complementary to that on the first string: red opposite to green, yellow opposite to blue. Now take the strings apart, and next to each string, make up a new string by following the same rules of complementary pairing, red opposite to green, yellow opposite to blue. You now have two pairs of strings. Each pair, comprising one old string and one new complementary string, is a perfect replica of the original pair. This is exactly how gene replication works, except that instead of beads of four colours there are chemical units of four shapes. The material that is made of these four units is called DNA, and genes are made of DNA. The order, or *sequence*, in which the chemical units occur is unique for each gene, and the chemical shapes dictate complementary pairing and very accurate replication.

Two examples can illustrate the kind of functions that genes specify. Both examples are of mountaineering interest: the first concerns oxygen transport.

Haemoglobin

Oxygen is carried from the lungs to the rest of the body via haemoglobin in the blood. In haemoglobin the oxygen binds reversibly to iron. The iron is held in a substance called haem, which in turn is held in a much larger substance called globin. In haemoglobin there are actually two types of globin, called alpha and beta, and there are two of each of these per complete haemoglobin molecule. This seemingly complicated structure determines the precise affinity of haemoglobin for oxygen, enabling efficient uptake in the lungs and release in the tissues.

Genes come into this scheme of things as follows. Each of the two types of globin is made from smaller units called amino acids, about 140 per complete globin. There are 20 chemically different amino acids, but it is the sequence in which they are assembled that is critical, just as with letters of the alphabet. The alpha and beta globin sequences are different from each other. Each of the two sequences, alpha and beta, is encoded in a separate gene.

There are also other globin genes. One of them encodes a globin called gamma, which is used instead of beta in the foetus. The resulting foetal haemoglobin has higher oxygen affinity than the mother's haemoglobin, enabling transfer of oxygen from maternal to foetal blood. Yet another globin gene specifies myoglobin, a transient oxygen store in muscle, relatively abundant in red muscle and especially in the diving mammals, whales and seals.

Rhodopsin

The second example of a gene concerns night vision. The eye has an exquisitely sensitive detection mechanism which makes it possible to see in very low levels of illumination, such as starlight on a glacier. The detector is called rhodopsin. In rhodopsin a molecule called retinal, a derivative of vitamin A, is surrounded by a larger structure called opsin. Retinal strongly absorbs light. Capture of an incoming photon of light causes retinal to flip shape, with consequent change of shape in the surrounding opsin molecule. This response triggers a cascade of further processes that result in a nerve impulse travelling from the retina of the eye to the brain. The summation of all such events gives us our picture of the (night) world.

Opsin and globin are both members of a large class of substances called proteins, all of which are made from the same set of 20 amino acids, but in a unique order for each protein. In opsin there are about 350 amino acids, and their order is totally unrelated to globin. Opsin is encoded by its own gene. There are also three other opsin-related genes. Their proteins are present in the retina in smaller amounts than rhodopsin, and they generate signals only in daylight. Each of these three additional detectors responds maximally to light of different colour, and together they mediate colour vision.

Many thousands of proteins go to make up a human being. Each protein has its own unique function, for example in digesting food, in extracting energy from the products of digestion, in muscular movement, in conducting nerve impulses, in fighting infections and so on. Each protein is encoded by its own gene.[2]

47. *Olan NW face, Dauphiné.* (Guy Muhlemann) (p 104)

48. *Guy Muhlemann on NW face of Aile-froide.* (Simon Richardson) (p 104)

49. *Ailefroide NW face, Dauphiné.* (Guy Muhlemann) (p 104)

50. *Grandes Jorasses N face after storm.* (Simon Richardson) (p 104)

51. *Grandes Jorasses from Petites Jorasses. Walker Spur and Shroud profiled right, Hirondelles ridge centre, E face on left.* (Simon Richardson) (p 104)

52. *Pelvoux: Joy Hunt on the Col Temple-Ecrins. In the background the Arête de la Momie, 1950.* (John Hunt) (p 113)

53. *The Schalihorn summit ridge. From L: Joy Hunt, Basil Goodfellow and Frankie Mayo, 1951.* (John Hunt) (p 113)

54. *With Charles Warren below the Arbengrat on the Obergabelhorn, 1951.* (John Hunt) (p 113)

55. *Basil Goodfellow on the N ridge of the Weisshorn, 1951.* (John Hunt) (p 113)

56. *From Piz Giuv, looking S to the Portilücke and the peaks beyond.*
(David Brett Duffield) (p 120)

57. *Looking W from Konkordia.* (David Brett Duffield) (p 120)

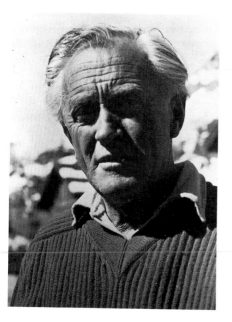

*58. Bernard Biner, Bergführer Zermatt.
29 December 1900 – 9 April 1965.
Gedenket seiner im Gebete.* (p 129)

59. Hotel Bahnhof, Zermatt. (Perren-Barberini, by permission) (p 129)

60. *Jubilee procession, 15 July 1990. 125th Anniversary celebrations for Edward Whymper's first ascent of the Matterhorn, 14 July 1865. L to R: Paula Biner, Peter Ledeboer, John Hunt, Stephen Venables (part hidden), Tony Streather, John Whyte.* (p 132)

61. *A meeting between Nigella Hall and Antoine Carrel, with Mike Esten (centre).* (Tony Welling) (p 132)

62. *Michael Binnie on the N pillar of the E peak of Piz Palü.* (Tom Sancha) *(See also photo No 84)* (p 135)

63. *The town of Melnik in the Pirin mountains.* (J W Gajewski) (p 155)

64. *Vasilyashki Cirque and Todorini Lakes. Mt Kamenitsa (2822m), Mt Yalovarnika (2763m), Mt Zybyt (2650m). In the background Mt Kuklite (2686m).* (J W Gajewski) (p 155)

Gene ancestries

All human genes have long ancestries. For example, haemoglobin is present in all vertebrates, and a primitive form of globin is present in invertebrates. Thus an ancestral globin gene must have considerably preceded the origin of vertebrates, and globin genes must have been around for about 1000 million years. Most or all human genes can be traced back to ancestries from the beginnings of vertebrate evolution, many of them to the evolution of nucleated cells and some of them to the origins of life. The subcellular component that I and my colleagues had been studying is called a ribosome, a piece of machinery that is at the centre of the assembly line for all proteins. Its role is so fundamental that the origins of ribosomes must have been closely linked to the origins of life some 3500 million years ago.

Occasionally errors do occur in gene replication. Some errors are lethal and do not survive. Others are tolerated and some may be advantageous. Aberrations are of several kinds, ranging from incorporation of a wrong chemical unit at a particular site in the gene (called a point mutation) to duplication of an entire gene. The multiple human globin genes arose from successive duplications from an ancestral gene, followed by independent mutations. Thus the alpha, beta and gamma genes are related by descent.[3]

The rates at which mutations accumulate in genes are generally extremely slow. The rates can be measured by determining the sequences of the chemical units in the genes that encode the same protein in different animals, such as man, chimpanzee, mouse and frog. (Small samples of blood can supply sufficient DNA for the analysis.) Many such comparisons from a large number of genes show that to achieve divergence at one per cent of positions (or to change the colours of one per cent of the beads, using the earlier analogy) takes anything from one million years to 50 million years for different genes. Often the changes that do occur are such as to cause minimum effect on the function of the protein. These numbers explain how features in the design of some biological structures are stable over vast periods of time.

Genes and species

A difficult question remains: if most vertebrate animals contain most of the same (or functionally related) genes, why are there so many different vertebrate species? Notwithstanding Darwin's *Origin of Species* and much that has been written since, the processes leading to the origin of new species remain mysterious. The central problem lies in the extreme complexity of the interactions that are involved between large numbers of genes and proteins in the development of an organism.

Approaches to an answer are likely to come from three directions. First, duplication and divergence of genes as mentioned above provides a mechanism for some diversification of functions. Second, some genes produce proteins that are specifically involved in the activation of other genes during development. Some mutations in such genes (in fruit-flies, for example) exert major effects on the developmental pathway. Possibly other changes accumulated during evolution might exert subtle developmental effects, and many such changes might contribute to species divergence.

A third source of biological variation may arise from the following relatively recently discovered properties of DNA and its behaviour. All genes are DNA, but not all DNA is genes. In man and in other animals the genes are linked to each other by long tracts of extragenic DNA. The extragenic DNA accumulates changes much more rapidly than the genes themselves, and its function is largely unknown. Increasingly, however, regions are being discovered within extragenic DNA that modulate the activities of genes, with regard to 'turning on' or to the quantity of a protein that is produced. This extragenic DNA affords potentially enormous territory for the evolutionary testing of changes in complex regulatory interactions among genes, such as those involved in developmental pathways. It is likely that biological variation leading to the appearance of new species is at least partly linked to changes in the rapidly evolving extragenic DNA.

Species exist for finite periods before being replaced by new species. Genes are passed on not only from individual to individual but, often with relatively little change, from species to newly evolved species. In contrast to the great evolutionary stability of most genes, species survival times are often of the order of a few million years before new species take over. Geographical factors play an important role in speciation, by isolating populations in which DNA variations may arise and become fixed. It may not be fortuitous that species lifetimes, as opposed to gene lifetimes, are often roughly comparable to the timescales for substantial geographic changes by the processes described above.

This discussion has traversed some distance from sunrise on Mont Blanc, but it is an interesting reflection that the analysis of life at the level of the precise structures of genes and DNA is leading to new and deep insights into life's origins and most ancient features, its long history, the emergence of new functions and new levels of complexity, and the mechanisms whereby we perceive and interact with the world around us.

NOTES

1   The Earth's magnetic field has reversed in direction several times during geological history. Magnetism in the direction of the prevailing field becomes 'frozen' into basaltic rocks when they first form. The distribution of normal and reversed magnetized bands outwards from mid-ocean ridges, detected by measurements at the sea surface, together with the reversal times calibrated from land-based rocks of known ages, gives the rate of sea-floor spreading.

2   In a gene, a triplet of chemical units encodes each amino acid. This is indicated in the 'red, blue, green;' analogy above by a semicolon after every third colour. There are 64 such different triplets. Each of the 20 amino acids is encoded by one or more triplets, and the code linking

particular triplets to particular amino acids is (almost) invariant throughout nature.

3   A group of genes can be recognized as being descended from a common ancestral gene not only because the genes specify related functions, but also from features of their internal structure called introns, which occur in precisely homologous locations in related genes. Introns are tracts of DNA that interrupt the continuity of the coding sequences. For example the coding regions of globin genes come in three blocks, with an intron separating the first and second blocks and another intron separating the second and third blocks. For a fuller account of introns in genes see P Chambon, 'Split Genes', *Scientific American* 244(5), 60–71, 1981.

C E Montague – Mountaineer and Writer

SCOTT RUSSELL

In the early 1930s Montague's *In Hanging Garden Gully*[1] was almost prescribed reading for us fledgling mountaineers. It is probably the best-known and the most enjoyable of his mountain stories. Writing in the first person, he describes meeting at Ogwen a botanist who had an injured knee which could not bend, no mountaineering skill and a passion to see the plant Lloydia in its native habitat. With a borrowed rope they set off for Hanging Garden Gully. The botanist was not a restful companion; catching sight of plants, he scrambled across almost holdless ground to admire them. But he eventually arrived safely at the top. Then, seeing a splendid patch of Lloydia a few yards away, he rushed joyously to admire it. He was still roped up, the rope tightened, he fell over and was fielded rolling down the slope.

Montague told the story so vividly that, at first, I thought that he had described a real event. But some years later I met a retired civil servant whose total lack of imagination or sense of humour made him seem a reliable witness. He told me that he had no interest in plants and, having a stiff leg, had previously made only one climb – being hoisted up and down Mont Blanc by two guides. By chance, at Ogwen, he met Montague who agreed to take him up Hanging Garden Gully. Montague's enthusiasm had amused him and he recalled, laughingly, how when he reached the top his leader had given a shout of pleasure and rushed to admire a carpet of Lloydia in full flower. Forgetting that he was still tied to the rope which tethered him, he fell over. Perhaps this is one reason why Montague never wrote 'straight' accounts of his climbs, wishing to keep to himself the incidents which inspired his stories. Beyond this, his modesty may have made him think that no one would be interested in his own doings. Unfortunately for us, he never contributed to the *Alpine Journal*.

Charles Edward Montague was born in Ealing on New Year's Day 1867; both his parents were Irish. His father had been a Roman Catholic priest but doctrinal doubts, including (it seems) opposition to celibacy, led him to renounce his calling. CEM was taught at home by his father until he was 12 years old and then went to the City of London School. At 18 he became an exhibitioner at Balliol; he narrowly failed to get a First in Greats. He played rugby, rowed for his college and enjoyed squash, tennis and swimming. One incident in Oxford, to which he never referred in later life, was the rescue of a drowning man in the Isis for which the Royal Humane Society gave him its

Bronze Medal. Politics attracted him and he became a rather left-wing liberal. He retained his interests in strenuous open-air activity and in politics throughout his life. An Oxford friend, R R Marett, later Rector of Exeter College, wrote thus of him:

> He was the best-tempered fellow in the world and always full of fun. Cheerful, sympathetic, humane, with a pretty wit and a tireless body, he was the friend and companion that it was the dream of one's youth to find in Oxford (quoted by Elton[2]).

CEM's ambition was to be a journalist and, in 1890, C P Scott gave him a post on the *Manchester Guardian*. In time he became the paper's chief leader-writer and acted as Scott's deputy in his absences. Apart from the period of the First World War, CEM remained with the *Guardian* until he retired in 1925. Elton[2] described his career in journalism.

CEM was anything but a militarist. He had been critical of British policy in the Boer War but in 1914 his attitude was very different. He wrote: 'Europe must either smash German Junkerdom or be smashed by it.' Even though he was a married man – he had married C P Scott's daughter – with seven children, he was determined to join up, dyeing his greying hair in a not very successful attempt to conceal his age. Eventually he became a private in the 24th (Sportsmen's) Battalion of the Royal Fusiliers. The early part of his army life delighted him. In 1917 he wrote nostalgically in his diary:

> That old time seems like one's youth; it was merry and friendly and full of the vague thrill of greater experiences lying ahead. Most of us privates had gone back, as by a miracle, to the irresponsibility of childhood . . . we got up like children by order and, when the day's work was done, it was all rest and play. I remember, in May and June 1915, the half-hour before lights-out was blown on the bugle, the thirty men going to bed laughing, chaffing and singing together and telling stories and there were nightingales singing in the trees outside. It's all gone as childhood does.

This simple freedom was short-lived. Soon, promoted sergeant, he was injured in an accident while demonstrating the use of grenades. He blamed himself but did not receive the reprimand he expected. After a month in hospital he contrived to avoid a period of sick-leave so that he could go to France with his battalion. His injuries, not yet fully healed, caused trouble and with difficulty he persuaded a medical officer – who called him a fool – that he was fit to go to the trenches. Within two months he caught trench-fever and, when recovered, the doctors marked him 'permanent base'. The prospect of spending the rest of the war, safely, as a provo-sergeant was anathema to him and he managed to be transferred to the Intelligence Corps in which he was commissioned, becoming eventually a captain. In France he grasped every opportunity to be in the front-line, thus giving local colour to press releases which he wrote. Soon he had more important duties – censoring journalists' dispatches and leading 'distinguished visitors' to the front – these included senior officers, politicians, newspaper proprietors and writers. One of CEM's charges, Bernard Shaw, wrote thus:

> Finding him [CEM] just the sort of man I like and get on with I was glad to learn that he was to be my bear-leader ... The standard joke about Montague was his craze for being under fire, and his tendency to lead distinguished visitors, who did not necessarily share this taste (rare at the front), into warm corners. Like most standing jokes it was inaccurate but had something in it. War is fascinating even to those who, like Montague, have no illusions about it, and are not imposed on by its boasting, its bugaboo, its desperate attempts to make up for the shortage of capable officers by sticking tabs and brass hats on duffers ... its holocaust of common men for nothing ... its vermin and dirt and butchery and terror and foul-mouthed boredom ... neither of us ever asked the other 'And what the devil are *you* doing in this galley?' ... We had come to the theatre to see the play, not to enjoy the intervals between the acts, like fashionable people at the opera (quoted by Elton[2]).

CEM's rather free interpretation of the instruction that he should guide his charges 'within the limits of safety' became well known; Field Marshal Haig commented on it, when CEM called on him to deliver a dispatch.[2]

He was sometimes irked by what he regarded as his sheltered life on the staff, and made unsuccessful attempts to be returned, as a sergeant, to his battalion. In 1918 he wrote in his diary:

> Can all the daring of soldiers and men rescue the staff from the judgement they call down by their littleness, their spites and jealousies, their decoration hunting and their past idleness ... Because I am 50 I must live among the *embusqué* (shirkers) and not with the friends I came to love and honour since I came to know the depth of their courage and patience in the trenches. It is cheap to murmur against this. It is like trying to combine my inglorious safety with a little aspiration after self sacrifice. But I do mean it.

At the end of the war CEM received a Military MBE as well as two mentions in dispatches. He was a little entertained to be made a Knight of the Order of the Crown of Romania (with swords) because he bear-led a Romanian General.

In 1922 he wrote of the war, largely from the viewpoint of other ranks, in his aptly titled *Disenchantment*.[3] Several years later he pilloried bellicose newspaper owners, who had irritated him during the war, in a novel, *Right off the Map*.[4] It contains a description of men making their way through very steep country, in nearly total darkness, which may awake memories for many mountaineers.

It seems that CEM's interest in mountains did not develop until after he went to Manchester, but it soon grew rapidly. The Lake District, North Wales and, still more, the Pennines – to him the backbone of England – were close at hand. Regrettably, he left no detailed record of what he did, but from passing comments in his writings it is clear that he came to know these regions well and that his visits to the hills were strenuous. He developed a keen interest in topography and maps, writing:

> Unless you are a mountaineer, an engineer or a surveyor, the odds are that the great illumination will escape you, all your life; you may return to the grave without having ever known what it is like when the contour lines sing together like the biblical stars.[5]

Even a bicycle ride from Manchester to London was an exciting experience, and so was a walk on the top of the Pennines; your footsteps on the boggy moss could influence the drainage of water to east or west.

CEM first visited the Alps in 1891, starting in Chamonix, the Aiguille du Moine being his initial climb. In seven seasons up to 1906 he made 29 ascents, including some Chamonix Aiguilles, Mont Blanc, Monte Rosa, traverses of the Matterhorn and Zinalrothorn, the Rimpfischhorn, the Obergabelhorn, the Eiger, the Schalijoch and other passes. He was then elected to the Alpine Club and later served on its committee. He made six subsequent visits to the Alps and, except for the war years, it was rare for him to not be in either the Alps or the British hills at least once each year. All his alpine climbs were by standard routes. In his first seasons he had employed guides but later he dispensed with them, his wife being a frequent companion. We know nothing of his other companions in the Alps, but Geoffrey Winthrop Young and Albert Hopkinson enjoyed his company.

Among British rock-climbers Siegfried Herford was his closest friend. They had met apparently when Herford was a schoolboy, 24 years younger than CEM. It seems that Herford's father, a professor in Manchester, had brought them together. Herford's climbing standard came to greatly exceed that of CEM but they remained close friends and, when war came, Herford followed him into the same company of the Royal Fusiliers and was killed in action. CEM presented to a chapel in Manchester a stained-glass memorial window which showed Herford climbing; it is now in the Outward Bound Centre in Eskdale. CEM also wrote a tribute to Herford for a Memorial Book arranged by the Fell and Rock Climbing Club. Herford comes through as a splendid climber and companion.

CEM's climbing stories give the impression of vivid authenticity, equally in the approach to a mountain and on the climb itself. His enthusiasm is infectious and the atmosphere he creates is as realistic as that which A E W Mason achieved in his account of an ascent of the Brenva ridge on Mont Blanc.[6] And Montague has a pleasant sense of humour, for example:

> The Swiss are inspired hotel-keepers. Some centuries since, when a stranger strayed into their valleys, their simple forefathers would kill him and share out the little money he might have about him.

Now they know better. They keep him alive writing cheques. He
has risen in economic value from the status of a hare or a wild
pigeon to that of a milch cow or, at lowest, a good laying hen.[7]

Montague's most memorable climbing stories are *In Hanging Garden Gully*,[1]
the ascent of the 'Dent Rouge' in *The Morning's War*[8] and *Action* which gives
the title to the last volume of stories which he wrote.[9] They contrast much in
mood. *Hanging Garden Gully* is pure pleasure and fun. The 'Dent Rouge' climb
is based on an ascent of the NE ridge of Mont Collon which he had made. He
describes a daunting expedition in very poor snow conditions. The author may
have added to the height of the gendarmes but none the less gives an authentic
impression of a severe expedition when the climber's only aids were an ice axe,
nailed boots and a hemp rope.

Action is about an elderly climber whom Montague called Bell. He had
just had a mild stroke. His wife was dead and his children had drifted away; the
prospect of becoming immobile terrified him and he decided to make an end by
attempting an ice climb, which he knew was beyond his powers but which he
would make every effort to achieve. He chose the steepest slope on the Zinal
side of the Schalijoch. When he felt about to collapse an ice axe shot past him
and he heard a cry for help. This galvanized him into action: he shouted that he
was coming and chipped steps up the ice bulge which rose before him. A woman
was dangling, helpless, on a rope held by her husband from above. Bell held her
while the husband cut a secure anchorage to bring them up. The wife fell asleep
soon after they reached a hut. Her husband was a Harley Street specialist and he
and Bell settled down to talk over the day's events. Unguardedly, Bell gave
himself away by saying that there was no route on the face on which they had
met. He confessed what he had planned to do and admitted that, when in
action, the consequences of his stroke had not worried him. Their conversation
ended with Bell saying that he was 'sticking on'. An almost melodramatic story,
but it lived when I first read it. Montague died a few months after the story was
published. Had he been pondering, at least part of him, how he would like to act
if he knew that years of immobility would lie ahead? This seems perhaps more
likely as Montague and his creation Bell had several characteristics in common.

The *In Memoriam* notice on Montague in this journal[10] suggested that
with Leslie Stephen he was among the Club's eminent writers. You must read
Montague to decide if you agree.

It is a pleasure to express my thanks for the help I have received from
Montague's daughter, Mrs Rose Elton, and her niece Mrs Susan Adams; they
answered many questions and permitted me to read and quote from
Montague's war diary. I am grateful also to the archivists of the Alpine and Fell
and Rock Climbing Clubs and to Outward Bound, Eskdale.

REFERENCES

1   C E Montague, 'In Hanging Garden Gully', in *Fiery Particles*. Chatto and
     Windus, 1923.

2 O Elton, *C E Montague, A Memoir*. Chatto and Windus, 1929.
3 C E Montague, *Disenchantment*. Chatto and Windus, 1922.
4 C E Montague, *Right off the Map*. Chatto and Windus, 1927.
5 C E Montague, 'When the Map is in Tune', in *The Right Place*. Chatto and Windus, 1924.
6 A E W Mason, *Running Water*. Hodder & Stoughton, 1907.
7 C E Montague, 'Up to the Alps', in *The Right Place*, Chatto and Windus, 1924.
8 C E Montague, *The Morning's War*. Methuen, 1913.
9 C E Montague, *Action*. Chatto and Windus, 1928.
10 *AJ*40, 369–370, 1928.

Seracs

HAMISH M BROWN

Over-investment in machinery brought about the financial crisis in Danny Peplinska's scrap-yard on Firth Street East. Danny loved handling the cool, metallic atoms and could never resist a machine which could cut, flatten or melt the metals he recycled from our waste society. When an out-of-breath jogger stopped at his gate Danny noticed his apparent interest and invited him in to see round the yard.

Ivor Bentley-Crowcombe, a popular artist in his own right, ran an internationally renowned gallery of modern art in Bristol but was frequently gallivanting about Britain, Europe and America. Ivor had studied at Grenoble in his early twenties and had climbed in the Dauphiné regularly but the only reminders of those days were the many mountain paintings and sculptures he'd acquired.

One day his wife had commented that he was 'becoming as broad in the beam as he was in the brain' so, piqued, every day since he had dutifully put in a run, no matter where he was, no matter how tight his schedule.

Ivor had been visiting the friendly Kirkcaldy Art Gallery, officially to discuss a coming exhibition, unofficially to drool over the extensive collection of Peploes, so it was late afternoon before he set off along the sands under the Esplanade. The tide forced him off the shore and he then found himself toiling up an unexpectedly steep brae. He turned off – and so came on Danny's yard.

He stood, breathless, fascinated by the weird tangle of shapes, the unintentional geometrics, the frightful grace of powerful machinery. 'Must be money in scrap' ran through his mind, art and finance being the right and left ventricles of his existence. He gladly followed Danny round the yard.

One machine was effortlessly slicing thick power cable ('the Knowles cutter goes through it like butter' Danny chirped), a man in goggles was cutting inch-thick iron plate with a blue flame, a furnace suddenly opened and lava flowed. Ivor walked in awe. He could quite understand Danny's fascination with the job. Suddenly he stopped.

Before him was a stack of cubes of what looked like tangled and crushed silver snakes. They were beautiful. They were desirable. Danny smirked: 'Aluminium core: stripped by the Vortex, cut by the Baby Knowles, cubed by the Sondheimer Press'. In Ivor's eyes however they appeared as objects born of the high Alps: bold hunks of glacial ice, sculpted by time and sun and motion. Beautiful indeed.

'How much?' Ivor blurted out and was soon deep in an aspect of the business which he never underestimated. The next day his overloaded Transit headed south while Danny was left chuckling over a £300 windfall which he badly needed. Ivor made three groupings out of his haul, welding the aluminium in places (not easy) and finally calling them *Seracs I, II and III.*

Seracs I he set up on his own patio in the Cotswolds and Seracs II went to the gallery in Bristol, of course.

Seracs III was dispatched to London, with a stylish coloured brochure showing alpine glaciers, an appropriate modern poem and pictures of the various stages of his work on the sculpture. The work was snatched up at once by an American collector for a bargain £30,000.

On the same day as Seracs III was sold Danny Peplinska was officially declared bankrupt.

A Bibliography of Privately Printed Mountaineering Books

A Revision

EUGENE P MECKLY

Author's Note: *This bibliography which first appeared in AJ57, 391–396, 1950 has now been revised and corrected. It has been compiled from the Alpine Journal, Appalachia, the catalogues of the libraries of the Alpine Club and the Swiss Alpine Club, and various booksellers' catalogues. The list includes privately printed books that relate to mountains, mountaineering exploits, and the men who took part in these exploits; and it includes all English books and those foreign books listed in the sources consulted. General references which have been consulted are listed at the end. The author would be grateful to receive any corrections, additions or notes to this list at 15 Westfield Road, Fletcher, NC 28732, USA.*

Abbot, Philip Stanley
> *Addresses at a memorial meeting of the Appalachian Mountain Club, October 21, 1896, and other papers.* Reprinted from *Appalachia*. Boston, 1897. Privately issued.

Abney, Capt
> *Private Menu for the guests of Capt Abney at a dinner at his house on 15 December 1898.* Drawing of the Dru above menu. Only 18 of these were issued.

Aitken, Samuel
> *Among the Alps. A narrative of personal experiences.* ppxii, 119. 73 plates from V Sella's photographs. Privately published, nd.

Atkins, Henry Martin
> *Ascent to the Summit of Mont Blanc, on the 22nd and 23rd of August, 1837.* Edited by JGC. 8vo, pp49, 2 litho plates. London, 1838. Not published.

Atkinson, Edwin (Felix) Thos
> *Notes on the history of the Himalaya of the N-W P, India.* 2 vols, 8vo. Privately printed, St-Leonards-on-Sea, 1883.

Autumn Rambles; or, fireside recollections of Belgium, . . ., Switzerland, the Italian Lakes, Mont Blanc, and Paris. Written by a Lady, for private circulation in aid of the Rochdale relief fund. ppvii, 217. Rochdale, printed by Wrigley, 1864.

Backhouse, (W)
A Holiday Visit to some Continental Cities, and the Savoy Alps and the Rhine, in August and September, 1869. 8vo, pp56, 1869.

Baker, G P
Mountaineering Memories of the Past. Privately printed, 1951. Book form of the next entry.
Mountaineering Memories of the Past. Pamphlet. Privately printed, 1942.

Barry (Dr Martin)
Ascent to the Summit of Mont Blanc, 16th-18th of 9th month (Septr), 1834. 8vo, pp40, 2 litho plates. Privately printed, London, 1835.

Basterfield, G
Songs of a Cragsman. 12 songs of the Hills, privately published by the author, 1935.

Beetham, George of Wellington
First Ascent of Mount Ruapehu, New Zealand, and a Holiday Jaunt to Mounts Ruapehu, Tongariro and Ngauruhoe. 1878. Introduction by T E Donne. 8vo, pp40. 2 plates, sq. Privately printed, Harrison, London, 1926.
Printed by Mrs Beetham for presentation to personal friends.

Bellows, William
Zermatt and the Matterhorn. pp19, 4 plates. Privately printed, 1925.

Bent, Newell
Jungle Giants. Tall 8vo, cloth, pp255, illus with photos. Privately printed, 1936.

Beraldi, (H)
Cent ans aux Pyrénées. 7 vols, 8vo, Paris, 1898–1904. 300 sets privately printed.
Le Passé du Pyrénéisme. 10 vols, 8vo, Paris, 1911–31. Privately printed.
Balaitous et Pelvoux. 2 vols, folio, Paris, 1907–10. Privately printed.
Ramond (Baron L). Au Pic du Midi (1787–1810). Trente-cinq voyages. 8vo, Paris, 1922. 25 copies privately printed.

Blakeney, Edward Henry
Alpine poems. pp39. 60 copies printed at the author's private press, Winchester, 1929.

Boeck, Kurt
Himalaya Lieder und Bilder. pp74, 20 plates. Privately printed, Haessel, Leipzig, 1927.

Bonaparte, Prince Roland
Le Glacier de L'Aletsch et le Lac de Marjelen. 4to, pp27, 3 plates. Printed for the author, Paris, 1889.

Bonney, T G
Memories of a Long Life. 8vo, ppiv, 112, vii, Metcalfe, Cambridge, 1921. 350 copies privately printed.

Booth, Alfred
Some Memories, Letters and other Family Records. Written and arranged by his daughter Harriet Anna Whitting. 75 copies privately printed. Henry Young & Sons Ltd, Liverpool, 1917.

Booth, Margaret
   An Amazon Andes Tour. 8vo, pp148, red cloth. Printed for the author by
   Edward Arnold, London, for private circulation, 1910.
Botfield, Beriah
   Journal of a Tour through the Highlands of Scotland, during the Summer of
   MDCCCXXIX. 8vo, pp376. 500 copies printed for private circulation by
   the author. Johnstone, Edinburgh, 1830.
Bourrit, M-T
   Extrait du voyage de M Bourrit en Piemont par la Mer de Glace de
   Chamouni. pp8. Privately printed, nd but September 1787.
   See Montagnier
Bree, Rev Wm Thos.
   Nugae helveticae. Scraps gathered during a tour in Switzerland in the summer
   of 1855. 8vo, pp21. Printed for private distribution. Newman, London,
   1856.
(Brigg, W A)
   Iter Helveticum. 8vo, pp88. Privately printed, Keighley, 1887.
Brydges, Sir Egerton
   Letters from the Continent. pp177. Kent, printed at the private press of Lee
   Priory by John Warwick, 1821.
Buel, O P
   An Account of the Ascent of Mont Blanc October 3rd and 4th, 1866 by O.P.
   Buel. Privately printed pamphlet, republished from the Troy *Daily News*
   and Public Spirit.
(Bulwer, J R)
   Extracts from my Journal M.DCCC.LII. 8vo, pp56, illustrations. Privately
   printed, Norwich, 1853.
Bunnell, J F
   Rock Climbing Guide to Hong Kong. Privately printed, Hong Kong, 1959.
Butler, Arthur Gray
   Zermatt Churchyard. 8vo, pp2. Privately printed, Cambridge, 1909.
Cameron, Una
   A good line, written and illustrated by Una Cameron. Privately printed,
   1932.
Carr, (Alfred)
   Adventures with my alpenstock and knapsack; or, a Five Weeks' Tour in
   Switzerland. 12mo, pp76, wrappers. Privately printed, York, 1875.
Chevassus, E
   Notice sur Lons-le-Saunier-les-Bains . . . notamment: les Roches et Grottes
   de Baume. . . 8vo, pp53, map, ill. Privately printed, (1900).
Clark, (Jane Inglis)
   Pictures and Memories (Travel and climbing adventures of a member of the
   Alpine Club, written by his wife). Colour plates. Privately printed, 1938.
Clarke, (W B)
   Recollections, 1828. Being lines written in recollection of a journey up the
   Rhine and of travels in Switzerland. 8vo, privately printed, Manningtree,
   1828.

C(lowes, G, Junior)
Forty-six Days in Switzerland and the North of Italy. 8vo, ppxii, 102, illustrations. Privately printed, William Showers and Sons, London, 1856.

Cook, (Charles)
Three weeks in Switzerland and lines on 'The Prisoner of Chillon'. Privately printed, London, nd, (c1878).

Coolidge, Rev W A B
Climbs in the Alps made in the years 1865 to 1900 by Coolidge. 8vo, pp23. 100 copies privately printed, J E Francis, London, 1900. 2nd impression revised, 50 copies.

A list of the Writings (not being Reviews of Books) dating from 1868 to 1912 and relating to the Alps or Switzerland of W.A.B. Coolidge. pp37, 150 copies privately printed, Jakober-Peter, Grindelwald, 1912.

Die Petronella–Kapelle in Grindelwald. 200 copies privately printed, Grindelwald.

See Gardiner, Frederick

Cordier, S F
Excursion en Suisse. pp76. Privately printed, Poignee-Darnauld, Sainte-Menehould, 1846.

Courtenay, Bryson H
Rock Climbs Round London. Illustrations, illustrated covers. Privately printed, 1936.

Cowles, Elizabeth
Alpine Beginner. 40 unnumbered pages, wraps, illustrations. Privately printed, c1938.

C(uchetet), Charles
Souvenirs d'une promenade en Suisse pendant l'année 1827; Recueilis pour ses amis. 8vo, pp257. 30 copies printed, Paris, Duverger, 1828.

Cursory notes of a nine weeks' tour. pp140. Privately printed, Hernaman, Newcastle-upon-Tyne, 1834.

Das, Sarat Chandra
Narrative of a Journey to Lhasa, and Narrative of a Journey round Lake Palti. Reports privately printed by the government, 1890.

Devonshire, Georgiana, Duchess of
The Passage of the Saint Gothard. With an Italian translation by G Polidori. Folio, pp41. 50 copies printed by W Bulmer and Co, Cleveland Row, St James's, London, for Gameau and Co, 1803.

Docharty, W M
A Selection of some 900 British and Irish Mountain Tops. Compiled and arranged by W M Docharty. pp124, illustrations. Privately printed, the Darien Press, Edinburgh, 1954.

The Supplement to a Selection of some 900 British and Irish Mountain Tops, and a Selection of 1000 Tops under 2500ft. 2 vols. Illustrations, panoramas and maps. Private circulation only. The Darien Press, Edinburgh, 1962.

(Drinkwater, Miss)
Poetische Reise. 8vo, ppiv, 125. Illustrated by E F H(adow). Privately printed, London, 1837.

Drumlangrig
'*Memoires of my Lord Drumlangrig's and his brother Lord William's Travells Abroad for the Space of Three Yeares, beginning Septr. 13th 1680.*' From a Ms book in the charter room, Drumlangrig Castle. Preface by Hew Dalrymple. Small 4to, ppviii, 75, frp and one plate. Privately printed, 1931.

Ehrman, Louise S
Adventures in the Great Outdoors. 12mo, cloth, portrait, np, privately printed, nd.

Elliott, Rev J M
Ascent of the Matterhorn, July 24, 1868. Reprinted from *Once a Term; or, the Brighton Coll. Chronicle,* July 1869. Folio, pp3. Privately printed, London, 1910.

Farquhar, Francis
First Ascents in the US 1642–1900. Privately printed, The Grabhorn Press, Berkeley, California, 1948.

Fellows (Sir Charles)
A Narrative of an Ascent to the Summit of Mont Blanc. 4to, ppvii, 35, plates. Privately printed, London, 1827.

Fisher, Joel E
Problems in the Geology of Mountains: five theses. 8vo, illustrations, diagrams. Collected, re-edited and privately published, May 1944.

Fitzpatrick, T C
A Memoir. Portraits. Privately printed, Cambridge, 1937.

Fletcher, F P
My Out-of-Doors. pp178, photos. Privately printed, nd, (c 1920s).

(Forbes, Murray)
The Diary of a Traveller over Alps and Appennines; or, Daily Minutes of a Circuitous Excursion. 4to, ppviii, 170. Privately printed, London, 1824.

Fox, Joseph H
Holiday Memories. ppvi, 47. Privately printed, Wellington, Som, Tozer, 1908.

Freshfield, (Douglas W)
Across country from Thonon to Trent; Rambles and Scrambles in Switzerland and the Tyrol. 8vo, pp134, 3 maps. 50 copies privately printed, London, 1865.
Quips for cranks and other trifles. ppx, 112. Privately printed, (Clowes, London), 1923.
A Tramp's Wallet. Not published.
Catalogue of a collection of photographs by Signor V Sella and Mr E Garwood, taken during the tour of Kanchinjinga, made in 1899 by Mr Douglas W Freshfield. With a preface. 8vo, pp24. Privately printed, London, Spottiswoode, 1900.

Gaillard, E and Montagnier, H F
Lettres de H B de Saussure à sa Femme. Edited by EG and HFM. Privately printed, Chambery, 1937.

Gallet, Julien
Julien Gallet, Dans l'Alps Ignorée. Explorations et Souvenirs. 300 copies
printed, Imprimeries Réunies, SA, Lausanne, 1910.
Gardiner, Frederick
The Alpine Career (1868–1914) of Frederick Gardiner. Described by his
Friend, WAB Coolidge. pp75, portrait. 50 copies only printed for private
circulation, 1920.
Gardner, (JD)
*Ascent and Tour of Mont Blanc, and passage of the Col du Géant, between
Sept. 2nd and 7th., 1850*. 32mo, pp60. Privately printed, Whittingham,
Chiswick, 1851.
Geikie, (Sir Archibald)
Memoir of the late James David Forbes. 4to, pp38, with bibliography.
Privately printed, Edinburgh, 1869.
Gosse, Dr Philip
Notes on the Natural History of Aconcagua Valley. Privately printed, 1899.
Gray, Jonathan
Letters written from the Continent, during a Six Week's Tour, in 1818. 8vo,
pp119. 50 copies printed by Blanchard, York, 1819.
Hanley, J Frank
A Day in the Siskiyous, An Oregon Extravaganza. 4to, cloth, colour plates
and other photos. Privately printed, Indianapolis, 1916.
(Harrison, F)
Among the Mountains. ppiv, 55. Privately printed, 1892.
(Hawes, Benjamin)
*A Narrative of an Ascent to the Summit of Mont Blanc, made during the
summer of 1827 by Mr. William Hawes and Mr. Charles Fellows*. 4to,
pp35, illustrations, panorama. Privately printed for Benjamin Hawes by
Arthur Taylor, London, 1828.
(Hayward, A(braham))
Some Account of a Journey Across the Alps in a Letter to a Friend. 12mo,
pp44. Privately printed, Roworth, London, 1834.
This is the first edition. Fifty copies of a second, corrected, edition were
afterwards printed, for which the whole type was reset.
H(evat), K(irkwood)
My Diary. Notes of a Continental Tour. Privately printed, 1878.
Hollier, Richard
*Glances at various Objects, during a Nine Weeks' Ramble through Parts of
France, Switzerland, . . . and Holland*. 4to, pp244, 100 copies printed, for
private distribution only, by James Moyes, Took's Court, Chancery Lane,
London, 1831.
Hooker, William Jackson
Journal of a Tour in Iceland, in the Summer of 1809. 8vo, pp496, coloured
plates. Printed by J Keymer, King Street, Yarmouth, 1811. Not published.
Hooker, William Dawson
*Notes on Norway: a Journal of a Tour to the Northern Parts of Norway, in
the Summer of MDCCCXXXVI*. 8vo, ppiii, 127, 4 lithographic plates.
Unpublished, Richardson, Glasgow, 1837.

Howard, Wm
> *A Narrative of a Journey to the Summit of Mont-Blanc, made in July 1819.*
> 12mo, pp49, 1 plate. Privately printed, Baltimore, 1821.

Howard, W D and Lloyd, F H
> *Photographs among the Dolomite Mountains, etc. 1865.* The subjects, 23 in
> number, are privately printed.

Howell, George O
> *Recollections of a Visit Abroad, being notes of a scamper through Switzer-*
> *land, etc. during the month of August 1894.* pp73. Privately printed,
> Plumstead, 1895.

Ives, H L
> *Reminiscences of the Adirondacks.* 8vo, cloth, pp124, illus, portrait.
> Privately printed, Potsdam, NY, 1915.

Jenkins, Dulcibel
> *Chronicles of John R. Jenkins, Mountaineer, Miner and Quaker.* pp130.
> Edited and privately published by Dulcibel Jenkins, np, 1987.

Journal of a short excursion among the Swiss landscapes. Made in the summer
> *of the year ninety-four.* 12mo, pp132. Privately printed, Barlow, Dublin,
> 1803.

Kothari, Jehangir H
> *Impressions of a First Tour Round the World in 1883 and 1884.* 8vo, ppvi,
> 284. 300 copies printed for private circulation, London, 1889.

(Lascelles)
> *Sketch of a Descriptive Journey through Switzerland.* 8vo, pp84. Printed for
> the author by Cooper, Graham, London, Sept 1796.

Lakeman, T A
> *Of Hills.* A collection of mountain photographs, mostly Himalaya, with
> commentaries and verse. Privately published, London, nd.

de Lassus, B
> *Minuit & aurore au sommet du Grand Vignemale.* 8vo, pp34. 50 copies
> printed, Abadie, Saint-Gaudens, 1892.

Letters from Switzerland 1833. pp170. Printed by W Hasper, Carlsruhe, 1834.
> Unpublished.

Lewin, W H
> *Climbs.* ppXVI, 226, illus, portrait. Published privately, Smith's Bookstalls,
> 1932. Limited edition of 250 copies.

Longman, William
> *A Lecture on Switzerland.* 8vo, ppvi, 90. Privately printed, London, July
> 1857.

Longman, William and Henry Trower
> *Journal of six weeks' adventures in Switzerland, Piedmont, and on the Italian*
> *Lakes.* 8vo, pp123, map. Privately issued, London, 1856.

Lurani, Francesco
> *In memoria di Francesco Lurani Cernuschi.* pp86, portrait. Privately printed,
> 1913.

Major, C I Forsyth
> *Materiali per servire ad una storia degli Stambecchi.* pp56, litho. Privately
> printed, Pisa, 1879.

Manton Smith, J
> Jottings on my Journeys in Switzerland. Privately printed by the author, 1896.

(Mathews, William)
> Lecture on the Glaciers of Switzerland. 8vo, pp29. Privately printed, Hepworth, Tunbridge Wells, 1902.

(Matthews, George)
> Rough Notes of a 'Lark' among the Fiords and Mountains of the North. Printed for private circulation by Francis D Finlay, Calendar-Street, Belfast, 1845.

Maus, Octave
> Savoie. 37 plates. 100 copies printed, Fleury, Paris, 1911.

Mayhew, H and A
> Mont Blanc. A comedy, in three acts. First produced at the Theatre Royal, Haymarket, Whit Monday, 25 May 1874. 8vo, pp63. Privately printed, London, 1874.

Mayo, Lawrence Shaw
> Three Essays. ppx, 94, portrait. Privately printed, Boston, 1948.

Memoir of the Rev J M Elliott. Privately printed, Brighton, 1870.

Meyerstein, (E H W)
> The Climbers. (An Ode on the Eton Masters who lost their lives descending the Piz Roseg on August 17, 1933.) 4to, pamphlet, pp6. Privately printed, 1934.

Montagnier, Henry F
> Lettre de M. Bourrit à Miss Craven sur deux voyages faits au sommet du Mont-Blanc; l'un par M. le Professeur de Saussure, l'autre par M. le Chevalier Beaufoix, et Relation de celui que M. Bourrit a fait en Piemont par la fameuse mer de glace du Montanvert. pp 19. Privately printed, Biancheri, San Remo, 1911.

40 copies of the above have been reprinted by Mr H F Montagnier.

Moore, (A W)
> The Alps in 1864. A Private Journal. 8vo, ppvi, 360, maps, illus. Privately printed, London, 1867.

Muir, H Moncrieff
> A Tour in Switzerland in the Summer of 1895. pp32, wrappers, 3 photos, portrait, frontis. Privately printed, nd.

Muir, (J.)
> Notes of a Trip to Kedarnath and other parts of the Snowy Range of the Himalayas. 8vo, pp72. Privately printed, Edinburgh, 1855.

N(ewall), Maj-Gen D J F
> Preliminary Sketches in Cashmere; or Sciences in Cuckoo-Cloud-Land. 8vo, ppx, 86, illus, map. Privately printed, I W Brannon, Newport, 1882.

North Wales: Tour through Part of North Wales, October, 1827. sm4to, 8 plates. Privately printed, 1829.

Nutting, Helen Cushing
> To Monadnock. The Records of a Mountain in New Hampshire through Three Centuries. Privately printed by the compiler, 1925.

A Peek at the Mountains: the Journal of a lady. pp34. For private circulation, Hewitt, Leicester, 1871.

Petrie, P J W de C
Farewell to the Mountains. Diary of a Himalayan Journal. ppxii, 34, illus. Printed for private circulation, London, 1940.

Philips, (Francis)
A Reading Party in Switzerland: with an account of the Ascent of Mont Blanc, on the 12th and 13th of August 1851. 8vo, pp49. Privately printed, Manchester, 1851.

Pickman, (Dudley Leavitt)
Some Mountain Views. 12mo, illustrated. 500 copies, privately printed, Boston, 1933.

Pigeon, (Anna) and Abbot, (Ellen)
Peaks and Passes. 8vo, pp31. Privately printed, London, 1885.

Poles and Tails; or, English vagabondism in Switzerland, in the summer of 1854. By two of the vagabonds. 8vo, pp81, 3 plates. Printed for private circulation, Billing, London, 1855.

(Porter, Edward C)
Six Letters Relating to Travel, 1865–1869 by Josiah Gilbert. sm8vo, pp41. 150 copies privately printed, January 1954.

Pretyman, Herbert Edward
Journal of an Expedition to the Kittar Mountains in 1891. pp50. Printed for private circulation only, London, November 1892.

Proctor, A Phimister
An Ascent of Half Dome in 1884. Privately printed, the Grabhorn Press, San Francisco, 1945.

R, L N R
A short account of our trip to the Sierra Nevada Mountains. 8vo, pp89. Privately printed, Martin, London, 1884.

Rackham, H
Thomas Cecil Fitzpatrick: A Memoir. pp47, portrait. Privately printed, Cambridge University Press, 1937.

Raffles, W Winter
Zermatt, with the Col d'Erin and de Collon; and an ascent to the summit of Mont Blanc. Two letters addressed to the editor of the *Liverpool Times.* 8vo, pp22. Privately printed, Liverpool, 1864.

Reid, J
A Tour in Switzerland. Wood engravings. Privately printed, 1878.

Reilly, A Adams
The Chain of Monte Rosa.
From the *Carte Federate* of Switzerland, combined with an actual survey of the Italian side made in 1865 by A Adams Reilly. (Scale of original 1:50,000 but reduced by photography for private circulation to about 1:116,000.)

Richardson, W L
This World So Wide. Grey printed boards. Privately printed, Chicago, 1922.
Good Adventure. Blue printed boards. Privately printed, Chicago, 1925.

Ritchie, Richmond
  Record of an Ascent. Privately printed, London, 1961.
Rivington, (Alexander)
  Notes of Travels in Europe in the Years 1856–1864. 8vo, ppxxxix, 276, illustrations. Privately printed, London, 1865.
(Rowell, R and F E)
  Recollection of our midsummer ramble in two parts. Part 1 by the printer; Part 2 by his wife. Printed for private circulation by Robert Rowell at Rock Cottage, Ventnor, Isle of Wight, 1873.
Russell, Henry
  Souvenirs d'un montagnard. pp416. Laheugue, Pau, 1878.
  La vente de cette ouvrage est interdite.
Sandberg, G
  An itinerary of the route from Sikkim to Lhasa, ... 8vo, pp29. Privately printed, Baptist Mission Press, Calcutta, 1901.
Schlagintweit, (H and Robert)
  Reports on the last Journeys and the Death in Turkistan of Adolph Schlagintweit. 4to, pp18. Privately printed, Berlin, 1859.
Schmidl, A
  Reisehandbuch durch Erzherzogthum Oesterreich mit Salzburg, Obersteyermark und Tirol. 8vo, ppxviii, 504. Privately printed, Guns, Reichard; Volckman, Leipzig, 1834.
Schuster, Arthur
  Indian Sketches. 21 coloured plates. Privately printed, 1908.
Sims, Col Charles
  The Pyrenees. A poem written in 1849. 8vo, pp13, 5 lithographs by Mr C H Sims. Privately circulated, 1887.
Smith, (Albert)
  Mont Blanc. Privately printed, London, 1852.
Sopwith, T
  A Month in Switzerland in 1874. pp75, map. Privately printed, Hexham, 1875.
Sowden, (G S)
  Recollections of Holiday Tours in Switzerland. Frontis, and 3 illustrations. Privately printed, 1890.
Standen, R S
  A Trip to the Harz Mountains in the Summer of 1860. pp41. Privately printed, Oxford, 1862.
  Continental way-side notes: The diary of a seven months' tour in Europe. 8vo, ppviii, 344. Printed for private circulation, London, 1865.
Stanley, (Rev E)
  The Mauvais Pas, a Scene in the Alps. Illustrating a Passage in the novel of Anne of Geierstein. 8vo. Privately printed, Macclesfield, c1830.
The Story of Mont Blanc and a Diary to China and back. By the late Albert Smith. 8vo, ppxvi, 299: 60; illus. For private circulation, July, 1860.
Sundt, Eilert
  The First Winter Ascent of the Aconcagua, September, 1915. pp8, 32 photographs. Privately printed, Buenos Aires, 1915.

Sutton, (G) & Noyce, (W C F)
  Samson. Privately printed, 1960.

Talfourd, (Sir Thomas N)
  Recollections of a First Visit to the Alps, in August and September 1841.
  12mo, pp193. Privately printed, London, 1841.

T(hioly), F
  Excursion en Suisse et en Savoie. 8vo, pp64, illus. (Privately lithog, Genève,
  1859.)

Thorington, J Monroe
  Mountains and Mountaineering. A List of the Writings (1917–1947) of J
  Monroe Thorington. 150 copies privately printed, 1947.

Tombazi, N A
  *Account of a Photographic Expedition to the Southern Glaciers of
  Kangchenjunga in the Sikkim Himalaya.* 4to, ppx, 80, map and 62
  photographs. 150 copies printed for private circulation, Bombay, 1925.

Tomlin, James
  Notes from a traveller's Journal, during an excursion in Norway and Sweden.
  8vo, pp204. Privately printed, Woodfall, London, 1852.

Tonnelle, Alfred
  Journal de Voyage. Privately printed, 1859.

Undrell, Capt J
  An Account of an ascent to the summit of Mont Blanc, in August, 1819. In
  'Annals of Philosophy', London, etc. NS, vol1, no5, pp373–383. This
  'Account' was also privately printed.

Veneon, (Jean)
  Tschingel. 8vo, pp9, illus. Privately printed, Grenoble, 1892.

Vignet, L
  *Les étapes d'une berline a travers le Tyrol, l'Engadine et les Grisons, juin
  1864.* Lectures données à la section lyonnaise du CAF. 8vo, pp67. 300
  copies privately printed, Pitrat, Lyon, 1880.

(Ward, Mrs)
  Memoirs of Kenneth Martin Ward. Illus. Privately printed, 1929.

Whitney, Josiah Dwight
  Names & Places, Studies in Geographical & Topographical Nomenclature.
  12mo, pp239, index, only 100 copies. Privately printed, 1888.

Whymper, Edward
  A Letter Addressed to the Members of the Alpine Club. pp16. Printed for
  private circulation, London, 1900.
  A right royal mountaineer. 8vo, pp23. Privately printed and published,
  Clowes, London, 1 February 1909.

Wickham, Robert S
  *Friendly Adirondack Peaks. A Book concerning Walking Trips among
  seldom climbed Mountains.* Privately published, Adirondack Mountain
  Club, 1924.

Wigram, (Mrs)
  Memoirs of Woolmore Wigram, 1831–1907. Privately printed, 1908.

Wilbraham, E B
> *Narrative of an Ascent, etc.* Privately printed from the 'Keepsake'.

Williams, William
> *My Summer in the Alps.* 1913. pp21, illus. 300 copies on Dutch handmade paper privately printed for the author by Frederick Fairchild Sherman, New York, MCMXIV. 50 additional copies on Dutch handmade paper privately printed for the author by Frederick Fairchild Sherman, MCMXIV.
>
> *Mountain Climbing, 1899 and 1905.* Privately printed, 1906?
>
> *Mountain Climbing. 1921–1925.* 250 copies privately printed, 1926?
>
> *A Summer Trip to Ecuador.* Privately printed, 1924?

Wills, (Alfred)
> *The Ascent of Mont Blanc, together with some remarks on glaciers.* 8vo, pp90. Privately printed, London, 1858.

Wilson, Claude
> *An epitome of fifty years' climbing.* pp118. 125 copies printed for private distribution, 1933.
>
> *Mountaineering.* With illustrations by Ellis Carr. 8vo, ppvi, 208. 50 copies were printed on handmade paper, not for sale. London and New York, 1893.

Wilson, H Schütz
> *A fine pair of horns, being the Weisshorn and the Matterhorn.* 8vo, pp23. Privately printed, London, 1873.
>
> *Eisleben or Stormont and Whitemont, An Alpine Sketch.* 8vo, pp31. Privately printed, London, 1873.
>
> *Eisleben. No 2. The Alps in sadness.* 8vo, pp31. Privately printed, London, 1873.
>
> *A bivouac on the Rothhorn.* 8vo, pp30. Privately printed, London c1874.

Woelflin, E
> *Une ancienne mesure de la hauteur du Mont-Blanc.* 8vo, pp9. 20 copies printed, Thomas Malzeville-Nancy, 1909.

Wright, Robert Alderson
> *A Little Known Ascent of Mont Blanc.* Privately printed pamphlet.

Wright, Wilhelmine Gerber
> *The Haunted Mountain and other Poems.* Privately printed, 1935.

Young, Bert Edward
> *Edward Whymper, Alpinist of the Heroic Age.* pp9. Nashville, Tennessee, 1914. Reprinted from *Popular Science Monthly*, June 1913, for private circulation.

Young, Henry
> *A Record of the Scientific Work of John Tyndall (1850–1888).* pp38. 200 copies printed for private circulation, Chiswick Press, London, 1935.

GENERAL REFERENCES

T G Brown and G de Beer,	*The First Ascent of Mont Blanc.* London, OUP, 1957.
W A B Coolidge,	*Swiss Travel and Swiss Guide-Books.* London, Longmans, 1889.
B Dobell,	*Catalogue of Books Printed for Private Circulation.* London, 1906. Published by the Author. Republished by Gale Research Co, Detroit, 1966.
J Martin,	*Bibliographical Catalogue of Privately Printed Books.* 2nd edition, 1854. Reprinted by Johnson Reprint Corp, NY, 1968.
C E Mathews,	*The Annals of Mont Blanc.* London, Unwin, 1898.
H F Montagnier,	'A Bibliography of the Ascents of Mont Blanc from 1786 to 1853'. *AJ25*, 608–640, 1911.

The London Dinner

ANNE SAUVY

(Translated by Ernst Sondheimer)

Strange as it may seem, it's because the lightning had struck, high up in the north face of the Aletschhorn, on 13 August of that year, that I found myself, on the 1 December which followed, clad in a dinner-jacket which didn't belong to me, driving by night across London through the late autumn fog.

The lightning had hit a party which, right from the start of the route, had been several ropelengths ahead of us, having started from the Hollandia hut whereas we had come from the Konkordia. Nothing had forewarned us of the sudden arrival of the thunderstorm which, indeed, moved away again as fast as it had come. We got away, Jean-Claude and I, with a good shake-up and a bad fright, but the other pair was closer to the ridge and was not so lucky. We moved up to them in a fierce little hailstorm and found them in rather bad shape. One was British and the other German; both were suffering from slight burns. The German had lost his ice axe. The Brit had lost the use of one arm and had sprained an ankle: he had been hurled several metres down the slope and owed his life to the ice screw to which he had been belayed and which had held firm.

We were in a remote spot, and it would have taken too long to alert the mountain rescue. Besides, the two casualties wanted to move on, and seemed just about fit enough to do so. We decided to rearrange the ropes: Jean-Claude took the German under his wing, and I the Britisher. In this way we managed the rest of the face without too much trouble. Also the weather had turned fine again, and the whole situation appeared less dramatic than it had done earlier. We moved up the ridge together but soon, as my rope was the slower of the two, I told the other pair to move on at their own pace and wait for us from time to time; it seemed pointless for them to stay always close to us.

Injured as he was, my partner climbed with plenty of spirit. He didn't even want to stop for any length of time, judging that his ankle would only become more painful as soon as it was no longer heated up by the exertions. I kept well above him so that I could check any slip, and thus had plenty of time to have a good look at him. He was a man in his forties, in whose lean face sparkled two large grey eyes. He wore the ragged clothes traditionally sported by the British: patched trousers, an ancient, faded sweater with frayed cuffs, a greenish cagoule, its rents and tears stuck together with crossed bits of sticking-plaster . . . In the underground you might have given him a small coin. But he spoke excellent French, and so I thought – I don't quite know why – that he must be an academic. It was just an idea that crossed my mind, but of course I had other things to do than ponder about his life history. The first priority was to reach a safe haven before nightfall.

It is 2500 metres down from the top of the Aletschhorn to Belalp, 2500 metres of ridges, snow slopes, glaciers, scree, and mountain-paths at the end. It goes on for ever. . . Nevertheless, we were in time to catch the last cable car, and there we found Jean-Claude's party waiting for us.

From here a complicated sequence of trains could have taken us to Grindelwald, but our British friend was generous enough to summon a taxi. He was feeling better and some movement had returned to his arm but, worn out by the big effort, he slept throughout the journey. We asked to be dropped off at Stechelberg where I had left my car, and there we took leave of our new friends. Poking about in a dusty pocket of his rucksack, my Briton extracted a wallet – a magnificent one, I can tell you – and pulled from it a visiting card which he gave me with his profuse thanks. I scribbled down for him my own address on the back of a hut receipt. And I wasn't half surprised when I took in, a bit later, both his name and his title: our ragamuffin was called Lord Whichunt. [*Author's note*: this name is not a reference to Lord Hunt (of Everest), but a family joke concerning a cousin of the author.]

And that's why, having been invited by my new friend to the Annual Dinner of the Alpine Club, I was crossing London, sitting next to him, at the beginning of the following winter . . .

I had arrived by air a few hours earlier, and had to leave again next day. It was a bit foggy but the weather was unseasonably mild, and we had the windows open. I had worked for two years in America and so my English was quite fluent, but I had never been to London. The city seemed enormous . . . From time to time I gave a startled jump, not being used to people driving on the left (I did my best to conceal this from my friend), but I was much entertained by the famous red two-storeyed buses, the tall policemen with their extra-tall helmets, the streets with their rows of dozens of identical houses, distinguished only by the colours of the front doors deep inside their pillared porticos. I was delighted to be there and to be about to take my place in the bosom of such an illustrious gathering; indeed I felt that I had entered the world of Phileas Fogg . . .

The dinner was held in a large building near the Thames, and we were directed to a hall on the ground floor where drinks were served. As I walked into this room I gave a start of surprise. A few moments earlier I had reflected that I was about to join the most ancient of all alpine clubs, but it had not occurred to me that the people I would meet there would themselves be so ancient . . . By and by I was to discover the reasons for this. The cost of the dinner – or so I heard – was twenty-five pounds, and no doubt the younger members of the Club knew of better ways of spending such a sum. And then, it is in later years that one really likes to meet fellow-survivors of the passage of time.

At any rate, my host was – apart from myself – one of the youngest members present. He had warned me beforehand that he would not be able to be with me all the time, having duties to carry out in the Club, and I had assured him that I would have no problem in entertaining myself. And indeed, he was soon surrounded by people and carried off far away from me, but I wasn't in the least bored. It was absorbing to study the crowd which thronged the room, mostly men in their dinner-jackets, more rarely ladies in long dresses. And this gathering was, dare we say it, of such a venerable age that it seemed hard to recognize the connection between so many worthy ancients and the rough reality of the sport of climbing. I just couldn't imagine that all these fragile patriarchs, squeezed into their gala outfits, could ever have been battling against the storm which lashed their thin anoraks, soaked in wet snow and stiff with ice ... The only thing here that might conjure up the image of snow was the immaculate whiteness of the many heads of hair ...

There was gin and sherry on offer. I took a gin-and-tonic and, glass in hand, steered through the crowd, trying to visualize the early life of the veterans I brushed past, seeking without success to put names to their faces. As time went on, I began to imagine that I could decipher various adventures written into those deep wrinkles and into the corner of a smile. I was particularly fascinated by a smallish greybeard who must have been close to a hundred years old. Firmly pressed against the serving table, talking to nobody, he concentrated on getting hold of the maximum number of sherries which he gulped down to the last drop and, as soon as he had put down one glass, he was already reaching for the next.

Having watched these goings-on for some time, I went to study the table-plan which was pinned up in a corner of the room. We were about a hundred and thirty diners; amongst them I recognized the Liechtenstein Ambassador and various famous names in mountain history. One of these attracted my attention: that of James Eccles. In the second half of the nineteenth century there had been a well-known mountaineer of that name. Asking myself whether this could be one of his descendants, or whether it was a case of pure coincidence, I looked for Lord Whichunt to ask him about it, but he couldn't tell me. Doubtless this James Eccles must be some kind of greatgrandson or greatgrandnephew of the Victorian mountaineer, for he was one of the Club's invited guests for the evening and was going to propose the last toast. But, apart from Colonel Edward Masonridge, who had been in contact with him but was unfortunately confined to bed this evening because of an attack of gout, nobody there knew anything about this James Eccles. Anyway, we would doubtless find out in the course of the last toast, and that would be enough to satisfy my curiosity.

Banging a little hammer to ensure silence, a master of ceremonies now informed us that dinner was served in a room on the third floor. At the same time he asked the young ones if they would be so kind as to leave the one and only lift for the use of the older guests. The young ones! It was, in truth, a weird doddering band which tackled the task of mounting the large stone staircase, doing their best to demonstrate by this heroic climb that some of their vital functions were not yet defunct. It was a moving sight, and I didn't dare think of the scene in the lift ...

We looked for our places on the long tables, decorated with anemones. A group of waitresses, dressed in black with white aprons, watched our entrance with curiosity. The Reverend J F Tindicott said Grace, after which we sat down with a great shuffling of chairs. I was next to Lord Whichunt and, as soon as everyone had inspected the menu, I began to make contact with my other neighbours. One of them had been a member of Tilman's expedition to Everest, another had spent a whole summer working up at the Vallot Observatory without once coming down, a third seemed to have explored every single mountain on Earth . . . The talk flowed easily, even if some hands cupped to ears were a reminder that hearing had not improved with the years . . . And I felt that I was myself a living part of a little piece of alpine history, when it was pointed out to me that yonder venerable diner, his shirt-front so stylishly adorned with little starched pleats, was the last man to have seen Mallory and Irvine alive in 1924, or that this other one, with a white beard reaching down to his bow-tie, had pioneered the first ascent of a route which, even today, was not often repeated.

From where I sat I could comfortably observe the small grizzled sherry-swigger. He had been amongst the last to slide into his seat on the top table, just as Grace was being said, and since then he had not missed a single mouthful. Having guzzled with a healthy appetite the vol-au-vent which started the meal, he noticed that the lady next to him had not touched hers, and – having whispered a few words into her ear – he had, with a conjuror's skill, carried out a rapid switch of plates . . . At the same time he was swigging the Chablis, beckoning to the waiter as soon as his glass was empty. Between courses he broke off pieces of bread, munching them with evident relish. I noticed that, on several occasions, his neighbours made efforts to engage him in conversation, but to no avail. The only response was a slight shake of the head which quickly discouraged all approaches. On the other hand, I was pleased to see him enjoying several helpings of his veal escalope with mixed vegetables. After the Chablis he took equal pleasure in the Château Camarsac which went with the main course, draining it to the last drop. For dessert he went straight for the apple-pie, dousing it with lashings of cream, and, when the liqueurs came round, he helped himself to a huge, brimful glass of brandy. Here and there cigars began to appear in the dining room. Our friend pulled from his pocket a small pipe of distinctly antique design. The time for the after-dinner speeches had arrived.

The President dealt quickly with the first three toasts, addressed respectively to Her Majesty the Queen, the members of the royal family and the Club's guests. This gave me a moment of intense inner joy: contemplating the whole gathering as, upstanding, it declaimed with one voice 'The Queen', I pictured to myself the ribaldry and catcalls which would accompany a similar toast to the President of the Republic in any gathering of French mountaineers, be they ever so aged . . .

The fourth toast, to the Principality of Liechtenstein, went on and on . . .

When it finally seemed to be coming to an end, my little elderly friend extinguished his pipe, leapt to his feet with vigour and, without a single note to assist his memory, started to propose the fifth toast, that of the Alpine Club. The start was traditional: 'Your Excellency, my Lords, Ladies and Gentlemen . . .'

And then, straightaway, he started to talk of mountains, real mountains, and – whether or not he was related to his illustrious namesake – it was obvious that he knew what he was talking about. The picture he drew for us of the early years of the Club was gripping, full of life. Never before had I understood so well the passion which had animated the first British alpinists.

The speaker recalled for us the long journey they had had to make, by boat, steam train and coach, to reach the Promised Land. He described in detail the primitive shelters which got established, one by one, around the fringes of the mountain ranges. He recounted the history of the fierce competition for the first ascents, and the battles amongst rival climbers for the services of the best of the Swiss or French mountain guides. He reminded us of the inadequacy of the early primitive equipment, the drawbacks of hobnailed boots, the fragility of long ice axes with wooden shafts, the permeability of hemp ropes which soaked up the water and then froze, going stiff as iron bars. He spoke of the trouble caused by that heavy white tent which, on Whymper's advice, he had acquired for himself, only to find at the end of the day that it was more of a hindrance than a help.

I saw eyes opening wide in the audience. But stupefaction reached its height when James Eccles – for there could be no doubt about it, it was he himself, there amongst us in person – calmly undertook to tell us the tale of his first ascent of the Peuterey Ridge with the Payot brothers, on 31 July 1877, giving us first of all some hitherto unpublished details about their two earlier attempts, and then reconstructing for us, with a superb flight of eloquence, the full story of this great climb, performed more than a century ago.

We felt we were on the climb ourselves . . . We shivered with him in the icy cold of the bivouac . . . We could see the blue splinters of ice, spraying out under the guide's ice axe . . . We balanced gingerly on the verglas which coated the rocks . . . We suffered thirst because the water in the flask had run out . . . And finally, we felt the deep emotion which came with the realization that no further obstacle stood between us and victory . . . Entranced, spell-bound, we relived one of the great moments of alpine history.

James Eccles's eyes shone with pleasure as he described for us the relatively easy crossing of the big cornice which opened the way to Mont Blanc de Courmayeur . . . And he finished his talk with an earnest appeal.

'And right on the summit of Mont Blanc,' he said, 'what do you think we found? The pure, radiant whiteness of the peaks? The unspoiled solitude of the mountains? The wild appeal of the heights? Not a bit of it! What awaited us on the top, which had been reached that day via the normal route by three big parties, complete with guides and porters, what we saw there was filthy snow, trampled all over by dozens upon dozens of boots, soiled with food scraps, refuse and bottles which nobody had taken the trouble to remove! And will you believe that, in order to escape from that disgusting spectacle, we had to climb down again a bit, on the Miage side, before we could enjoy our victory in a more welcoming spot. And that we said as a joke, but not without a touch of bitterness, that soon the Mont Blanc range would have to be submitted to inspections by the Health Department! And that was in 1877 . . . So I now put the question to you – to you, the young. What have you really managed to do in the meantime to preserve the mountains in that pure, unspoiled state which is their essence? And what are you *now* going to do about it? Think about it. And whilst I am waiting, I raise my glass to our dear old Club.'

'The Club,' repeated the audience, who had risen to their feet.

Silence fell, and James Eccles, his head raised a little, seemed still to be focusing his intense gaze on some snowy ridge or some corner of the sky. The assembly did not disturb his reverie, and we could all count the twelve strokes of midnight drifting in through the half-open windows.

As soon as the last stroke had died away, James Eccles was no longer with us. He had suddenly dissolved, the way a light mist evaporates in the sun's rays.

And not one word could be heard as the guests, struck dumb to a man, slowly left the dining room.

On the staircase, Lord Whichunt was one of the first to regain his voice. He whispered in my ear: 'I do hope that you have enjoyed our old British customs.'

One Hundred Years Ago

(with extracts from the Alpine Journal)

C A RUSSELL

(Plates 83–86)

Although the weather experienced in many parts of the Alps during the opening days of January 1891 was unsettled, with reports of violent winds and very low temperatures, conditions slowly improved as the month progressed and several winter expeditions of note were completed. In the Mont Blanc range on 14 January Paul Güssfeldt with a party including Emile Rey and David Proment made the first winter ascent of the Grandes Jorasses, reaching the summit by way of the SW face. The ascent was carefully planned and 'a great track had been made by a party of men sent some days before to clear the way as far as the Italian Club hut.' Any route to Pointe Walker, the highest peak, is a fine expedition and the climb was a considerable achievement, even for this formidable party.

Later in the month Güssfeldt, with Rey, Proment and two porters climbed the Gran Paradiso. 'The ascent of this peak by Dr Güssfeldt on January 25 last, though not the first that has been made in winter, deserves record as a remarkable performance.' The party succeeded 'after two false starts, in getting off from the Rifugio Vittorio Emanuele a few minutes before midnight on the 24th, reached the summit at 4.30, remained there twenty minutes and returned to the Rifugio at seven, thus accomplishing the whole excursion before sunrise. They were, however, favoured with a brilliant moon.'

In the Bernina Alps on 20 February Mrs Elizabeth Main[1] and W H Bulpett, with Martin Schocher and Martin Weibel, completed the first winter traverse of the three summits of Piz Palü and the first winter ascent of the central, highest, peak. Starting from the Boval hut the party reached the W ridge at the Bellavista pass. 'The day was warm and still, the ridge in an excellent state and the rocks free from ice. From the highest peak to the third peak took more than one and a half hour, owing to the icy condition of the ridge and the consequent step-cutting. After spending some time on the third peak, the climbers left it at 2.00P.M. and all went well till they were within a few feet of the point at which the ridge is generally finally quitted. Here an enormous bergshrund had split the slope asunder, and the party were forced on to the Italian side of the arête in order to turn it. The slope was of smooth blue ice, and took nearly an hour's hard work in step-cutting before it could be descended, though the distance was only about 30 feet.'

As the winter snows receded it was hoped that conditions during the climbing season would, at the very least, be better than those experienced throughout the Alps in the previous year. It is clear, however, from the following account that such hopes were not fulfilled.

The past season in Switzerland will long be remembered by Alpine climbers as the one in which all previous records of bad mountaineering weather were broken; and no less an authority than Melchior Anderegg, the great Oberland guide, speaks of '1891' as being the worst of all the many seasons he ever experienced in the Alps since he began climbing in 1858. It is hardly an exaggeration to say that, with the exception of occasional breaks of fine weather, two days out of every five were bad ones; and this, together with the unusual quantity of snow and verglas on the rocks, combined to make the ascent of the more difficult peaks almost impossible. The mere fact that only five ascents were made of the Matterhorn (a peak which in ordinary seasons is climbed between twenty and thirty times) shows what unfavourable conditions mountaineers had to contend with. These ascents were made by the easiest route from Zermatt, whilst no one succeeded either in crossing the great mountain or in reaching its summit from the Italian side. In the Oberland and at Chamonix, both guides and amateurs watched for the sunshine which never came, in spite of the misleading hopes so often held out by their aneroids and by those weather signs which for years past have always been held to be infallible.

In such circumstances, it was not surprising that many parties were confined to the lower peaks. In the Pennine Alps two new routes were recorded in the chain of Les Maisons Blanches, the rock peaks at the head of the Corbassière glacier below the N flank of the Grand Combin, and on 21 July G W Prothero and Walter Leaf with Clemenz Zurbriggen made the first ascent of Le Ritord, on the ridge to the north of that chain. In the Arolla district on 27 July A G Topham with Jean Maître and Pierre Maurys completed the first traverse of the ridge between the Pointe des Genevois, the highest peak of the Dents de Perroc, and the central peak or Dent de Perroc. Further east several new climbs were completed by determined parties. On 18 July C H Gould and George Broke, with Adolf Andenmatten and Aloys Burgener, made the first recorded ascent of the upper section of the SW ridge of the Strahlhorn, above the Alderhorn, and on 15 August Ludwig Norman-Neruda and May Peyton, his future wife, with Christian Klucker reached the summit of the Pointe de Zinal by way of the unclimbed S ridge. On 25 August a direct route was forced up the steep NE face of the Alphubel, above the Längfluh rocks, by A F de Fonblanque with Xaver Imseng and Isidor Bumann.

A few days later, on 2 September, a party including C G Monro and O G Jones, with Antoine Bovier and Pierre Gaspoz, made the first recorded ascent of the Dent des Rosses above Ferpècle and on 3 September Monro and Jones, without guides, completed the first ascent of the E ridge of the Grande Dent de Veisivi on their way to Arolla. The party then crossed to the southern side of the

65. *Alpine flora of Yulong Shan (at 4000m), with Rhododendron adenogynum.* (Tony Schilling) (p 63)

66. *Left, Rhododendron adenogynum.* (Tony Schilling) (p 63)

67. *Abies delavayi.* (Tony Schilling) (p 63)

68. *Clematis montana.* (Tony Schilling) (p 63)

69. *Rhododendron telmateium.* (Tony Schilling) (p 63)

70. Paeonia delavayi. (Tony Schilling) (p 63)

71. Cypripedium margaritaceum. (Tony Schilling) (p 63)

72. *NW flank of the Yulong Shan and Yangtse.* (Tony Schilling) (p 63)

73. *Campsite in the Nyanchen Thanglha range.* (Margaret Clennett) (p 75)

74. *Approaching the Goring La pass.* (Margaret Clennett) (p 75)

75. *The limestone crest of the Jura west of Chasseral.* (Kev Reynolds)
(p 152)

76. *The lip of the Creux du Van, rock-climbers' playground in the heart
of the Jura.* (Kev Reynolds) (p 152)

main chain and Monro later recalled that 'we left Arolla feeling sad, for the previous evening, at table d'hôte, we had seen a dreadful sight, in the shape of an individual, of the male sex moreover, in full evening dress. The significance of this incident was enforced by the recollection that the last time I had fed at that table I was clad in a somewhat airy costume consisting chiefly of stockings and mackintosh.' On 10 September, starting from an establishment 'in which an all-pervading bovine odour was present, which was not wonderful, inasmuch as through the extensive chinks in the flooring the backs of the cows could easily be seen', the party approached the S side of the Grand Combin massif where Jones and the two guides made the first ascent of the SE ridge of the Combin de Grafeneire.

The one region 'which was blessed with a modicum of the fine weather denied to so many other quarters of the Alps' was the Dauphiné and it was here that the principal expedition of the season was completed. On 13 July J H Gibson, with Ulrich Almer and Fritz Boss, made the first traverse of the E, summit ridge of the Meije from the Grand Pic or Pic Occidental to the Pic Central. It was only the second time that the ridge had been traversed, the route having been completed in the reverse direction by the guideless party of the Zsigmondy brothers and Ludwig Purtscheller six years earlier. Addressing the Alpine Club in the following year Gibson explained that after reaching the Grand Pic by way of the Promontoire spur they were able to examine the real turning-point of the climb,

the western face of the westernmost tooth. We noticed at once that a few feet below the top there hung what was apparently a fragment of Zsigmondy and Purtscheller's rope, but whether our way was clear or not it was impossible at that distance to tell. But what struck us more than anything was that we saw we were not to be the first party to try the arête that season. Right along the crests of the two western and across the northern faces of the two eastern teeth – that is to say, along the identical route we proposed to traverse – ran a continuous well-defined line of footmarks. That the party, whoever it was, had not got any further, however, was evident at a glance. The snow of the Brèche Zsigmondy was untouched, and we might still hope to be the second party to traverse the whole length of the ridge.

After descending safely to the Brèche Zsigmondy the party 'advanced towards the rocks of the westernmost tooth, our excitement rising as we neared them. If the rocks would "go" at all, it was at one place, and one place only; a narrow crack, which, starting from near the base of the crag, runs diagonally upwards towards the left for about fifteen feet or so, and then bends round on to the northern slope of the tooth.' With considerable skill Almer climbed the crack and worked his way up the slope to the top of the tooth. Gibson added that 'the slope is tremendously steep, the rocks loose and ice-coated, and there is not a good grip to be got anywhere. I can confidently recommend the view of La Grave and the valley of the Romanche to be seen from this coign of vantage; but it is too theatrical for people troubled with weak heads.' Before completing the route the party looked along the ridge to the Pic Central.

> The situation is a striking one. On the left was the slope of 70° up which we had just come, on the right the continuous wall of precipice that forms the southern face of the mountain, at our backs was the cliff that overhangs the Brèche Zsigmondy, and in front of us lay the sharpest knife-edge I have ever seen. The mystery of the footmarks I spoke of before was now cleared up: a party had indeed been on the ridge – not of men, but of chamois.

The traverse from the Grand Pic to the Pic Central, still regarded as one of the finest expeditions in the Alps, was an outstanding achievement for the period, comparable in historical importance with the first traverse of the ridge.

Other climbs of note in the Dauphiné were the first ascent of the NW face of Pointe Durand, the lower summit of Mont Pelvoux, by F E L Swan with Pierre Gaspard père and Maximin Gaspard on 10 July and an ascent of the unclimbed NE ridge of Le Plaret on 18 July by the guideless party of G H Morse, C H Pasteur and J H Wicks.

Despite the unfavourable weather a number of new expeditions was completed in other districts. In the Graian Alps on 3 August G Stallard and A L Ormerod with Johannes Ogi-Müller and Abraham Müller made the first traverse of Mont Herbetet, ascending the E ridge and descending by way of the NNE ridge. In the Bregaglia group A von Rydzewski with Klucker and Mansueto Barbaria reached the summits of several unclimbed peaks including the Torrone Centrale, at the head of the Forno glacier, on 8 July and, on 12 July, the Punta Pioda di Sciora in the Sciora chain. In the Austrian Alps V J Pillwax with S Huter and P Untersberger made the first ascent of the S face of the Grossglockner, crossing the long couloir – now known as the Pillwax couloir – which divides the face below the Obere Glocknerscharte. The S face is nearly 600m high and the first climb, like the first ascent of the couloir in the E face by the Pallavicini party 15 years earlier, was a remarkable achievement in advance of its time.

In the Dolomites the highest point of the Fünffingerspitze or Punta delle Cinque Dita, which had been climbed by the guideless party of Robert Hans Schmitt and Johann Santner in the previous year, was reached by no less than four parties at the end of the season. On 4 September Norman-Neruda, accompanied by Klucker, approached the peak from the north hoping to make the second ascent. In a paper read before the Alpine Club in the following June Neruda recalled that after Klucker had led up a series of difficult chimneys in the N face they were both surprised to hear voices. On completing the climb Neruda found that the Dutch climber Jeanne Immink – who was to make the first winter ascent of the Croda da Lago on 10 December – and her guides Antonio Dimai and Giuseppe Zecchini had arrived at the summit a few minutes earlier after making the second ascent of the route on the S side taken by Schmitt and Santner. Neruda added that the Fünffingerspitze 'is the most difficult rock-climb I have ever done. The Kleine Zinne, the Croda da Lago, the Cima di

Canali, the Cima della Madonna, and other peaks of reputed great difficulty I have climbed cannot for one moment be compared with it; in fact, they are mere child's play by its side.'

Following his ascent to the new Vallot observatory and the summit of Mont Blanc in the previous year Dr J Janssen, the astronomer, 'was struck with the advantages to science of an observatory on the actual summit.' After the necessary funds had been raised preliminary studies were carried out by A G Eiffel, the celebrated engineer. 'Here especially it was essential that "the house should be founded on a rock", and the first point to ascertain was how near the rock approaches to the summit of the Calotte.' During August and September a tunnel was driven through the ice, many of the workmen being incapacitated by frostbite.

M Eiffel had determined that, in order to be successful, a platform of rock must be found at a depth not exceeding 12 mètres below the surface. The tunnel in the ice was commenced on the N side towards the Petits Mulets, at an elevation of 14 mètres below the summit, and was carried horizontally for 29.4 mètres, till the boring corresponded with the actual summit, but no rock had been found. Though the gallery was subsequently carried 23 mètres further beneath the snow, still no rock was touched.

Janssen then decided to erect the observatory on snow and a wooden hut 'capable of accommodating two persons, with an arrangement whereby any vertical or horizontal movement can be observed' was placed on the summit.

As work on the tunnel progressed a hut built on a proper base was being completed not far away. 'The Turin section of the C.A.I. opened in August a hut on a spur of the Aiguille Grise, on the right bank of the Glacier du Dôme, at a height of about 10,500 feet. This hut is known as the *Capanna del Dôme*.' The first party to ascend Mont Blanc from the Dôme, or Gonella, hut was that of Francesco Gonella who with Julian Proment and Joseph Croux reached the summit on 13 August. Further along the chain the construction of another famous refuge was completed at Gressoney. 'When the Queen of Italy visited that place on August 15 it was put together, and, after an open-air Mass had been said near it, her Majesty was pleased to "christen" it in her own name, and it will be known as the "Capanna alla Regina Margherita".'

On 10 July the death occurred of Alexander Seiler, the great hotelier who as the hospitable proprietor of the Monte Rosa Hotel had welcomed many climbers to Zermatt. Writing in the *Alpine Journal* Leslie Stephen described Seiler as 'the best of all landlords of Alpine hotels' who in spite of change had 'preserved the qualities which had first gained for him the respect and friendship of a whole generation of travellers.'

Later in July a major engineering project which had been completed received official approval. 'The Federal Inspector of Railways has been over the new line from Viège to Zermatt, and authorized its being opened for passenger traffic; trains are now, therefore, running daily.'

In the Caucasus equally bad weather was experienced by Gottfried

Merzbacher and Purtscheller who, with the guides Johann Kehrer and Johann Unterweger, were the only climbers to visit the range. Despite unfavourable conditions this determined party climbed extensively, attaining the ridge between the two summits of Ushba on 24 July during an attempt to reach the S, higher, summit (4710m) and scaling Elbrus (5633m) and other high peaks. On 21 August the party completed the first ascent of the central and highest peak of Dongus Orun (4454m) in a bitter NW wind. After three hours of mixed climbing

a rock ridge was gained which abuts right against the peak. This ridge was narrow and broken by all sorts of obstacles. The rocks were covered with powdery snow, slightly frozen. Immediately below the peak the ridge rose steeply in a series of smooth bossed rocks, covered with snow and ice. The ascent of these was plainly difficult and dangerous; a couloir which offered an alternative route was only to be reached by a dangerous traverse. Meanwhile Unterweger had climbed the first cliff, and thought it would be better farther up. The rest followed, to find things only got worse – advance was doubtful, retreat impossible. The ascent of 120m took two hours, and not for a moment were they out of danger. When the upper snow-slopes were reached they sank in deep, but it seemed an easy promenade to the N peak, and along a broad ridge to the central peak.

After Purtscheller's departure Merzbacher and the guides travelled for some distance along the chain, climbing Kasbek (5047m) on 30 September and, on 4 October, completing the first ascent of Gimarai Khokh (4776m).

In October Francis Younghusband crossed the Karakoram on his way to India after wintering in Kashgar and continuing his exploration of the Pamir region. After ascending a valley near the Wakhjir pass his party reached the head of a glacier where a magnificent view presented itself. 'Here we were among the real mountain monarchs once more. We saw before us an amphitheatre of snowy peaks glittering in the fading sunlight, and at their foot one vast snowfield, the depository of all their surplus snow and ice. This nook of mountains was the very Heart of Central Asia.'

Gilgit was reached on 13 October and a few days later Younghusband crossed the last pass on his way south.

Another journey had been accomplished; all the difficulties and all the anxieties of it were now over. The sun set in a glow of glory. The snows of the mountain summits were tinged with ruddy hues, the fleecy clouds overhead were suffused in ever-changing colours; then slowly the peaks in the distant east grew grey, the warm tints faded from the scene, one by one the stars pierced through the skies, and night settled down upon the mountains.

Still further afield two famous mountaineering clubs were founded during the year.

The New Zealand Alpine Club is now fairly launched. At a meeting held on July 28, at Christchurch, twenty-seven members and five 'subscribers' were elected, rules were considered and adopted, and officers were appointed. Mr L Harper is president; Mr A P Harper, secretary; Mr G E Mannering, editor of the journal. 'Subscribers' will have the privileges of the club, but no voice in its management.

Interest in the Southern Alps was increased by the publication of Mannering's book *With Axe and Rope in the New Zealand Alps* in which he gave a spirited account of his own experiences in the region.

In South Africa the formation of a mountain club had been suggested by the botanist Dr Rudolph Marloth and in September the suggestion was taken up by the *Cape Times*. At a public meeting held in Cape Town on 9 October a provisional committee, which included Dr Marloth, was elected and 60 members were identified. On 4 November the Mountain Club of South Africa held its first meeting, electing Sir James Sivewright, a member of Cecil Rhodes's cabinet, as the President. Sir James was the first of many distinguished public figures, including Rhodes himself and J C Smuts, who have belonged to the ranks of the Mountain Club.

At home an important climb was completed in the Lake District on 27 July when W P Haskett Smith, Geoffrey Hastings and W C Slingsby made the first ascent of the North Climb on the Pillar Rock. The climb was a remarkable feat for the period and Haskett Smith advised that 'it should not be touched except by experienced climbers.' At Easter Jones, accompanied by W E Sumpner, made his first ascent of the Napes Needle, a climb which he repeated with Sumpner a few days later. On the Isle of Skye a notable achievement was the first crossing of the Thearlaich-Dubh gap in the main Cuillin ridge by J N Collie and W W King with John Mackenzie.

In September an event of considerable interest was the publication in the *Scottish Mountaineering Club Journal* of 'Tables giving all the Scottish Mountains exceeding 3000 feet in height', the lists compiled by H T Munro. The tables were soon in demand and the climbing of 'Munros' has become a popular pursuit.

By August 1891, when celebrations were held to mark the sixth centenary of the Swiss Confederation, Zermatt and the other great Alpine centres were already experiencing the process of inevitable change described by Stephen as 'only part of a much wider change, of which it is useless, and would therefore be idle, to complain.' It seems appropriate to conclude this account with the following extract from a review which appeared at the end of the climbing season.

The railway to Zermatt has been completed, and the little village which remained so long the stronghold of Alpine climbers is at last invaded by enterprising tourist agents and their following, whom they tempt to visit the valley by inducements similar to those held out to the thousands who pass 'nine hours at Brighton for three shillings.' Grindelwald, too, is a railway terminus, and the red and white posts one sees from the road near Sallanches warn us that the same fate is in store for Chamonix. Still, the rising generation of climbers ignore these changes, and flock in numbers to the old 'Playground of Europe.' In spite of the altered surroundings the great snow peaks seem to afford as much pleasure and enjoyment to them as they did to the little band who first made war against the mountain giants.

REFERENCE

1   Better known as Mrs Aubrey le Blond, the founder and first President of the Ladies' Alpine Club.

(*Editor's Note.* This article is the twenty-first in an annual series which started in 1971. On the occasion of this 'coming-of-age' I would like to express, on behalf of the Alpine Club, our thanks to our member C A Russell for his contributions, invariably prepared with meticulous care and always of great historical interest.)

AREA NOTES

COMPILED BY A V SAUNDERS

The Alps 1990

LINDSAY GRIFFIN

The recent mild winters and the general lack of snowfall throughout the Alps have brought dismay to the hearts of the *piste* skiers. Alpinists, however, attempting ascents in December and January, have been delighted by the quasi-summer conditions. Unfortunately the knock-on effect has been to create exceptionally dry conditions during the summer months. Large expanses of bare rock are now viewed with amazement by those expecting the usual snow and ice slopes. This appears to be most marked towards the western end of the chain (especially in the Ecrins Massif), where stonefall has now become serious and danger areas are being established on routes of all grades that were until recently considered 'objectively safe'. This current trend suggests that many of the lower-altitude ice/mixed routes might become a thing of the past for the alpinist visiting the range during the more traditional holiday periods.

Gradings quoted below are UIAA unless otherwise stated.

Mont Blanc

Additions to the repertoire of 'Short Rock-climbs' are countless. Route diagrams of the fine granite towers, such as the Trident du Tacul or Pt 3014m on the Evêque above the Charpoua, show a myriad of dotted lines. Included is a Topo showing a very worthwhile and highly recommended outing at a reasonable standard on the excellent granite of Pt 3014m. Romain Vogler has again played a prominent role in this type of development and has also created a fine new line on the Pt de L'Androsace (300m French 6c). The latter lies above the glacial basin of Combe Maudit which is still wonderfully unfrequented.

In 1989 the Swiss climber P Steulet freed the Darbelley route on the N face of the Petit Clocher du Portalet to give the massif's first-ever French 8a. This year T Renault and A Ghersen produced the second when they climbed the short yet vicious front face of the second gendarme on the Cosmique arête (Aiguille du Midi) to give 'Digital Crack'.

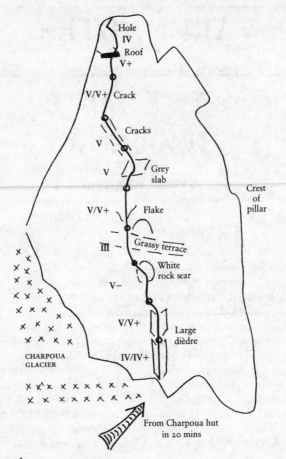

Hole
IV
Roof
V+
V/V+ Crack

Cracks

V

V

Grey
slab

V/V+

Flake

III

Grassy terrace

White
rock scar

V−

V/V+

Large
dièdre

IV/IV+

Crest
of
pillar

CHARPOUA
GLACIER

From Charpoua hut
in 20 mins

L'EVÊQUE WEST FACE
Pt 3014m
'MONSEIGNEUR LEFEBVRE' TD − 300m V+
P AND G BORNET, 28 July 1988 Rappel Descent

On the Brouillard face of Mont Blanc, both the Red and Right-hand pillars have received additions from the ever-productive Piola–Anker team, with the crux moves going at a reasonable (for these days!) VI+/VII−. The Garbarrou–Long on the Red Pillar is rapidly becoming a modern classic. On one occasion three teams were seen to be simultaneously engaged on the route and one of these, rappelling from the summit of the pillar, made the round trip from the Monzino hut on the same day! It is reported that all the necessary pegs are now in place on the big aid pitch. If this is the case, the difficulty associated with this time-consuming section has been significantly reduced.

A British team, attempting to repeat the Grassi route Etica Bisbetica on the Right-hand pillar, was stopped low down by stonefall which appeared to originate from the depression left of the true crest of the upper pillar. In the lower section the correct line was difficult to locate but sported at least one double bolt belay 'in an area with an embarrassment of good cracks'. The original Bonington route was thought to give a safer and probably better line. This year, approaches to pillars could be made from the Eccles by rappelling the monster rimaye from an *in situ* stake.

Two significant events occurred on the Central Pillar of Frêney: the first winter ascent of the Jori Bardill route by R Escoffier and Ghersen on 9 January 1990 and, during the summer, the first recorded free ascent of the original route. The latter was a well-known problem that, perhaps surprisingly, had not been solved earlier. The crux, (not surprisingly) the chimney pitch through the roof above the Chandelle, was given a French 7a+ grading by Alexis Long.

On the Grand Pilier d'Angle the super-route Divine Providence was soloed by Jacques Lafaille on 4–5 August and then, shortly afterwards, climbed almost completely free by Renault and Ghersen. The sixth pitch on the Red Wall now becomes the crux at French 7c – an appalling thought at that altitude! The recalcitrant pegs (two or three) lie in a damp roof, and it is thought that very dry conditions would be needed to eliminate this short aid section.

The higher mixed routes were in good condition during the continuous fine spell that affected the massif during much of August. Rob Durran, climbing perhaps the most popular route on the Grand Pilier – the Dufour–Frehel with the Direct Finish – recommends a horizontal traverse from Col Moore to the foot of the face. This is quicker and avoids the rather serious difficulties that seem to be encountered these days on the several rimayes below the face. It is, however, still 'decidedly heart-in-mouth'! Eight hours from the Trident hut (which was unguarded this summer) to the Peuterey ridge, and then a further five hours to the summit. This last section, in high winds, was in many ways the most demanding part of the ascent.

Durran also notes changes to some of the more traditional classics. The top section of the Rocher du Mont Blanc route is really quite steep for its lowly PD grading, and the seracs at the exit from the Brenva Spur are now much harder than they were several years ago. This summer they appeared to be far more extensive, and at one point they contained a seemingly unavoidable overhanging wall – albeit with a good landing!

Gabarrou and Grassi still continue to discover those ephemeral ribbons of ice that occur during the spring. On Mont Maudit the last unclimbed couloir on the 'Three Gendarmes' fell to Gabarrou, Gourdini and Passino on 16 May. This is the steep narrow runnel between the Central and Left pillars. It is 400m and took 11 hours which is a long time for Gabarrou; so the climb must be hard! The August/September edition of *Vertical* gives a good overview of the range with full descriptions of many of Gabarrou's new gully lines throughout recent years.

The Bonatti route to the summit of Pt Whymper on the N face of the Grandes Jorasses received its third ascent with a fine solo effort by S Svetičič. This, together with his winter ascent of the Eiger, will continue to enhance the considerable reputation of Eastern Block mountaineers.

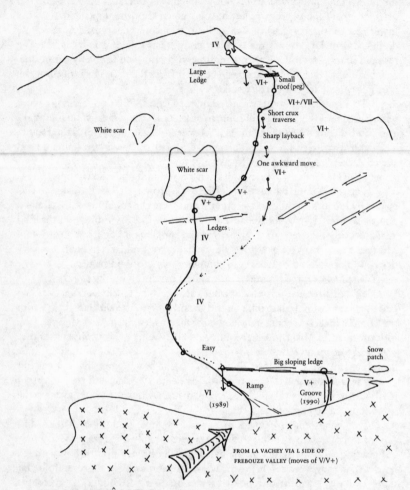

IV

Large
Ledge

VI+

Small
roof (peg)

VI+/VII−

Short crux
traverse

VI+

Sharp layback

White scar

One awkward move
VI+

White scar

V+

V+

Ledges
IV

IV

Easy

Snow
patch

Big sloping ledge

VI

Ramp

V+
Groove
(1990)

(1989)

FROM LA VACHEY VIA L SIDE OF
FREBOUZE VALLEY (moves of V/V+)

AIG DE L'EVÊQUE Pt 3019m
E FACE 'CRESSWELL ROUTE' TD VI+/VII− c500m
T PENNING AND A TIERNEY, 24 July 1990 Rappel Descent

Two significant events have taken place on the W face of the Petites Jorasses. On 15 January Piola and H Bouvard made the first winter ascent of the Czech 1976 route. In the summer Piola and Sprüngli created 'Anouk'. This is a 21-pitch route with unavoidable moves of VI. The climbing is sustained at VI+ to VII−, with a small roof of VII+. What is so special about this ED(1) line? The answer lies in the fact that the route is protected by 108 *in situ* bolts! Recently many top Swiss climbers have harshly criticized their countryman who, with this offering, has created the first '100-bolt' route in the massif. However, it is a reflection on the current popularity of 'safe' climbing that the route has already been repeated 25 times. The rappel anchors, down the line of ascent, are reported to be excellent!

Now into a quieter corner of the range. In 1989 Tony Penning and Pete Cresswell were climbing unroped up the first section of a proposed new line on the E face of the Aiguille de l'Evêque above the Frebouze glacier basin when, tragically, Cresswell fell to his death. Penning returned with Andy Tierney in 1990 and on 24 July climbed the face, finishing at Pt 3019m to the east of the main summit. The approach to the area beneath the face (from La Vachey via the L side of the valley below the glacier) is quite serious as it involves a 50m runout at around V/V+ beneath some hanging seracs. It is almost certain that the Aiguille has never been approached from this side before and that this is the first route on this vast face. There is some good climbing on sound granite and a Topo is included.

Lastly, let's try something different! Descents on a surf-ski have now been made of the N faces of the Plan, Pain de Sucre, Midi (Mallory route) and the Jager couloir on Mont Blanc du Tacul. The French skiers Govy and Ruby have been the main activists.

Bernese Oberland

A remarkable *enchainement* was achieved by Michel Worth on 16 September 1989 when he completed, solo, the N faces of the Mittaghorn (700m TD+), Grosshorn (1200m TD+) and Lauterbrunnen Breithorn (1050m ED) in a total of 17 hours. Better still, he descended from each summit by the rather old-fashioned means of down-climbing the easier northern flanks of the peaks that lie between the routes. Quite a contrast to the usual parapentes, hang-gliders, helicopters etc that often accompany these exploits nowadays.

On the Eiger, S Svetičič made the first winter solo ascent of the Harlin route.

Bregaglia/Bernina

Snow conditions on the classic routes in the Bernina remained very good until late in the season, but the weather seemed rather less predictable here than in the Western Alps. Notable omissions in the Bregaglia included the snow-patches usually present on the approach to the NE face of the Badile from the N ridge and the more famous one on the Cassin route itself. There was very little evidence of the snow dome on the summit of the Cengalo by the end of August. With current glacial recession this area has a definite sub-alpine feel and any ice climbing has become rather impractical after mid-June.

New bolt-protected routes are being worked out on steep slabs of the Spazzacaldeira, and the Albigna valley is by far the most popular in the range. Excellent all-free climbs that have much attention from local climbers but are largely unknown to visiting British alpinists are: The Kasper Pillar on the Frachiccio (VII); Leni route (VI/VI+), Felici (VI) and Nigg direct (VI−) on the Spazza. Here the famous Fiamma still gives a steady pitch at V, while the Dente has come under the scrutiny of the sports climber and gives a well-bolted final pitch at VI+. The superb granite of the Bio Pillar is very popular and, in keeping with exploration in the Mont Blanc range, two routes were equipped and climbed this summer on the slabs below the Albigna hut.

On the south side of the range, the Vinci route on the Cengalo (VI+) has impressed many parties. Certain authorities have coined that wonderful expression 'one of the best rock climbs of its type in the Alps'. Outside of the Mello, climbs in these southern valleys seem little frequented by non-Italian alpinists. The range has still not received the thorough grooming that has been applied to, for example, the Chamonix Aiguilles, and much scope remains.

Dolomites

A significant achievement on the S face of the Marmolada was an ascent of the Koller–Sustr route, 'The Fish' by Roger Everett and Mick Harris, 24–26 July 1990. Although it has been climbed completely free (VIII+/IX−: Mariacher 1987, see *Mountain 132*), most parties will be forced to use a fair amount of aid, and two good skyhooks are essential. All belays are in place and the route is well equipped with rappel points all the way to the major terrace after pitch 21. However, as the line is neither obvious nor straight, a good memory of the ascent route is required for any retreat. Two to three days should be allowed for a complete ascent but a fast party with minimal gear, capable of climbing British 6b quickly and/or skilled with skyhooks, should be able to reach the terrace and rappel off in one day. The crux is above the whale-shaped niche (The Fish) at 500m. The original description and grading (VII and A1) are pure fantasy. Parties making recent repeat ascents of some of Koller's and other Czech routes in the Bregaglia have also found them badly undergraded. With little *in situ* protection the harder pitches can be very bold. The climbing is continually excellent, mostly on perfect rock and of a difficulty which matches many a bolted crag (but without the bolts!). A revised description now follows but is likely to be at the upper limit of its grade (1000m VII A3 24hr).

Marmolada South Face

Attraverso il Pesce (The Way through the Fish). ED sup. (Koller, Sustr, 1981)

Start R of an obvious brown water stripe and wire cable which descend from the téléphérique station. Scramble up to the undercut start at a block on the ledge, about 50m right of the brown stripe. (Peg runner in overhang.)

1. 50m. Climb over the bulge (VI+, loose), then go up over a second bulge (VI) to easier ground. Continue direct to sloping ledge and peg belay.

2. 15m. Go easily up left to an easy open groove. Belay below a steep flake crack.

3. 40m. Climb the crack (V+) and continue to a narrow ledge. Move left to a peg belay.

4. 15m. Easily up to the next ledge, then right for a few metres, past a vague pillar, to another peg belay.

5. 45m. Climb the right side of the pillar leftwards (V+) to reach a crack. Follow this (V) to a stance between small roofs.

6. 45m. Zig-zag up to a bulge (IV+), over this on R (V) to a groove leading L and finally back R (IV+) to a stance below a smooth bulging wall on the L.

7. 20m. Climb up, then trend R below the bulging wall (IV) to reach a sloping ledge (a vague terrace which crosses the whole face). Belay on the R.

8. 50m. Step back L, over a bulge (V) and into a long chimney corner which is followed direct to a stance under a bulge (V).

9. 35m. Continue up the corner which bends rightwards (V) (or climb the crack on the R, V+), then traverse delicately R (V+) to a stance under a bulge.

10. 25m. Climb the bulge leftwards (VI−), then the wall above (VI), then trend L to a small stance level with a line of niches on the R.

11. 35m. Continue direct, then trend slightly R to pass a small roof on the R (VI), then up to a peg belay.

12. 35m. Climb a crack and wall (VI−) to an easier groove leading to a bulge. Traverse delicately R 4m (VI−), go over the bulge, then boldly L to a smooth wall. Climb this (VI+) to reach a flake on the R, then traverse L to a belay below bulges.

13. 20m. Climb over the bulge on the L (VI+) to a small ledge. Traverse L across the wall (VII) to a crack. Climb this (A3) to exit over a bulge to another cramped stance. (Friend 1 useful; the difficulty will vary greatly depending on the length of slings in place on the next belay. The second part of this pitch follows a seepage line and will rarely be dry.)

14. 30m. Step left to a short flake. Climb direct up the wall for 4m (VII), then move L to the L hand of two shallow niches. Climb the bold wall above to a peg belay in an amazing position on the L (VI).

15. 45m. Climb the slabby wall on the R of the shallow groove above for 15m to peg and thread runners (VI+). 7m above on the L of the groove is another peg. Reach this by a combination of hard free and aid climbing (A3, skyhook essential). After the peg, trend up and R, then up directly to pegs below a bulge (VI+).

16. 25m. Traverse the wall on the R (A2, skyhooks) to holds leading up and R into the Fish (VI). Continue to the R end of the Fish.

    10–12 hours seems a reasonable time to here for a sac-hauling team; bivouac possible. Abseil escape would be awkward from the Fish, although another route does come up directly. It would be better to retreat after pitch 15, or after pitch 17.

17. 40m. Exit the R side of the niche. Climb the wall direct (VII, bold) to a peg, then make a long unprotected traverse L above the Fish (VI, then easing). When above the L end of the Fish, climb the wall above, past a break, to a hanging stance and peg belays (A3, skyhooks).

18. 45m. Climb the wall above (A2, skyhooks) to easier free climbing up to scoop (VI). Move left (VI) then diagonally up and left for 15m to a peg (A3, skyhooks and awkward nuts. There is another peg horizontally L from the scoop; this is off route.) Now move R across the blank wall (A3, skyhooks) to holds leading to peg belays.

19. 40m. Climb the slabby wall above to a peg (VI–). Tension almost horizontally leftwards for 10m to a crack (A3 and VII, skyhook useful). Climb the crack to a stance on the L (VI).

20. 15m. Traverse back R to the crack, then up to the large roof. Undercut R and pull round to a stance immediately above (VI).

21. 45m. Descend a little, then traverse R to the bottom of a corner. Climb this direct, then over an overhang (AO and V, or VI+) to easier ground and a large terrace and excellent bivouac sites.

    Allow 5–7 hours from the Fish. Abseil escape based on the line of the route is possible from here.

22. 20m. Start 15m R of the bivouac cave. Climb a wall (VI), then move L to the bottom of a corner.

23. 30m. Climb the corner direct over a number of bulges to easier ground (VI).

24. 45m. Climb the slabs above, trending slightly L (III).

25. 45m. Continue in the same line to a stance below steep walls (III).

26. 45m. Climb the overhang on the L to the bottom of a corner line slanting R below steep walls (V+). Continue up the corner (IV).

27. 45m. Follow slabs on the R (III).

28. 30m. Move R on to slabs on the front face, and up to a line of grooves (III).

29. 45m. Climb the grooves and a fine white slab, trending back L to the corner line (IV).

30. 45m. Climb the chimney (IV).

31. 45m. Continue up the chimney to a bay below overhangs (IV).

32. 30m. Climb the overhanging crack on the L (V+) to a stance above.

33. 20m. Continue up the chimney, then move out R to a corner (IV).

34. 30m. Climb the corner for 10m, then swing back L into and up the chimney (IV+).

35. 35m. Continue up the chimney to a stance below where it narrows and overhangs (IV).

36. 40m. Climb the outside of the narrowing (IV+), then easily up broken ground.
37. Continue up, then move L towards a ridge on the L (II).
38. 40m. Go through a hole in the ridge, traverse along a wire cable, then up a short gully to the ridge line (II).
39. 40m. Negotiate rock, metal ladders and the guide rails of the téléphérique housing to reach the glacier (II and AO).

Allow about 6 hours from the terrace, giving about 24 hours climbing time in total. Awkward spacing of the only reasonable bivouac sites means that this may have to be spread over 3 days, especially if afternoon storms threaten.

Józef Nyka adds:

The Yugoslav climber Slavko Svetičič completed the first solo ascent of the Harlin route on the N face of the Eiger, in a single 26-hour push starting at midnight on 13/14 January 1990. The crux section in the lower part is above the Eigerwand station (VI+, A2). The second crux, 200m high, is below the Spider. The pitches above the Spider involved strenuous hard ice climbing of 70 and 80°.

On 13 and 14 January 1990 the 'classic' Heckmair route was climbed by Marija Frantar from Yugoslavia, accompanied by Dare Juhant.

On 11 October 1990 Catherine Destivelle completed the first female solo of the Bonatti Pillar (SW buttress) on the Petit Dru (3733m). She started the climb at 11.30am and reached the summit at 3.50pm. The ascent was made free and without protection, except for the 40m Fissure des Autrichiens, where rope and pitons were used. The first free ascent of the Bonatti Pillar was made in 1982 by Marco Pedrini and Silvio Vicari with a 7a variant to the right of the Austrian Crack.

Lindsay Griffin would welcome further information and new route descriptions for publication in these pages and the forthcoming guidebook to the Bernina/Bregaglia at: 2 Top Sling, Tregarth, Bangor, Gwynedd LL57 4RL.

South America 1990

EVELIO ECHEVARRÍA

The number of visiting expeditions to the Andes seems to have remained static or, perhaps, suffered a diminution. However, this picture may be erroneous, since repeats of the old classic routes that are carried out routinely are often not reported. The search for new routes and for new peaks did suffer a reduction, undoubtedly because the great ranges and ice walls of Peru have been partially closed to climbers for political reasons. The weather picture is still not clear, since the seven Andean countries have climbing seasons during very different periods of the year, but it can be said in general that the weather is both opposing and co-operating with mountaineering. Drought, the great curse of the planet since 1985, continued through 1990. Andean rivers, locally regarded hitherto as unfordable during the climbing months, may now be crossed on foot, a great help to Chilean and Argentinian mountaineers. On the other hand, dry weather has prevailed during most of the various precipitation seasons, particularly in Chile and Argentina, the only Andean countries with an established ski industry. And waves of bad weather unexpectedly hit several Andean ranges at the peak of the dry season. This was particularly true in south-east Peru and most of Bolivia during 1990. In the latter country snow reached down as far as the streets of La Paz, an unusual occurrence. Intense cold and strong winds were also typical of the Peruvian and Bolivian dry seasons during June and July.

The political situation has remained fairly much the same as before, but climbers will be glad to learn that very popular areas such as the Cordilleras Blanca and Vilcanota of Peru, for several years regarded as unsafe, are now returning to normality. On the other hand, general costs have risen. Inflation in nearly every Andean country has been climbing faster than the exchange rate of the dollar, the currency foreign tourists use. The high cost of gasoline has affected transportation in general.

On the brighter side is the increase of the number of local mountain guides, now being controlled by an association, as well as of visiting expeditions from other Latin American countries which, because of the local support they receive, will create everywhere an atmosphere increasingly receptive to foreign visitors in general.

Activities listed below belong to the calendar year 1990, unless otherwise stated. Most of this information was supplied by Professor H Adams Carter, Editor of the *American Alpine Journal*, by friends from Venezuela (José Betancourt), Peru (Walter Lazo), Argentina (Marcelo Scanu, Claudio Bravo and Luis Alberto Parra) and at times some reports were collected by the author himself, when travelling in South America.

Venezuela

The Sierra de la Culata runs roughly east to west and is situated north of the Andean city of Mérida. It contains the largest number of peaks over 4000m in the country. On 12 December 1989 José Betancourt climbed alone the massive rock mountain Pico Mina de Hierro (4582m), located near the eastern end of the Culata. It seems to be a first ascent. Betancourt and a woman climber, Isabel Suárez, climbed the N face of Pico El León (4746m), a new route. The latter peak belongs to the Sierra Nevada de Mérida.

Peru

Apart from a good many repeats of very worthwhile classic routes, particularly in the Cordillera Blanca, the only reports on ascents of new peaks were filed by the Club de Montañeros Américo Tordoya, of Lima. Five of its members staged a traverse of the Cordillera de la Viuda, located east of Lima, and accomplished there in August 1989 the first ascent of Cerro Nevería (5050m) and of Cerro Azul (5100m). The traverse took the party from the railway station of Chicla in a north-west direction to the town of Canta.

Bolivia

Foreign visitors who hastened to Bolivian peaks a little too early were fortunate with the weather, since snow-storms repeatedly hit the great ranges of this country shortly after the beginning of the climbing season in June, and wintry weather continued to the end of July. The great peaks of the Cordillera Real, in particular, offered now a double challenge, due to the cold. However, no new ascents have been reported in that immense area. In the Cordillera de Quimsa Cruz, south of Illimani, two Britons, Angus Andrew and Neil Howells, made in the third week of June the first ascent of the S face of Nevado Nina Collo (5280m), also a third ascent. In the same district, Evelio Echevarría, alone, climbed on 26 June the square rock block of Cerro Chamacani (5200m), a first ascent. Chamacani is located on the WSW side of the big lake Chatamarca which overlooks the Amazonian basin. The same mountaineer made on 7 July the second ascent of Cerro Mamani (c5400m), in the southern end of the range. It had been climbed in September 1939 by the two athletic Germans Wilfried Kühm and Josef Prem, whose cairn was found on the top.

Argentina

As has become customary in the last few years, the greatest and most varied Andean mountaineering activities of the year took place in this country. In the north, eight members of the Club Andino Tucumán led by veteran Dr Orlando Bravo attempted to ascend the very respectable mountain put at 6660m and located south of Ojos del Salado, in the Catamarca province. This mountain has been variously named Nevado del Cazadero, Cerro Walther Penck and Cerro Tunupa. The Tucumán climbers were chased down from a height of 6500m by deep snow. Daniel Villagra, one member of the group, made alone the first ascent of Cerro Pabellón (c5900m), situated east of Lake Laguna Negra (January 1989).

In the district east of the city of San Juan a large joint Argentinian–Italian expedition of 20 persons led by Dr Franco Cremonese headed for the Cocota valley and, from a camp at 4900m above its sources, a party of 10 members, including two women, reached on 3 January the summit of the little-known Cerro Olivares Sur (5850m). Other peaks also ascended by expedition members were Points 5500, 4600 and 4400m.

Aconcagua had another new route inaugurated on its flanks. The SE ridge, which overlooks most of the S face of the mountain, was climbed for the first time by the Argentinians Carlos Domínguez and Mauricio Fernández, who placed six camps to reach the summit after laborious work, on 21 January. They descended via the normal route.

Luis Alberto Parra, the well-known expert on Aconcagua, submitted a report stating that 353 expeditions visited Aconcagua during the major part of the local season (December to February). Of 1244 participants, 121 were women. Three climbers perished in this last season, thus bringing the total number of victims of Aconcagua to 57. The Argentinian Daniel Alessio accomplished his fifth ascent of the mountain, now breaking the speed record previously held by the American Marty Smith. Alessio recorded the new time of 6 hours 7 minutes for his ascent from Plaza de Mulas to the summit.

Immediately south of Aconcagua and of the Mendoza river there was activity that concentrated on new peaks. The results were as follows:

La Jaula chain: the brothers Federico and Pablo González climbed four peaks, varying from 5200 to 5500m (estimated heights) in this district, located south of the railway station of Punta de Vacas (March 1990).

Las Cuevas district: Evelio Echevarría made alone the first ascent of Cerro Negro del Inca (4432m), situated south-east of the border settlement of Las Cuevas, and of Cerro Peñas Coloradas (4200m), north of the same place (December 1989-January 1990).

Cerro Sosneado group: another large Argentinian–Italian party, led by A Toujas and F Santon, carried out climbing and exploration in the southernmost Andes of the province of Mendoza. In the Sosneado group, team members made the first ascent of Cerro Pire (3850m), Cerro de la Natividad (3810m) and of an unnamed mountain 4250m high, all located on the north-east bank of the Atuel river (March 1989).

Chile

The main event of importance for the Patagonian year 1989 was the climb of the north-west spur of Cerro La Fortaleza (2754m). Italians Fabio Bristot, Roberto Cazan and Bruno de Dona were in the Paine district in the spring (November) for four weeks. They placed 300m of fixed ropes (which they removed on the descent) as they worked their way up the spur in bad weather. Taking advantage of an unusual windless day they climbed almost without stopping for 14 hours, reaching the summit on 26 November.

Also in the October–November months of 1989, a Japanese expedition engaged the company of the Chilean Patagonian veteran Eduardo García, a companion of Eric Shipton, and moved into the area where the Shipton party had been at work in 1962. Three of the Japanese reclimbed Cerro 2469m, highest in Tierra del Fuego, whose name is under scrutiny by the Chilean geographic authorities, since the name Darwin does not seem to apply to it. The party also made the second ascent of Monte Luna (c2300m) which the Shipton–García party knew as Darwin III.

New maps and new heights

Several Andean countries are mapping their territory on a scale of 1:50,000. A recent Argentinian official army map lists Ojos del Salado as 6862m high (thus confirming the earlier Chilean figures of 6863 and 6870m), and Nevado de Pissis, third highest in the American continent, as 6882m high. This would give Pissis the second highest elevation after Aconcagua. Chilean figures had given it 6779 and 6780m.

Until the methods used for this new survey are published, it seems only reasonable to recommend caution regarding the acceptance of these new figures.

H Adams Carter adds:

In South America Matt Culberson and his wife Julie made a very difficult new route on El Altar in Ecuador and then ascended the previously unclimbed western rib of the massive W face of Huayna Potosí.

Mark Nawrocki, Geoffrey Bartram and Robert Parker climbed a new route in the Cordillera Real of Bolivia, the W ridge of the N wing of Condoriri. In the Paine Towers of Chilean Patagonia, Jay Smith and Scott Cosgrove completed a remarkably difficult new route on the Torre Central de Paine. They named their route, which ascended the spectacular NW buttress for 18 pitches, the 'Wild, Wild West' route. They could climb on only four of the 62 days they spent in the region. They fixed rope in weather which was even more doubtful than is usual for the region. Before dawn on 7 January 1990 they climbed the fixed ropes to their high point and continued on to the summit after 18 hours of climbing. After a descent halfway down the route, they bivouacked. The next morning they completed the descent, removing all their fixed ropes.

Józef Nyka adds:

On 14 June 1990 the Yugoslav climber Pavle Kozjek made what was probably the first solo ascent of the American route on the 900m high S face of Chacraraju Este (6001m). Despite its steepness (55–65°), the bottom part of the face was covered with heavy snow. But the crux of the route was the 150m high summit wall, reaching 80–85° and cut by a rock barrier. The route was first climbed in 1978 by Steve Brewer and Mark Richey. Kozjek classified it ED with some V–V+ sections. The delicate corniced ridges of the mountain were very dangerous, and he was forced to descend by the ascent route.

Kozjek later made an eight-hour ascent of Artesonraju (6025m) by a 1000m high face of 50–60° where he had to fight against deep snow. Another objective was the 1500m N face of Huascaran Sur (6750m). Unfortunately, the central part was continuously swept by falling ice and rock, and the climb had to be given up half way.

Morocco 1990

HAMISH M BROWN

I spent several months in winter/spring 1990 exploring some of the lesser-known ranges of the Atlas mountains: the Jbel el Kest in the Anti Atlas, Jbel Siroua (Sirwa), and many of the highest peaks of the western Atlas – Imaradene, Wajir and Askawn on the Tichka Plateau and Tinergwet above Taroudant. With two days of rain this was a contrast to the UK's remorseless bad weather, and it is the availability of almost unlimited rock-climbing or alpine-type ascents, of long traverses above 3000m, or demanding but grand trekking *in our winter* which I feel needs to be emphasized. Because of the availability of English-language guides the Toubkal region is busy, albeit with little effort at originality, new routes etc, while these many, equally fine, areas lie fallow. The Moroccans are waking to the fact of the alpine delights they hold, so there is an added incentive to go *now*, before too much becomes organized and the priceless heritage of a thousand-year-old way of life disappears.

We were able to test some of the people as well as places recommended in the Morocco Notes of the last *AJ*, and I heartily endorse these. We made a week-long trek taking in the summit of remote Jbel Siroua (Sirwa) and Ahmed, from the Auberge Souktana at Taliouine, organized the mules and tents – and gave us superb *cuisine* each night. With three British and three Berbers it was a closely-knit group and most enjoyable. We camped each night in sites of character and walked through some remarkable landscapes, with fields of saffron, Morocco's one cliff-village, gorges and conglomerate pinnacles, kasbahs, and a last day of memorable mud! Highly recommended for fit parties.

We then used Aziz, from Taroudant, to explore the western end of the Atlas. He favours using local houses/food/mules etc, an interesting contrast. In March the Tichka Plateau was snowbound and Aziz's main task was to organize *camionette* (pick-up) transport into the hills via Tigouga and then mules to help us reach the snowy heights. We bivouacked on the plateau and climbed several peaks on its rim, the plateau in reality being the upper *valley* of the Oued Nfis. Both rims drop with dramatic steepness on the outside, and many of the crests would offer days at a stretch of snowy alpine-style traversing, all at 3000m or above. Imaradene (Tassiwt, 3351m) was the highest and best of the peaks on the northern rim, giving a long day on crampons – wishing for skis! We descended into the exquisitely beautiful Medlawa valley, crossed to Imoulas further west and, with mules and then packing, got in a position for Tinergwet (3551m), the highest in the area, the horned peak so well seen from Taroudant.

North of the Nfis and the Tizi n' Test (pass) road from Taroudant to

Marrakech lie Igdat (3616m) and Erdouz (3579m), the highest peaks west of
the Toubkal massif. These were climbed by taking mules from Imlil, crossing
the Tizi Mzic, Tizi n' Ouarhou and Tizi n' Iguidi (splendid country) to reach
Ijoukak, then up the Nfis to the confluence of Nfis and Ougdempt. The latter
gave a grand approach route and then the ridge east of Igdat was crossed to
descend to the Nfis via Tifni. An account of this trip should be in the *SMC
Journal* for 1991.

Imouzzer, an exciting morning ride up in the hills from Agadir, is famed
for its waterfalls, honey festival and delightful hotel. This year we followed a
piste eastwards and, with one bivvy *en route*, walked out to the Agadir–
Marrakech road – an excellent warm-up trip, or coda before flying home.

In February, with another friend, I managed to spend several days
climbing the highest summits of the Jbel el Kest range, the best of the Anti Atlas
above Tafraoute and the Ameln valley. Rock ridges and faces abound, none
climbed, and a marvellous lure at that time of year.

Well east, on the south side of the Central Atlas, the Todra and Dades
gorges offer sheer walls which are remarkably accessible, yet seldom climbed.
Morocco, the nearest country with such a contrasting culture, peoples and
climate, deserves to be far better known. The above were all climbed in the
period February–June. By June the plains are desert hot, so summer is not a
good period to visit. October–November is practicable, but the landscape is
burnt up and the glory of the snow and the vivid greens and blossoms of spring
are absent. So, if you want a real winter break, here is the place to go. After 25
years of doing just that, I find it more alluring than ever. I am very happy to pass
on practical information, addresses, details of maps, etc. Contact (SAE please)
21 Carlin Craig, Kinghorn, Fife KY3 9RX (0592–890422).

New books:

I have seen two new publications, both covering the Bou Goumez/M'Goun
area. The first is a well-illustrated account of personal travels by a regular
visitor, Odette Bernezat: *Hommes et Vallées du Haut-Atlas*. Editions Glenet,
BP177, 38008 Grenoble-Cedex, France (98FF). The second is a 94pp, colour-
illustrated, well-mapped guide to a selection of multi-day treks, *Randonnées
Pédestres dans le Massif du Mgoun* 1990. Published in Morocco. (Copy in AC
Library.)

Karakoram 1990

PAUL NUNN

(Plates 87, 88)

After several years of relatively poor weather there were better summer conditions. Greg Child stated that, on the north side of K2, 'we enjoyed relatively good weather from 4 July to 20 August.' This led to an interesting and varied crop of routes and some impressive near misses.

The greatest prizes were, perhaps, two ascents of K2 from the northern side. A large Japanese expedition led by Mr Fukishima climbed a new line up the N face, joining the N ridge at around 7700m. After reaching a snow dome at c7000m this followed almost exactly the same line as that attempted by the Poles in 1982, and branched left up a long diagonal couloir to the N ridge at 7700m. From Camp 5 at 7950m, Hideki Nazuka and Hirotaki Imamura reached the summit on 9 August. This was a large expedition involving 12 Japanese and 15 Sherpa climbers. They were on the mountain 100 days, fixing rope and establishing five camps. The summit pair used oxygen.

An American–Australian group comprising Steve Swenson and Phil Ershler (USA) and Greg Child, Greg Mortimer, Lyle Closs, Dr Peter Keustner and Margaret Werner tried the N ridge. They used four high-altitude porters to help establish base on the K2 glacier, and suffered difficulties with the Shaksgam river on the approach. It then took 47 days to reach the summit, fixing rope low down and using old ones higher up. They had three camps, the highest being close to the site of the Japanese Camp 5. Child, Mortimer and Swenson reached the top at 8pm on 20 August. They descended in the dark, to spend a night in an abandoned Japanese tent at 8000m. Child reported: 'The route was quite steep, but sheltered from the prevailing south-westerly winds . . . Our opinion is that it offers a safer way up K2 than the southern side, though more technical, remote and expensive!'

Carlo Pinelli led the *K2 Libre* clean-up expedition to the S side of the mountain. This 'Biella Wilderness'-inspired venture sought to clean the Abruzzi in its lower reaches, and to take out as much detritus as could be managed. In part a symbolic action, launched in Europe with great fanfare by the Aga Khan, it removed about 400 porter-loads of junk. One wonders, though, whether more benefit might be achieved by specifically encouraging all expeditions to do their part, rather than by introducing new armies of porters in the old-fashioned style to the sensitive areas. A small American expedition led by Douglas Dalquist was unsuccessful on K2.

There was much action in the Gasherbrum range. Wanda Rutkiewicz and Ewa Pakiewicz climbed a couloir by a new variation on Hidden Peak (Gasherbrum I), this being Rutkiewicz's sixth 8000m peak. An 11-member

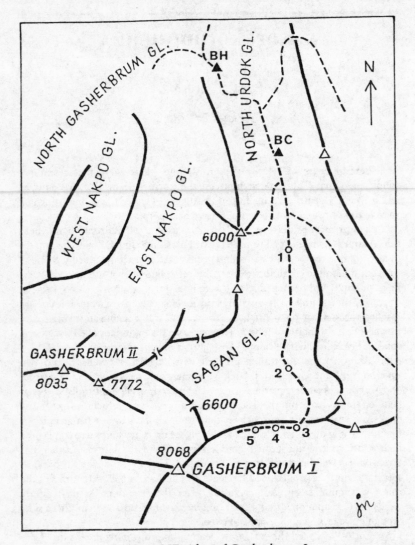

Route to NE ridge of Gasherbrum I.
First attempt 1990 by Japanese

Korean party led by Keon Jung Youn repeated this variant. On the W ridge the
Okayama University Alpine Club led by Haruhisa Kuroda and involving 12
climbers was successful. Base was set up on 24 May. They took a different route
from that of the Yugoslav ascent of 1977, placing two camps before joining it at
the snow dome at 7200m. After setting up two more camps, Camp 4 being at
7600m, three Japanese and two high-altitude porters set out for the summit on
15 July. Takahiro Katayama, Tomoyuki Yamanei, Ali Raza and Rajab Shah,
who at 40 was the oldest, reached the summit. Hidehiko Tajiri turned back at

around 8000m, but Yamanei reached the top without oxygen. The party claimed that the previous Yugoslav climbers went up this ridge only from the snow dome to 7600m, and that this was the first true ascent of the W ridge.

Most novel was the exploration and attempt on Gasherbrum I from the Chinese side by a 12-climber Japanese party led by Hiroshi Yashima and Koichi Otomo. Base was at only 4100m, and the Sagan glacier required a further base established at 4400m on 28 June. A further two camps were then set up at 4750m and 5000m in a difficult glacial approach. They attempted the NE ridge of Gasherbrum I for the first time, ascending steep ice to reach it and setting up camps at 5400m and 5700m by 20 July. Yashima was badly injured in a snow slide, but Camp 5 at 6100m was set up on 4 August. Then dangerous conditions were encountered on the ridge leading towards the summit, and on 9 August the attempt was abandoned. The party made reconnaissances of the glaciers and lower peaks north of the Gasherbrums which ought to be valuable to future visitors to that extremely remote and difficult region.

On Gasherbrum II, Georg Rudiger, a member of a Polish international expedition, reached the top on 18 July from Camp 3 via the western side of the summit cone, a new route. He suffered frostbite and was eventually helicoptered by the Pakistan Air Force from Base Camp.

The Muztagh Tower was repeated by a Swedish expedition. Base was established on 10 July at 4700m, and the party found the route through the Chagran icefall long and tedious, a total of 22km from base to Camp 3 on the mountain. Five camps were set up, and 1200m of fixed rope were used. The Swedes put Camps 1 and 2 north of the Chagran glacier, unlike their predecessors, and made a shortcut up the great couloir at the base of the Muztagh Tower. This they thought less demanding and less avalanche-prone than the original British route on the opposite side of the Chagran. Magnus Nilsson reported: 'In spite of collapsing seracs on the ridge, some mildly frostbitten fingers and a fixed rope that broke during rappel, the team suffered no severe incidents. They reported the extremely loose rock on Muztagh as the major hazard. A lot of snow on the ridge enabled them to avoid most of the rockclimbing, but this on the other hand built up the dangerous seracs mentioned . . . Camps were established at 6800m on 11 August, 7100m on 15 August and the summit was reached on 17 August. The party was led by Ola Hillberg.'

On the Great Trango Tower Takeyasu Minamura led a six-member attempt on the Norwegian NE pillar pioneered originally by Doseth and his partner who died on the descent. Four climbers climbed 11 new pitches (5.12.A2) to the right of the original line on the lower wall, and finished the climb after 27 days' climbing on 17 August. They turned back a few pitches below the NE peak, as their time had run out. The leader Minamura soloed a 27-pitch route on the E face of the Trango Tower to the right of the Kurtyka route (VII.5.10.A4), reaching the top on 9 September. An attempt to parapente off failed, and Minamura was stranded on a ledge. Masonori Hoshina and Satoshi Kimoto then climbed the British original route with three bivouacs and reached him, seven days after the aborted descent. On 17 September they began the descent of the Yugoslav route and reached Base Camp next day.

Also on the Trango Tower a Swiss expedition led by Philippe Scherrer succeeded. A Spanish group climbing on Trango Great Tower and Uli Biaho is reported to have failed.

In the Choktoi–Panmah glaciers areas two Basques, Jon Lazkano and Javi Mugarra, climbed the prominent rock tower of 6100m by an 800m route (6a+. A3+), fixing the lower part with 600m of rope and making a final 22-hour push. Base had been established on 24 June. Doug Scott led another attempt on the great ridge of Latok II (the American Ridge), but without success in heavy snow early in the season. Their cook, Sher Mohammad, died on 26 June when he fell into the Braldu river. In the same area approached from the Biafo glacier Hans Lanters and Roland Beckendam, supported by Gaby Jobses and journalist Joos Philippens, tried Baintha Brakk ('the Ogre'), reaching 6100m on the S pillar. The rock of this route was climbed in 1983 by a French party. They set up base on the Uzun Blakk on 26 June and set up two camps, the top one being just under the pillar at 5912m. Roland Beckendam reported: 'We fixed 900 feet of rope in the 40 to 50-degree couloir leading to Camp 2. 7 and 8 July saw us proceeding up the first 900 feet of the pillar, which we fixed with ropes. It contained a 300-foot high wall of A2–3 difficulty, probably the most time-consuming part of the route. Now everything was ready for an alpine-style push from the end of the fixed ropes towards the summit. Apart from some minor snowfalls the weather had been good, but during our resting period at Base Camp it snowed and rained almost continuously. On 15 July we went up under a blue sky for the summit attempt. Unfortunately the weather broke again next day and we had to sit out snowfalls and very strong winds at Camp 2 for four days.' Thereafter their luck continued poor and, after recovering food from below swept away in the air-wave of a serac fall, bad weather caught them again on the pillar and forced a retreat to base. A final summit attempt was foiled by an upper food dump being destroyed by ravens, and by variable weather. Their Base Camp was plundered by the local bear(s?), who are increasingly aware of the welfare benefits which expeditions and treks provide. Also on the Ogre a Bavarian party led by Michel Lentrodt climbed very high on the Yugoslav route, stopping only 200m from the summit.

Further west another Dutch party made the first ascent of the S pillar of Kanjut Sar II. The five climbers set up base on 1 July at 4500m on the Khani Basar glacier. Two camps were made on the SW ridge and three weeks were spent supplying them. Then bad weather foiled a first attempt. Between 26 and 29 July they succeeded, bivouacking three times *en route* to the summit. H C Freie reported: 'The problems were mainly rock (7–/A1, some ice (55°)). After the second bivouac Peter Kok descended alone because of what later appeared to be pulmonary oedema. On 29 July the others reached the summit (6831m) at 4pm and descended the next day.' Thus Freie, Franck van de Barselaar, Franck Schmitt and Pieter de Kam made the second ascent of this peak, by a new technical route. Further west Alain Vaucher led a 10-member Swiss party in a successful ascent of Bularung Sar (7200m).

Early in the year a French party made a new ski traverse in the spring. Reaching Askole on 31 March the *Groupe Universitaire de Montagne et Ski* Expedition traversed the Biafo, Simgang, Nobande Sobande, Chiring, Sarpo

Laggo, Karfogang and Muztagh glaciers, to finish on the Baltoro. This new high route, a companion to that pioneered by Galen Rowell and Ned Gillette from Kaphalu to Hispar, was completed by 25 April when the six-man party led by Claude Pastre re-emerged at Askole. Temperatures ranged between −15°C and −30°C, and there was some good weather, but also a lot of fresh snow. Norwegian pulkas were used, and there were dangerous crevassed sections, on the Skam La, the Chiring glacier and a steep descent on the S side of the E Muztagh pass. The maps are reported very inaccurate around the Muztagh passes. The W Muztagh seems to be 5700m, not 5370m, nearer to the Sarpo Laggo than indicated by the Duke of Spoleto (1:75,000) and Istituto Geographico Militare (1:100,000) maps. Miyamori (1988, 1:100,000) is thought to be more accurate.

14 expeditions were allowed to attempt Nanga Parbat in 1990. Anton Golner led 17 Slovenes who followed the Schell route (UIAA III-IV(V)) on the 4500m Rupal face, one of the world's highest mountain walls. This was the first Yugoslav ascent of Nanga Parbat, and the first female ascent of the Rupal face. Marija Frantar has past experience in the Alps, including the N face of the Eiger last winter, in the Soviet Pamir and Tien Shan, and was the leader of a Yugoslav womens' expedition to Annapurna South (7219m) in 1986.

Below the Diamir face there was filming of a BBC reconstruction of Albert Mummery's disappearance, involving Charlie Houston, Chris Bonington and Sigi Hupfauer, with producer Richard Else and Jim Curran as climbing camera. They reported disgusting refuse at base, much of it associated with this year's expeditions and including medical syringes and other items traceable to the 11 doctors who visited this summer.

In the Hushe–Kaphalu region there were many parties. An important attempt was made at a big new route on K7 (7100m). Dai Lampard, Bob Wightman, Bob Brewer and Luke Steer spent 20 days in a big single push, climbing 88 pitches of difficult but good rock to a 6200m col below the 'Fortress' climbed during the Japanese first ascent. Though only 100m of hard climbing remained they had to retreat, as Wightman had lost a rucksack and had been without a sleeping bag for five days, and they had run out of food. Most of this climb went free despite its iced-up appearance. The small trips included one by Ian Stewart and Neil Wilson, who climbed for six weeks at the head of the Charakusa glacier in July and August and claim the first ascent of Point 6248m north of the Charakusa, via a (Scottish) grade 3 route on the S face of 1000m. The route was climbed at night on 18–19 August, with descent by the same route. Victor Radvils led a British attempt on Trinity Peak (6800m). He injured his shoulder early. The other members continued but were unsuccessful.

In Hunza, Ultar I (7388m) defeated Tsuneo Hasegawa's small Japanese party. Paolo Civera's Sondrio (Italian) group succeeded on Alstor-O-Nal (7403m), but another Italian group failed on Shakaur (7116m). A West German group led by Alfred Fendt climbed Sharagrar (7403m).

This appears to have been a relatively good year, though conditions seem to have been poor early in the season and better later. The pattern of activity was broadly conventional, with 56 expeditions in the field, and considerable concentration on the lower 8000m peaks. K2 was underattended, and five fatalities were reported, four on the mountains and one in the river accident mentioned above. Applications for 1991 seem to follow a similar conventional pattern.

Footnote. At the time of writing full details are not available for the East Karakoram, and from the numerous visitors to peaks below 6000m. Maciaj Berbeka's Polish-British winter expedition to the Rupal face of Nanga Parbat is reported to have failed because of bad conditions.

H Adams Carter adds:

American Jeff Lowe and Frenchwoman Catherine Destivelle were filmed by David Breashears while they climbed the Nameless Tower of the Trango Towers. They climbed the Yugoslav route on the S face free. I suspect that Jim Bridwell and Breashears, who has climbed Everest twice, may also have reached the summit and had even more difficult climbing during the filming. A group of young climbers took advantage of not having to pay a peak fee for peaks just under 6000m in the region near the Biafo glacier. Peter Gallagher and Robert Warren made an alpine-style ascent of the Ogre Stump on 29 June. John Catto, Steve Wood, Gallagher and Max Kendall climbed Lupkilla Brakk by a new route on 6 July. Warren, Gallagher and Wood completed a seven-day, 33-pitch climb of a spire they called 'Deck of Cards'. They rated the climb as VI, 5.11, A4. Not all expeditions were successful. Thor Kieser led parties that got high on Rakaposhi and Trisul but did not reach the summits.

Nepal 1990

BILL O'CONNOR

Most of the news from Nepal in the spring was about politics, not peaks. The growing pro-democracy movement, centred naturally on Kathmandu and Pokhara, resulted in rebellion and the spilling of a great deal of blood by the military and police that was barely reported by the British media. A few pre-monsoon expeditions were effected, trying to get in and out of Kathmandu whilst a curfew was enforced to keep westerners off the streets. Trekking companies reported a slight drop in business as 'mail order mountaineers' fearful for their safety opted to stay away. However, by the time the post-monsoon season ended, a fear both of flying and falling had been overcome, resulting in the busiest climbing season ever in the Nepal Himalaya. In all 78 expeditions visited the country, with a total of 553 climbers more or less active. This represents a 30% increase over the 1989 post-monsoon season.

Predictably, established routes on 8000ers attracted the most attention. Most ascents were repeats of established routes and have been well documented in magazines.

Everest Records

A somewhat dubious record was set on Everest. Between 4 and 7 October no fewer than 31 climbers reached the summit via the South Col route, with over 100 waiting in the Western Cwm! Marc Batard was the only climber in 1990 to reach the summit without supplementary oxygen; this during his failed attempt to climb both Everest and Lhotse within 24 hours. In all, eight nations reached the top, and the successful included the youngest-ever summiteer: 17-year-old French schoolboy Jean Noël Roche, accompanied by his father Bertrand and a brace of married couples – Mr and Mrs Stremfelj from Yugoslavia and American Cathrine Gibson with her Russian husband Aleksei Krasnokutsky.

Lhotse South Face Solo

What Messner dubbed the 'problem for the year 2000' was climbed solo without 'tinned air' by Tomo Cesen. This undoubtedly represents a significant breakthrough in contemporary Himalayan climbing and was the most notable achievement of the year. Sadly, some French alpinists and media have, for no apparent reason other than sour grapes, tried to cast doubt on Cesen's ascent. However, other leading activists including Profit, Beghin and Escoffier have spoken out strongly in favour of Cesen.

Lhotse's South Face, the world's highest, has been the setting of successive attempts, sieges and failures over many years. Undoubtedly, its time had come, for during the post-monsoon season a large Soviet team succeeded in making a second ascent of the face by a new line, using siege tactics and oxygen. Evidently the Soviets are keen to build on their mammoth successes on Everest and more recently Kangchenjunga.

Cho Oyu (8201m) and Xixabangma (8027m)

Voytek Kurtyka, Jean Troillet and Erhard Loretan made an early and fast ascent of the previously unclimbed 2000m SW face of Cho Oyu between 19 and 20 September. On 2 and 3 October the same trio climbed the S face of Xixabangma via a couloir to the right of the Yugoslav pillar, in a single 18-hour push.

Trekking Peaks

There has been an increase in the numbers climbing the so-called Trekking Peaks. For years these 18 summits have been neglected by all but the trekking agencies and a few *cognoscenti* like Jeff Lowe for whom small has meant both beautiful and a crop of technical first ascents. Undoubtedly the publication of Bill O'Connor's definitive guide to the peaks has focused attention on their unclimbed possibilities, their relative cheapness and their lack of organizational red tape. The fact that the MEF and BMC are willing to grant-aid 'expeditions' with worthwhile projects on Trekking Peaks has also stimulated a little interest.

Illegal Ascents

Several accidents and at least one fatality to a Briton attempting to climb without a permit occurred last year. Alpine and solo attempts on trekking and other peaks have been increasing, and the temptation to have a go without the bother of getting a permit is very strong, particularly when the climb can be completed in days or perhaps hours. I have spoken to the Minister at the Nepal Mountaineering Association, and they are perfectly aware that illegal ascents occur and have hinted at measures being taken against an offender's national organization or fellows.

Peaks, Permits and £'s

Permits for Trekking Peaks have always been issued to all applicants without it resulting in any real problems. The majority of permits are in any case granted to trekking agencies, inevitably for commercial groups; Island Peak, Mera Peak and Tent Peak being the most popular. Permits for the 108 expedition peaks were previously granted, we were led to believe, on a first-come, first-served basis; one permit for a particular route up the mountain being granted for a given season. However, a recent change in this policy has resulted in multiple permits being granted for the same peak and route at the same time. Obviously the Nepalese wish to increase their hard cash income from their finest asset, and this is the simplest and quickest way of doing that. On many mountains it has little effect, since the majority of peaks on the list hardly earn their keep. On the other hand, Everest, Makalu, Dhaulagiri, Ama Dablam, Pumori and a handful of the 'sexy' summits attract a lot of applications, with the result that Base Camp can now be occupied by several expeditions. It was reported that seven groups queued for the NE ridge of Dhaulagiri, that another seven teams were encamped at the small tarn below the SW ridge of Ama Dablam, and that no less than 12 expeditions were active on Pumori.

Despite the Minister reminding me that climbing was about camaraderie, I had to inform him that rivalry had always been an essential motivator in mountaineering. Certainly my own experience on Ama Dablam in 1989 was that two expeditions on a route that was well defined and with limited camps leads to problems, perhaps the kind seen on K2 a few years ago. The unacceptable alternative suggested at the NMA was that perhaps expeditions would like to pay more for the privilege of exclusivity?

Józef Nyka adds:

On 23 and 24 April Krzysztof Wielicki soloed a new route on the E face of Dhaulagiri (8167m) to 7800m, descending by a previously equipped descent route. The new route lies to the left of the 1980 Kurtyka–MacIntyre route.

India 1990

HARISH KAPADIA

So much is happening in the Indian Himalaya that it is difficult to cover it all immediately. I begin with some important climbs of 1989 which escaped attention last year.

First, two peaks in the east. The fifth ascent of Pauhunri (7125m) on the Sikkim–Tibet watershed was made on 1 November 1989. Base Camp (5099m) was established at Chholamo, with two more camps at 5343m and 6209m on a col. 500m of rope was fixed. From this northern col the peak was reached in 7½ hours by Nawang Kalden, Nima Wangchu and Pasang Lakhpa, all instructors at the Sonam Gyasto Mountaineering Institute at Gangtok, Sikkim. The 21-member expedition was led by Sonam Wangyal.

In Arunachal Pradesh, Gori Chen II (6488m) was climbed by an Assam Rifles team led by Commandant N Sherpa on 6 October 1989. This 20-member team made Base Camp at Chokarsan on 2 October. Establishing two more camps, a party led by Naik Sonam Lepcha scaled an unnamed peak (6247m) on 4 October. Finally they followed the SE ridge over Pk6247m to reach the summit at 1.30pm. This is a rare climb in this difficult area where no mountaineering party has been allowed.

There may be some good omen in this for mountaineers. The government is considering the selective opening of these areas in the future. In 1991 a strong Indo–Japanese team has permission to attempt the Kangchenjunga E face, while another Indo–Japanese team will raft down the Brahmaputra from the border across Assam.

In Gangotri, three South Koreans made an ascent of the W face of Bhagirathi III (6454m), a first-ever big-wall, alpine-style ascent by South Koreans. A British team failed on the E ridge of Meru (6300m), but two of their members made a rapid ascent of Bhagirathi II by the E face. Nearby, Shivling West (first ascent by Bonington–Fotheringham) was climbed by the Americans via the SE ridge–E face in September 1989.

Far in the west, Carl Schaschke led a British team which climbed an unnamed peak (6230m) in Kishtwar. A Scottish team led by Graham Little was active in the area north of the Dharlang nala, Kishtwar during September 1989. They climbed 'Rohini Shikhar' (5990m) and 'Sentinel Peak' (5950m). These were perhaps the last climbers in these areas, for political troubles will rule out any visits to Kishtwar and Kashmir for some time to come.

The summer of 1990 began with sad news. As I was trekking up to Tapovan in Gangotri, a helicopter ferried out the body of a Spanish climber who had died of oedema at Base Camp. Another three-member Spanish team

77. *First ascensionist Hans Wongtschowski. Grosse Spitzkop, 1946.* (Else Wongtschowski) (p 160)

78. *NW face of the Grosse Spitzkop, showing the final sections of the original route coming round from the left skyline. Schreiber's W face route is the diagonal line in the shade on the right.* (Michael Scott) (p 160)

79. *Antarctica: view from the summit of Vinson Massif, 4895m.* (Oswald Oelz) (p 173)

80. *The N side of Aconcagua, 6960m.* (Oswald Oelz) (p 173)

81. *Mont Blanc Brenva Face, July 1977.* (Ted Maden) (p 182)

82. *'Folding and Crumpling': Zanskar Himalaya, July 1988.* (Ted Maden) (p 182)

83. *Alphubel NE face (L) and N ridge.* (C A Russell) (p 215)

84. *Piz Palü (L) and Bellavista pass.* (C A Russell) (p 215, p 135)

85. *Grand Combin, with (upper R) SE ridge.* (C A Russell) (p 215)

86. *Pillar Rock from the east with (R) N face.* (C Douglas Milner) (p 215)

87. *Gasherbrum I from the Duke of Abruzzi glacier.* (Paul Nunn) (p 239)

88. *Baintha Brakk (The Ogre, 7285m).* (Paul Nunn) (p 239)

89. *Annapurna Reunion, 14-17 June 1990.* (p 311)

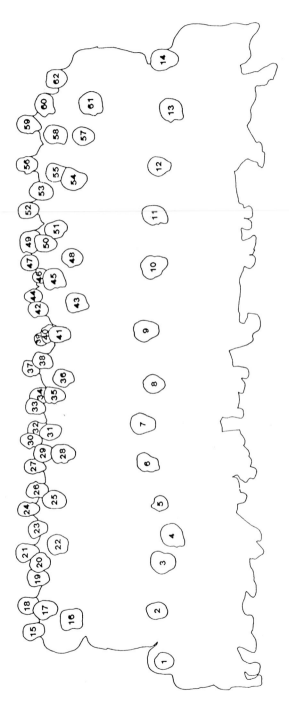

ANNAPURNA REUNION, 14-17 JUNE 1990

1	....	23	André Roch	43	....
2	Nimi Sherpa	24	Ernst Reiss	44	Tony Streather
3	Jeanne Franco	25	Mohan Kholi	45	....
4	....	26	....	46	....
5	Junko Tabei	27	Tomo Cesen	47	Robert Paragot
6	Maurice Herzog	28	....	48	Francis de Noyelle
7	Marcel Ichac	29	....	49	....
8	Reinhold Messner	30	....	50	....
9	Edmund Hillary	31	Yutaka Ageta	51	....
10	John Hunt	32	John Boyle	52	Norman Hardie
11	....				
12	....			53	Nick Clinch
13	....			54	Fritz Wintersteller
14	....			55	Wojciech Branski
15	....			56	Pete Schoening
16	....			57	....
17	Maurice Herzog			58	Kazimierz Olech
18	Marcel Ichac			59	Kurt Diemberger
19	Reinhold Messner			60	George Band
20	Edmund Hillary			61	Andrzej Zawada
21	John Hunt			62	....
22	John Boyle				

NB Can you help to complete the above list? Please send names to the Editor.

90. *Mount Washington, July 1990: members of the New England Chapter of the American Alpine Club and the Alpine Club. From L: Michael P Ward (AC), Charles S Houston (Hon AC, AAC), Bradford Washburn (Hon AC, AAC), H Adams Carter (Hon AC, AAC), Robert H Bates (AC, AAC). (p 311)*

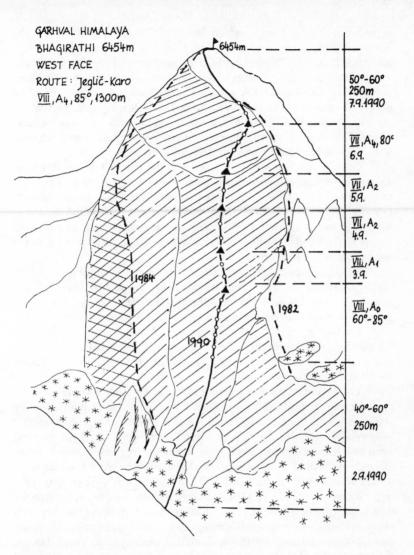

GARHVAL HIMALAYA
BHAGIRATHI 6454m
WEST FACE
ROUTE : Jeglič-Karo
VIII, A4, 85°, 1300m

6454m

50°-60°
250m
7.9.1990

VII, A4, 80°
6.9.

VII, A2
5.9.

VII, A2
4.9.

VII, A1
3.9.

VIII, A0
60°-85°

1984

1982

1990

40°-60°
250m

2.9.1990

left for Meru leaving behind a note but failed to return. No trace of them has been found despite searches. On Sudarshan Parbat, an Indian climber succumbed to oedema bringing the total number of deaths in Gangotri in May 1990 to five. The rest of the team climbed Sudarshan Parbat (6507m) on 30 June.

But things improved, and some excellent climbs followed. One of the best climbs was again the W face of Bhagirathi III by two Yugoslavs, Silvo Karo and Janez Jeglič. In six days they climbed a new line on the 1300m face, with five bivouacs, reaching the summit on 7 September 1990. (To top it all they immediately left for Everest, which Janez climbed on 7 October!) Nearby Bhrigupanth (6772m) was climbed on 26, 28 and 30 August 1990 by an Indian team from Pune. They climbed by the S face, the route of the first ascent in 1980 by the American women's team of Arlene Blum. On 26 August Dr S Mate, Mohan Patel, Ms Chandraprabha Aitwal, Sange Dorje and Sange S climbed the peak. Five members, including the leader Dr D T Kulkarni, made the climb on the 28th, followed by another four members on the 30th. This was the sixth ascent of Bhrigupanth and the fourth by the south route. A two-member British team led by Robert Blackburne failed to climb this peak.

Other British teams were also active in the area. A four-member team attempted the pillar of Bhagirathi III, to the left of the Scottish route. They were stopped by altitude sickness. On Shivling another British team attempted the N face after the original objective, Thalay Sagar, had proved either too difficult or too dangerous. A team of 11 RAF and 10 Indian mountaineers attempted Kamet by the W ridge. Two summit bids were thwarted only 130m below the top by high winds and extreme cold.

Nilkanth (6596m) by its southern approaches has attracted British climbers. After the abortive attempt in 1989 (Duncan Tunstall), a nine-member team led by Roy Lindsay attempted the SE ridge. They reached the second pinnacle at 5730m. An American attempt was also beaten back a little earlier.

Abi Gamin (7355m), Sri Kailash (6932m), Kedar Dome (6831m) and Satopanth (7075m) were climbed with regularity by both Indian and foreign teams. Other peaks attempted were Panchchuli II, Nandabhannar, Mukut Parbat and Yanbuke.

Two important climbs were achieved by Indian teams on peaks that had defeated many in the past. Swargarohini I (6252m) is a small but technically challenging peak (in fact a group of five peaks) which has been attracting mountaineers for decades. J T M Gibson and many other parties have attempted it from different sides. Eight mountaineering instructors from the Nehru Institute of Mountaineering, Uttarkashi, UP, achieved the first ascent on 3 May 1990 on their training course. They made Base Camp (4300m) in the upper Ruinsara valley on 25 April. Advanced Base (5000m) was located on the way to the eastern col of the peak. Challenging rock-climbing followed on a steep rock wall with the aim of locating Camp 1 on the eastern col. However, paucity of time did not allow that and all the trainees were sent down. Finally, the instructors started for the peak from ABC itself on 3 May. They went over the rock wall with the help of the ropes fixed earlier, reaching the col at 10am. The slope eased above the col. They continued in two ropes of four climbers each and climbed over a series of snow-plateaux. They overcame a final bergschrund 25m below the summit, reaching the cornice five metres below the peak. The summiteers were Sqn Ldr A K Singh (leader), Maj A S Sandhu, Sonam Sangbu, Rattan Singh Chauhan, Ranveer Singh Negi, Chewang Norbu and Surat Singh Chauhan. Each was a highly experienced climber. This was a finest first ascent, fittingly in the Silver Jubilee year of their Institute.

Later a team sponsored by the Indian Mountaineering Foundation, led by S P Chamoli, climbed Swargarohini II (6247m) and III (6209m) in June.

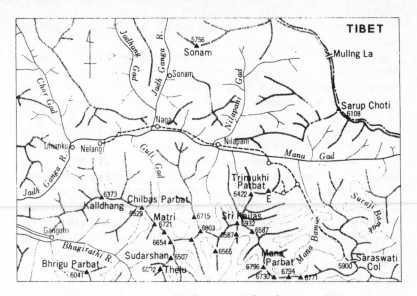

Mana gad area, Garhwal

A two-member team (Harish Kapadia and Monesh Devjani, with two porters) from Bombay explored the Jadh ganga–Mana gad area in May. This was the first visit since J B Auden's in 1939. From Bhaironghati they entered this restricted valley bordering Tibet. Going east, Base Camp was established at 4200m. Advanced Base was a little ahead of Tridhara. After a detailed recce of this unknown area they climbed 'Nandi' (5795m) on 28 May 1990, with Pasang Bodh and Yog Raj. This peak is north-east of Trimukhi Parbat (6422m). On 30 May Monesh Devjani and Pasang Bodh climbed Trimukhi Parbat East (6280m) by the steep E face. Both climbs were first ascents. Finally, on 4 June all four reached 'Saraswati Col' (5900m) at the head of Mana gad. The possibility of the existence of such a col was mentioned by J B Auden. This unexplored high col leads from Mana gad to the Saraswati valley (Badrinath). It overlooks the Mana pass. The team brought back excellent records of many unclimbed peaks in the area and also found many marks of snow-leopards and bears.

Continuing in the same vein, a four-member Indian expedition from Bombay, led by Ajit Shelat, explored the unvisited Kalla Bank glacier, north of the Nanda Devi sanctuary. Two attempts were made on Lampak (6181m) by the SE ridge. A high point of 5880m was reached. Both attempts were aborted because of bad pre-monsoon weather.

Kagbhusand (5830m) is a small but challenging rocky peak near Kamet. It was climbed by Eric Shipton in 1931, after his first ascent of Kamet. Now a seven-member team sponsored by the Himalayan Club scaled the peak on 28 September 1990 without the help of Sherpas or high-altitude porters. From the Deoban glacier on the Banke Plateau, E Theophilus, Depinder Kapur and Divyesh Muni reached the top at 5pm after 10 hours of climbing over steep terrain. Most of the route above Camp 1 was climbed using rock-shoes, and the rock-climbing was mostly VS and HVS with one pitch of E1 as per British standards.

With so much happening in the Garhwal, the talk of closing the Gangotri area was alarming. It was argued that trekkers and mountaineers caused little ecological damage compared with lakhs of pilgrims who visit the holy shrines. Saner counsel prevailed and, though stringent conditions will be imposed, they will in no way affect mountaineers and climbing teams. Talk of opening the Nanda Devi sanctuary remained inconclusive.

In the other areas, one important climb was achieved in Sikkim. Chummakhang East (6050m) was climbed by a party led by P M Das of the Sonam Gyasto Mountaineering Institute. Base Camp (4200m) was established on 3 June, only two hours beyond the roadhead at Yongdi near the Tista river. They followed the SE face and ridge, establishing Camp 1 at 5200m. On 13 June they made the first ascent of the peak in a six-hour push. 300m of rope was fixed. The main peak of Chummakhang (6212m) (also known as Laschi) was first climbed by H W Tilman in 1938. In 1946 T H Braham and party were beaten back by the difficulties of the icefall and heavy snow. The present expedition is the only party reported on this peak since then.

Far to the west, Dharamsura (6445m) saw two ascents, by an Indian team from Calcutta on 18 June, and by the British (Captain Adrian Phillips) on 29 June. Another British team (S J Bell) failed in two attempts on 29–30 June to climb Shigrila (6247m) in Lahul. Ali Ratni Tibba (5470m), the famous shapely pinnacle, beat back a spirited four-day Indian attempt (Mohit Oberoi) on 19 May.

A seven-member Indian team led by Dhiren Pania made the fourth ascent of Shigri Parbat (6526m) at the head of the Bara Shigri glacier in Lahul. They established camp at Concordia and climbed the S face to a prominent col. The summit was climbed via the SW ridge by Dolphy D'Mello, Vasant Dalvi, Tikam Ram Thakur and Singhi Ram on 24 August. This peak was first climbed by Joss Lynam in 1961.

Other smaller climbs in Lahul included M5 (6370m) and Fluted Peak (6137m), and in Spiti there were ascents of Chau Chau Kang Nilda (6303m), Marshu Rang (5639m) and Kala Rang (5913m), and an attempt on Sudh Parbat (6200m). All these were by Indian teams.

In the scholarly fields, *Exploring the Hidden Himalaya* (Soli Mehta and Harish Kapadia) was published by the Himalayan Club. It covers the Indian Himalaya and many unknown peaks in it. A large number of books on the ecology and environmental aspects of the Himalaya were published in India this year. As usual, some are excellent but many cover no new ground.

During the year A B Ghoshal, Hon Treasurer of the Himalayan Club, passed away. M L Saha, a noted authority on the Himalaya, died in Calcutta. Both had done a lot for the range. Far away in the UK Gordon Osmaston and J B Auden died. Both had a strong affiliation with India. Osmaston was in the Survey of India and responsible for the survey of many areas of the Indian Himalaya. J B Auden was with the Geological Survey of India and had explored Gangotri, the Jadh ganga and Lamkhaga valleys along with Nepal. A high and difficult col leading from Rudugaira to the Bhillangna valley, crossed by him, is named 'Auden's Col'. Both will be remembered here for their love of India.

As the helicopter ferried the body of the Spanish climber, I was talking to a middle-aged lady from South India who had spent the full winter at Tapovan (Gangotri) for spiritual gain. With few resources she stayed in a cave to experience what was written in the ancient Indian texts. According to her experience it is only by respecting nature that one can understand its strength. Where well-equipped mountaineers had perished, she had survived the worst with humility. Any lessons for us, mountaineers?

Miscellanea 1990

We are grateful for the following additional information, received from H Adams Carter (Nos 1–4) and Józef Nyka (Nos 5–6).

1. *Alaska*. American John Phelan and Briton Dave Sharman did a splendid new route on the SE face of Mount Foraker (5303m). It took them six days of climbing, mostly on very steep snow and ice. Not only did they have severe difficulties during the ascent – on the descent of the SE ridge they were plagued by bad weather and ran out of food. Foraker's Pink Panther route on the E face received its second ascent, by Dave Harries and Chris Smith. A couloir on the W face of Dan Beard was climbed for the first time by a party led by Carol Snetsinger. Mark Bebie and Bill Pilling took five days to make a new route on the S ridge of Mount Augusta. The descent via the first-ascent route on the N ridge left them on the side away from their Base Camp, and they had to traverse some 25km around the N and E sides to get back.

2. *Canada*. Dan Mazur led a party that made the ascent of Mount Steele, while Willy Orr's group climbed Mount Logan (5951m), Canada's highest peak, by Independence Ridge. Probably the most notable climb in this season in North America was the second ascent, and the first in alpine style, of the Hummingbird Ridge of Mount Logan, made during the second half of April by American Dave Nettle and Canadian Geoff Creighton. They gained the ridge via a different start from the original one. Their route followed a steep icefall couloir and 60° ice face for 1500m before joining the ridge at 4265m. From that point to 4900m the difficulty was very great. The ridge then became somewhat easier up to 5325m, where they emerged on the summit plateau. They reached the summit on 29 April, seven days after leaving Base Camp. They descended the E ridge, which took four more days on very short food rations.

3. *Antarctica*. In January, Mugs Stump did some remarkable solo climbing near the Vinson Massif. He made the second ascent of Tyree by an extremely difficult new route, the 2500m-high W face. This was done on the same day that New Zealander Rob Hall soloed the Chouinard route on Mount Shinn, adding a direct line to the summit. At the same time Dr Geoffrey Tabin ascended the Vinson Massif. Tabin is believed to be the first American to have reached the highest point on all seven continents (counting the Carstensz Pyramid and not Mount Kosciusko as the highest point in Australasia).

4. *The Pamir*. Mark Twight climbed a new route on the N face of Pik Vorobyova, a climb of 800 vertical metres which involved 90° ice. With Ace Kvale he climbed the Czech route on the N face of Pik Kommunizma.

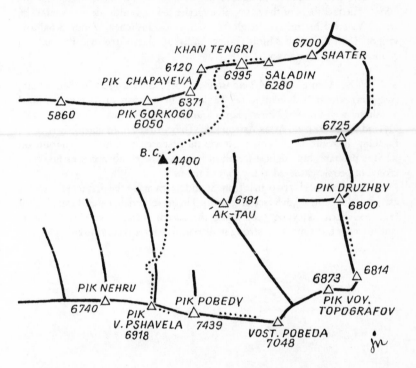

5. *Tien Shan*. In August a team from Kazakhstan achieved an astonishing success, completing an alpine-style ridge traverse comprising 12 of the highest peaks of the central Tien Shan, from Pik Pobedy to Khan Tengri. The five-man team spent 15 days generally over 6000m, traversing 73·6km of ridges and summits.

Their Base Camp was at 4400m on the Zvezdochka glacier. Six men started on 6 August, climbing towards Pik Vazha Pshavela (6918m). During four days they traversed Pik Pobedy (7439m). Beneath Pik Pobedy East (7048m) they were trapped for a day by bad weather; all equipment became soaked through. They crossed Pobedy East and descended to the Chon Teren saddle (5488m). Here icy storm forced the retreat of one member of the team, who suffered frostbite. On 12 August the others climbed the ice ridges of Pik Topografov (6873m) and camped in the summit area. The weather deteriorated again, and until 19 August they had to fight on the high ridge against cold, storm and snowfall. Only one day allowed climbing during the whole of the day. The 12km section from East Shater (6700m) to the foot of Khan Tengri was particularly exhausting. The ridge was covered with 90cm-deep snow, heavily corniced and prone to avalanche. On 20 August they crossed Saladin Peak (6280m) and Khan Tengri (6995m), and at midnight they staggered into Base Camp.

This was the most remarkable success of the year in the mountains of the USSR. The members of the team, all experienced high-altitude mountaineers, were: Valeri Khrichthaty (leader), Andrey Tselinshchev, Zinur Khalitov, Grigori Lunyakov and Murat Galiev. Sadly, the last three died in a fall on Manaslu in October 1990.

6. *Norway*. According to *Aftenposten* of 30 January 1990, the 600m-high, steep and extremely difficult icefall Tågfossen in the Møre district was climbed by three well-known Norwegian mountaineers, Andreas Fredborg (28), Øyvind Vadla (28) and Aslak Åstrop (28). They worked hard during three days, finishing the route on 28 January. It was the first ascent of this superb route on what is probably the highest icefall in Europe. The climb was watched by a crowd of people gathered at the foot of the fall.

Simultaneously, two girls from Sunndalsøra made the first female winter ascent of the 350m-high S face of Skardfjell in the Innerdalen area. Grete Nebell (24) and Berit Skjevling (26) made the ascent during two days. This is considered a fast time for a strong male pair in winter conditions.

Mount Everest
Foundation Notes 1989–90

EDWARD PECK

The following notes summarize reports from expeditions which have received the approval of the Mount Everest Foundation, and this is in most cases accompanied by a grant. MEF approval is generally an important first step to seeking assistance, financial or otherwise, from firms or other organizations. It should be noted that the MEF only 'sponsors' expeditions in exceptional circumstances, e.g. the 1981 Mount Kongur Expedition.

Copies of the full reports of the expeditions briefly summarized below are lodged, when available, with the Alpine Club Library and the Archives Section of the Royal Geographical Society, and may be consulted in these places. Some expeditions will already have been described in the *Alpine Journal* and in mountaineering periodicals.

The expeditions summarized in the following notes took place between April 1989 and October 1990 (with one belated exception). These notes are compiled from reports received up to 1 December 1990.

America, North and South, including Arctic Regions

88/35 *British Huayhuash Expedition* (July-August 1988)

This four-member party was obliged to abandon their proposed route on the S ridge of Seria Norte, but succeeded in climbing the S face of Nevado Sarapo (6127m) in the Huayhuash area of Peru.

89/24 *Flight of the Condor (mountaineering and parapente)* (July-August 1989)

After acclimatizing with ascents of Huayna Potosí (6080m) and Ayllayco (5500m), this four-member team went on to climb Viluyo (III and I), Hancopiti (VIII and I), Ancohuma (6427m), the N peak of Illampu, and finally Illimani (6487m), with some innovatory parapenting on the descent.

89/25 *South Patagonian Ice-Cap Expedition* (October–December 1989)

This three-man party did not achieve their main objective of a return crossing of the S Patagonian ice-cap (Chile), between latitude 51°S and 51°10′S, or to reconnoitre the Cerro del Diablo, but they did succeed in establishing a new route from the Torres del Paine National Park up the E side of the Tyndall glacier, when eight days were spent in bad weather on the ice-cap.

89/32 *Bath University Apolobamba Cordillera* (July–September 1989)

After climbing Huascaran Sur in Peru, this four-member team moved to the Cordillera Apolobamba in Bolivia, where they achieved the first ascent of the N ridge of Cololo (5915m), the second British ascent of Nubi (5710m) and the first ascent of the SW ridge of Palomani Grande (5768m).

89/48 *Loughborough Students Andes*

Part 1: July–August 1989. This eight-member team from Loughborough spent six weeks in Bolivia, climbing in the Cordillera Apolobamba where they made the first British ascent and traverse of Huelancalloc (5836m), the third British ascent by the W ridge of Cololo, and first ascents of 10 other summits, including Mita (5500m), three unnamed peaks of 5375m, 5370m and 5305m, and the second ascent of Iscacuchy (5650m).

Part 2: October–November 1989. Four members from Loughborough continued to the Torres del Paine National Park region in Chile to make a successful first ascent of the NW face/N ridge of the Cerro Negro (2100m) on the N ridge of the Paine Grande, a new route on the Trident, and repeated the S ridge on the formidable Torre Norte.

89/51 *Sangay* (November 1989)

This six-member scientific group carried out a study of phytosociology and the morphological assessment of plants of the paramó in the areas of Laguna Estrallada and Lagune Verde in the Sangay National Park in Central Ecuador. They also studied the limnology of three lakes and four river systems, collected data from five forest sites (550 trees), and recorded six soil profiles.

90/1 *Southern Ocean Mountaineering Expedition* (December 1989–February 1990)

This five-member team explored the Allardyce and Salvesen ranges in South Georgia, succeeding in their objective of a first ascent of Mt Carse, also first ascents of Mts Vogel and Kling and some unnamed outliers.

90/7 *Tierra del Fuego Expedition* (January 1990)

This three-member party resumed attempts made in 1988 on Monte Roncagli (2300m) in the Cordillera Darwin. Based on Yendegaia Bay on the Beagle Channel, they succeeded in the first ascent of Roncagli on 14 January 1990 via the Dartmoor glacier and the N ridge to the N top. They also made the first ascent of Pico Pais de Galles, E of the Stoppani glacier.

90/13 British Mount Foraker (Alaska) (May–June 1990)

This two-man party was anticipated by two days in their proposed first ascent of the SSE 'French' ridge of Mt Foraker. Instead they climbed the SE ridge of Mt Crosson, retreated owing to technical difficulty on a new route on the WSW buttress of Mt Hunter, and were also turned back by bad snow conditions on a new route on the SE face of Mt Foraker.

90/24 Northern Group East Greenland Expedition (July–August 1990)

This nine-member group climbed some 15 of the significant peaks in the previously unvisited northern area of the Kronprins Frederik mountains of East Greenland.

Himalaya

89/4 British Gangotri (Sumeru Parbat) (August–September 1989)

This eight-member team abandoned their attempt on the W face of Sumeru Parbat, but succeeded on the hitherto unclimbed S ridge, without however proceeding to their ultimate objective of a first British ascent of the summit.

89/5 and 89/5A Blackspur Makalu Expedition 1989

Though this expedition was unsuccessful in its main objective of traversing Makalu, two members made a first ascent of the W face of Kangchuntse (Makalu II). The accompanying nutritional expert brought back a detailed valuable report on the 'Nutritional and Calorific Intake on a High Altitude Expedition', drawing the conclusion, *inter alia*, that periods of rest at Base Camp should be used to restock the high protein, fat and carbohydrates that are vital to replenish body glycogen and fat reserves for continued extreme high-altitude activity.

89/11 Manaslu NE Face (September–November 1989)

This 13-member party climbed in independent groups of two or three. Heavy snow throughout September made the face avalanche-risky. After establishing Camp 3 at 7700m under the ice cliffs, two groups attempting to go higher were forced by high winds and bad snow conditions to abandon the attempt.

89/16 British Langtang Lirung (September–November 1989)

This eight-member party laid determined siege to the formidable SE ridge of Langtang Lirung (7234m). One member succeeded in the first British ascent (sixth in all) by this ridge; two others reached within 100m of the summit.

89/21 *Scottish Garhwal Expedition* (September–October 1989)

This four-member climbing party attempted the first British ascent of Bhrigu-panth (6772m), in the Gangotri area, by the SE face, but turned back at c5900m in the couloir below the S col.

89/35 *British Manaslu SW Face* (September–October 1989)

This lightweight attempt by two climbers established Advanced Base at 4350m, fixed ropes up the rock pillar to 5200m, and from a bivouac at 6500m attempted to push along the horizontal ridge to the summit, but could not complete the climb owing to the excessive length of the route.

89/38A *UK–New Zealand Lobuje East (6119m)* (October–November 1989)

After climbing the S ridge to the false summit (6070m), this four-member team made an extensive reconnaissance of routes on the W and E faces. Ice conditions caused them to abandon a new route on the W face at 5070m, and also an attempt on the E face by the Lowe–Kendall couloir.

89/41 *British East Ridge Meru Expedition* (August–September 1989)

Unstable snow conditions prevented this nine-member team from achieving their objective of the first ascent of the E ridge of Meru (6672m, Gangotri area); they turned back at 6300m. Some had the consolation of reaching the summit, or close to it, of Bhagirathi III (6512m).

89/43 *British Winter Taboche Expedition* (November–December 1989)

All members of this British–West German team (three UK, one German) succeeded in the first ascent of Taboche (6501m) in Sola Khumbu; two by the SE ridge on 11 December; two by a new route on the SE face.

89/45 *Hagshu Peak Expedition* (August–September 1989)

This five-member team accomplished their objective of the first ascent of Hagshu Peak (c6300m) from the north. A first attempt by the NW ridge and across the E face was abandoned, but the second team succeeded in reaching the summit by the E face.

89/58 *Hagshu N Face Expedition* (June–July 1989)

This three-man team, despite logistic and metereological difficulties, managed to climb well over half way up the formidable N face of Hagshu before turning back after three nights of storm.

90/4 *British Army Gyachung Kang Expedition* (April–May 1990)

This 12-member Service party forced a way through the wide icefall by its W end. Two members reached a high point of 7100m on Gyachung Kang (7922m) before turning back because of avalanche and snow conditions.

90/17 *New Zealand Everest Expedition* (April–June 1990)

This nine-member team attempted the traditional route on the N face of Everest, but approaching it by the Middle Rongbuk glacier and left-hand start of the Great Couloir. One member reached the top of the Third Step at 8730m but turned back rather than proceed alone. Others retreated on a second attempt owing to absence of bottled oxygen.

90/22 *TWTCC Expedition to Central Lahoul* (September–October 1990)

This five-member group abandoned their proposed first ascent of the N face of Minar in favour of the SE ridge of Mulkila. Three reached the col below the summit pyramid at c6100m.

90/31 *British Army Tilicho Peak Expedition* (September–October 1990)

This Service party came close to succeeding in their objective of the unclimbed S face of Tilicho peak, having overcome all serious difficulties before having to retreat at 6600m owing to a non-fatal accident.

Karakoram

89/36 *London University Expedition to East Karakoram, Charakusa Valley* (July–August 1989)

This 11-member party trekked in the area of the Gondokoro, Chogolisa and Charakusa glaciers, climbing Nayser Peak (5500m) and Gondoro Peak (5800m). They made the first ascent of Point 5500m which they named Senate Peak in honour of London University.

89/44 *Hushe Valley Expedition* (August–September 1989)

This six-member party concentrated on the Aling glacier system, a tributary of the main Hushe valley, and made what they believed to be the first ascent of Reed Peak (5625m). They also carried out an extensive reconnaissance of the Aling valley, sighting many impressive unclimbed peaks.

89/47 *International Hushe Valley Expedition* (July–August 1989)

This 15-member party had as its objective the Charakusa and other spires. Heavy snow and poor rock caused retreat on the Charakusa spires, on Namika and on Sulu (6010m), but a group succeeded in climbing the N ridge of the fine granite Nazer Peak (5800m).

90/15 *Batura Glacier Expedition* (June–August 1990)

Members of this five-member team climbed a 5450m peak at the head of the Pir nala on the watershed between the Batura and Lupgha valleys, a twin-peaked summit of 5800m, and two 6000m peaks around the Miniapin glacier.

90/16 *British Trinity Peak Expedition* (August–October 1990)

Owing partly to bad weather and partly to an accident (non-fatal), this seven-member party did not establish itself very high on their objective of the unclimbed SE face of Trinity Peak (6800m) at the head of the Chogolisa glacier; but they reckoned that their intended route was feasible.

90/21 *British K7 Expedition* (July–August 1990)

This strong four-man team attempted the second ascent of K7 by the unclimbed SW ridge, described as superb climbing on high quality rock. After 14 days on the ridge, including 'five nights without a pit', they retreated from the Fortress.

90/29 *Nanga Parbat Geomorphological Expedition* (September 1990)

This two-woman team successfully carried out their planned sampling of (a) glacially-ground silt and (b) silt produced by cold-weathering process on five moraines or debris fans of the Hange, Rupel, Shaigiri, Sacha and Rakhiot glaciers and their valleys, on SW Nanga Parbat. They found it difficult to test rock for thermoluminescence in field conditions.

90/30 *NUMC Malangutti Glacier Expedition* (June–August 1990)

This three-member team succeeded in their objective of climbing unclimbed peaks in the Malangutti glacier area, in particular Mt Neverett (5700m). They also made the second ascent, by a new route, of Shufktin Sar.

Elsewhere: Central Asia and South-East Asia

90/12 *British Speleological Expedition to North Vietnam* (March–April 1990)

This nine-member caving team explored the 'classic' river cave of Phong Nha ('Teeth of the Wind'), and surveyed and photographed 18km of other caves in various karst areas of N Vietnam, particularly Quang Binh Province. Despite political difficulties, this was a successful speleological reconnaissance in unknown country.

90/18 *British Turkestan Expedition* (June 1990)

This two-man party achieved a successful new line on the N face of Ak Su (5355m) and explored the potential of this area, noting numerous unclimbed faces and peaks.

90/28 *USSR/British Pamir Caving Expedition* (July–August 1990)

17 cavers divided their time between the exploration of caves in (a) the Kirktau Plateau at the W end of the Zeravsankij mountains in Uzbekistan, finding three new pot-holes; (b) the Arabika Massif in the W Caucasus; and (c) the Ukraine.

90/36 *ASPEX '90 Anglo–Soviet Pamir Caving Expedition* (July–August 1990)

11 British pot-holers co-operated with 10 Soviet speleologists in a preliminary exploration of an extensive cave system in the limestone wall of the Hodja Gur Gur Ata Plateau (3921m) in the Bajsuntai area of Uzbekistan.

Appendix: Mount Everest Foundation to administer Alison Chadwick Memorial Grant

In 1978 Alison Chadwick, a British climber, died close to the summit of Annapurna I, whilst a member of the successful American women's expedition. Three years earlier, together with Janusz Onyszkiewicz (her Polish husband) and Wanda Rutkiewicz she had already reached the summit of Gasherbrum III – at the time the world's highest unclimbed summit, and probably for ever the highest virgin summit climbed by a woman. A Memorial Fund was instituted in her name, which provided 'grants to further British and Polish women's mountaineering in the world's greater ranges, ie further afield than the Alps'.

At the end of 1990, the entire assets of the fund were very generously passed to the Mount Everest Foundation who intend, as far as possible, to adhere to these guidelines.

The MEF exists to support British and New Zealand applicants proposing to climb new routes on high remote mountains: the Foundation will now consider expeditions in which there are both Polish and British (or New Zealand) women members (or a single member) for the Alison Chadwick award.

Applicants should apply to the MEF for an 'Application for Grant' form: their eligibility for the 'MEF Alison Chadwick Memorial Grant' will be considered automatically during the screening process.

Requests for forms should be made to the Hon Secretary of the MEF, giving details of the intended objective. They must be completed and returned to him by 31 August or 31 December of the year preceding the expedition. Early applicants will be interviewed in November and the later ones in March. It is advisable to submit applications as early as possible.

MEF Hon Secretary: Mr W H Ruthven, Gowrie, Cardwell Close, Warton, Preston PR4 1SH.

Book Reviews 1990

COMPILED BY GEOFFREY TEMPLEMAN

Elusive Summits
Victor Saunders
Hodder & Stoughton, 1990, pp191, £14.95

This is very much a book of our time and a model of its genre. It tells of four lightweight, alpine-style expeditions to the Karakoram. All the routes described were of the highest standard of difficulty and epics abound. So far, no big deal; lots of young mountaineers have been going to the greater ranges on exactly this sort of expedition during the last decade.

What raises this book head and shoulders above the run-of-the-mill is that Victor Saunders is not only a hard climber but an unusually percipient and humorous writer. This is a happy and rare combination of talents which I shall allude to later.

In this, his first book, Saunders has got most things right. Each expedition gets about 50 pages. This ensures that the narrative is concentrated and it avoids the inescapable padding of 'the expedition book'. Saunders is commendably frank – bearing in mind that the totally honest autobiography has yet to be written. He has that knack, brought to an art form by Tom Patey, of exposing, almost caricaturing, his friends' quirks. As with Patey, it is done with disarming humour and kindliness. With a sophisticated, and often self-deprecating, sense of humour he reveals the absurd and the illogical in many expedition situations and attitudes. This is delightful leavening.

His writing is crisp, even staccato, and he frequently surprises with a sudden oblique view of a scene. For instance, when a falling stone knocks a tooth out, he climbs down 'trailing blood, spit and self-pity'. Or, after a claustrophobic bivouac during a good three-day Karakoram blizzard, the asthmatic, self-confessed hypochondriac sums it up: 'for three days storms and headaches beat like angry fists at my eggshell universe'. You will have to look very hard for clichés. He has a sharp ear for dialogue, particularly in the funny bits.

Now to the nuts and bolts. The first expedition was to Uzum Brakk (6642m), or Conway's Ogre, in 1980. The story starts with the dramatic rescue of a Japanese climber from a neighbouring expedition who had lain injured in a crevasse for nine days. They climb a new route on the E face but fail to make the summit. The descent is hairy.

Next came the higher Hunza peak of Bojohaghur (7329m) in 1984. There is a hilarious scene when Chris Watts falls off a cramped bivouac and dangles below an overhang, still in his sleeping bag. He jumars back without getting out! Again they climbed the route but were unable to make the summit.

In 1985 it was Rimo I (7385m), this time with Stephen Venables who managed to drop his rucksack at a pregnant moment when the summit might have been within grasp. This is also described in Venables' *Painted Mountains*, and the two accounts bear tolerable similarity.

Finally, Spantik (7072m) in 1987. The well-known photograph of the Golden Pillar which they climbed tells it all. The headwall is 4000 feet of stomach-turning verticality. Saunders' partner was that superb and colourful mountaineer, Mick Fowler, who, of course, provides ample material for the by now familiar Saunders treatment. Their commitment was awesome. Towards the top of the headwall they climbed near-vertical shale down which an abseil retreat would have been impossible. On the descent (at last Saunders made the summit on this one!) they abseiled into unknown country down irreversible ice cliffs.

There are eight pages of colour pictures, too many of them reduced to quarter page and thus losing their impact.

To return now to the theme of the climber/writer: Victor Saunders is certainly to be congratulated on a splendidly crafted first book. He now joins the ranks of my currently favourite mountain writers: John Barry and Stephen Venables. The Club is fortunate to have such members. Victor Saunders was recently on an expedition to Makalu. I wonder what he will make of that?

Mike Banks

Coming Through
Andy Fanshawe
Hodder & Stoughton, 1990, pp218, £14.95

This is Andy Fanshawe's first book. The majority of the 218 pages are concerned with his five climbs on Chogolisa and Menlungtse, but there are also soul-searching passages on incidents such as a fatal accident involving his closest friend and his struggle to come to terms with his lack of success on his 1989 expedition to Makalu.

Andy writes well. I'm not sure about the title, but this is a lucid, descriptive book which covers a whole lot more than straightforward technical climbing stories. It exudes a youthfulness and vitality which very much captures the sense of wide-eyed excitement experienced by those exploring the Himalaya for the first time. From the harsh heat of Islamabad to the crisp coldness of high altitudes the sense of adventure and need for excitement shines strongly through.

The book starts by recalling days in Chamonix and scenes so familiar to many. Hard up but fun, lots of excitement; maximum value from minimum experience.

Gradually, of course, other opportunities arise; Andy meets Hamish Irvine (by climbing up his ropes whilst *in extremis* on Point Five) and together they organize what is to be Andy's first trip to the Himalaya. A bold first traverse of 7600m high Chogolisa and the subsequent death of Liam Elliot on Broad Peak bring mixed emotions which Andy explores with an endearing openness.

Contact with Chris Bonington via Andy's work as National Officer of the British Mountaineering Council results in his inclusion on Chris's 1988 expedition to Menlungtse and culminates in the first ascent of the W summit of the peak with Alan Hinkes who had been employed as the accompanying reporters' mail runner.

Again Andy successfully steers clear of the potentially monotonous blow-by-blow account of the climb and revealingly projects the personalities of those involved, their reactions to the mountain and his emotions at seeing first-hand the shattered remains of the Buddhist monasteries destroyed by the Chinese cultural revolution in Tibet.

Both ethnic and mountaineering scenes are well portrayed by colour photos, and the whole book adds up to a very attractive package. Above all else it is immensely readable – there are few climbing books that I have read so avidly. Recommended.

Mick Fowler

Mallory of Everest
Dudley Green
Faust Publishing Company Ltd, 1990, pp141, £8.50

Sixty-six years after his disappearance on Everest, this is the third book to be written in English about George Mallory. Any appraisal, therefore, must inevitably invoke comparison with its two predecessors – the 1927 memoir by David Pye, and the biography by George's son-in-law David Robertson in 1968, both acknowledged by the present author amongst his sources.

Dudley Green, a life-long enthusiast for the Mallory story, has now produced a fuller account of George's life, especially its earlier part, than Pye, and in shorter format than Robertson. By drawing on a number of sources still extant but hitherto untapped, and in particular by first-hand up-to-date contacts with surviving members of the families of George and Ruth, the author has brought to light much new material and many previously unpublished photographs. The result is a highly informative and readable biographical sketch comprising 141 pages of text, a short useful index and more than 40 illustrations. The author's researches, particularly those relating to Mallory's life before Everest, provide justification enough for yet another book on what some might consider an already overworked chapter of mountaineering history.

'Other climbers,' said David Robertson in 1968, 'have gone on talking about George Mallory as if the decades were only years'. But that is no longer true, for one may encounter many of today's climbers and still more members of the public who seem quite unacquainted with the story. Dudley Green's method is to allow his subject to spell out his character and philosophy by means of first-hand quotations from writings and letters – an approach which reflects much painstaking investigation and absolves the book, although presented in somewhat popular form, from any charge of deficiency in depth.

Something must be said about the illustrations. Unpublished photographs of outstanding interest include several family, school and university groups; a 1911 Pen-y-pass picture of George with Cottie Saunders (later Lady O'Malley and writer 'Ann Bridge'); another from Pen-y-pass showing George at the wheel of his Model T Ford in 1919, with Geoffrey Winthrop Young beside him and five other members of the party, including Ruth, trying to get them started with a combined 'push-job'. There is also a splendid full-face photograph of Sandy Irvine, one of George as a subaltern and a quite new one of Ruth.

But in its production the book is disappointing – the presentation is not worthy of the material. The binding, in rather unattractive sheets of plastic-coated card more suited to a guidebook than to a serious work, and the quality of most of the illustrations falls far below those of Pye and Robertson. The briefest glance at the three books is enough to confirm this: for instance Winthrop Young's famous photograph of Mallory descending the Moine Ridge, reproduced in all three, is outstandingly good in Pye, where, as its composition obviously requires, the picture is vertically projected. In Robertson composition and definition are superior to Green, but in both these the impact is much diminished by the horizontal projection.

Mallory of Everest, excellently titled, deserves better of its binding and illustrations, and if it is welcomed as it should be in the world of climbing books and by the wider public let us hope for an improved second run, bound (please) in hardback.

It is good to hear that two of George's three children, Clare (b1915) and John (b1920) are still with us. For them this book will bring back treasured memories of the unforgettable story in which their father was *primus inter pares*; and for the rest of us a fresh and invigorating look at the two men who may have climbed Mount Everest 29 years before its summit could, beyond all doubt, be said to have been reached. The unanswerable question remains, and in a concluding postscript Dudley Green wisely leaves it with Noel Odell, last to see them alive on their final journey.

Edward Smyth

The Pundits: British Exploration of Tibet and Central Asia
Derek Waller
University Press of Kentucky, 1990, ppviii+327, $30

Through the many books on Himalayan and Central Asian explorations there runs a persistent, strong, yet discontinuous and often invisible thread – the story of the Pundits.

Although Hari Ram (M-H or No 9) in the late 19th century ascended the Dudh Kosi, crossed the Nangpa La, visited Tengri on at least two occasions and travelled through South Tibet, thus circumnavigating Everest, there is only a passing reference to him in the appendix on surveying in the first book on the exploration of Everest from Tibet, and, indeed, Shipton in his account of the exploration of the Nepalese side of Everest in 1951 does not mention this Pundit at all.

One difficulty in finding out about the Pundits is that their work was clandestine; they were secret native surveyors employed by the Survey of India; yet there is a paradox. Why was their work so often recorded, albeit by their case officers, in geographical journals? Why was the Pundit Nain Singh given the Gold Medal of the Royal Geographical Society, which he richly deserved? Surely this is as public an announcement of his exploits as it is possible to have.

The Pundits owed their existence to the expansion of Russia from Europe to Central Asia in the late 19th century. The Government of India knew very little about the topography and political allegiances of the vast, remote and strategic land into which Russia was moving, so it became of paramount importance for them to gain as much information as possible. As British surveyors in these regions were either murdered or politely returned, the Survey of India decided to use local natives for this hazardous work. After selection these men were trained in basic clandestine survey techniques at Dehra Dun, their work was tested, and then they were given specific assignments, lasting months or years.

The North-West Frontier was the first target and Abdul Hamid, the first Pundit, travelled to Yarkand. Unfortunately, on his return over the Karakoram Pass he became ill and died under suspicious circumstances. Another attempt to explore the Oxus and Pamir was made by a 'Pathan of the Native Sappers and Miners' who was dispatched from Peshawar towards Chitral. A family blood feud caught up with him, however, and he was murdered. 'The Mirza' followed and reached Kashgar by a circuitous route via Kandahar, Kabul and the Wakhan Corridor. After four months in Kashgar he returned via Yarkand and Leh, being away for two years. Despite initial misgivings, his survey measurements were finally accepted by the geographical establishment in the UK and Montgomerie (who was in charge of the Pundits) read a paper on the Mirza's explorations at the Royal Geographical Society in 1871. Both were congratulated on their work. The Mirza was sent on a second exploration to Bokhara in 1872–73 but was murdered *en route* whilst he slept. Further work on the North-West Frontier was carried out by the Havildar, the Mullah and others, but as the area was becoming increasingly penetrated by British military expeditions, the efforts of the Pundits were then concentrated on Tibet.

For this purpose Tibetan-speaking inhabitants of the high Himalayan valleys, many from the Milam area, were recruited by Smyth, the Education Officer of Kumaon. Initially Nain Singh and his cousin Mani Singh were chosen. Neither was new to surveying, both having accompanied the Schlagintweits in Ladakh and the Stracheys in West Tibet. This was the start of a most fruitful period in Central Asian exploration and many members of the Singh family were involved.

The Pundits crossed and recrossed the Himalaya and the Tibet plateau, they visited and mapped Lhasa, the gold fields of Thok Jalong in South Tibet, discovered the Gangdise and Nyenqentangla ranges, followed the course of the Tsangpo almost to the plains of India, explored Bhutan and established a remarkably comprehensive picture of Central Asia and Tibet for the Survey.

Perhaps the most remarkable journey was that of AK, Kishen Singh, described in my article on pp 49–62 of this volume. When AK returned to India 4½ years after he had left, he was destitute, in rags, and so physically exhausted that it was feared he might die. Despite being robbed by both his companion and brigands, and being searched and detained more than once under grave suspicion, he retained all his notebooks and virtually all his instruments. He was a man of great integrity: on his return he was asked if he had any debts, for often the Pundits had to sell items or borrow money; AK said he had none. The distance covered on this journey amounted to 2800 miles which, when added to his previous exploits in South Tibet and Tengri Nor (which he circumnavigated) and his journey to Khotan on the Forsyth Mission, meant that he had surveyed more of Central Asia than any other Pundit, even his illustrious cousin Nain Singh. He was honoured with Gold Medals by the Italian and French Geographical Societies, but not by the Royal Geographical Society – an astonishing omission. AK retired to Milam, where he was visited in 1905 at a nearby village, Mansiari, by Tom Longstaff who was on his journey to Western Tibet and the attempt on Gurla Mandhata.

Professor Derek Waller, in a labour of love over many years, has given the first complete account of the Pundits' explorations, and what comes through the pages of this academic and thorough work is the sheer persistence, ingenuity, resourcefulness and bravery of these remarkable men. This book is a considerable work of scholarship with 40 pages of references, and all who are interested in the exploration of the Himalaya and Tibet should be greatly indebted to the author for his detailed account which clarifies and expands an important period in Central Asian travel.

Michael Ward

Exploring the Hidden Himalaya
Soli Mehta and Harish Kapadia
Hodder & Stoughton, 1990, pp213, npq

High Asia. An Illustrated History of the 7000 Metre Peaks
Jill Neate
Unwin and Hyman, 1989, ppx+213, £25.00

Exploring the Hidden Himalaya is principally about the lesser known parts of the range. It includes the Indian Karakoram and Sikkim, but excludes all of Nepal and Bhutan. The format is that of chapters outlining the history of exploration in each of the massifs. A narrative style is adopted; the book is meant to be read, not just picked over for bare information. The text is well supported by photographs and maps, though there is a gap between Lahul and Kishtwar. I suspect that the mapping was based on the commercially available material, which also has a similar gap. It would have been helpful if the maps could have folded out, as almost constant reference to them is required in the reading of the text.

The strength of the book lies in the authors' commitment to their subject. Harish Kapadia is *the* authority here. He has contributed to the subject with his prolific excursions into untracked territory, and his explorations are always backed up with meticulous research. Harish has not only done more than any one else on these lesser peaks, he knows more about them too.

In spite of its title, Jill Neate's book is less a history than a survey of the 7000m peaks from the Soviet Pamir to Minya Konka on the far eastern edge of the Tibetan plateau. Neate has included the unclimbed and unattempted peaks and has listed intriguing mountains about which almost nothing seems to be known. I cannot decide whether she has done mountaineering a great service or a disservice. I will certainly always have a copy of her books to hand when looking for Himalayan projects (her bibliography of mountaineering literature has long been a favourite of mine); on the other hand, it distresses me that every other Himalayan peak-bagger will have access to the same information. The format is that of an encyclopaedia, with beautiful photographs, and sketch maps that for my taste are too small in the area they cover to be really useful.

Both books are highly recommended.

A V Saunders

My Tibet
The Dalai Lama, introduction and photographs by Galen Rowell
*University of California Press, Berkeley, 1990,
pp159, 108 large colour plates, 2 maps, $35*

The fourteenth Dalai Lama, spiritual leader of Tibetan Buddhists, has become more widely influential in exile than he could have become in Tibet. He writes with gentle passion, and is respected and revered throughout the world. Quite possibly these essays may do more to rescue our threatened environment than the actions of noisier organizations.

This is an incandescent book. Accustomed as we have become to Galen Rowell's brilliant photography, these many plates have that special clarity of the pure atmosphere in high Tibet; the colour is faithful and composition superb. The pictures glow. Rowell ranges widely: from limitless horizons, crystal snow summits, intimate portraits of indigenous birds and beasts and people, to a large and unusual portfolio of Tibetan monks, pilgrims, shrines and ceremonies. His genius has captured the beauty, the wildness, the spiritual quality of poor tormented Tibet, making a luminous background for the simply phrased message of the Dalai Lama. In his introduction Rowell outlines enough Tibetan history to give us background for the plates and for the messages which match them. He describes the humour, the wisdom and the joy in the midst of tragedy which pervades this most human of spiritual leaders. This is not a book for mountaineers or travellers alone – it is a message for all the world.

Charles Houston

High Altitude Medical Science
Edited by G Ueda, S Kusama, N F Voelkel
Sinshu University, 1988, npq

This book is the Proceedings of an International Symposium on High-Altitude Medicine held in November 1987 at Matsumoto in Japan.

The majority of papers are from Japanese workers and all are in English.

It is the Japanese counterpart of the now well-established Hypoxia Symposium held every two years in North America at Chateau Lake Louise.

Essentially for medical scientists, this book covers many aspects, both clinical and experimental, of cold and oxygen lack in man and animals. In particular there are three papers on high-altitude adaptations in the pika, a primitive species native to high altitude for 37 million years and distributed world-wide. Like the yak it appears to be genetically adapted, not having to any degree enlargement of the right heart which is found in non-adapted species like man.

This book is a welcome addition to the growing corpus of work on an increasingly important subject.

Michael Ward

A Manual of Modern Rope Techniques for Climbers and Mountaineers
Nigel Shepherd
Constable, 1990, £8.95

Once I thought myself competent with ropes, and as I remain alive it cannot have been a complete illusion. Climbing before nuts required ingenuity unless you were brave, and some of the latter tended not to be around long.

Then protection and security in movement on mountains was attempted by much the same methods as now, but the tools were simpler and sparse. In consequence ingenuity with the rope itself and with the few slings usually carried was at a premium, and the costs of lack of imagination could be long delay, a cold bivouac or worse. Securing protection with four or five slings, rattling flakes and chockstones and knout-like knots stuck into cracks was a high art, from Siegfried Herford and Fred Pigott to Joe Brown and the dawn of our more democratic age. None should delude themselves that the progress of protection has been cost-free. Immense artisanal ingenuity went into protecting climbs and escaping from them when technological means were so slight.

There is maybe little to be read into a cover shot of slate endeavour on a book that has relatively little to say about the specifics of modern harder extreme climbing. Indeed, the world with a lightly out-of-focus bolt close at hand seems remote from much of the book. The bolt-ladder specialist needs relatively few of these techniques, requiring instead enough strength, concentration on where to pull up next and on what, and someone holding the rope who will remember to clip in the sticht plate and, preferably, stay awake. Most of the world is elsewhere, bigger, more unstable in essence, moving, tumbling, decaying, swept by weather and wind. The most permanent-looking of rock citadels tempt believers in permanence to doom or disillusion.

So this book gives more thought to movement than to sitting in a crowd. Chapters on snow, rock and ice anchors, jumaring, abseil, recovery of a partner on rock and ice, these are of the essence of moving through the firing line of the real mountain, and most rock, environments. What shines through is the author's practical experience, the lessons drilled in from real hard times. Most experienced climbers know many techniques, but most are happily rusty from infrequent use. Nigel Shepherd's guiding is the key to these sections. Nothing concentrates the mind better than being attached for days on end to varieties of people who may or may not be as competent as they think, may or may not do as they are advised, and may or may not be of assistance in an emergency. Old guides used to keep them on tight handheld strings, for easier disposal if their security could no longer be assured. There is no doubt that exposure to these situations, often in objectively dangerous places, brings out wisdom in those who survive.

One admirable result is the explanation of a wide range of techniques, and illustrations support these. Another is a short way with manifest impracticalities, and scepticism about techniques that might just be used if all else has already failed. On rescue in particular I liked (p157): 'Do not underestimate the difficulties of hoisting someone without assistance. What is essentially a simple system to set up is extraordinarily difficult to effect.' He can say that again! As one moves on to areas long rusty, this commonsense gives some confidence.

In the areas I know best, ascending and descending rocks, mountains and all sorts of tottering places as quickly as my lungs and muscles allow, while seeking to evade an oft-expected brush with eternity, this is a well considered, clearly argued and ordered text. Take 'Moving Together' and 'Glacier Travel'. Both are as essential as ever to expeditious ascent anywhere but in a klettergarten. Maybe at one time the joint stresses upon not falling and keeping the rope reasonably closely managed between climbers were not necessary. Now they are, as the transition from small-scale to motion on mountains is a bigger leap.

This text is good value. If some of the rope rigs look likely to baffle my memory, that is my problem rather than the author's.

Paul Nunn

Mountains and Other Ghosts
Dermot Somers
Diadem Books, 1990, pp224, £12.95 (hb), £8.95 (pb)

Dermot Somers is a good friend, and it might have been sensible to refuse Geof Templeman's request to review this book. But my sympathy for all editors who have to extract material for deadlines overruled my hesitation. I leave it to readers to decide if I am biased.

The book contains 14 short stories. Most have a mountain background, but only four or five could be described as 'climbing stories'. Many have an Irish background but are not the less universal for that. Don't expect peaceful stories – they are almost all full of tension: I don't mean characters hitting each other, but tense in many ways, physical – a car chase, death in a storm, the Eigerwand – and mental – young offenders, the ingrained tensions of rural Ireland.

For me, anyway, each story needed reading twice; the first time because I couldn't stop, the second time (or perhaps the third) to get full value from his evocative use of words, and to extract his full meaning. I remember reading some early writings of Dermot's – adjectives piled on adjectives. In these stories every word is important, and none is redundant. Scenes are set in clipped, yet fully descriptive phrases. This works for dialogue too, which is always wholly realistic, recognizable.

The stories range very widely. *Nightfall* is an ascent of the Eigerwand against the background of a nuclear war; a hugely emotional situation which the writer has the capacity to master. *The Island* takes a group of juvenile delinquents on 'Adventure Skills', which bring out and heighten all their latent hostilities almost to killing point. *The Old Story* retells the well-known story of Art O'Neill and Hugh O'Donnell, escaping from Elizabethan Dublin Castle, and O'Neill's death from cold on the snowy Wicklow hills; by interleaving with a group of today's walkers, Dermot points up our Irish preoccupation with the past.

For successes, I score 12 out of 14. *A Taste of Honey* is too sweet. According to the 'blurb', *The Lug Walk* pokes 'gentle fun'. For me, the fun was quite ungentle: the main character is unpleasant and stupid, but he is treated by the writer with a total contempt which revolted me.

English readers should not be put off by the first story in the book. The publisher did Somers a disservice by placing it there, since the casual reader may well dismiss the book as another outpouring of Irish Republicanism. It isn't; the story simply shows in an Ulster context how nearly all humans react when they feel themselves isolated.

I think this is a great collection; stories which I have read several times and know I will want to read again. There is not much mountain fiction about which I would say that.

Joss Lynam

Ten Letters to John Muir
Terry Gifford
Burbage Books, 1990, pp16, £2.50 (£5 Limited Edition)

One has little hesitation in commending this poetry as among the best written by an English climber in 200 years. This may seem faint praise: writing standards have not usually risen with climbing standards, as has been pointed out by this reviewer before. But even a casual reading of these *Ten Letters* shows a poet in full control of language, rhythm and narrative – the things that make poetry what it is. 'Written to the founding father of Yosemite National Park in its centennial year', this booklet is by no means a pompous panegyric, as one might expect. Rather, contrasting the idyllic wilderness known to the pioneer with the horror-show known to us as Yosemite National Park, and written with an exact knowledge of English prosody that would shame some better-known poets, it is a suitable statement for our times. One hesitates, as ever, to quote out of the context of the whole rhythmic structure. But it is fair to contrast a well-mulled couplet, chosen at random, 'Your "ramble" up from the Valley/ To spend a night on this bare mountain' (seven beats carefully spaced with two groups of two short syllables, and one group of two long syllables) with ...

Ronnie Wathen

Hanging in the Balance
Andy Miller
Amcott Press, 1988, pp22, unpriced

... with another couplet, again chosen at random: 'Since then we have computed permutations on our balance sheet. And lost our love in Equity, Assurance and Dual Benefit'. Here there seem to be about a dozen beats (give or take two?) and no rhythmic tension, internally or externally to other lines coming before or after – and precious little sense either. But most of this booklet is prose anyway and, to judge it as purely that, it is laboured with the faults all too common in the climbing magazines of today – and therefore deserving censure. One would strongly suggest that this is not this writer's best work, and that he learn a few lessons from the master Terry Gifford, and read a lot of other good writers besides: to structure his paragraphs, put verbs in his sentences, avoid the self-pitying mode and, at the end of the day, choose a decent typeface, and not dot-matrix! Apart from this, he shows much promise and the accounts of rock-ascents and marriage-descents are gripping.

Ronnie Wathen

Coleridge. Early Visions
Richard Holmes
Hodder & Stoughton, 1989, pp409, £16.95

'The Mountain air is not congenial to opium eating' says Leslie Stephen, rather tartly. He is surely right, but unfair by implication to Coleridge. On the other hand, countless people have found the poet himself addictive. Most such will have already read this biography, which has won praise and prizes for its perceptive approach to this 'rare, anomalous, magnificent, interesting, curious and tremendously suggestive character'. This goes well outside the scope of the *AJ*, but anyone who is interested in the origins of climbing should certainly read this book.

Two Reverend botanists seem to have beaten Coleridge to graded rock when they found a way up Clogwyn du'r Arddu, no less, in 1798, making use of a leather belt for security on the crux. Characteristically, the pursuit of science was the excuse given for enjoying a dangerous adventure. The poet was ranging the Quantocks by then, and next year he began the Lakeland fell-walking which led to his famous scramble on Sca Fell on 5 August 1802. This involved the first recorded descent of Broad Stand, and thus got him an additional scrap of immortality (in the FRCC guide). His notebooks and a letter written on the summit may still be read. At one moment Coleridge writes: 'There is a sort of Gambling, to which I am much addicted; and not of the least criminal kind for a Man who has Children and a Concern. It is this. When I find it convenient to descend from a Mountain—, where it is first *possible* to descend, there I go, relying on fortune for how far down the possibility will continue.' In the description which follows he comes to a point at which he thinks himself cragfast. The pressures of fear and loneliness threaten to overcome him, but he is able to control his panic, and his delight in this seems to be a step in his struggle to direct his whole artistic life in face of the disintegrating forces which are working on it. This is a key passage in Romantic Literature, but the situation might be recognized by many a more prosaic climber, who has ever got himself somewhere he did not intend to be.

A few weeks later Coleridge is again on the crags:

'I have always found this *stretched* and *anxious* state of mind favourable to a depth of pleasurable Impressions—.' It has a modern feel. We are up-and-away from the Picturesque Tourists who then saw the mountains through their Claude Glasses, and now do so in their wing-mirrors.

Francis à Court

One Step in the Clouds
An omnibus of mountaineering novels and short stories
Compiled by Audrey Salkeld and Rosie Smith
Diadem/Sierra Club, 1990, pp1056, £16.95

Unsure of my companions and with a heavy heart, I shouldered my rucksack (with its 1056-page volume) from the AC Librarian, tried not to look her in the eyes, and cycled home. Was mine to be the first ascent of the Anthology Wall, or had the ladies (the Compilers) already done it? A moot point. I could not trust my companions (the Writers). Their lack of experience of the world, nostalgic reading habits, and brain-exhaustion (in some cases permanent) from altitude, would strain my resources as their Reviewer. I sat down to a bivouac of coffee and earplugged Gulf News in the living room.

I was resigned to a hard, perhaps lethal climb up this Anthology Wall. The 'topo' or Introduction was wayward. Looking up the Face, I could not locate some pitches: they were from some other mountain! – for example, *Green Mars* and *Damnation of Mr Zinkler*. I began climbing, placing an ill-omened foot on the avalanche-debris of Joe Simpson's *Meltwater*.

Suddenly my heart lifted, as I reached the first stance and saw ahead of me the shoot-from-the-hip thriller *B-Tower West Wall* (Peter Lars Sandberg). 600ft of sheer, steely prose at night, with a scared killer as second, led to the foot of Anne Sauvy's *La Fourche* with its interesting opening moves about the Chamonix weather – which I could have quoted at length here, were it not for my scruples against the use of fixed rope. I didn't care for the next two pitches, David Roberts's *A Storm in the East* which was schoolgirlish, and G J F Dutton's *Midges* which left me glad I hadn't washed (thus I retained my midge-repelling odours). I hauled myself up K V Crocket's *October Day*, surprisingly easy despite its baggage of memories and soggy prose – and took a thermos-break.

Pitch 7 was a corker, *Ulrich the Guide* (or *The Mountain Inn*): it's Maupassant, who perfected the solo short story ascent single-penned, didn't he? It's a masterly brew of mountain error and terror, which ends in madness (as did Maupassant). On cue, the American Jeff Long follows with his *Virgins of Imst*. I was really beginning to enjoy the climb. Gone was that unaccountable feeling of wanting to be off the mountain, of not wanting to complete this book (no doubt it would return). I wanted to rope back down this pitch, repeat it, locate its secrets, do it better. But ahead the Irishman Dermot Somers, disguised for *The White Graph* as an ageing Salford rockjock, was leading arrogant Youth up a variant to the Fissure Brown – a perfect study of how to burn out a bastard.

A frisson of thrill is in Anne Sauvy's *Time Reversal*. Step past the *Big Mistake* and if you don't jump *In the Crevasse* with Ben Saunter you pendule on pitch 12 on to a ghastly accident in *Summertime* with Al Alvarez. After that, the famous crux *In Hanging Garden Gully* may disappoint, both the rope antics and the prose palling, where once we giggled at C E Montague's joke. David Craig's *The Escapist* is modern, but it too may fade in time, with its view of rock-climbing as substitute marriage-battle. This is followed by one of the most intriguing sections of gymnastics in the entire Range, an excerpt from M John Harrison's *Climbers*: Gaz and Sankey are the first real people I've met on this Big Wall and they may well be the last. Savour their horror-show, Britain, while you can, with its greasy, *Sun*-reading Public . . .

Ahead lies the Holmesian *Case of the Great Grey Man* by Robin Campbell, and you should not be put off by its starting on a sofa, for soon we are enmeshed in Highland mist, where there is a most interesting move involving the use of live human bodies as balloon-ballast. Brain-damaged in a car crash, Davie stumbles through Gordon Thomson's *Children Like Climbers Often Fall*, on a 2000ft Grade V night-time ice-climb with two male nurses.

Perhaps the only British climber ever to have had the tortured detachment essential to creative writing was Menlove Edwards: his grim, secretive *Scenery for a Murder* could provide discussion for a whole night in a bivouac. The angle eases for a few ropelengths, past suspect *Cannibals* by Jeff Long, and a nutty priest in *No Gentlemen in the Himalaya* by Greg Child, and Balti porters ruminating *In Another Tongue* on sahibs' motives, and the tribulations of Sherpas in Elaine Brook's *Rites of Passage*, and a snow-slog through a Hiawathan sex-legend, *The Way of the White Serpent* by John Daniel. Now, as the headwall looms, Anne Sauvy's *2084* provides light satire of a future of government-regulated climbing, resulting in the worst massacre in mountaineering history when the computer fails. A ropelength of Sci-Fi slabs called *Bright Fire, Bright Ice* (Charles Hood) has what some might unfairly assume to be a Bonington character committing suicide in Outer Space, but suddenly we are back with Alvarez in the familiar rock-grind, *Night Out*, but without the late Mo Anthoine's wit. An old 'un in Dave Gregory's *The Old Man's Pigeon Loft*, young and old 'uns in John Long's *For Everything Its Season*, some travel stuff and ascents into madness on *Leviathan* (Geof Childs), a blocked lavatory cleared by *The Bronx Plumber* who turns out to be Mallory, by Guy Waterman who turns out to be Irvine, and a final little fillip with a ghostly hitchhiker who may or may not be Irvine, *In Gentle Combat with the Cold Wind* (Jeff Long again), bring us, without any alarming headwall it turns out, to summit snows in sight now. These stretch up at the easier angle of six novellas and one play. One of the novellas is Elizabeth Coxhead's *One Green Bottle* (1951). The play is in fact Maurice Wilson talking to Maurice Wilson.

But before I could taste these reverse-slope delights, I was plucked from the Face by the *AJ* Editor in a helicopter.

Ronnie Wathen

In Balance. Twenty years of mountaineering journalism
Peter Gillman
Hodder & Stoughton, 1989, pp252, £12.95

Anyone who has been a regular reader of the *Sunday Times* over the past 20 years will be familiar with the mountain writings of Peter Gillman. Whenever any event of importance has occurred in the mountain world, Gillman could be relied upon to present a balanced view in good journalistic prose, of interest to both layman and *aficionado* alike. Being a climber himself, although not a great one, as he himself would be the first to point out, his articles were always free from the gaffes committed by so many journalists attempting to write on climbing. There are some 40 articles collected in this book, not only from the *Sunday Times*, ranging from early ones such as Harlin's death on the Eiger, Maestri on Cerro Torre and the Old Man of Hoy TV Circus, to comparatively recent ones on the K2 tragedies and Venables's success on Everest. In between are items on lesser hills and events, including some of the author's own exploits, which make for equally interesting reading.

The Picturesque Scenery of the Lake District
Peter Bicknell
St Paul's Bibliographies, 1990, pp198, £40

Once again our member Peter Bicknell has regaled us with a book to do with his chosen theme and lifelong interest, this time a bibliography of all the delightful early guides and illustrated books to do with the Lake District.

This is a scholarly book, and a highly important work of reference. It is delightful to browse in it and to look at the illustrations. But, above all, it is Peter's introductory essay that ought to be read. Nobody else has ever introduced us to all the romantic, artistic and literary history of the Lakes in quite the same way. This essay should be essential reading for any lover of the English Lake District and its artistic and literary traditions.

The book is sumptuously produced and does credit to the publishers. We should be grateful for this, because it is a book that was really worth doing well.

Charles Warren

Dust and Snow. Half a Lifetime in India
C Reginald Cooke
Privately published, 1988, pp8 + 338

The author of this sumptuously-produced, leather-bound volume of memoirs has published it himself, to tell his story of half a lifetime in India. Apart from a break of a few years in England for education, the whole scenario is India, but it stops short at Independence when Reginald Cooke decided to accept the post of Chief Engineer of Posts and Telegraphs in Pakistan and moved to Karachi. Life under the new bureaucracy was not attractive, however, and he soon moved back to England for good.

Whilst the major part of the book is concerned with life and work in India, interest for climbers centres on three chapters. The first recounts the second ascent of Kolahoi (5437m) in the Pir Panjal, made with Wigram Battye in 1926. In 1935, with Gostav Schoberth, he made an ascent of Kabru (7316m), finishing the climb alone. This was the highest solo ascent until Hermann Buhl climbed Nanga Parbat in 1953. Finally, in 1937, the author went on an expedition with John and Joy Hunt to develop a new route on Kangchenjunga. Their exploration around the Zemu and Twins glaciers and various training climbs are described, but any attempt on the N ridge of 'Kanch' proved impossible. The author then went off to make a hazardous trip through the Umaram valley. These historic exploits make fascinating reading and, indeed, the whole book is an excellent memoir of an era that now seems so long ago.

Geof Templeman

Wayward Women
Jane Robinson
CUP, 1990, ppxvi + 344, £17.50

Jane Robinson worked for a number of years in an antiquarian bookshop specializing in travel. Thus her main interest was in books, and her original intention was to write a bibliography of travel books written by women. The trouble was, she started to read the books, and became so fascinated by the authors and their adventures that it turned into a reference work on the travellers themselves and their writings. Several years of painstaking research later, here is the result, and it makes fascinating reading. In all, I added up that there must be some 400 authors included, each having a list of her travel books, followed by a potted biography and details of her travels. All sorts of travellers are included, from Abbess Etheria's pilgrimage to the Holy Land in the 4th century, via Mary Kingsley's African journeys and Amy Johnson's flights, to Julie Tullis on K2. Titles such as *How I Shot my Bears; Or, Two years' Tent Life in Kulu and Lahoul* and *Diary of an Idle Woman in Constantinople* abound and, as the author says, it was titles like these and *On Sledge and Horseback to Outcast Siberian Lepers* and *To Lake Tanganyika in a Bath Chair* that started her reading. A trawl through the book, purely from a mountaineering books point of view, has failed to reveal any omissions. It is a monumental piece of research and a delight to dip into.

Geof Templeman

The Corbetts and other Scottish Hills – Scottish Mountaineering Club Hillwalkers' Guide – Volume Two
Edited by Scott Johnstone, Hamish Brown and Donald Bennet
Scottish Mountaineering Trust, 1990, pp250, £14.95

The first volume of this book, *The Munros*, was reviewed in *AJ92*, 256–7, 1987, and Volume Two is every bit as good and follows the same layout. The editor of the first volume has been joined for the second by two co-editors, and the names of the writers which are listed in the section headings add up to no fewer than 30. This has had the result of a fine variety of style, so lacking in some guidebooks. The final product is absolutely splendid.

Good routes are described on every Corbett, and in addition 62 other outstanding hills have been selected from all over Scotland and its islands, many of them in remote and little visited places. This book will lead to many pleasant surprises.

Errors in the text are minimal and insignificant. The hill on p216 is north-east (not north-west) of Loch More, and this is obvious on the route map. All Jim Renny's route maps throughout the book are as excellent as ever. In the Index on p250 Mealisval (in the Outer Hebrides) is indeed way out, the reader being directed to p2246 (should be p246 of course).

On Broad Law (p16), the Radar Beacon on the top is so unobtrusive that it is not mentioned, but it is worth noting that there is a road up to it, down which you can walk 4km to the Crook Inn in Tweedsmuir.

Ivan Waller

Scotland Coast to Coast. A long distance walk from Glen Shiel to Arbroath
Hamish Brown
Patrick Stephens, 1990, pp224, pb, £6.99

This book is the result of Hamish Brown's efforts to find a route across Scotland from coast to coast which can be accomplished in a fortnight's walking and which has a place to stay, whether B & B, cottage or hotel, at the end of each day. At the same time, knowing the author, the route had to be through the best scenery available within those parameters. Hamish has crossed Scotland on foot each year for the past 12 years, but he did this particular walk in 1988. His descriptions give a clear guide to the route, with maps and photos, and with alternatives of both route and accommodation (camping sites etc) for those of a hardier disposition.

Adventure Treks. Nepal
Bill O'Connor
Crowood Press, 1990, pp160, pb, £9.95

There is a proliferation of Himalayan trekking books at the moment, but this is a good one, the first in a projected series of 'Adventure Treks'. The author selects 10 itineraries, each one having a map, general description, superb colour photos and delightful drawings, with a summary of details at the end. General trekking information is given in a final chapter. Having watched leeches crawl over my boots in exactly the same spot by the new bridge over the Modi Khola as described by the author, I can vouch for the accuracy of his descriptions!

Dzieje Polskiego Towarzystwa Tatrzanskiego. (The History of the Polish Tatra Association)
Władysław Krygowskì
'Kraj' Kraków, 1988, pp148, pb

The Tatra Association, founded in 1873, spread to having a mountaineering section in 1903. This book traces the history of the Association up to 1950.

Footpaths of Europe: Walking the Pyrenees (GR10)
Trans Bob Hosea, Helen McPhail & Suzanne Davies
Robertson McCarta, 1989, pp222, £9.95

Walking the GR5: a) Lake Geneva to Mont Blanc. Trans Simon Knight
b) **Modane to Larche.** Trans Helen McPhail
Robertson McCarta, 1990, pp a) 190, b) 200, £11.95 each

Three volumes in the *Footpaths of Europe* series, published in conjunction with the *Fédération Française de la Randonnée Pédestre*, with IGN Orange series 1:50,000 maps to all sections of the routes and adequate descriptions. Separate 'blocks' give information on what you may expect to see along the way. A very useful series.

High Summer. Backpacking the Canadian Rockies
Chris Townsend
Oxford Illustrated Press, 1989, pp160, £12.95

This is the story of the author's successful attempt to walk the 2500 km along the spine of the Canadian Rockies in one push, from the US border in the south to the Liard river close to the Alaskan border in the north. For the southern part, Townsend was just another walker, but after Jasper he was virtually on his own, with only the bears and other wild life for unwelcome company, and a few small towns, home to miners, loggers and hunters, where he could provision and recharge his batteries.

On Lower Lakeland Fells. The 50 Best Walks
Bob Allen
Michael Joseph, 1990, pp224, £12.99

This book follows the author's excellent *On High Lakeland Fells* with a selection of walks for less energetic souls, the average height being 1500ft and the walks short and circular. Whilst it is unlikely to appeal so much to *AJ* readers, many of the walks described are little gems, and the whole is illustrated by Bob Allen's excellent photos.

The Himalayan Experience. An Introduction to Trekking & Climbing in the Himalaya
Jonathan Chester
Harrap Columbus, 1990, pp224, pb, £12.95

Yet another book giving a very good general introduction to trekking and climbing in the Himalaya, this one has a couple of extra features – short accounts of individual expeditions by others such as Doug Scott, Greg Child and Warwick Deacock, and the photos. The author is described as being 'Australia's leading adventure photojournalist', so you would expect his photos to be good, and they are superb, helped by the large format. Most people who buy the book will do so, I suspect, because of its illustrations.

The Mountains of Europe
Ed Kev Reynolds
Oxford Illustrated Press, 1990, pp208, £19.95

Kev Reynolds has assembled a team of 13 writers, in addition to himself, to tackle the 19 chapters of this guide to the mountain areas of Europe. Of these 14, half are AC members, and a further five have provided photos – whether that proves anything, readers can judge for themselves! It is certainly a stylish book, with a large page size and good reproduction of excellent photos. The four main mountain areas of Britain are taken first, followed by Norway, and then the main central part of the book is, naturally, on the Alps – eight sections, three by Reynolds himself, two by Douglas Milner, and one each by John Brailsford, Cecil Davies and the late Dudley Stevens. The final grouping is of less popular areas (to British mountaineers anyway), the editor taking the Pyrenees – naturally – and Corsica, and Victor Saunders the Caucasus. The Carpathians, Picos de Europa and Greece are also covered. To cover such a vast amount of ground in 200 pages means that details of each area must of necessity be fairly brief, but the expertise and style of each author is such that the essence of each group of mountains has been well caught. This, added to the factual information given at the end of the book, will whet anyone's appetite for a visit.

Zanskar. A Himalayan Kingdom
Olivier Föllmi
Thames & Hudson, 1989, not paginated, £28

Olivier Föllmi has been to Zanskar each year for the past 10 years, including three winters there. He became completely enchanted with the people of this isolated area on the western border of Ladakh and, as an accomplished photographer, was able to make an extraordinary record of his time there. The resulting coffee-table book of 103 colour photographs is superb. Those of the people are fascinating, but it is the landscape shots with incredible subtleties of light and shade that stick in the memory. A book to dip into again and again.

Classic Walks in the Pyrenees
Kev Reynolds

Classic Walks in the Yorkshire Dales
Walt Unsworth
Both, *Oxford Illustrated Press, 1989, pp144, £16.95 each*

These two volumes are the seventh and eighth in the 'Classic Walks' series. They follow the usual format of very brief technical details of location, etc, of each walk, followed by a detailed description, rudimentary map and a selection of mostly good photos, many in colour. The two are obviously different in content; Unsworth's of mostly shorter walks, although with one or two *tours de force* such as the Three Peaks, over an extended Yorkshire Dales which includes the Howgills, whilst Reynolds includes a number of multi-day tours starting with the Pyrenean Traverse (7–8 weeks!).

The Loneliest Mountain
Lincoln Hall, photos by Jonathan Chester
The Mountaineers in America, Simon & Schuster in Australia, distributed by Cordee. 1989, ppxvi + 232, £19.95

Mount Minto is one of the world's less accessible mountains, situated by the western shore of the Ross Sea in Antarctica, the highest peaks in this coastal range of North Victoria Land. Although three of four peaks in the range had been climbed, Minto had rebuffed four assaults, only one of which had even reached the base of the mountain. Lincoln Hall and Greg Mortimer originally planned their expedition for 1986/87 but, for various reasons, it was early 1988 before they, with nine companions, sailed out of Sydney Harbour in a small boat on a return journey of 2500 miles to Minto. This book tells, in journal form, of their epic voyage, followed by their 150km trek to the mountain and eventual success on the 4000m summit. The story is well told and, with photos by Jonathan Chester, one knows beforehand that the illustrations will be excellent.

Trekking in Pakistan and India
Hugh Swift
Hodder & Stoughton, 1990, ppxviii + 510, pb, £10.95

This book is a vast compendium of information on trekking in the mountains of Northern Pakistan and India, and a companion volume to that on Nepal, West Tibet and Bhutan already published. Originally published by Sierra Books, some of the introductory chapters on trekking are the same as in the other volume, but, provided the information given is good, as here, why not repeat it? Descriptions of country, people and the treks themselves are comprehensive, as are the chapters on medicine, natural history and languages. A book to be recommended.

Camera on the Crags
Alan Hankinson
Silent Books, 1990, pp176, £19.95

Third, enlarged edition of the book of photos by the Abraham Brothers, originally published in 1975. The addition is a 32-page section of alpine photographs which once again show the artistic and technical skill of the brothers, and their perseverance in humping their equipment around. There is an interesting picture of Whymper in Zermatt in the early years of the century, and of George Abraham himself with his guides who accompanied him on an epic ascent of the Matterhorn in 1898. It is somehow surprising to see him looking so young!

The Northwest Highlands
D J Bennet and T Strang
Scottish Mountaineering Trust, 1990, pp342, £17.95

The SMC are continuing their new series of district guides in the same excellent format as the first – the Islands. This one covers everything on the mainland west and north of the Great Glen, quite a tall order, but everything is adequately, if briefly, covered. Each chapter has a general introduction followed by sections on access, public transport and accommodation. Then come separate descriptions of each major mountain with routes, and final notes on Paths and Walks, and Climbing. The illustrations throughout are excellent.

Adventure Treks. Western North America
Chris Townsend
Crowood Press, 1990, pp160, pb, £9.95

First of a new series of trekking books edited by John Cleare, this one features 10 treks from the Californian Sierra Nevada to Mount Robson on the British Columbia–Alberta divide, via Colorado, the Wind River Range, the Cascades, the Selkirks and most other important ranges in between. As the shortest is 85 miles (the longest is 256) over very rugged country, these are demanding treks. Each section is well described with excellent colour photos.

Matterhorn Vision
Brian Bonner
Woodgate Press, 1990, pp86, pb, npq

For many years Brian Bonner had nursed an ambition to climb the Matterhorn, but it was not until 1965 that he decided to put his thoughts into action. It took 15 years. Admitting that he is no mountaineer, he took the only route open to him – hiring a guide and slowly working up to his goal each summer holiday. This book is the story of the partnership between Bonner and Ivo Perren, their attempts on the mountain and final success in 1980. There is a good description of the Hörnli ridge, excellent photos, and useful notes on training walks and climbs, guides' fees and so on. As with many 'private' books of this type, it suffers from a rather too-enthusiastic style and a surfeit of CAPITAL LETTERS!, but, for sheer determination, it is a tale that takes some beating.

The Magnificent Mountain Women. Adventures in the Colorado Rockies
Janet Robertson
University of Nebraska Press, 1990, ppxxiv + 220, 54pp b/w photos, $21.95

The Colorado high country is a wild, enticing area which has long attracted adventurous spirits, but, until now, little has been known of the part women have played in opening up the area. From 1858, when Julie Archibald Holmes, a suffragist, climbed Pikes Peak, to the free-climbed ascent of the Diamond on Long's Peak by Louise Shepherd and Jean Ruwitch in 1980, this book tells their story. It isn't all climbing, though. Included here are the stories of some three dozen women who, in addition to climbing, hiking or skiing, went to act as guides, practise medicine, botanize, paint or set up homesteads. Some were visitors, such as the English tourists Isabella Bird and Rose Pender, whose published exploits were well known. Others, however, were locals, unknown outside the area until this book. A 54-page section of historic photos completes a very readable history.

Mountain Environments
John Gerrard
Belhaven Press, 1990, pp318, £30

The author, who is from the School of Geography at Birmingham University, has written an 'examination of the physical geography of mountains'. Covering geo-ecology, weathering, hydrology, slope form, glaciation and volcanoes, amongst other aspects of mountain formation, it is a very technical book, with a 44-page bibliography for those wishing to take the study further.

Himalayan Enchantment. An Anthology
Frank Kingdon-Ward. Ed John Whitehead
Serindia, 1990, ppxviii + 254, £16.95

Frank Kingdon-Ward excelled as a botanist, explorer and writer, his greatest love being for the area of the Eastern Himalaya where Assam, Tibet, Burma and China meet. He spent almost 50 years undertaking 25 major expeditions, and collected and numbered over 23,000 plants, an incredible achievement. His books have long been sought after, and this present volume is an anthology of his writings taken from 13 travel books and other sources.

Icewalk
Robert Swan
Jonathan Cape, 1990, pp254, £15.99

When Robert Swan reached the South Pole in 1986, as told in the book *In the Footsteps of Scott*, he was already considering plans to become the first man to reach both poles on foot. In March 1989 he set off with an eight-man international team for the 500-mile crossing of the Arctic Sea. It took them two months, and they made it on 14 May. The book gives a graphic description of the hardships of arctic travel, both of the illnesses suffered by the team members and the extreme difficulties of the terrain. Based on the diaries of all the members, it has many excellent colour photos.

Tales of Many Mountains
Norman Croucher
Amanda Press, 1989, pp279, pb

This book, privately published by Norman Croucher, is mainly a compilation from three earlier books – *Shin Kicking Champion* (1971), *High Hopes* (1976) and *A Man and his Mountains* (1984). As such, there is little new material in it, but all three books are now out of print and, apart from telling a marvellous story of incredible achievement, it possibly benefits from the condensing and tightening-up of the material. Early days in this country and the Alps are followed by a number of South American expeditions culminating in the ascent of Aconcagua. Climbs in Kashmir are also described, with finally an ascent of Muztagh Ata, and bits and pieces from Croucher's personal life form a fascinating linking narrative. Copies can be obtained from the author at 8, Woodville Gardens, Ealing, London W5 2LG, price £11 including p+p. (Cheques to be made payable to Norman Croucher.)

Kingdom of the Sun God. A History of the Andes and their People
Ian Cameron
Century, 1990, pp224, £19.99

A coffee-table-sized book telling the story of the Andes through the ages; but, whereas most books of that genre rely on pictures to tell the story, this is solid but very readable text, albeit with a few excellent colour photos and text illustrations thrown in. It is all here, from the pre-Inca civilizations, through the conquistadores, Bolivar and other revolutionaries, to the great naturalists and, finally, the cattle barons, spoilers of the rain forests and tourists of today. A chapter on mountaineers in the Andes deals with the exploits of Whymper, Hiram Bingham, Fitzgerald, de Agostini and Shipton.

Women Climbing. 200 Years of Achievement
Bill Birkett and Bill Peascod
A & C Black, 1989, pp192, pb, £12.95

Bill Birkett and the late Bill Peascod took on a difficult task when they decided to write a history of women climbing, knowing that they might get criticism from all sides. In the event, they haven't done a bad job, although the end result makes for a rather patchy and irritating read. Their method is to choose one particular climber from a period, write about her in some detail, but insert other paragraphs on 'lesser' climbers active at the same time. In the Miriam O'Brien chapter, therefore, you also get short items on Pat Kelly and the Pinnacle Club, Dorothy Pilley and Dorothy Thompson. Thirteen 'major' climbers are featured, starting with Lucy Walker and finishing with Louise Shepherd, and each is dealt with fairly thoroughly. A book of this type obviously requires a vast amount of research, but it is a pity that numerous small errors have been allowed to creep in – the first ascent of the Matterhorn is stated to have been in 1868, for instance, and Jill Lawrence was born in both 1950 and 1959!

L'Oberland Bernois à Skis
Daniel Anker & Hans Grossen
Denoël, 1990, pp240, npq

This, the latest – and 26th – in the *100 Plus Belles* . . . series from Denoël gives, as you might expect, 100 ski runs and descents in the Bernese Oberland. Produced to the usual high standard, each alternate double page is in colour, with good illustrations and either map or diagram as appropriate.

Classic Rock Climbs in Northern England
Bill Birkett
Oxford Illustrated Press, 1990, pp128, £16.95

This is the third in the 'Classic Rock Climbs' series, all, incidentally, written by Bill Birkett. The format is as before, and the area covered is the North Yorks Moors, Lancashire, the Peak District, Yorkshire, Cumbria and Northumberland. Obviously, with such a wealth of climbing, the author has to be very selective, but there is something here for everyone, including a few 'lesser-knowns' for non-locals.

Bhutan and the British
Peter Collister
Serindia Publications/Belitha Press, 1987, ppxiv + 210, npq

This is the story of Anglo–Bhutanese relations over the past 200 years or so, particularly the part played by the official missions which started in 1774. The East India Company were naturally the first to be involved, seeking their ubiquitous trade routes, and relations went from good in the early days to bad (the war of 1864–5), and finally back to good again, when Britain is again helping Bhutan with education and in other ways. There is no mountaineering as such in this book, but it includes a wonderful set of photographs taken in 1905–08 by John Claude White and some drawings by Julian Burton.

Dolbadarn. Studies on a Theme
Ed Paul Joyner
The National Library of Wales, 1990, ppxxviii + 100 + 16 colour plates

John Ruskin e le Alpi
Museo Nazionale della Montagna 'Duca degli Abruzzi'. Monograph No 74, 1990, pp74

Two slightly similar studies on themes of painters in mountain locations, the first being issued to complement an exhibition, 'Castell Dolbadarn Castle', organized by the National Library of Wales in 1990. Six authors cover the various ways in which artists have portrayed this famous landmark between Llynau Peris and Padarn, our own member Peter Bicknell giving a comparison between picturesque treatments of this castle and similar paintings in the Lake District. The second volume is a catalogue of the exhibition 'John Ruskin e le Alpi', and forms the latest in the long list of alpine publications issued by the museum. Both books are beautifully illustrated.

A Lakeland Mountain Diary
A Harry Griffin
Crowood Press, 1990, pp224, £14.95

For 40 years, Harry Griffin has been writing his Lake District 'Country Diary' for *The Guardian* every other Monday, and this is the second published collection, covering the last 15 years. The extracts, each of some 250–300 words, are arranged in order of the months of the year, giving an overall picture of the Lakes at all seasons, in the author's polished prose. Little footnotes bring some entries up to date, and the final entry is a rather poignant one, recording the move, at 80, from his fellside home to a town flat in Kendal. Whiteside Pike and others can still be seen, however, over the rooftops!

Everest (2nd edition)
Walt Unsworth
Oxford Illustrated Press, 1990, ppxvi + 704, £19.95

In his review of the first edition of this book, Peter Lloyd said that he regarded it 'as a notable achievement', being the outcome of four years' work. The work goes on. Some 130 additional pages have been added to bring the story up to 1988–89, the major part of the book being a straight reprint of the earlier edition. You cannot, however, buy the later chapters as a supplement, but have to pay nearly £20 for the whole thing and throw your previous copy away! However, the new edition is well worth it for it contains, in addition to the story of the later expeditions, no fewer than 145 pages of Appendices, Bibliography and Notes & References. These include further information on the original chapters, summaries of all expeditions, route diagrams, lists of first ascents, fatalities and so on, plus a very detailed bibliography. A notable achievement indeed.

Himalayan Trekking Maps
Air-India (Obtainable from Robertson McCarta,
122 Kings Cross Road, London WC1X 9DS. £30 + £3 p+p)

Air-India engaged a cartographer to produce a portfolio of trekking maps for
the Himalaya, with the co-operation of the Surveyor General of India and the
Indian Department of Tourism and Ministry of Defence. There are 30 three-
colour maps in a 19″ × 14″ format covering the Indian, Nepalese and Bhutanese
Himalaya to varying scales, and with main trekking routes clearly marked.

Dal Cervino al Monte Rosa
Photos: Davide Camisasca; Text: Luciano Caveri
Pheljna Aosta, 1990, not paginated, limited edition, npq

The description 'coffee-table-book' doesn't really do justice to this volume,
which is a really sumptuous production. It consists of 40 colour plates, all
superb photographs superbly reproduced, of the Matterhorn–Monte Rosa
region,varying from wide mountain shots to atmospheric views of villages and
'still-lifes'. A truly beautiful book, but, as with many of these specialist limited
edition works, one wonders who will buy it – too big as it is to fit on a normal
shelf and, in its accompanying box, too heavy to carry around.

Geology of Nepal Himalaya and Adjacent Countries
Chandra K Sharma
Sangeeta Sharma, Kathmandu, 1990, ppx + 482, npq

Dr Sharma is a well-known Nepalese scientist, currently working in the Water
and Energy Commission Secretariat of the Nepalese Government. This, his
tenth book, is a detailed geology of the Nepal Himalaya, crammed with tables,
maps and figures, and including a 25-page bibliography. All geological aspects
are covered and, whilst it is not possible to give a detailed review here, anyone
interested in researching the geology of a particular area will find this book
particularly useful.

Les Grandes Heures des Alpes
Max Chamson
Perrin, Paris, 1990, pp480, npq

M Chamson has written a number of books on mountains and travel, and this
current volume is really a general history of the Alps from the earliest days. It
includes some slightly unusual chapters, such as one on Hitler and the Alps and
'The last hours of Mussolini', but, needless to say, most chapters concern de
Saussure, Whymper, Bonatti *et al.*

The following guides and other books have also been received:

First Aid on Mountains. Basic Treatment for climbers, hill walkers and those on expeditions. Steve Bollen. BMC, 1989, pp41, £0.95

More Scrambles in the Lake District. R Brian Evans. Cicerone Press, 1990, pp192, £8.95

Rock Climbing in Scotland, a selected guide. Kevin Howett. Constable, 1990, pp14 + 468, £9.95

Rock Climbing in Snowdonia. Paul Williams. Constable, 1990, ppxxxvi + 460, £9.95

Eastern Baltoro Mostagh. 1 & 2. Jan Kiełkowski. Przewodnik Alpinistyczny, Düsseldorf, 1989/1990, pp48, pb, in Polish. (Mainly Broad Peak.)

The Atlas Mountains. A Walker's Guide. Karl Smith. Cicerone Press, 1989, pp127, £9.95

Gogarth. Various authors. Climbers' Club, 1990, pp304, £10.95

Tremadog and Cwm Silyn. Mark Pretty, Dave Farrant and Geoff Milburn. Climbers' Club, 1989, pp328, £10.95

Rock Climbing in Northern England. Bill Birkett and John White. Constable, 1990, pp444, £9.95

The Mountains of England and Wales. Volume I, Wales. John & Anne Nuttall. Cicerone Press, 1989, pp256, £8.95

Fair Head. Ed Clare and Calvin Torrans. FMCI, 1989, pp192

Atxarte. Escuela de Escalada. Jose Zuazua. Vitoria–Gasteiz, Bilbao, 1989, pp208 (Topo guide to the Atxarte region, in Basque and Spanish.)

Fifty Best Hill Walks of Britain. John Cleare. Webb & Bower, 1990, pp208, pb, £9.99 (Paperback edition of the book published last year.)

The Hillwalker's Handbook. Steve Ashton. Crowood Press, 1990, pp160, pb, £9.95 (Paperback edition of the 1987 hardback.)

The Walker's Handbook. Hugh Westacott. Oxford Illustrated Press, 1989, pp316, £12.95 (Third, hardback edition of the book originally published by Penguin in 1979.)

Mountain Photography. David Higgs. The Mountaineers (in USA), Diadem, 1990, pp10 + 110, pb, £9.95 (New edition of the book first published by Longman in 1983.)

The Pyrenean Trail GR10. Alan Castle. Cicerone Press, 1990, pp176, £6.95

Randonnées Pédestres dans le Pays du Verdon. J Alor, C Catrisse, A Lucchesi. Édisud, 1990, pp184, npq

Climbing Terms and Techniques. Ken Crocket. Patrick Stephens, 1990, pp160, £12.99

Welsh Winter Climbs. Malcolm Campbell and Andy Newton. Cicerone Press, 1990, pp248, £11.95

Best Walks in Southern Wales. Richard Sale. Constable, 1990, pp288, £8.95.

Snow and Ice Climbing. John Barry. Crowood Press, 1990, pp144, £9.95. (pb, 2nd edition.)

Tour of the Queyras. A Circular Walk in the French Alps. Alan Castle. Cicerone Press, 1990, pp152, £5.95

Les Calanques de Marseille. CAF Editions Jeanne Laffitte, 1990, pp64, 50F

Costa Blanca Climbs, including Majorca. An Introductory Guide. Chris Craggs, Cicerone Press, 1990, pp128, £6.95

French Rock Climbs. Martin Atkinson. Cordee, 1990, pp144, £7.95

Kinder and Bleaklow. Ed Geoff Milburn. BMC, 1990, pp416, £11.25

Alpine Pass Route. Switzerland. Kev Reynolds. Cicerone Press, 1990, pp168, £6.95

Borrowdale. R J Kenyon. F+RCC, 1990, pp324

100 Classic Climbs. Yorkshire and the Peak District. Gritstone. Steve Ashton. Crowood Press, 1990, pp272, £10.95

Long Distance Paths. South East England. Alan Castle. A & C Black, 1990, pp160, pb, £9.95

Exploring Idaho's Mountains. A Guide for Climbers, Scramblers & Hikers. Tom Lopez. The Mountaineers, 1990, pp288, pb, $16.95

Monte Rosa & Mischabel. Gino Buscaini. CAI/TCI, 1991, pp688

Alpi Marittime. Euro Montagna, Lorenzo Montaldo & Francesco Salesi. CAI/TCI
Vol I – From Colle di Tenda to Colle Ghiliè, 1984, pp476
Vol II – From Colle Ghiliè to Colle della Maddalena, 1990, pp664, L56,000

In Memoriam

COMPILED BY GEOFFREY TEMPLEMAN

The Alpine Club Obituary		Year of Election
Sir Douglas Laird Busk		1927 (Hon 1976)
Phyllis B Munday	Hon LAC	1937
Paul Bauer		1933 & 1953
Stephen David Padfield		1976
Guy Dufour		1968
The Very Rev Harold Claude Noel Williams		1958
Robert Carmichael Stuart Low		1983
Dennis Kemp	ACG	1953, 1967
Esme M Speakman	LAC	1946
Francis Hugh Keenlyside		1948
Countess Dorothea Gravina	LAC	1955
Thomas Fitzherbert Latham (d 1987)		1955
Johannes Adolf Noordyk		1974
William J March		1987
William David Brown		1949
Maurice Bennett		1959
Richard Ayrton		1956
Irene Poole	LAC	1931
Leslie Ashcroft Ellwood (d 1988)		1923

The tribute to J Monroe Thorington, who died in 1989, was received anonymously from America; I am pleased to be able to print it here.

J Monroe Thorington 1894–1989

Dr Thorington was born at Philadelphia in 1894. His grandfather, who joined a fur company out of St Louis in 1837 and spent two years on the Western Plains, became US Senator for Iowa, and was American Consul on the Isthmus of Panama during the French administration. His father, James Thorington, served as surgeon of the Panama Railroad during this period before coming to Philadelphia.

The subject of this memoir graduated from Princeton in 1915, received his MD from the University of Pennsylvania in 1919 and, after residency at the Presbyterian Hospital, began the practice of ophthalmology. During 1917 he worked at the American Ambulance Hospital, Neuilly-sur-Seine, and then for six years he was Instructor in Ophthalmology at the University of Pennsylvania and became Associate Ophthalmologist at the Presbyterian Hospital.

Two summers of his youth, spent in the Bavarian Highlands, aroused his interest in mountaineering, a sport which dominated his vocational life. 15 seasons were spent in the Canadian North-West, during which he explored much of the Alberta–British Columbia watershed between Mt Assiniboine and Mt Robson, making about 50 first ascents, including Mt Barnard, Mt Lyell, Mt Saskatchewan and North Twin, the latter the highest summit entirely in Alberta. He also visited the Interior Ranges of British Columbia, with five seasons in the Purcell Range, many names of peaks suggested by him being accepted by the Geographic Board of Canada. He was the author of *The Glittering Mountains of Canada* (1925), *The Purcell Range of British Columbia* (1946), and the translator and editor of *Where the Clouds Can Go* (1935). He also wrote the standard guidebooks on climbing in the Rockies of Canada and the Interior Ranges of British Columbia, both of which went through several editions.

He climbed and travelled in the Alps as well, and was familiar with the major groups between the Dauphiné and the Grossglockner. He wrote *Mont Blanc Sideshow* (1932) and *A Survey of Early American Ascents in the Alps* (1943). A list of his historical and other papers issued in 1967 contained more than 275 titles. He had also made ascents in the English Lake District, Norway, Swedish Lapland and Sicily.

Dr Thorington was a member of the German–Austrian Alpine Club (1910), the Swiss Alpine Club and Mazamas (1914), the *Club Alpin Français* and the American Alpine Club (1918) and the Alpine Club of Canada (1919). He was chairman of the NY section of the latter (1930–32), and became an honorary member in 1949. He served as editor of the *American Alpine Journal*, 1934–46, as president of the American Alpine Club, 1941–43, and became an honorary member in 1949. He was elected to the Alpine Club in 1927, and was made an honorary member in 1946. He was one of a small group of Americans who flew to London in November 1957 to attend the AC centenary. He was also an honorary member of the Alpine Ski Club and the Appalachian Mountain Club. He was a Fellow of the Royal Geographical Society, a member of the Wilderness Club (Philadelphia), the Explorers Club (NY) and edited the Bulletin of the Geographical Society of Philadelphia (1922–31). He was also an Hon Trustee of the International Folk Art Foundation, Santa Fe, New Mexico.

In Canada and the Alps he climbed with many members of the American Alpine Club, and his topographical knowledge enabled him to bring his parties to desirable areas, a number of ascents being made without guides. A peak in the Purcell Range officially bears his name.

In 1925 he married Christine Rehn of Philadelphia, who accompanied him on travels which included Central and South America, North Africa and the Near East.

Sir Douglas Busk KCMG 1906–1990

Douglas Laird Busk was born on 15 July 1906 and died at Chilbolton on 11

December 1990. He went to Eton and New College, Oxford, and spent a period in the USA as Davison scholar at Princeton.

He joined the diplomatic service in 1929 and gained wide experience in Iran, Hungary, South Africa, Japan, Turkey and Iraq before succeeding to ambassadorial posts in Ethiopia, Finland, where he was knighted, and Venezuela.

Although a fluent writer and stickler for the proper use of the English language and generally a master of his field, as wittily recorded in two of his later books, *The Curse of Tongues and Some Remedies* (1965) and *The Craft of Diplomacy* (1967), he would not wish to be remembered solely for a long and distinguished diplomatic career. He was at his best in posts where his natural bent for travel, exploration and mountaineering could usefully be combined with the job. In Iran he climbed Demavend and explored the Throne of Solomon range. Memories of his early climbs and travels in the Pyrenees, the Alps, the Rockies, South Africa's Table Mountain and the Drakensberg are captured in *The Delectable Mountains* (1946).

Those who served with him in Ethiopia will not forget his meticulous organization of safaris to all parts, his collection of topographical information on a countryside then still inadequately mapped and his encouragement of his staff to do the same. More than that, in 1953 he travelled by road from Addis Ababa to the Mountains of the Moon in Ruwenzori and, with Arthur Firmin, climbed two hitherto unidentified peaks on the S ridge of Mount Stanley. They dutifully submitted to Her Majesty that these might be called Elizabeth and Philip, linked by the Coronation glacier. This proposal was approved, and these names now appear on official maps. These East African travels are recorded in Busk's delightful book *The Fountain of the Sun* (1957), with outstanding photographs (and charming line drawings by his wife Bridget).

On his last ambassadorial appointment, in Venezuela in the early 1960s, he lost no time in organizing regular visits with groups of like-minded friends to the attractive Andean city of Mérida and its surrounding mountains. From a camp beside the Timoncito glacier, first ascents were made of the rock spire of El Vertigo and the SW face of El Abanico. After the day's climb, paper-thin slices of Swiss Bündnerfleisch – imported in the diplomatic bag – were welcome supplements to the evening ration of Johnny Walker.

On another occasion Mérida University students were introduced to ice-climbing techniques and the use of crampons. Then, in 1963, he was able to divert Eric Shipton, who was *en route* to Patagonia, and mastermind a rare winter weekend ascent of the 5000m Pico Bolivar with a team of expatriate petroleum engineers from the oilfields beside Lake Maracaibo. To his great delight, the citizens of Mérida recognized his enthusiasm for the place and its people by honouring him with the freedom of the city.

Returning to Britain, he devoted much of his time and personal generosity to the Royal Geographical Society and to the Alpine Club. The Society made him an Honorary Vice President. Through the Margaret Busk Fund, grants helped young people on expeditions. The Busk Medal, which he initiated in 1975, is awarded annually for 'geographic field work and conservation research'. He was nominated by the Society and was an energetic

Chairman of the Mount Everest Foundation which was set up jointly by the Society and the Alpine Club after the first ascent of Everest in 1953 to assist British and New Zealand expeditions to the mountainous regions of the world. Although it mostly assists small expeditions, the MEF has also supported some major ascents such as Kangchenjunga and Annapurna S face, for which he chaired the managing committee.

Busk was elected to the Alpine Club in 1927 while still an undergraduate, became Vice President in 1965 and an Honorary Member in 1976. His application for membership included a first winter ascent of the N face of the Pic du Midi d'Ossau in the Pyrenees. He also became a member of the exclusive French *Groupe de Haute Montagne*.

His greatest contribution was to the unique Alpine Club Library where he succeeded Lord Tangley as Chairman, after it had been set up as an educational charity. Under his direction, and also through his personal generosity, funds were raised and a magnificent 600-page catalogue published, the first since 1899. Its publication in 1981 was marked by an exhibition, *The Treasures of the Alpine Club*, displaying texts of early ascents and travels from the 16th to 19th centuries and sketches and paintings by the likes of Whymper and Ruskin.

As early as the 1920s he was experimenting with infra-red photography in the Pyrenees, and in the 1960s he was conducting comparative tests of stoves in the high Andes of Venezuela. Wherever he climbed and travelled, he brought a warm-hearted, versatile and continually enquiring mind. He developed a close friendship with the Argentière guide Armand Charlet, with whom he climbed in the Mont Blanc massif and of whom he wrote the sympathetic *Portrait d'un Guide* (1975). Busk's epitaph might be his comment on a happy climb with Charlet on the Charmoz: 'We lived as only the gods can do, and my mood was such that I would not have bartered all the peaks in Christendom for one of those precious minutes.'

He married in 1937 Bridget Hemsley Thompson, a partnership which lasted for 53 happy years, and is survived by her and two daughters.

George Band and Edward Peck

Peter Lloyd writes:

I would like, if I may, to add a short personal note on Douglas Busk, for my memories go back even further than Ted Peck's, to family holidays in the Alps, and it was with him that I had my first proper 'season'. This was in 1925 and it was mountaineering strictly in the old tradition for we engaged Heinrich Burgener, son of the great Alexander, whom we had got to know the previous year when Neddy Eaton, then Hon Sec of the Club, took us with him on climbs in the Lötschental. Burgener was twice our age, a heavily built powerful man, and with him there could be no question of sharing the lead or forming a balanced partnership. Neither of us climbed that way again, for while I turned to guideless climbing, Douglas developed his long and felicitous partnership with Armand Charlet, facilitated by the house in the Chamonix valley owned by his aunts, *les demoiselles des Praz*.

Douglas was very much a member of the Establishment so it was curious that when, on his retirement from the chairmanship of the Library Committee during Emlyn Jones's presidency, some of his friends gave a dinner for him, the talk centred largely on his role as a rebel protesting at the domination of the Club by the older generation as typified by the members of the Alpine Dining Club. The rebels' banded together in the late 1930s to form 'The Young Shavers', dining together at a Mayfair pub before AC meetings, while the ADC was meeting at the Reform or another Pall Mall club.

Douglas and I never climbed together after these early days and our paths did not cross again till the 1970s and 1980s, the time of his great work for the Library and the MEF. Few men have done as much in their labours and their benefactions for the AC and for mountain exploration. But some of us will also remember and mourn him as a loyal friend, a man of the highest standards and an entertaining companion.

Phyllis B. Munday 1894–1990

Phyllis Munday, who was elected an Honorary Member of the American Alpine Club in 1967, died on 11 April 1990. Born in Ceylon in 1894, she spent most of her life in Canada. An active member of the Alpine Club of Canada, which she joined in 1921, she and her husband, Don, made numerous first ascents in the Coast Mountains of British Columbia. Among these was Mount Munday (later so named for the Mundays) in 1928. The Mundays are probably best known for their pioneer exploration of Mount Waddington (Mystery Mountain) and the Waddington area, later described in Don Munday's *The Unknown Mountain*. Phyllis Munday's article, 'First Ascent of Mt Robson by Lady Members', appeared in the 1924 *Canadian Alpine Journal*. She also wrote for the Ladies' Alpine Club, of which she was elected an Honorary Member in 1937. 'Mount Queen Bess' was published in the 1944 *LAC Yearbook* and 'Mount Reliance: A Letter from Canada' in 1948.

Although she did not climb actively in later years, Phyllis Munday continued her involvement with the Alpine Club of Canada, most notably as editor of its *Journal*, from 1953 to 1969. She also served on the Climbing Committee and, later, received all the club's honours, serving as Honorary President since 1972. She is survived by a daughter, Edith Wickham.

(*Courtesy American Alpine Club*)

Paul Bauer 1896–1990

Paul Bauer is dead. The great Himalaya-Bauer is no longer with us. In 1987 I had the good fortune to become personally acquainted with him, as a guest in his house on the edge of Munich, when he was made an Honorary Member of the Austrian Alpine Club. Otherwise I would have said: 'What, was he still alive?' Somehow, ever since I started climbing, his name has had for me the aura of something 'big'. Paul Bauer was then already a relic from that heroic period of discovery, when the Himalaya were still *terra incognita* and not yet the target for treks by all and sundry. That makes it difficult to realize that this man was also our own contemporary!

After a 93rd birthday celebrated in good spirits, and a short illness from which he appeared to have nearly recovered, Paul Bauer died peacefully on 9 January 1990 in Munich, in the circle of his family. This marked the departure from the scene of the Nestor and the last of the great German Himalaya pioneers.

Already in 1919, when he returned from captivity after the end of the First World War, Bauer was filled with the burning desire to venture into the mountains of the world and to open access to the high peaks of Asia for German mountaineers. In 1928 the Caucasus was for Paul Bauer the first attainable goal of this kind, just as it was for me 30 years later. Our tracks, though greatly separated in time, met on the NE ridge of Shkara. The Caucasus was his springboard for the Himalaya.

In 1929 and 1931 Paul Bauer led the two expeditions to Kangchenjunga which after heroic battles and difficult ice climbing reached heights of 7400m and 7700m on the NE spur (Camp XI, 7360m).

In 1932, at the Los Angeles Olympic Games, Bauer received the Gold Medal of the literary competition for his book *Um den Kantsch*. In 1936 a small expedition to Sikkim led by him made the first ascent of Siniolchu (6879m). In 1937 he led the recovery expedition to Nanga Parbat which dug out the seven mountaineers and nine Sherpas who had been buried by a huge ice avalanche in Camp IV, and in 1938 he was again active on Nanga Parbat as leader of an expedition.

The list of the names of his companions reads like a *Who's Who* of the leading German–Austrian mountaineers of that time: among them Eugen Allwein, Peter Aufschneiter, Fritz Bechtold, Adolf Göttner, Hans Hartmann, Karl Kraus, Hermann Schaller, Hias Rebitsch, Ludwig Schmaderer and Carlo Wien. Although the time was not yet ripe for an 8000m summit, the experience gained by these expeditions formed the basis for the successes of the 'decade of the 8000ers' which started in 1950.

It would go far beyond the scope of an obituary to give the details of these Bauer expeditions; they can be found in his four books. His Himalayan expeditions are described together in the book *Paul Bauer* which was produced by our member [of the Austrian Alpine Club] Gerhard Klamert and the German Himalaya Foundation on the occasion of the 90th birthday of the great man. Paul Bauer had in fact been, in 1936, one of the founding members of the Foundation.

In the Second World War Bauer was for much of the time Director of the Army Mountain Training School in Fulpmes, and in between he served as a major in the fighting in the central and western Caucasus.

Paul Bauer, a notary by profession, had been a member of the Austrian Alpine Club since 1929, his final membership number being 19. On 12 February 1987 he was made an Honorary Member of the club. The same distinction was bestowed on him also by the AAVM Munich, his section of the DAV and the mountaineering club GORSKI of Warsaw. In England he was received by members of the royal family, and he nearly became vice-president of the Alpine Club, so steeped in tradition. All this underlines the international stature of the deceased. Together with his family, the Austrian Alpine Club and many mountaineers everywhere mourn the departure of a great pioneer of the Himalaya and an outstanding man.

Erich Vanis

(We thank Peter Rieder for permission to publish this translation of an obituary in the *Österreichische Alpenzeitung*, March/April 1990, and Norman Dyhrenfurth for his assistance in the matter.)

Robert Carmichael Stuart Low 1912–1990

Michael was my closest friend and climbing companion for nearly 60 years. We had both climbed one or two basic alpine peaks in 1925–6, he being introduced by his father who had made the second or third ascent of Mt Cook in New Zealand and had a wide acquaintance of the well-known figures of that era such as Norman Collie, Harold Porter, Claude Elliott and Frank Smythe.

He introduced me to rock-climbing in what might be described as the Abraham era, but above all it was his native Scotland that he loved. We had many trips to the wilder parts of the Highlands and Islands, usually by boat and often with OUMC companions like David Cox and Elliott Viney.

We celebrated our last summer of freedom in 1934 in the Lofoten Islands before being incarcerated in our jobs. I made some original routes like the traverse of Trakta in Øst Vågoy and the first British ascent of Stetind on the adjoining mainland (not to mention that of the Svolvaer Gjeita).

But thereafter, incarcerated was the word; for engineers who actually produced things, unlike their so-called professional colleagues, were limited to two weeks annual holiday and one Saturday off per month. With no air travel to speak of, mountaineering outside Europe was not on and even reaching the Alps left little enough time for climbing.

I remember one such fortnight just before the war stopped play, when we made the Dolomites in 26 hours non-stop, three up, in a Morris 8. We were nearly arrested on the Brenner as we crept under a hedge of sunset Nazi salutes and Fascist clenched fists. Enjoyable climbing though – Langkofel Nordwand, Fünffingerspitze by the Schmitt Kamin and the Adang Kamin on the Rotspitze.

Michael had a distinguished war; special operations in Singapore, evacuated just in time with a wound; then N Africa and Italy where the same leg was hit again under Monte Cassino and where he was awarded an MC.

After demob he returned to British Rail and, following several management assignments, ended up as Engineering Director. As a second career after retirement, he virtually created what is probably the most successful UK naturalist trust, BBONT.

As holidays became more reasonable he always spent them in the hills, whether in the Bernese Oberland, Austria, the Jotunheimen, Corsica, Canada or Switzerland. Later on he managed some seven trekking expeditions to the Himalaya and an abortive attempt on Chuli East.

Always remaining fit since his days as an Oxford rugger blue, he celebrated his 70th birthday by ascending Galdhøpiggen in two-thirds of guidebook time, and I don't think his 1930 ascent and descent of Glamaig from

Sligachan after Sunday lunch was ever equalled by anyone other than one of General Bruce's Sherpas.

An all-round mountaineer more attracted by the mountains themselves and their wild life than by difficult routes to their summits, great fun to be with – I sometimes felt in his presence that I had postponed my maturity for 75 years!

Alan Pullinger

Esme Speakman d 1990

Esme's first alpine climbing season was in 1934 and from that date until the 1960s and later she was in the Alps or further afield almost every year, apart from the war years, and there were not many months in the year when she was not climbing in Britain.

She climbed most of the big peaks in the Alps and records first ascents on the Grand Cornier, and on peaks in Turkey, Greenland and Glencoe. She climbed El Teide in Teneriffe, Adam's Peak in Ceylon, in the Tatra, the Andes, Iceland, and the Himalaya. There cannot be much doubt about her devotion to mountains and to adventurous travel. One of her last adventures, a camel trek in Algeria, was in 1988.

Esme was a fine photographer, professionally trained, and had an impressive collection of slides of her travels, which made good lectures.

Her usual unruffled calm could be disturbed. I remember witnessing a wrangle at the shop in Moscow airport over the price of caviar, conducted in broken English and Polish. This became so heated that I began to think that Esme might be led away in handcuffs.

As with another well-known member of the Ladies' Alpine Club, Una Cameron, it is difficult to think of Esme without an accompanying cat – though obviously not in the Alps. On my first holiday with her in her caravan in Scotland, I remember chasing an indignant cat among the car wheels just moving in a long queue towards one of the many West Highland ferries. Her cats were as characterful as she was.

Scotland will be a sadder and duller place without Esme's elegance, wit, distinctive personality and generous and imaginative hospitality.

Margaret Darvall

Francis Hugh Keenlyside 1911–1990

Francis Keenlyside was an undergraduate of Trinity College, Oxford, during the 1930s, but he was never a prominent member of the OUMC – if, indeed, he ever belonged to it. His Alpine Club proposal form reveals a walking holiday in the Alps (and also an ascent of the Great Pyramid) in 1938, two or three small guided climbs in 1939, and two good seasons immediately after the Second World War. The first of these (1946) was guideless, with John Barford, Michael Ward and Peter Knock in the Dolomites, and the second (partly with a guide) in the Valais. He was elected to the Club in 1948. Incidentally, in the following year he was a member of a large guided party which spent 30 hours on a dramatic traverse of the Täschhorn, by the Teufelsgrat, with descent direct to

Randa, in storm conditions and with one of the party badly injured by stonefall. He described this expedition in an article in the *Climbers' Club Journal* 1949, entitled 'A Minor Memory of the Mischabel'.

During the war years he was able to climb a good deal in both the Lake District and North Wales. With strict petrol rationing in force, this must have meant facing many long blacked-out train journeys for the sake of, perhaps, only 48 hours in the mountains.

At Oxford Francis took a First Class degree in Philosophy, Politics and Economics, which reflected the fact that he was a man of notable intellectual, as well as practical, ability. When the war broke out he was earmarked for planning work in one of the Whitehall departments and was therefore never in uniform. Afterwards he became Managing Director of the Union Castle Shipping Line for a number of years, but in the early 1960s he decided to set up a business of his own in Rhodesia. From there he made trips to England only three or four times a year; and when he eventually retired, and came back to Europe permanently, he went to live in Andorra. Consequently he had not been a familiar figure at AC occasions for a good many years. He continued, though, to be greatly interested in AC affairs, and in 1988 at the time of the survey of members' views on the question of the future location of the Club premises he wrote a masterly letter advocating the importance of the Club's remaining in London.

He was a man of scholarly, even rather austere, appearance, and an entertaining and witty companion, although it might be true to say that he did not always suffer fools gladly. The very diversity of his abilities may have prevented him from achieving his full potential. In the end he became a businessman, but he was equally suited to being either an academic or a top civil servant.

In his early days he was very much a Climbers' Club man; he was Hon Secretary of that Club from 1946 to 1949, and he edited the *Climbers' Club Journal* from 1950 until 1954. It was in that year that he took over the editorship of the *AJ* from T Graham Brown, and he edited two issues of the journal per year until his departure abroad in 1962.

The journals which he produced may seem old-fashioned now, and certainly they contrast strongly with today's magnificent single annual volume (which has the advantage of being commercially published). Even as early as 1969, with the publication of Alan Blackshaw's first one-volume number, they began to look antiquated. But Keenlyside's period as editor was a significant one. Since the Second World War, British mountaineering in the Alps had moved into a different, more modern world – one which demanded the acceptance of artificial techniques and a reappraisal of what were, and what were not, legitimate mountaineering objectives. And the point in brief is that it was under Keenlyside that the *AJ* began to reflect these modern attitudes and positively to welcome them. In lesser matters, too, such as format and presentation, he gave the journal a more up-to-date image. Hitherto, the list of contents of each issue had appeared on the outside of the front cover; he altered this. He dropped (as being no longer true) the phrase 'by members of the Alpine Club' which used to follow the sub-title 'A Record of Mountain Adventure and

Scientific Observation'. He also introduced a hard green cover for those who preferred it.

The most notable, as well as the most sumptuous, of Keenlyside's journals was, of course, the Centenary number (November 1957), which incidentally included a series of seven articles, all by eminent members, of the detailed history of the Club from the beginning. Naturally, the following number (May 1958) is largely devoted to reporting the various celebrations, including the special reception in the Great Hall of Lincoln's Inn, which was a royal occasion. Among various photographs of this historic event, it is highly appropriate that (between pp86 and 87) there should be a striking photograph of Francis himself, presenting a copy of the Centenary number to HM the Queen.

David Cox

Ian McMorrin writes:

I first met Francis Keenlyside in 1970 in what was then Rhodesia. He was living with his second wife, Joan, and their adopted daughter, Simonetta, in a house set amongst red- and brown-leaved Msasa trees with lovely views towards bare granite hills. I remember the house being filled with bright African sunlight and the music of Mozart. At the time Francis was Managing Director of an export company and, perhaps more interestingly, dabbling in liberal politics. He was giving economic advice to, and contesting a seat for, a newly-formed Centre Party which, under the leadership of Pat Bashford, a tobacco farmer, was struggling to give a voice to those people (mostly white) who could see where the politics of Ian Smith was taking the country. As he almost certainly expected, the 1970 General Election proved disastrous for his party. It was also disastrous for Francis. He became ill and, probably as a direct result of his having broken ranks with the white business community, felt it necessary to leave the country. He spent a brief period in Johannesburg before returning in 1972 to live with Joan and Simonetta in West Herefordshire. It was here that Francis wrote *Peaks and Pioneers*, a sympathetic and finely perceptive history of mountaineering. Five years later the family emigrated once again, this time to Andorra where Francis lived for the remainder of his life. Essentially an intellectual, even an ascetic, Francis seemed happiest with his books and music, or teaching French to Simonetta. His love and enjoyment of mountains were similarly intellectual, and I remember him once saying, not long before his departure for Andorra, that mountains were important to him primarily because, in some way, their outlines defined his existence.

Dorothea, Countess Gravina d 1990

Ivor Richards's lines about the earlier Dorothea give an idea of the qualities they shared – unquenchable enjoyment of mountains and adventurous travel and refusal to be defeated by age:

> The glacier our unmade bed
> I hear you through your yawn:

'Leaping crevasses in the dark
That's how to live' you said.

And:

We have them in our bones:
Ten thousand miles of stones.

Her climbing started at four years old, on the roof of her home in Yorkshire. In the 1920s she travelled in South and East Africa and climbed Kilimanjaro, possibly the first ascent by a woman. From 1934 to 1939 she lived in the Italian Tyrol and climbed and ski'd in the Alps, ski mountaineering with her uncle Binnie, a founder member of the Alpine Ski Club, and with her husband, also a very competent skier.

At 50, in 1955, she joined a beginner's course in rock-climbing with Gwen Moffat, who found her the oldest and keenest of the group, and probably the most competent. She joined the Ladies' Alpine Club that year and the Pinnacle Club the next. From that time she climbed and travelled compulsively. In 1956 she climbed in the Alps and Britain and did several guideless ascents with her son Chris, including the Matterhorn and Monte Rosa.

In 1959 she joined the Women's International Cho Oyu Expedition and took over the leadership after the leader, Claude Kogan, Claudine Van der Straten and two Sherpas had died in avalanches. She climbed to 7300m on the rescue attempt.

In 1962 she led the Pinnacle Club Jagdula Expedition to West Nepal, which climbed Kagmara I, II and III and an unnamed peak of 6410m, all first ascents. She was on all the tops except the last one, which she missed through temporary illness. Dawa Tensing was the Sirdar on this, his last expedition. Dorothea contributed generously to the fund set up to help him in illness and old age.

In 1963 she was President of the Pinnacle Club and rode out to the Alps on a moped for a PC/LAC Meet in Zinal. In 1966 some young tigers met her for the first time on an LAC Meet at Saas Fee and were impressed by her fast and competent climbing, particularly her lead on the N ridge of the Weissmies, where she raced ahead of other parties. The verdict was: 'We were very proud of Dorothea.' She was unique too in carrying a tent and firewood up to huts and camping outside. Those who drove with her found her fast driving more frightening than any climb – but it never led to disaster.

1967 was a good year, with a traverse of the Weisshorn by the Schaligrat, and the Peuterey with two bivouacs in bad weather.

In 1970 Dorothea travelled to S Africa to visit her Aunt Marjorie, mostly by native bus and lorries. In 1971 she took a bus from Clapham Common to Agra – 'so much more amusing than flying' – and across Iran and Afghanistan to Kathmandu. She engaged two Sherpas to trek with her to Everest Base Camp. She went on to make a circuit of Annapurna and climb Dambusch Peak – nearly 6000m. She continued to S India, mostly by bus, then by cargo boat to Mombasa. She visited Tanzania, Zambia and the Victoria Falls, with some climbing on and around Table Mountain. She was back in Europe for the LAC Dolomite Meet, including the traverse of the Fünffingerspitze.

In 1976, at 71, she was still climbing and camping. She attended the ABMSAC Meet in 1989, her last Alpine Meet. In 1990 she bullied her doctor into giving her a certificate of fitness for an RGS cruise to the Antarctic. He was wrong – she had no time to make this trip before she died.

Margaret Darvall

William J March 1941–1990

'Big Bill' March, who died in Canada in early September at the age of 49, was one of those rare mountaineers able successfully to combine the role of achiever with that of educator in our anarchistic sport. Indeed for a while he was a legend in both top-flight climbing and top-rung outdoor education, fields that rarely overlap here in Britain.

An ebullient London cockney who became addicted to climbing while reading geography at King's College London, Bill initially was a teacher on his home ground in the East End. Meanwhile he spent some time as a volunteer instructor at Plas y Brenin and made his first alpine climbs in the Dolomites. But the mid-1960s saw a burgeoning interest in the value of outdoor education, and in 1969, after a spell as a staff instructor at Edinburgh's Benmore Centre in Cowal and a further PE qualification at Loughborough, he joined the staff of Glenmore Lodge, the Scottish Sports Council's prestigious mountaineering centre in the Cairngorms. Later, when Fred Harper became Director, Bill became his deputy.

The celebrated veteran Creag Dubh climber Johnny Cunningham was a fellow instructor, and he and Bill formed a brilliant climbing partnership. Hitherto Scottish ice climbers had excelled at vertical step-cutting, but Cunningham had practised front-pointing on the unrelenting walls of Antarctic icebergs. He and Bill re-curved the picks of their axes in a bunsen flame and took to carrying a file to hone their crampon points during climbs. With his youthful ebullience Bill soon emulated Cunningham's technical brilliance and further developed his innovative techniques on steep ice. The result was a proliferation of superb new winter routes and a major revolution both in ice-climbing standards and speeds. Possibly the most notable of these routes was The Chancer on Hell's Lum but he also made the first repeat of Tom Patey's fabulous Crab Crawl traverse of Creag Meagaidh. After breakfast one day Cunningham and March drove from Glenmore to Fort William, climbed two of the longest and most difficult ice routes on Ben Nevis and returned to the Lodge for tea – this at a time when the BMC were pleading for a hut on the Ben to enable climbers to complete one route in daylight hours!

Meanwhile Bill was busy communicating this new approach to ice-climbing both to his students and to the mountaineering world at large. His definitive instructional book *Modern Snow and Ice Techniques* appeared, and another valuable classic, *Modern Rope Techniques in Mountaineering*, soon followed. He qualified both as a Mountain Guide and as a member of the Scottish Mountaineering Club – the latter probably a more elusive qualification for a mere Sassenach. And he married Karen, a Canadian girl whose North American attitudes were to have a profound influence on his later career.

Though a talented instructor and administrator, Bill had little sympathy for unnecessary bureaucracy, and a disagreement with the Scottish Sports Council over his participation in the ill-fated 1974 RAF Dhaulagiri IV expedition led to his resignation from the Lodge. During the expedition he was lucky to escape an avalanche accident which killed several Sherpas on fixed ropes but which he considered avoidable, and this strongly coloured his future attitude to Himalayan climbing and its attendant risks.

Bill and Karen moved to Pocatello in the American west, to run the ambitious Outdoor Programme at Idaho State University. Here he took his Master's degree and absorbed the refreshing American attitudes to Risk and Outdoor Education. This stage in his career enabled him to widen enormously his mountaineering, kayaking and wilderness experience, both with students and with local climbers, especially the celebrated Colorado mountaineer and hardwear designer Bill Forrest, who became a close friend.

In two busy years Bill accomplished a fine series of summer and winter ascents. He repeated such classics as The Nose of Yosemite's El Capitan and the Black Ice Couloir on the Grand Teton (the first British ascent), besides pioneering new climbs in the wilderness ranges of the Wind Rivers, the Saw Tooths, the Lost River Range and Zion. He became 'known' in American mountaineering circles.

In 1976 the Directorship of Plas y Brenin, the Sports Council's National Mountain Centre in Snowdonia, fell vacant, and Bill was head-hunted for the job. It was a delicate task, fraught with problems such as the dichotomy between the educationists who controlled the Centre and the mountaineering community it was supposed to serve. He was shocked to discover that his mountaineering instructors were unionized, with overtime payable for such things as rescue call-outs. Bill did much to heal the rift and re-establish the Brenin's credibility, hosting international climbing meets and throwing open the lavish facilities to ordinary climbers. But it was an uphill task, for his integrity would allow no compromise and he felt unsupported from above and sniped at from the flanks. When he ordered some feral goats marauding the gardens to be shot, a major furore resulted; he managed little challenging climbing, and became disillusioned. After only 18 months, he resigned.

With his wife, Bill now returned to North America where he had been offered an Associate Professorship at Calgary University, co-ordinating the Outdoor Pursuits Programme of the Physical Education faculty. Based so close to the foothills of the Rockies, Bill fell on his feet. Before his first university term had even started he had ticked off the formidable N face of Mount Temple, and swift ascents followed of Mount Robson's Kain face, the N ridge of Assiniboine and the E ridge of Bugaboo Spire, with 'before breakfast' times that astonished the locals. Canada was his scene, his extrovert personality suited the big country and its wilderness, and the university was broadminded enough to allow him his head. He took Canadian nationality. Before long he had repeated the long and desperate local 'full-pitch-vertical' ice climbs such as Polar Circus and Takakkaw, often in company with his old friend Rusty Baillie. Several new routes on large and remote mountains helped cement his now formidable reputation in North American mountaineering circles. But his metier had now become adventure in general, with climbing and kayaking its typical expression.

Selected as members of the 1982 Canadian Everest expedition, Bill and Rusty made a new ice route on Chimborazo and then a serious attempt on the SW buttress of Nuptse as training climbs. When the original leader was fired, Bill was invited to replace him, an offer he could not refuse despite his qualms about big expensive 'national' expeditions. That the expedition was successful, putting the first two Canadians and four Sherpas on the summit of Everest, says much for Bill's leadership ability. Nevertheless four men died, the team was split by disagreement, the weather was dreadful and the mountain in dangerous condition. It was all that he disliked about mountaineering, and it went against the grain to discover himself and the two summiteers national heroes on returning to Canada. Nevertheless, Bill continued to climb and to climb hard. He made frequent return visits to Britain to see his parents, to climb with old friends and revisit old haunts. With Karen he walked much of the South-West Coast Path, and only a month before his death he was enjoying a sun-scorched sea traverse on the Swanage limestone. A sabbatical sojourn in Australia was in the planning stage. But his family now occupied first place and he devoted himself to his wife Karen and young son Tony.

A gentle giant, Bill March was a gregarious man, wonderful company, a teller of good stories and an enjoyer of good ale. His distinctive cockney accent marked the focal point of many a mountain bar and enlivened many a cold bivouac. On the mountain he was the very best of companions, unflappable, powerful, always super-fit and above all safe. It is ironic that, having survived at the sharp end of a dangerous profession for 30 years, he should have died suddenly from a cerebral aneurysm while relaxing on a canoe expedition with his students at Toby Creek in British Columbia.

John Cleare

William David Brown 1908–1990

I would not like to let the death of David Brown go by without some comment by me because, in the 1950s and thereabouts, we climbed together a good deal in the Alps.

I can remember an excursion into the Dauphiné when we climbed Whymper's classic route up the Pelvoux, the Pic de Neige Cordier and the Écrins. We then went round to the Promontoire hut to do the Meije but were stopped by bad weather. So we crossed the Brèche de la Meije to La Grave: a minor expedition.

Other excursions I had with him in the Dolomites. With that splendid guide Celso Degaspar, who had known Mussolini's son-in-law and entourage, we climbed the Punta Fiames, and then the very fine S wall of the Tofana di Rozes. I can't remember any other excursions with David after that, but I am almost sure that we climbed in North Wales together. I met him in London soon after he got married; but then my work took me out into Essex and our lives parted.

But David, what happy memories I have of times together, camping and climbing in the Alps!

Charles Warren

Maurice Bennett 1914–1990

... It is above all in the character – as a friend, that his memory will be cherished among us. The equanimity of his unfailing good temper, his pure, unselfish nature, his kindly and genial manner, the charm of his conversation, made him the most delightful and engaging of companions. He had the happy art of making friends wherever he went, and of winning the esteem and regard of all of every age with whom he came in contact.

Thus: from a famous obituary which seems as appropriate to the memory of Maurice Bennett as it did to that of our first secretary 100 years ago. If Bennett's name had been used instead of Hinchliff's, the saying would not have been less true. Wordsworth wrote: 'little, nameless, unremembered acts of kindness.'

In Maurice we have lost one of the stalwarts of the Alpine Club, willing always, and able, to pull his weight whenever called upon. Elected in 1959, he was soon involved in various offices. He became a trustee, a member of the House Committee, and AC representative (Chairman) on the London & SE Area Committee of the British Mountaineering Council. He also served on the committee of the Anglo-Swiss Society and on the advisory committee of the Bowles Mountaineering and Outdoor Pursuits Centre. Maurice himself wrote many of our obituary notices. His proposer and seconder for the Club were George Starkey and R C H Fox, and supporters M N Clarke, Dr A W Barton and Roy Crepin; well sponsored, some would say. By profession he was a solicitor, partner in a leading city firm, head of the department dealing with Company Law.

For 20 years prior to his election to the Alpine Club Maurice had been an active member of our offspring, the Association of British Members of the Swiss Alpine Club, in which he held many offices, Honorary Solicitor, Hon Joint Secretary for 11 years, President 1975–77. He played a prominent part in the negotiations leading to the acquisition of the Patterdale hut, giving the project his generous support, a project the like of which the AC would do well to follow.

I called the ABMSAC our offspring. In 1909 the feeling came to a head in the AC, led by prominent members, Clinton Dent (author/editor of the Badminton *Mountaineering* and *Above the Snowline*), J A B Bruce, Gerald Steel, A E W Mason (author of *Running Water*) that members using the Swiss huts should do more to support the Swiss Alpine Club; and so the ABM arose. Soon after this, £830 (at 25SwF to the £1) was raised to build the Britannia hut, and we are still rather proud of the fact. This of course was the small wooden edifice ... we are perhaps a trifle inclined to overlook the fact that the Geneva Section of the SAC, aided by the Central Committee, have spent a further £250,000 on the hut since; it is now one of the busiest huts in the Alps! Yes: we gave £500 in 1929 (half the cost of a reconstruction), Fr1000 for the Bétemps hut in 1930, and Fr 400 for Konkordia: we furnished the old table-tennis room at Britannia in 1959, and gave them a picture in 1984 . . . but . . .

We are not a 'Section' (one cannot have a section outside Switzerland), but an 'Affiliation'. Sections do maintain huts! I think I am expressing some of the 'Bennett' sentiments here.

I am now going to quote from the citation in the ABM Journal upon Maurice's advancement to the Presidential Chair in 1975 (quotes are enclosed in inverted commas). 'Club Presidents are not infrequently somewhat remote people to the majority of Club members. Nothing could be further from the truth in the case of Maurice Bennett. He always offered a warm welcome, and made new members feel at home. He shared our Alpine Meets regularly for many years, until declining health rendered this more difficult.' These had become joint meets with the AC, many people, of course, like Maurice himself, being members of both clubs. I have many happy personal recollections of his company, starting, I think, in 1959, the ABM Jubilee Meet at Saas Fee – with George Starkey in the chair. Harold Flook writes: 'Maurice Bennett was a great tower of strength to the Club and one recalls his kindly welcome and fund of stories and a memorable climb up the Weissmies in 1959, and burning the cardboard fuel container at the summit of the Mettelhorn some years later to make the kettle boil!' He took an active part in organizing many of these meets, had an extensive knowledge of the Alps, and could soon put us right on any topographical problem. I also remember desperate enthusiastic table-tennis rivalry at the Schweizerhof in Kandersteg.

'He served in the Royal Navy throughout the Second World War and saw service, *inter alia* in Malta and on Russian convoys and at the D-Day landing in Normandy. As an RNVR officer he commanded a tank-landing craft, and was Mentioned in Dispatches in connection with the Normandy landings.' A special form of mordant, but kindly, wit was his own. One story which has come down to us (by Wendell Jones) takes place whilst Naval Lieutenant Maurice Bennett was ferrying troops to the beaches: On a very rough day an army Colonel asked 'Do these craft often break in half?' 'No, Sir,' said Maurice. 'Only once.'

'In the years immediately before the war and for some years afterwards he enjoyed rock-climbing in N Wales on medium-grade classic routes. He had climbed extensively in the Bernese Oberland and Pennines and strayed into other areas of the Alps from time to time. The Oberland had always been his favourite, with the Mittellegigrat of the Eiger probably the pick of the routes.' Maurice was too modest about his climbing and seldom talked of it, but we find amongst many others:

> Finsteraarhorn
> Schreckhorn traverse
> Wetterhorn traverse
> Lauterbrunnen Breithorn
> Tschingelhorn
> Fletschhorn–Lagginhorn traverse
> Zinalrothorn

Rimpfischhorn
Petite Dent de Veisivi traverse, etc, etc.

But it was not only on the high peaks that Maurice was happy; all and every excursion amidst mountain scenery, every valley, every path, every stream, filled him with joy. We return to the obituary of 100 years ago – Leslie Stephen knew how to write – 'Whatever change may take place, the prosperity of the Alpine Club and of the pursuit to which it is devoted will depend upon the degree in which its members retain the hearty love of sublime scenery for its own sake . . . the intense enjoyment not only of the more startling adventures but of the quiet everyday incidents of life amongst the everlasting hills.'

'Maurice Bennett was a keen cricketer for over 30 years during which time he tried vainly a) to explain to fellow climbers what he could see in cricket and b) to explain to fellow cricketers what he could see in climbing.' AND he kept it up to the last: as recently as 1988 he missed the dinner because he was gallivanting across the Rockies.

Maurice was much loved. We are fortunate that his son David carries on the good work, Hon Auditor to the ABM since 1985; perhaps one day for the AC?

Farewell Maurice: We miss you.

F Paul French

Alpine Club Notes

(Plates 89, 90)

OFFICE BEARERS AND COMMITTEE FOR 1991

PRESIDENT	Lt Col H R A Streather OBE
VICE PRESIDENTS	The Rt Hon the Earl of Limerick
	Dr C R A Clarke
HONORARY SECRETARY	Dr M J Esten
HONORARY TREASURER	(to be appointed)
COMMITTEE: ELECTIVE MEMBERS	Ms M A Clennett
	C M Gravina
	G D Hughes
	L A Hughes
	H R Lloyd
	J R Mellor
	Mrs J Merz
	R Payne
	Cmdre M G Rutherford
ACG CO-OPTED MEMBERS	J L Bamber
	M A Fowler
HONORARY LIBRARIAN	D J Lovatt
HONORARY ARCHIVIST	E H J Smyth
ASSISTANT ARCHIVISTS	Miss M Darvall
	V S Risoe MBE
HONORARY KEEPER OF THE CLUB'S PICTURES	D J Lovatt
HONORARY EDITOR OF THE CLUB'S JOURNAL	Professor E H Sondheimer (until 31.8.91)
	Mrs J Merz (from 1.9.91)
ASSISTANT EDITORS	Mrs J Merz (until 31.8.91)
	A V Saunders
	G W Templeman

GENERAL MEETINGS OF THE ALPINE CLUB 1990

9 January	Victor Saunders, *Makalu 1989*
13 February	Mick Fowler, *Peak Bagging round the British coast*
13 March	Andy Cave, *Karakoram Alpine Style*
20 March	Professor G Allder, *William Moorcroft: Himalayan Explorer, Veterinarian and Surgeon* (extra meeting)
3 April	General Meeting (premises discussion)
10 April	George Band, *Kangchenjunga First Ascent*
8 May	Julian Freeman-Attwood, *South Georgia*
11 September	Jim Milledge, *Matelots, Medicine and Mountains*
9 October	Mike Banks, *Changing Greenland*
13 November	Lindsay Griffin, *The European Alps*
20 November	Italian Evening, *The Italian Side of Monte Rosa* (extra meeting)
24 November	General Meeting (premises discussion), Plas y Brenin
30 November	Annual General Meeting

CLIMBING MEETINGS 1990

| 17–18 February | ACG Winter Meet, Glencoe |
| 17–18 March | North Wales. Informal dinner with lecture by Paul Nunn, *On the Edge of the World* |

21 July-11 August	Bernina. Joint Meet with Climbers' Club and ABMSAC
21–29 July	Cornwall. CC hut, Bosigran. Family meet held jointly with Climbers' Club
29–30 September	Lake District. Informal dinner with lecture by Dave Wilkinson, *New Climbs in the Bernese Oberland*

A VISIT TO THE USSR, APRIL 1990

Our trip to Moscow and Leningrad was very interesting. The symposium in Moscow on early ascents of Ushba went well. Eugene Gippenreiter gave a full early history with generous emphasis on the 19th-century British pioneers. He also acted as interpreter for my account of our new route (and first British ascent) of the South Peak. Then followed a splendidly illustrated and lucid account (even to non-Russian speakers) by Vladimir Kiezel of the first Soviet mountaineers' ascent of the North Peak: not following Cockin's classic saddle route but the now more frequently climbed N ridge.

Later Gippenreiter and I had a long interview with Valery Sungerov of the official organization Alptour (5 Bol Rzhevskiy per, Moscow 121069) who offer a wide range of adventurous mountain tours in the Caucasus, Pamir, etc. They are trying to improve their marketing in Britain and the West. Present exchange rates could make such trips very good value.

In Leningrad we were looked after by Leonid Troshchinenko and his family. As a part-time job they do a lot of climbing on the onion domes etc of many old churches which are now under restoration and rehabilitation. I nearly managed to secure a huge bronze 'A' (for atheism) which they had just taken down from the Kazan Cathedral. Leonid T was chief cameraman on the successful Kangchenjunga expedition (see *AJ95*, 24–28, 1990/91). [Sadly, he died in the avalanche accident in the Pamir in summer 1990. *Editor*.]

We spent a very interesting two hours in the Moscow Museum of Mountaineering. We met there a partly French doctor who has lived in and around the N Caucasus for 50 years. She is soberly certain that there is a Caucasian yeti. She mentioned many witnesses and much interesting evidence but left us, still, at least agnostic.

Robin Hodgkin

ANNAPURNA PREMIER 8000M, CHAMONIX, 14–17 JUNE 1990

A high proportion of the French team which made the first ascent of Annapurna (8075m) on 3 June 1950 were mountain guides from the town of Chamonix below Mont Blanc. It was therefore fitting that a grand reunion to celebrate the 40th anniversary of the ascent should be arranged by the town under the auspices of its present Mayor, Michel Charlet. Sadly, only three of the original Annapurna team remained to participate: Maurice Herzog, the leader (who with Louis Lachenal reached the summit), Marcel Ichac, the cameraman, and Francis de Noyelle, the liaison officer and diplomat in India at the time. We later paid tribute to the memory of Louis Lachenal, Gaston Rébuffat and Lionel Terray who were all buried in the local cemetery.

It was therefore a happy and most generous gesture when the town decided to extend its invitation to a large number of prominent mountaineers, including all those who had first trodden the summits of the world's fourteen 8000m peaks. As Nick Clinch (Hidden Peak 1958) wrote when confirming his acceptance: 'The organization of such a celebration is far more difficult than organizing an expedition to 8000m-plus mountains.' The pert, obliging and inexhaustible Secretary General, Nadine Pachta, must have made hundreds of phone calls and written as many letters to gather us all together.

The British contingent consisted of John Hunt, Tony Streather, George Band, Norman Hardie (specially from New Zealand) and the omnipresent Chris Bonington, as usual efficiently combining pleasure with business in the form of a TV series on the history of mountaineering which involved him with two guides repeating Mummery's Crack on the Grépon, wearing ancient breeches and clinker-nailed boots. Even Ed Hillary had his arm twisted to break off his business in Toronto and fly for a day and a night to Chamonix; in compensation, on a brilliant Saturday morning, he was whisked by helicopter to the summit of Mont Blanc.

The highlight of the few days was planned to be a human chain from the top of the Aiguille du Midi *téléphérique* to the summit of Mont Blanc. Perhaps fortunately, the snow conditions did not permit this, and instead a few of us plodded partway up Mont Blanc du Tacul until lethargy overcame us. At one rest-point, in a group of half a dozen, Norman Hardie and I chanced upon three other Kangchenjunga climbers: the Poles Wojciech Bronski and Kazimierz Olech who made the South and Central Peaks and the Japanese Yutaka Ageta who climbed Yalung Kang. The week was full of encounters of this kind.

One morning we all met for photographs on the steps of the parish church; never before can such an august gathering of mountaineers have been assembled. I even resorted to autograph-hunting and within 20 minutes had collected over 50 signatures from participants of 34 major expeditions.

On other days time was filled with conference meetings, films and discussions: Expeditions and the Environment; the Role of the Sherpas; Culture, Religions and Traditions in Nepal; Expeditions and Sponsorship; High-Altitude Medicine. John Hunt had put together a charming account of the Sherpas with whom he had climbed over 50 years; unfortunately his slides had been inadvertently sent to Paris! Particularly memorable as an introduction to Charles Houston's talk on high-altitude medicine was the showing of his now classic film taken on the first 1950 foray up through Namche Bazar to the Everest icefall, with his father, Oscar Houston, Bill Tilman, a priest Anderson Bakewell and Betsy Cowles. (As Tilman relates in his *Nepal Himalaya*: 'Hitherto I had not regarded a woman as an indispensable part of the equipage of a Himalayan journey but one lives and learns. Anyhow, with a doctor to heal us, a woman to feed us, and a priest to pray for us, I felt we could face the future with some confidence.')

All this seemed but a prelude to the Gala Dinner on the Saturday night. *Moët et Chandon* flowed freely. Four of the best chefs in Chamonix had each contributed a course to the banquet. Then came the climax the media had been waiting for: presentation of eight Match d'Or Awards instigated by Paris Match and the Town Council for a variety of Himalayan achievements: the hardest routes, the greatest performance, the best man, woman, Sherpa, cameraman and, finally, the most likely Himalayan hero of tomorrow. We had been asked to send in our votes in advance for this bizarre series of Himalayan 'Oscars'. The mere concept had been enough to keep Joe Brown away. I almost expected to find Terry Wogan breathing down the microphone.

In the event, it was all handled surprisingly tastefully with impressive impromptu speeches by the recipients. By the end, the stage was crowded with a galaxy of talent, past and present: Maurice Herzog, Ed Hillary, Chris Bonington, Pierre Beghin, Reinhold Messner, someone on behalf of Wanda Rutkiewicz, Nimi Sherpa, Kurt Diemberger, Tomo Cesen, and relatives of the sadly departed Jerzy Kukuczka and Jean-Marc Boivin. We marvelled at the latest incredible solo achievements: Makalu S face Direct by Boivin; Jannu N face in under 48 hours and Lhotse S face in 62 hours by Cesen.

After we had said all our farewells at this unique happening, we strolled back well after midnight along the cobbled alleyway towards our hotel, wondering how on earth we could possibly cap all this for Everest in 1993!

George Band

AMERICAN ALPINE CLUB, NEW ENGLAND CHAPTER

In July 1990 Michael Ward visited Boston, Mass to help Bradford Washburn, former Director of the Museum of Science, with the second edition of the National Geographic's Everest Map, 1:50,000 (see *AJ95*, 246–247, 1990/91), and to give a seminar at the US Army Research Institute of Environmental Medicine at Natick. Over the weekend of 8 July he was a guest at Ad Carter's house at the foot of Mount Washington (which was ascended).

The party included Ad Carter (Editor of the *American Alpine Journal*, Hon AC), Professor Charles Houston (AAC, Hon AC), Bob Bates (AAC, AC), Bradford Washburn (AAC, Hon AC) and their wives. (See Plate 90.) Whilst the peaks, glaciers, weather and fauna of Alaska dominated the conversation, Everest and K2 were mentioned *en passant*.

Michael Ward

THE ALPS: POETS, PAINTERS AND TRAVELLERS, 16–18 NOVEMBER 1990

The Wordsworth Trust's special centenary exhibition was concerned with writers and artists inspired by the Alps in the late 18th and early 19th centuries, and included some of the Alpine Club's unrivalled set of platebooks. During the final weekend of this exhibition a well-attended Study Weekend was held at the

Prince of Wales Hotel, Grasmere. This was a most enjoyable and instructive event. The distinguished lecturers included our members George Band on 'Classic Alpine Climbs' and Jerry Lovatt on 'The First Ascent of Mont Blanc'. In connection with the exhibits, Janet Adam Smith spoke about depictions of the Mer de Glace, Charles Warren about editions of the poem 'The Passage of S Gotthard' by Georgiana, Duchess of Devonshire, and Peter Bicknell about other treasures of the AC Library.

ALPINE CLUB SYMPOSIUM 1990: NEW CHALLENGES IN NEPAL

This symposium was organized, in the spirit of its predecessors, to instruct younger climbers about a specific region of the Great Ranges. We concentrated largely on the lesser peaks of Nepal and strayed only occasionally on to 8000m summits. Around 120 people attended at Plas y Brenin, on Saturday, 24 November 1990.

Dr Charles Clarke introduced the meeting with a brief history of the Alpine Club and followed this with a talk on the geography of Nepal and its mountain groups along the main Himalayan ridge.

Bill O'Connor, author of *Trekking Peaks of Nepal*, reviewed the lower summits currently open to trekkers with a galaxy of photographs. Several of these peaks would provide major objectives for anyone.

A wealth of expedition, climbing and travel experience followed: Audrey Salkeld's journey through southern Mustang, Alan Hinkes's climbs on Makalu and Manaslu and Tommy Curtis's epic ascent of Kusum Kanguru N face in the Khumbu.

On environmental, social and political issues, Rob Collister and Doug Scott made us all realize some of the desecration of Nepal which has taken place during the last 30 years and the problems we shall all face in the future to preserve this mountain kingdom, dear to so many of us.

The Alpine Club's Himalayan Index, run by Michael Westmacott, was on display and was used during the meeting.

Bill Ruthven, Honorary Secretary of the Mount Everest Foundation, outlined the policies of the principal grant-giving body in Britain – and encouraged us all to provide prompt expedition reports.

The President, Lt Col Tony Streather, brought the meeting to a close and thanked both the speakers and our hosts.

The symposium proceedings, *New Challenges in Nepal*, edited by Roy Ruddle, will be published by the Alpine Club with financial assistance from the Mount Everest Foundation during 1991.

The event was organized by Victor Saunders, Sheila Harrison and Charles Clarke, with the assistance of the staff at Plas y Brenin. [They deserve warm thanks for their efforts. *Ed.*]

Charles Clarke

THE ALPINE CLUB LIBRARY

The bulk of the library is now in storage, where it will remain until new premises are available. Meanwhile a working library is in operation at 118 Eaton Square. The premises are cramped, but a good service is provided to expedition planners and others. The number of visitors has naturally fallen, but appears to be picking up again. We get rather more requests by letter or phone than before the move.

With the trauma of the move behind us, at least temporarily, work has been resumed on the archives and on cataloguing. A notable achievement has been increased income from reproduction of our photographs, with the help of Frank Solari, following reorganization and cataloguing of the collection. Sales of surplus books continue, and we are grateful for continuing gifts from members to augment the collection and to generate revenue.

Bob Lawford retired as Honorary Librarian at the end of 1990, having held the post for 21 years. The current good state of the library is due more to him than to anyone else. His contributions have gone far beyond the call of duty. While we were at South Audley Street, he brought order into the chaos of our store-rooms by building the necessary book-stacks with his own hands. He has re-bound books for us, made trolleys for stacking chairs, made show-cases for exhibitions which he has also helped to mount. He has catalogued the map collection and our many photographs. He has supervised the Librarian's work and solved so many of the day-to-day working problems that it is difficult to see how the AC office could function without him. Luckily for the rest of us, he will still be around after his retirement. He hands over to Jerry Lovatt, in time for the move to new permanent premises; it will be a very hard act to follow.

Michael Westmacott

THE HIMALAYAN INDEX

The computerized Index, available as part of the Library's information service to members and the general public, now comprises records of over 3500 ascents of or attempts on peaks over 6000m in the Himalaya and Karakoram, and a few in other parts of China. There are over 3000 references to the literature; almost all of these are in English so far, but we reckon that the great majority of expeditions from 1817 to 1989, and virtually all important ones, are covered. 1750 peaks have been identified and logged; in due course this number may be doubled after further exploration and research.

There is still a lot of work to do, on China, on journals in other languages, and on the numerous queries put on one side while the bulk of the data was being abstracted and entered. Meanwhile, there is a steady trickle of enquiries that can be satisfied from the Index, and more are anticipated when suitable publicity has been given to it.

Michael Westmacott

THE CORRESPONDENCE OF WILFRID NOYCE

Potential biographers of Wilfrid Noyce and students of climbing history will be interested to learn that a collection of his letters, covering the period from the early 1940s until his death, has been lodged in the archives of Balliol College, Oxford. Further information is available from: Ian Grimble, 14 Seaforth Lodge, Barnes High Street, London SW13 9LE.

FAREWELL AND HAIL

The present volume of the *Alpine Journal* is the last for which I am responsible. Editing five volumes of the *AJ* has been an exciting and rewarding experience which has taught me much about mountains and mountaineers and has brought me many new friends all over the world. I thank the Alpine Club for entrusting me with a post that has been occupied by so many illustrious predecessors, and all the people, too numerous to mention individually, who have given me their support with practical help, advice, encouragement and friendly criticism. I am very happy that Johanna Merz, who has been such an able Assistant Editor for the past four years, is to succeed to the editorship. I wish her every possible success, and I hope and believe that she will enjoy as much help and encouragement as I have received; an editor needs it.

Ernst Sondheimer

Contributors

SANDY ALLAN, married with two daughters, is a manager of the Access Engineering division of an oil-related company based in Aberdeen. His expeditions include ascents of the Muztagh Tower, Pumori S face direct and two visits to Everest's NE ridge.

VLADIMIR BALYBERDIN, trained as a computer engineer, is now a professional mountaineer, with numerous first ascents in the Caucasus, Alay, Pamir and Tien Shan. In recent years he has concentrated on climbing 7000ers in the USSR and 8000ers in Nepal.

PAULA BINER, a member of the well-known Alois Biner family who run the Hotel Bahnhof in Zermatt and sister of the late Bernard Biner, has long been a good friend to many British mountaineers.

MICHAEL BINNIE was brought up in India. He has climbed throughout Britain as well as in the Alps, Pyrenees, Kenya, Kashmir and Rajasthan (while teaching in India), Peru and Ecuador. He runs a unit for adolescent truants in Tower Hamlets.

DAVID BRETT DUFFIELD is a lecturer in the history of design in the University of Ulster. As David Brett he writes books, plays, articles and radio scripts, and he has climbed all over the place without much success.

DAVID BROADHEAD returned from Papua New Guinea to teach in Inverness, in the heart of his favourite Highlands. He has recently compleated his Munros, traversed the Rimpfischhorn, crossed the Hispar Pass, ski'd Galdhøpiggen and climbed Mount Whitney's Keeler Needle.

HAMISH BROWN is a travel writer based in Scotland, when not wandering worldwide or making extended visits to Morocco. Recent books include *Climbing the Corbetts, Hamish Brown's Scotland, The Great Walking Adventure,* and the anthology *Speak to the Hills.*

MARGARET CLENNETT works as a medical librarian in London. She spends most weekends on British hills, while her summer forays have included trips to Kenya, Tibet and the Karakoram.

EVELIO ECHEVARRÍA was born in Santiago, Chile, and teaches Hispanic Literature at Colorado State University. He has climbed in North and South

America, and has contributed numerous articles to Andean, North American and European journals.

MICK FOWLER is a Tax Office Manager in London. Since climbing his first new routes on shale (1976) he has enthusiastically explored rarely frequented climbing areas. Abroad his achievements include successes in the Himalaya, Africa, South America and the USSR.

JERZY GAJEWSKI, born in Cracow, belongs to the Mountain Tourism Committee of the Polish Tourist Association. He has written several books and many articles in tourist journals, and has wandered through mountains in Eastern Europe, the Alps and in Wales.

TERRY GIFFORD organizes the Festival of Mountaineering Literature at Bretton Hall College of Higher Education. His collection of poems, *The Stone Spiral*, was published in 1987 by Giant Steps.

LINDSAY GRIFFIN, after a lengthy alpine apprenticeship, has concentrated on remote ascents in the greater ranges, including 33 Himalayan peaks. He intends to continue until increasing age, unfitness and a long-suffering wife call a halt to this exploration.

JOHN HARDING is a solicitor, but was formerly in the Colonial Service in South Arabia. He has climbed extensively in Europe, Asia, Africa and Australasia.

ALAN HARRIS retired from British Airways in 1980. He will continue walking in high places for as long as he can. His plans include a return to the Gran Paradiso national park.

NIGEL HARRIS lecutures in Earth Sciences at the Open University. His recent research has focused on the magmatism of Tibet and the Himalaya. Field projects include a trans-Tibet geological traverse, granites of the Langtang valley and uplift of Nanga Parbat.

STEPHEN HART has climbed in the New Zealand, western and Julian Alps. He has participated in both NZ and British expeditions to Peru, the Hindu Kush and the Karakoram, preferring the lightweight approach on such trips.

DAVID HOPKINS, a mountain guide, tutor in education at Cambridge and a member of the Alpine Climbing Group, has led lightweight expeditions to Mount McKinley, Nanda Devi, Kusum Kanguru, Peak Lenin, and the volcanoes of Ecuador and Mexico.

JOHN HUNT (Lord Hunt of Llanfair Waterdine) has had a highly distinguished career in the army, the public service and as a mountaineer. He was leader of the British expedition which made the first ascent of Mount Everest in 1953.

HARISH KAPADIA is a cloth merchant by profession. He has climbed and trekked in the Himalaya since 1960, with ascents up to 6800m. He is Honorary Editor of the *Himalayan Journal*, and compiler of the *HC Newsletter*.

DAVID MACGREGOR teaches English and runs drama at Aldenham School, Hertfordshire. He has led many expeditions in the British Isles (particularly Scotland), and the Alps. The Chinese Pamir provided his maiden first ascents and extended his preference for mountain exploration.

TED MADEN, Professor of Biochemistry at Liverpool University, has climbed in the Pyrenees, Norway, USA, Canada and extensively in the Alps, and has compleated the Munros. With M Salim he solved the first complete structure of a vertebrate ribosomal gene.

EUGENE MECKLY was born in Pennsylvania and is a retired technical librarian living in North Carolina. He has been a collector of mountaineering books since 1947, specializing in Mont Blanc and privately printed works.

BRENDAN MURPHY is engaged in computer research at the University of Buckingham. Despite being a dedicated rock-climber, he has been spotted wearing crampons in Scotland, the Alps and the greater ranges.

PAUL NUNN PhD is principal lecturer in economic history at Sheffield City Polytechnic. His numerous climbs include first ascents of the British Route on Pik Shchurovsky and the SW Pillar of Asgard. He has been on eleven Himalayan expeditions.

OSWALD OELZ is Professor of Medicine at the University Hospital, Zürich, with a special interest in high-altitude physiology and medicine. His climbs include the first ascent of the Messner Couloir on Mount McKinley, Mount Everest, Xixabangma and Vinson Massif.

SIR EDWARD PECK was in the Diplomatic Service until 1975, when he retired to Tomintoul. He has climbed in the Alps, Turkey, Kulu, Borneo and East Africa. His object when serving abroad was generally to reach the highest point available.

KEV REYNOLDS had climbed in the Atlas, the Alps and extensively in the Pyrenees. For many years a Youth Hostel Warden, he is now a freelance writer and lecturer.

SIMON RICHARDSON is a petroleum engineer. He has survived several expeditions to the greater ranges, but now finds ever-increasing adventures on smaller and smaller mountains. His most recent bivouac was at an altitude of 15m on a Scottish sea-stack.

C A RUSSELL, who formerly worked with a City bank, devotes much of his time to mountaineering and related activities. He has climbed in many regions of the Alps, in the Pyrenees and in East Africa.

SCOTT RUSSELL'S expeditions in the 1930s included the Karakoram with Eric Shipton. In 1945 he emerged from a Japanese prisoner-of-war camp with the manuscript of *Mountain Prospect* in his haversack. Recently he produced a memoir of his father-in-law, George Finch.

ANNE SAUVY is a university lecturer at the Paris Sorbonne. She has climbed a lot in the Alps, mostly on ice, and is a French writer of mountaineering fiction. Her husband is John Wilkinson AC, ACG (qv).

TONY SCHILLING, a Deputy Curator of the Royal Botanic Gardens, Kew, has climbed in the Alps, Polish Tatra and Arctic Norway, and has led many botanical treks to Everest, Annapurna, Kangchenjunga etc, and botanical expeditions to Bhutan and South-West China.

MICHAEL SCOTT works for the Shell Company. He has been on expeditions to the Cordillera Blanca, the Cordillera Paine and Baffin Island, and was in 1976 the only person to have climbed all the 640 routes on Table Mountain.

VERA VASILJEVNA SHER, born in 1914, specializes in chemistry. A Master of Sport of the USSR in mountaineering, she has climbed in the Caucasus and the Pamir. She is the Honorary Director of the Central Museum of Mountaineering in Moscow.

STEPHEN VENABLES, besides enjoying several careers, all poorly paid, since leaving Oxford in 1975, has continued to ski and climb in the Alps, Andes and Africa, and has made ten expeditions to the Himalaya, written three books and climbed Everest.

MICHAEL WARD is a consultant surgeon who has combined exploration on Everest, the Bhutan Himal, Kun Lun and Tibet with high-altitude research – the mountaineer, *nolens volens*, being a model for sea-level patients with chronic heart and lung disease.

JOHN C WILKINSON is a don at Oxford, where he is senior member of the OUMC, and is married to Anne Sauvy (qv). He has had 27 Alpine seasons and has been on three expeditions to the Himalaya and Andes.

EDWARD WILLIAMS, Professor Emeritus of Nuclear Medicine (London), is now in Holy Orders. He has climbed in the greater ranges and has led, or been a member of, a series of mountain physiology expeditions, resulting in many scientific papers.

GUIDANCE FOR CONTRIBUTORS

The *Alpine Journal* has been published regularly since 1863 as 'A Record of Mountain Adventure and Scientific Observation'. The *Journal* has always been a record of all aspects of mountains and mountaineering and, although its main function is to record mountain adventure, articles on mountain art, literature, anthropology, geology, medicine, equipment etc are all suitable. Articles should be informative, and a good literary style is important. Scientific or medical papers should be of the general style and technical level of *Scientific American*.

Articles Articles for the *Journal* should normally not exceed 3000 words (longer articles can be considered in exceptional cases. Please indicate the number of words when submitting your article.)

Articles submitted to the *Journal* should not have been published in substantially the same form by any other publication. Authors are not paid for articles published in the *Journal*, but they do receive a copy of the issue in which their article appears. Please send articles direct to the Editor at 14 Whitefield Close, London SW15 3SS.

Typescript The complete typescript including the text of the paper, list of references and captions to illustrations should be typed on one side of A4 paper, at *double spacing* and with 20–30mm margins. Authors should keep a spare copy. Authors are asked, as far as possble, to adopt the *Journal*'s house style for proper names, abbreviations, mountain features, etc (for which recent copies of the *Journal* should be consulted). The Editor will advise if necessary, and she reserves the right to edit or shorten articles at her discretion.

Illustrations The number of colour photographs which can be printed is very limited and only top-quality photographs will be accepted. Prints should preferably be black-and-white, between 150 × 200mm and 220 × 300mm in size, and printed on glossy paper. Colour transparencies should be at least 35mm format and should be originals (not copies). A portfolio of up to 10 photographs should be provided. Maps and line drawings should be of a similar size to the prints and be finished ready for printing. Place-names appearing in the text, where relevant, should be marked on the maps also.

Each photograph should be clearly labelled with title, author and any copyright. This information should be typed on a separate sheet of paper attached to the photograph and not written on the back of the photograph itself. Routes of climbs should be marked on separate sheets of transparent paper.

Always take special care in sending prints through the post. Do include adequate stiffening to prevent folding and clearly label the cover: 'Photographs: Please Do Not Bend'. Do not include paper-clips or pins which could damage prints.

References Many articles do not require references. If other publications are referred to in the text, details should be given in a separate list at the end of the article (not as footnotes), and should be set out as in the following examples:

BOOKS   3 G B Schaller, *Mountain Monarchs*. Univ. Chicago Press, 1977, pp15–25 or: London (WS Orr), 1932.

JOURNAL ARTICLES   2 B C Osborne, 'Ladakh'. *Oryx17*, 182–189, 1983.
For *AJ* references, give volume number, first and last page of article, year: *AJ90*, 201–207, 1985.

Units   Metric (SI) units should be used throughout except when quoting original material which uses other units.

Biographies   For the 'Contributors' section of the *Journal* authors are asked to provide a 'potted biography', in not more than 40 words, and without using abbreviated style, listing what they consider to be the most noteworthy items in their career.

Deadline   Copy must be with the Editor by 1 January of the year of publication. Space in the *Journal* is strictly limited, and early submission improves the chances of acceptance. Articles for which there is no space may be considered for publication in a subsequent year.

Index

1991/2 Vol 96 Compiled by Marian Elmes